Technologies

Changing Our World

Christian Werner Loesch

Gerhard Chroust (ed.)

Technologies
Changing Our World

21 Perspectives
2000 – 2020

Bibliografische Information der Deutschen Nationalbibliothek:
Die Deutsche Nationalbibliothek verzeichnet diese Publikation in der Deutschen Nationalbibliografie;
detaillierte bibliografische Daten sind im Internet über dnb.dnb.de abrufbar.

Herstellung und Verlag:
BoD – Books on Demand, Norderstedt, Deutschland

ISBN: 978-3-7519-6769-3

PREFACE AND INTRODUCTION

This book is an extended version of the Book 'ICT Trends and Scenarios' [1] of 2017. Three more lectures have been added to the volume, covering now the years 2000 to 2020. It is a perspective view and venture that, as far as we know has never been tried before. A more than a duo- decennial overview of the evolution, status and future of ICT transgressing technology to economy, sociology and its way of changing our life personally and as society.

The lectures are designed to satisfy both the interested nontechnical as well as the knowledgeable audience, bridging this gap without compromising on the scientific depth, thus contributing to a better understanding of the present developments and the direction of future developments and the emerging dramatic changes.

It offers a powerful instrument of comprehension and an opportunity to analyze evolution, status, the challenges and expectations over this dramatic period. The multidiscipline approach enables an unbiased view on the successes and failures in technological, economic and other developments, as well as a documentation of the astonishing quality of technological forecasts. It could thus be the basis of a better understanding and prognosis.

Highlighting the dramatic improvement potential of the revolutionary developments from the computer becoming a network and the network becoming a social network or how information technology is even changing the way the world changes.

Many deep-impact innovations are reviewed. How information technology enabled advances in many fields from decoding the genetics to social networks, deep computing, robotics or emerging paradigms as Quantum technologies, Neuromorphic architectures to mention a few. Giving such a holistic view.

The impact literally reaches reaching from on the bottom of the sea beyond the sky, where ICT has enabled an unprecedented level of communications turning the world into a global village covered by a communication and but equally surveillance umbrella associated exposures and hazards threatening to our personal sovereignty and social life. Emphasizing the dramatic potential through rebooting the next IT revolution.

Commenting the scenario of the last decennia, we have the privilege of the presence of personalities who were eyewitnesses and even contributors to these developments enabling these lectures.

Special appreciation for their engagement and many valuable discussions goes "in parts pro toto" to Prof. Gerhard Chroust and Prof. Petr Doucek and their teams.

Christian Werner Loesch
September 2020

---

[1] LOESCH, C.W. , G. CHROUST (ED.) ICT Trends and Scenarios: Lectures 2000 - 2017 Books on Demand, Norderstedt, Germany, 2017 (hard copy and e-book).

A Word of Thanks

The innovations, observations, and analyses which are reported at conferences like IDIMT are based on the rapid growth of Information and Communication Technologies (ICT). It has caused the dramatic and often unbelievable increase in speed and capacity of the underlying computer hardware (transistors, chips, processors, and memory, etc.) . Despite the dramatic reduction of the price of mass produced circuits and storage units, the explosion of the costs for the total production (factories etc.) are also growing and this reduces the production market to a few big players. The economic parameters define which development roads are to be taken and at what speed. This broader context is essential in order to understand some of the widening directions into which the technological advances will take our economy, our technical activities and our society.

Since the year 2000 a special highlight of the yearly IDIMT–Conferences has been Christian Loesch's overviews of global technical, economic and/or business developments. In now 21 presentations Christian Loesch has provided the participants with broad and and insightful presentations explaining the major dependencies, driving forces, and obstacles for the future of ICT. Thanks to Christian's profound knowledge and his deep understanding of the international situation he has been able to imbed our discussion within the broader context of technological innovation and economic infrastructure.

Christian Loesch, 2007

As a service we reproduce his 21 presentations in this collection, It offers an excellent chance for a retrospective of the ICT scene and the associated technologies.

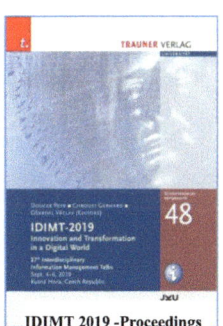

IDIMT 2019 -Proceedings

We want to thank Christian for his efforts in collecting the material and presenting it to the participants of the IDIMT conferences in short but important view beyond our immediate field of expertise. It has allowed us to take look behind the evolving scenes of the computer industry . and also offer an interesting view of the past evolution of this key technology. field.

Gerhard Chroust and Petr Doucek

Co-chairmen of the IDIMT Conferences

CONTENTS

The Seven locations of IDIMT Conferences

1993, 1994	Kubova Huť
2003 - 2007	České Budějovice
2008 - 2012	Jindřichův Hradec
1995 - 2002:	Zadov
2013	Praha
2014 - 2017	Poděbrady
2018 - 2020	Kutná Hora

IDIMT 2020

TECHNOLOGIES CHANGING OUR WORLD

Christian W. Loesch

IBM ret. CWL001@gmx.net

Keywords:

ICT industry and economy, future of microelectronics, more Moore and beyond Moore, emerging technologies, quantum, neurocomputing, sensors.

Abstract:

Based on an analysis of the economic status of the ICT industry, we will peruse the present status and future developments of microelectronics from "more Moore" to" beyond Moore". On the threshold of new computing paradigms we will look at emerging technologies, progressively important areas as communication and sensor technology as well as the arising challenges and problems.

1.   ECONOMIC SCENARIO

ICT industry has changed dramatically in the last few years, with 2019 being a turnaround year as shown by the economic developments of some key players of the industry below.

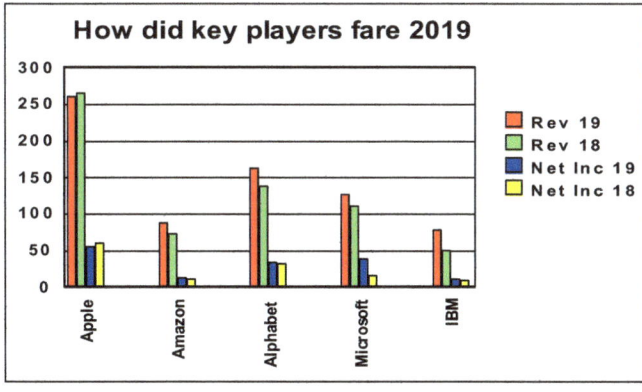

How and where are they achieving their impressive results:

Apple	- 4%
Amazon	+11%
Alphabet	+18%
Microsoft	+14%
IBM	+48%

- Apple: Diversifying
- Alphabet: Google, YouTube, etc. Adv.> 85% of rev.
- Microsoft: Most diversified, tax, five divisions each 20 %
- IBM: Not comparable due to new accounting standards

The worldwide market for chips has reached in 2017 the impressive volume of 412 b$ representing a rise of 21,6%. The IC market forecast (by IC Insights) for 2020 expected strong growth again of 8,0% and units shipments up 7,0%. In parallel a concentration process has reduced the number of leading edge chip manufacturing companies from 28 in 2001 to 5 in 2018.

Let's hope that these successes have been used by the industry to build the resilience needed to overcome the events of 2020.

1Q20 Top 10 Semiconductor Sales Leaders ($M, Including Foundries)

1Q20 Rank	1Q19 Rank	Company	Headquarters	1Q19 Total IC	1Q19 Total O-S-D	1Q19 Total Semi	1Q20 Total IC	1Q20 Total O-S-D	1Q20 Total Semi	1Q20/1Q19 % Change
1	1	Intel	U.S.	15,799	0	15,799	19,508	0	19,508	23%
2	2	Samsung	South Korea	11,992	875	12,867	13,939	858	14,797	15%
3	3	TSMC (1)	Taiwan	7,096	0	7,096	10,319	0	10,319	45%
4	4	SK Hynix	South Korea	5,903	120	6,023	5,829	210	6,039	0%
5	5	Micron	U.S.	5,465	0	5,465	4,795	0	4,795	-12%
6	6	Broadcom Inc. (2)	U.S.	3,764	419	4,183	3,700	410	4,110	-2%
7	7	Qualcomm (2)	U.S.	3,753	0	3,753	4,050	0	4,050	8%
8	8	TI	U.S.	3,199	208	3,407	2,974	190	3,164	-7%
9	11	Nvidia (2)	U.S.	2,215	0	2,215	3,035	0	3,035	37%
10	15	HiSilicon (2)	China	1,735	0	1,735	2,670	0	2,670	54%
—	—	Top-10 Total		60,921	1,622	62,543	70,819	1,668	72,487	16%

(1) Foundry   (2) Fabless

Source: Company reports, IC Insights' *Strategic Reviews* database

But the events of 2020 are changing the previous assumptions dramatically as shown below.

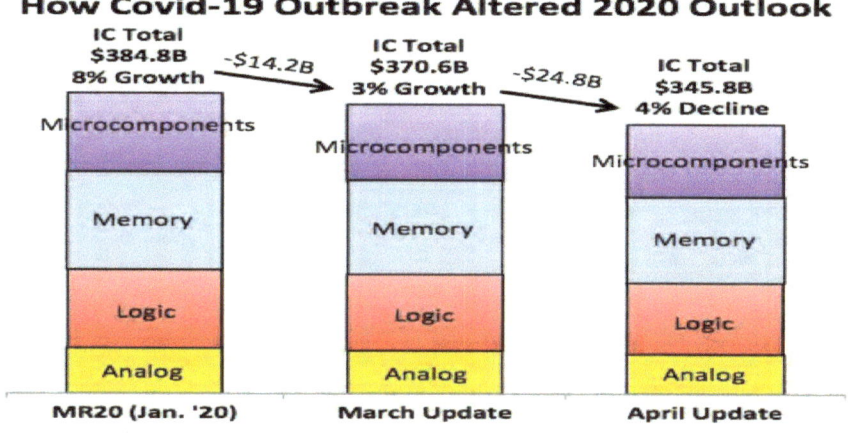

How Covid-19 Outbreak Altered 2020 Outlook

| IC Total $384.8B 8% Growth | -$14.2B → | IC Total $370.6B 3% Growth | -$24.8B → | IC Total $345.8B 4% Decline |

Microcomponents / Memory / Logic / Analog (MR20 (Jan. '20))
Microcomponents / Memory / Logic / Analog (March Update)
Microcomponents / Memory / Logic / Analog (April Update)

Source: IC Insights

2.   TECHNOLOGY

The twilight of Moore's law does not mean the end of progress. Innovation will continue, but it will be more sophisticated and complicated. Remember what happened to airplanes? A Boeing 787 doesn't go faster than a 707 did in the 1950s, but they are very different airplanes, with innovations ranging from fully electronic controls to a carbon-fiber fuselage. That may happen with computers. New EUV scanners will expand Moore's law for the anticipatable future, but nobody should overlook the equally impressive tacit advances in performance, e.g. the current Intel Core i3 processor is 32% faster than the first top of the line Intel Core i7 at half the power consumption only.

The chip making process is getting exceedingly complex, often involving hundreds of stages, meaning that taking the next step down in scale requires a closely intertwined network of materials suppliers and apparatus developers and manufacturers etc. to deliver the right new developments at the right time. If you need 40 kinds of equipment and only 39 are ready, then everything stops.

Leading companies, are trying to shrink components until they limits of the wall of quantum effects. The more we shrink, the more it costs. Every time the scale is halved, manufacturers need a whole new generation of ever more precise photolithography machines. Building a new fab line today requires an investment typically measured in billions of dollars, an investment only few companies can risk and afford this like INTEL, GLOBALFOUNDRIES, Samsung or TSMC. All of these companies rely on high volume manufacturing to finance the capital and the enormous R&D requirements to maintain their competitiveness,

Worlwide Wafer Capacity Leaders
(Monthly Installed Capacity in Dec 2019, 200mm-equivalents)

2019 Rank	2018 Rank	Company	Headquarters Region	Dec-2018 Capacity (K w/m)	Dec-2019 Capacity (K w/m)	Yr/Yr Change	Share of Worldwide Total	Inclusion or Exclusion of Capacity Shares from JV Fabs
1	1	Samsung	South Korea	2,934	2,935	0%	15.0%	
2	2	TSMC	Taiwan	2,439	2,505	3%	12.8%	shares of SSMC & VIS
3	3	Micron	North America	1,685	1,841	9%	9.4%	share of IM Flash in '18
4	4	SK Hynix	South Korea	1,630	1,743	7%	8.9%	
5	5	Kioxia/WD	Japan	1,361	1,406	3%	7.2%	

Source: Companies, IC Insights' *Global Wafer Capacity 2020-2024 Report*

The old market was characterized by producing a few different products, selling large quantities of them. The new market is producing a huge variety of products, but selling a few hundred thousand apiece, so costs of design and production has to be low. The fragmentation of the market triggered by mobile devices is making it additionally harder to recoup the investments. As soon as the cost per transistor at the next node exceeds the existing cost, the scaling stops. We may run out of money before we run out of physics.

Computing is increasingly defined by high-end smartphones, tablets, and other wearables, as well as by the exploding number of smart devices everywhere from bridges to the human body. These mobile devices have requirements different from their more sedentary cousins. The chips in a typical smartphone must send and receive signals for voice calls, Wi-Fi, Bluetooth and GPS, while also sensing touch, proximity, acceleration, magnetic fields, even fingerprints, demanding the device to host special purpose circuits. In this form the user value doubles every two years, Moore's law will continue as long as the industry can keep successfully marketing devices with new functionality.

Advanced Digital Computing (More Moore)

As shown below leading companies expect Moore to continue for years. Digital CMOS is currently at the 14 nm node with potential to scale to 3 nm by 2022. The challenges are materials and process variation to achieve these with new technology at acceptable tool and fabrication costs.

Logic/Foundry Process Roadmaps (for Volume Production)

	2015	2016	2017	2018	2019	2020	2021
Intel		14nm+	10nm (limited) 14nm++		10nm	10nm+	7nm EUV 10nm++
Samsung	28nm FDSOI	10nm		8nm	7nm EUV 6nm EUV	18nm FDSOI 5nm	4nm
TSMC	16nm+ FinFET	10nm	7nm 12nm		7nm+ EUV	5nm 6nm	5nm+

2.1   Emerging technologies and paradigms.

We are on the threshold of revolutionary new computing paradigms. We can look forward to a decade of multiple technologies going to revolutionize the world of computing over the next 5-10 years.

Over the last decades, intensive efforts have been made on enhancing the capabilities and performance potential of III-V wide bandgap material systems such as Indium Phosphide, Gallium Arsenide, Silicon Germanium, Silicon Carbide, Gallium Nitride, and Aluminum Nitride.

Parallel to this evolves the architectural approach: stick with silicon, but configure it in new ways to using 3D to pack more computational power into the same space. 3D sequential integration is an alternative to conventional device scaling. Compared to TSV-based 3D ICs, 3D sequential process flow offers the possibility to stack devices with a lithographic alignment precision (few nm) enabling a density >100 million/mm^2 between transistors tiers (for 14nm), to merge several technologies and materials with 3D sequential integration of various devices.

However, this rather works with memory chips, which do not have the thermal problem as they use circuits consuming power only when a memory cell is accessed.

We will also address some farther out are options and paradigmata like quantum computing, or neuromorphic computing. But most of these alternative paradigms has made it very far out of the laboratory.

Compound Semiconductor

Over the last several decades, industry, academia and government have collaborated to deliver the enhanced capabilities and performance potential of III-V wide bandgap material systems such as Indium Phosphide, Gallium Arsenide, Silicon Germanium, Silicon Carbide, Gallium Nitride, and Aluminum Nitride as well as recent work on ultra-wide bandgap compound semiconductors, subsystem and system levels.

Despite the potential for enhanced performance of III-V compound semiconductors, it has not been generally adopted for integration into consumer products. This is due to material complexity, high cost and a lack of requirements for the high power and advanced capability offered.

However, certain sectors in the commercial market have transitioned to compound semiconductor technology replacing silicon technology, specifically in wireless mobile communication infrastructure (base stations), CATV, IoT, automotive and energy sectors. As availability of compound semiconductor material continues to grow, specifically GaN/SiC, costs will decrease and integration into consumers' systems will gain popularity.

Emerging technologies that may radically change the IT scenario are paradigms that diverge from simple transistor based logic and operations. Advanced Research is apparent for spintronic majority gate technologies including spin-based logic, graphene-based Tunneling Field Effect Transistor (TFET) technology and novel material FETs technology.

The evolution of transistor architecture and channel materials (MOSFET)

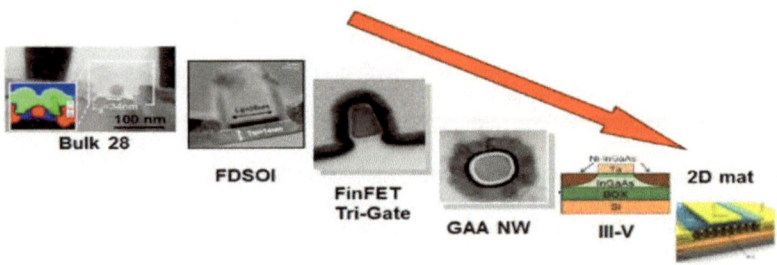

G. Ghibaubo, CNRS Grenoble

What makes these Nanotechnologies so appealing?

Remember: Carbon nanotubes (CNTs) are hollow cylinders composed of one or more concentric layers of carbon atoms in a honeycomb lattice arrangement, with a typical diameter of 1-2nm. Depending on the arrangement of the carbon atoms, the CNTs can be either metallic or semiconducting, and are considered both for interconnect or as field effect transistors (FETs).

The expected benefits of FETs over Silicon based devices are:

- High mobility is very high in carbon nanotubes, significantly higher than in any other material, enabling higher speed, or reduction of the operating voltage and lower active power (heat).
- The tube diameter is controlled by chemistry not by printing, allowing to reduce the body dimension beyond what is achievable lithography. This allows the fabrication of aligned arrays with high packing density.
- The intrinsic capacitance is a quantum capacitance related to the density of states and independent of electrostatics. The device capacitance could hence be much lower than the FinFETs gate to channel capacitances, reducing the switching energy.

Ferroelectric semiconductors and two-dimensional devices

Engineers at Purdue University and Georgia Tech constructed devices from a new two-dimensional material that combines memory-retaining properties and semiconductor properties using a newly developed ferroelectric semiconductor, alpha indium selenide. Noticeable applications would be: a type of transistor that stores memory as the amount of amplification it produces; and a two-terminal device that could act as a component in future computers using neuromorphic low-power AI chips as memristors as the neural synapses in their networks. Under the influence of an electric field, the molecule undergoes a structural change that holds the polarization. Even better, the material is ferroelectric even as a single-molecule layer only about a nanometer thick.

Digital reality, cognitive technologies, and blockchain are growing fast in importance. Virtual reality and augmented reality are redefining the fundamental ways humans interact with their surroundings, with data, and with each other. Cognitive technologies such as machine learning, robotic process automation, natural language processing, neural nets, and AI moved from highly special capabilities to tenets of strategy. These trends are poised to become as familiar and impactful as cloud, analytics, and digital experience are today.

Future memory technologies

MRAM has advantages over other memory technologies. Reading and writing data can be done at speeds similar to volatile technologies but consumes less power and, is nonvolatile, does not need a steady power supply to retain data.

MRAM stores information as the spins of electrons—a property related to an electron's intrinsic angular momentum. Most electrons in a ferromagnet point in the same direction. A currents magnetic field can cause most of those electrons to change their spins. The magnet records a "1" or a "0" depending on which direction they point.

But ferromagnets can be influenced by external magnetic fields, and the spins of adjacent ferromagnets can influence one another requesting enough space between them, limiting MRAM's ability to scale to higher densities for lower costs.

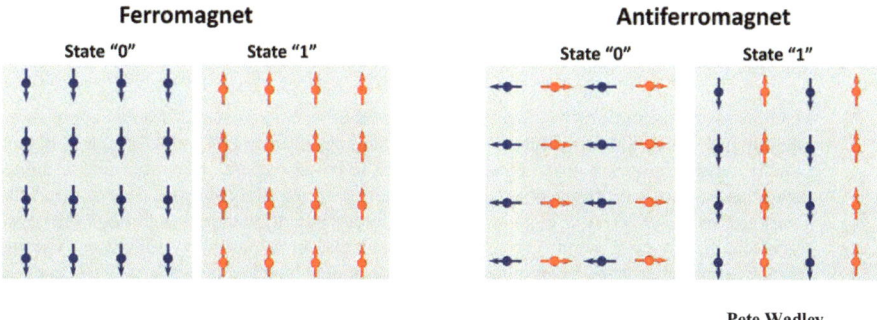

Pete Wadley

Ferromagnets [left] and antiferromagnets [right] can both store information in the spins of their electrons. But the orientations of those spins and their magnetic moments cancel out in antiferromagnets, making them impervious to external magnetic fields.

Antiferromagnets (metals such as Mn, Pl, Sn) do not have that problem. Electrons on neighboring atoms point opposite to each other and due to the dynamics of the spin in antiferromagnets are much faster, bits can be switched in picoseconds with terahertz frequencies. Theoretically, antiferromagnets could increase the writing speed of MRAM by three orders of magnitude. .

Analog Computing and Neuro-inspired computing

Analog, neuromorphic and quantum computing paradigms each involve alternative gate sets and architectures facilitating new computing paradigms. However new computing paradigms will also create additional security challenges beyond the ones already present with advanced CMOS. Current interests focus on machine learning and AI enabling applications, and the search for the hardware implementations.

- Analog computing is receiving increasing attention with advanced SiGe RF technology, hybrid digital/analog platforms, NEMs, photonics and superconducting electronics. This paradigm is particularly well suited for sensor applications and has significant power advantages for certain other applications as well.

- Neuromorphic and Neuro-inspired computing is experiencing rapid growth with major companies having intensive R&D efforts in this area (Google, Amazon, IBM, Microsoft etc.).

- The present digital technology falls short, partly because device scaling gains are no longer easy to come by, and the intractable energy costs of computation. Deep learning, using labeled data, can be mapped onto artificial neural networks, arrays where the inputs and outputs are connected by programmable weights, which can perform pattern recognition functions. The learning process consists of finding the optimum weights, however this learning process is very slow for large problems. Exploiting the fact that weights do not need to be determined with high precision, research has recognized that analog computation approaches, using physical arrays of memristor (programmable resistor) type devices could offer significant speedup and power advantages compared to pure digital, or pure software approaches

- Machine vision

  Machine vision technology has made great progress in recent years, and is now becoming an integral part of various intelligent systems, including autonomous vehicles and robotics. Usually, visual information is captured by a frame-based camera, converted into a digital format and processed afterwards using a machine-learning algorithm such as an artificial neural network (ANN). A large amount of (mostly redundant) data passes through the entire signal chain, however, results in low frame rates and high power consumption. Various visual data preprocessing techniques have thus been developed to increase the efficiency of the subsequent signal processing in an ANN demonstrating that an image sensor can itself constitute an ANN that can simultaneously sense and process optical images without latency. L. Mennel and his team (TU Vienna) demonstrated trained sensors to classify and encode images optically projected onto the chip with a dramatically increased throughput.

Impressed by these technological advances we have to keep in mind that most have evolved yet past the phase of a lab prototypes. The challenge may be 3D integration at affordable cost making organic materials an attractive candidate.

3. From Electronics to Photonics

Silicon photonics for optical quantum technologies is both technological as well as economically highly attractive. A fast expanding market both long-term with a CAGR 78–20 Fc of 8,6% and an accelerating growth rate in the last ten years up to 100%.This results in a continuous emphasis on future investment in R&D.(Statistics 2017).

Modern silicon photonics opens new possibilities for high-performance quantum information processing, such as quantum simulation and high-speed quantum cryptography.

- Solid state quantum memories based on electronic and nuclear spins are now becoming competitive for quantum repeater networks and distributed quantum computing
- Opto-electronic devices and 2D materials
  2D materials, such as graphene, provide new capabilities in communications, sensing, imaging, nonlinear optics, and quantum information devices. There are theoretically about 16000 materials are eligible as candidates for single or combined 2D i.e. multilayer materials.
- Silicon Lasers
  Silicon is the dominating and most thoroughly investigated material of microelectronics, seems to have another encouraging surprise ready. Emitting light from silicon has been the 'Holy Grail' in the microelectronics industry for decades.

Current technology, based on electronic chips, is reaching its ceiling. A limiting factor being heat, resulting from the resistance that electrons experience when traveling through the copper lines connecting the many transistors on a chip. To continue transferring more and more data, we need a new technique that does not produce heat as photonics.

In contrast to electrons, photons do not experience resistance. As they have no mass or charge, they will scatter less within the material they travel through, and therefore no heat is produced. The energy consumption will therefore be reduced. Moreover, by replacing electrical communication within a chip by optical communication, the speed of on-chip and chip-to-chip communication can be increased by a factor 1000. Data centers would benefit especially, with faster data transfer and less energy usage for their cooling system. But these photonic chips will also bring new applications within reach. Think of laser-based radar for self-driving cars and chemical sensors for medical diagnosis or for measuring air and food quality

Silicon's mature and large-scale manufacturing base could lead to implement a much needed reduction in the cost of photonic devices. Such a cost reduction can bring the power of optical networks to the desktop computer and to home systems. It could enable a new generation of electro-opto-mechanical chips that perform the job of today's complex systems at a fraction of the cost, size, and power dissipation.

Let us make a short review of the basic principles to explain the problem.

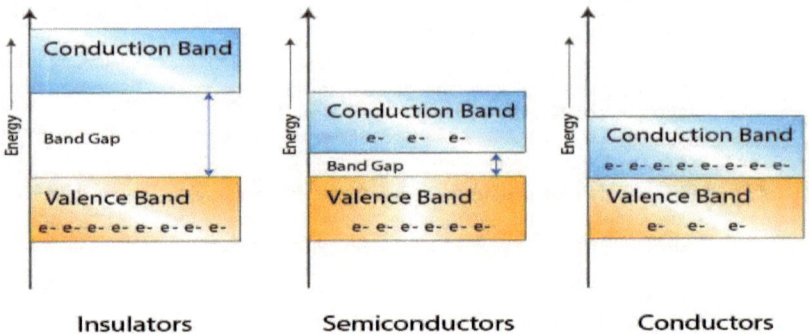

But reality is more sophisticated because unfortunately for our purposes, direct band gap light emission is necessary whereas Si has the property of only indirect bandgap emission.

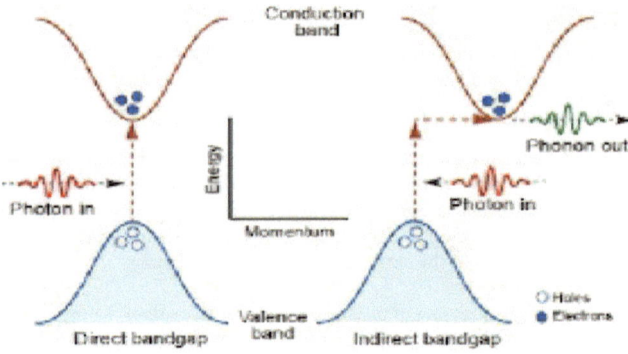

Unfortunately indirect bandgap semiconductors are usually very inefficient emitters. This problem been approached and resolved by an unusual approach. Researchers from TU of Eindhoven developed an alloy with silicon that has the desired properties to emit light and are now starting to create a silicon laser to be integrated into current chips.

Since QC and AI and related subjects have been covered in preceding IDIMT sessions only some additional comments:

Quantum-enhanced sensing

Quantum sensors enable unpaired precision measurements of time, fields, and forces for applications in the physical and life sciences.

QC (Quantum Computing)

QC continues to be perused with remarkable R&D (and PR) efforts to take advantage of the large parallelisms possible for complex optimization and factoring problems. It will not replace conventional computing but potentially offer superior performance for specific niche applications, rather than for the everyday digital computing tasks.

AI

AI is showing an impressive development. Factors responsible of its triumphal march are: more data, cheaper storage capacities and higher computing power (e.g. graphics card farms). They enable the use of AI processes in increasingly complex configurations. Experts differentiate between "strong AI", aiming to imitate human intelligence and "weak AI", which is used to make intelligent decisions for specific areas, such as the automation of processes, but strong AI is yet beyond the current technical possibilities. Unresolved fundamental problems ensure that it remains a theoretical game of thought for the foreseeable future, even if some of the reporting suggests otherwise. Weak AI, on the other hand, is an approach that plays a role in many applications today.

Further out in the long range future are "wet" technologies as the

Molecular computer

French scientists have built the first molecular computer using polymers to store data. They encoded and read the word the word "Sequence" in ASCII code using a synthetic polymer sequence, thus proving that it is possible to store information in polymer molecules. Given the size of each monomer unit of the molecule, this method would make the storage required for of each bit of information, a hundred times smaller than that of current hard drives.

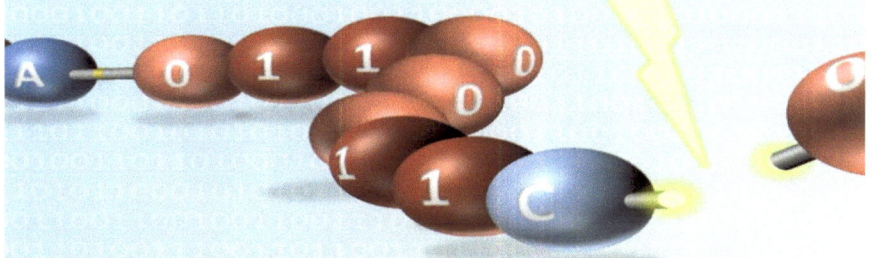

Source: NDIA

3.2. Lateral challenges, problems and risks emerging

New computing paradigms will create new security challenges. Analog computing, neuromorphic computing and quantum computing paradigms each involve alternative gate sets and architectures.

The advancement of such emerging technologies will likely outpace industry's ability to understand the related security threats as well as the readiness of adequate legislation.

Ecology is another important aspect i.e. finding alternatives for rare or toxic materials, and processes.

4. Communication (Connectivity and Advanced Logic)

Networking has lived in the shadow of the high profile technologies but this is changing even more drastically than forecasted Communication is overtaking the computer IC market segment already and is expected to race ahead of all other end-uses (2020 McClean Report).

The connectivity functions will be everywhere in the connected world, from the physical world, (things and persons, autonomous objects, (factory 4.0, autonomous vehicles...), the Cyber Physical Systems), cloud, (E-Health, Intelligent Transport Systems, E-Security, E-Functions and computing). The coming global skin of thousands of additional satellites will impact the scenario dramatically.

Expectations for the next 5 years (Source: Statistics 2017 but these figures may be dramatically impacted by Covid 19.

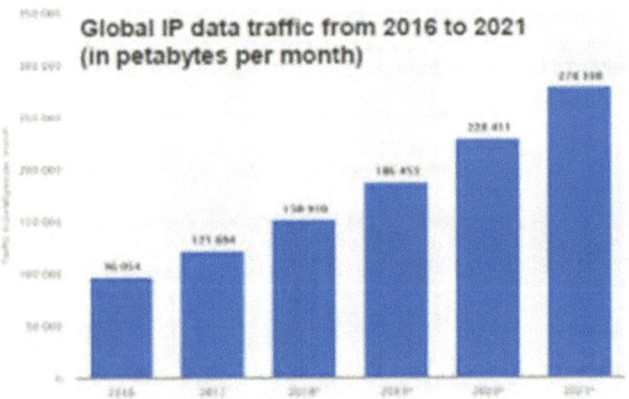

- Traffic   x 10000
- Energy/ bit   1/ 1000
- Connection density   x 10
- Data Rate/connection average   100Mb/s
- Data Rate/connection peak   10Gbs
- Latency   < 1ms
- Connected devices (w/o IoT)   x 100
- IoT connections   > 100 room

Technologies for Wireless applications (Indoor):

CMOS technology processes are the main circuit integration technology used and will continue the prevailing technology for the years to come. Challenges in this field will be the 3D integration in one low cost package. The best candidate for the economic point of view are organic materials, if they can demonstrate their technical capacity.

But the euphoric views and PR of some are met by the market participants with some skepticism. As the overhyped trends of 2020 have been quoted:

1. Augmented reality (39%)
2. 5G wireless technology (35%)
3: Biometric authentication (32%)
4. AI in the data center (31%)
5. Blockchain (31%)
6. Anything "as a service" (30%)

A astonishing approach for optical communication technology in the long run may come with

Vortex Lasers

Light has several degrees of freedom (wavelength, polarization, pulse length, and so on) that can be used to encode information. A light beam or pulse can also be structured to have the property of orbital angular momentum, becoming a vortex. Because the winding number of the vortex can be arbitrary, this technology opens the possibility to expand the channel capacity considerably.

5. Sensors

Global endeavors aim at more sustainable, ICT-enabled strategies for healthcare, energy and environment. Overall, connected objects, IoT, big data, software and algorithms, zero-power or self-powered sensors, sensor fusion, wireless sensor networks and system-in-package are all important for a future scenario. Improvements in healthcare sensor technology could drive an economic benefit of healthcare costs. Most of the sensors types mentioned below are similar and relevant for other industrial segments such as consumer electronics (MEMS accelerometers, magnetic, chemical and gyroscopes), industrial (image sensors), and environment (air quality gas sensors) and defense (LiDAR sensors).

This may enable a plethora of applications in the fields of energy and environment as:

- Automotive:

  - The road transport sector should be 50% more efficient by 2030
  - CO_2 emissions will reduce significantly (80% cars, 40% trucks)
  - Transport schedules (mobility) will be more reliable and traffic safety will improve. Industry expects autonomous cars to improve safety of passengers and pedestrians, reducing fuel consumption by 10% and cost of insurance by 30%.

- Sensors for internal system performance: Motion, Pressure and Position, Advanced Driver Assistance System (ADAS)

- Image (recognition), LiDAR and Infrared sensors

- Environmental monitoring
  -Gas and Particulate sensors
- Medical:
  -Physiological signal monitoring
  -Implantable sensors
  -Molecular diagnostics
  -Telemedicine (analyst and diagnostic systems).

- Quantum enhanced sensing
  -Quantum Radar
  An emerging remote-sensing technology based on quantum correlations (quantum entanglement) and output quantum detection, will allow the radar system to pick out its own signal even when swamped by background noise. This would allow to detect stealth aircraft, filter out jamming attempts, and operate in areas of high background noise.

6. Summary

The preceding review based on pre-Covid facts and figures of the computer industry has shown a healthy growing industry with resilience to economic challenges. We reviewed a broad spectrum ranging from the further extension of Moore as well as the plethora of options for beyond Moore through newly emerging technologies and new computing paradigms. The chart below shows a selection of the rich bouquet of potential present and future paradigms.

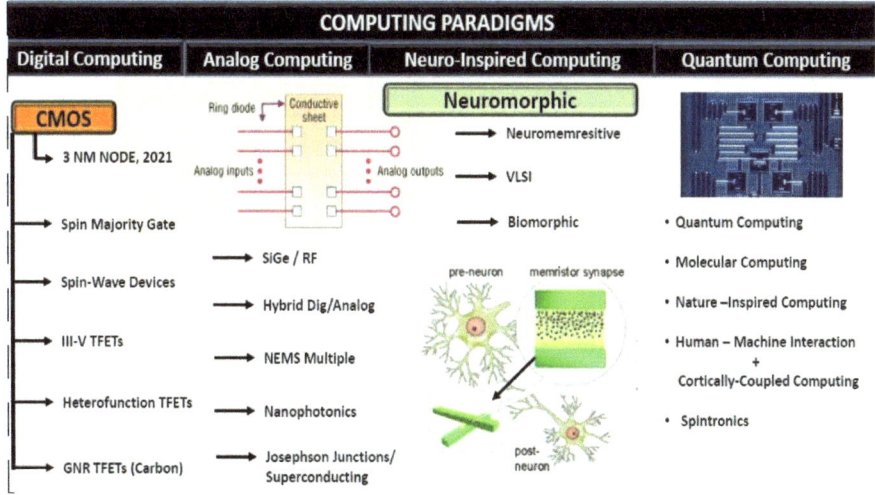

The impact of the pandemic crises shattered previous basic assumptions and made all forecasting difficult. Let us assume that in spite of unprecedented political actions, the related unemployment and debt avalanche the ingenuity and commitment of academic and all shareholders will overcome the present problems and exposures and enable the realization of the promising future outlined.

There is no shortage of ideas and potential and this should sum up to rebooting the IT revolution.

7. References

APPLE, Annual Report, 2019

ALPHABET, Annual Report 2019

AMAZON, Annual Report, 2019

BARDON, M .Garcia, IMEC 2019

BAKKERS, E. M. T. et alii, Direct Bandgap Emission from Hexagonal Ge and SiGe Alloys, 2020

BOTTI Group, Silicon Laser: Efficient light emission from direct band hexagonal SiGe Nanowires FSU

CHROUST G., ICT for resilience of Systems IDIMT 2015

CNRS Strasbourg and Marseille, Nature Communications 2019

MOORE S.K., Ferroelectric Semiconductors Could Mix Memory and Logic

NAKATSUJI S., Univ. Tokyo, MEINERT M, TU Darmstadt, Antiferromagnets the next step, IEEE Spectrum 2020

NDIA, Trusted Microelectronics, Joint Working Group 2017

NEREID, NanoElectronics Roadmaps for Europe, EU Horizon2020, 2019

REED, Technology and Information Services Inc. 2019

SOLOMON P., Analog Neuromorphic Computing using programmable resistor arrays, Solid State   Electronics 2019

WALDROP M., More than Moore Nature 530,144

YE LI G., Ferroelectric Semiconductors Georgia Tech.

ZHURUN et LI, Vortex lasers may be a boon for data,Science, May 2020

IDIMT 2019

ICT FUTURE SCENARIOS: VISIONS AND CHALLENGES

Christian W. Loesch

IBM ret.

CWL001@gmx.net

Keywords:

ICT economy, future of technology, applications, AI, QC, supercomputing, communication, and lateral ICT developments.

Abstract:

We will try by selected topics to cover of the present and future scenarios in ICT analyzing critically the economic and technological perspective as well as special topics as applications, AI, QC as well as well as supercomputing, communication and important lateral developments. It will be realistic review showing not only the achievements but also the challenges ahead.

1. Economy

In the last few years the ICT Industry has changed dramatically, to illustrate this lets have a look at the economic developments of some key players of the ICT Industry.

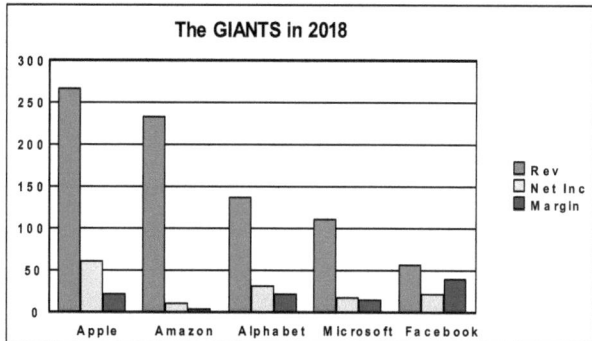

How do the "Big Five" accomplish their successes?

Apple: Phone 63%, Services 14% Mac 10%

Alphabet: Despite a wider umbrella name, ad revenue (via Google, YouTube, Google Maps, Google Ads, etc.) still drives 85% of revenue for the company

Facebook: Generates almost all revenue (98.5%) from ads, remarkably, as a free service the company generated more revenue per user than Netflix pay services.

Microsoft: Most diversified revenue, office products, server products, cloud, and Windows each around 20 %

The worldwide market for chips has reached in 2017 the impressive volume of 412 b$ representing a rise of 21,6% and is still continuing as shown by the table below.

The main players in the new IC technology industry structure are

2018 Rank	2017 Rank	Vendor	2018 Revenue	2018 Market Share (%)	2017 Revenue	2017-2018 Growth (%)
1	1	Samsung Electronics	75,854	15.9	59,875	26.7
2	2	Intel	65,862	13.8	58,725	12.2
3	3	SK hynix	36,433	7.6	26,370	38.2
4	4	Micron Technology	30,641	6.4	22,895	33.8
5	6	Broadcom	16,544	3.5	15,405	7.4

Parallel to this a concentration process has reduced the number of leading edge chip manufacturing companies from twenty-eight in 2001 to five in 2018.

2. Technology

Bipolar transistors (faster than MOS devices) were reaching the power limit by mid 90s, as reaction the CMOS technology was pushed by industry both for logic and memory devices. Again, power limits were reached at the middle of the last decade. No longer faster processors trigger the design of a new PC but the design of a new smartphone generates the requirements for ICs and components. This indicates the end of 2D topology and end of scaling as in history. The ICT Industry recognized very early in 1998 the need to restructure the MOS transistor and new worldwide approach to restructuring the transistor was 'equivalent scaling'. The goal of this program consisted in reducing the historical time of ~25years between major transistor innovations to less than half to save the semiconductor industry from reaching a major crisis.

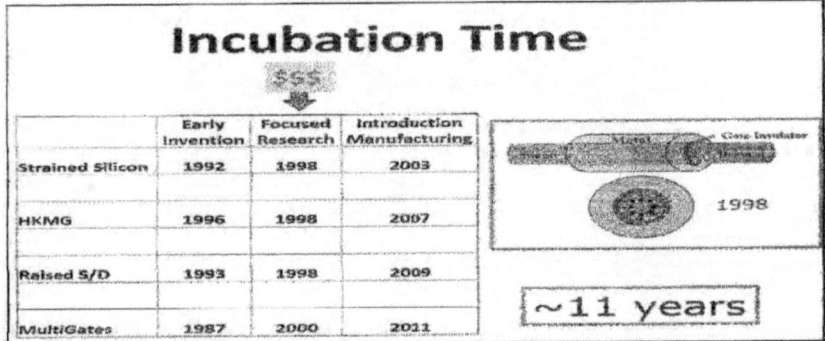

Strained silicon, high-κ/metal gate, finFET and the use of other semiconductor materials (e.g., Germanium) represented the main features of this scaling approach. All these new process modules were successfully introduced into high volume manufacturing. Additionally the industry itself

underwent an unparalled restructuring process, during the last decennium. Several developments revolutionized the ICT industry the way business is done. The advent and success of the combination of fabless design houses and foundries revolutionized the way in which business was done and heralded the coming of the new semiconductor industry.

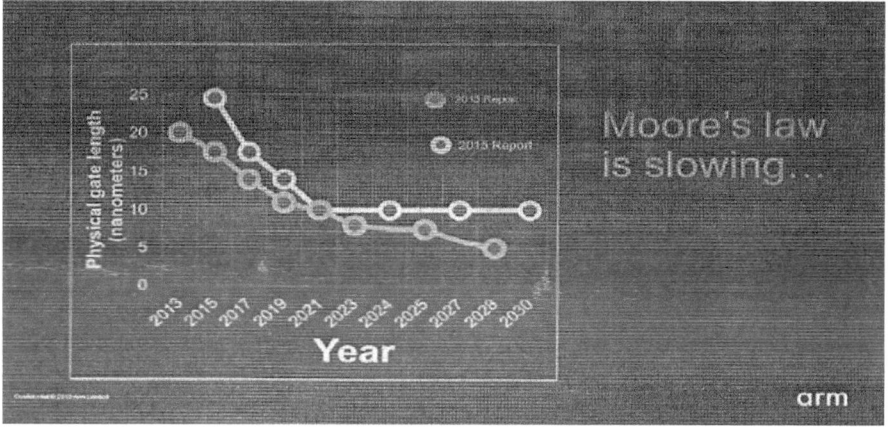

The restructuring of the ICT Industry, the Advent of fabless design houses and foundries as

- Fabless   Advanced Micro Devices and Apple Inc.
- Memory   Micron Technology and Samsung Electronics
- Foundries   Global Foundries and TSMC

TSMC has plans has reaching out for even a 3nm or 2nm technology and supplies Intel as well as for IBMs (7LPP,Power110 and Z15 chips) who is contracting out as well to Samsung

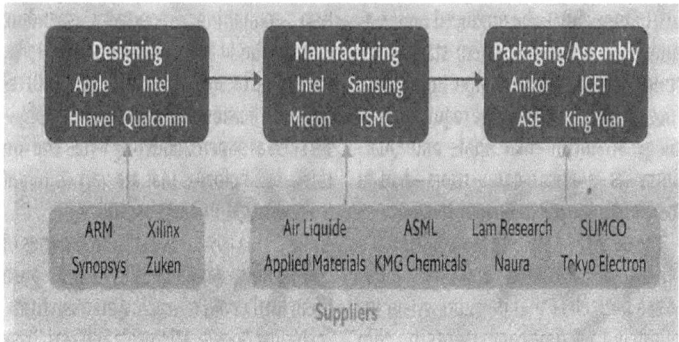

2.1. Future technology challenges

The next steps will be the integration of processor and memory, improving the bottleneck data in and out of the processor and is expected to enable improvements of 10-100 times.

Memory products have always been the leaders in transistor density (smallest feature pitch) and so it is not been surprising to realize that the solution to this problem came first from companies producing Flash memories. Flash products have been the technology leaders in pitch scaling since the mid-70's and they have already overcome the 2D limitations by aggressively implementing 3D memory cell strictures even 72-96 layers of Flash memory-cells have been demonstrated. It is anticipated that logic technologies will follow this transition.

Since the DRAM storage capacitor gets physically smaller with scaling, it is necessary to scale down significantly to maintain adequate storage capacitance thid means that dielectric materials with high relative dielectric constant (κ) will be needed. This material evolution and improvement will continue until 20 nm high-performance and ultra-high-κ (as Perovskite $\kappa > 50\text{-}100$) materials are realized.

These technological solutions will assure continuation of Moore's Law for additional 10−15 years!

While new creative 3D transistors memory cells aso. are revolutionizing the way ICs are produced, comes an old problem again.

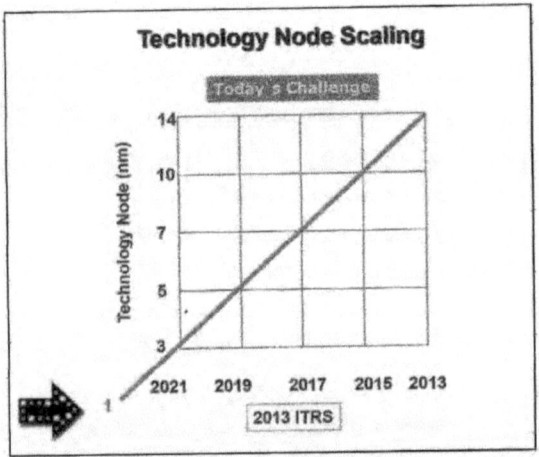

Nevertheless, just shrinking devices can result in unacceptable electrical performance. In addition, the necessity to use as many as 4-mask exposures to pattern a single layer is driving manufacturing costs towards levels no longer affordable. These considerations have driven the industry towards major innovations in device design as Flash memory products were becoming unreliable, because the physical size of the gate, where the bits were stored, was becoming too small (only few electrons could be stored). The industry is moving to three-dimensional (3D) flash memory to enable improved bit density on chips. Packaging is an additionally limiting factor in cost and performance for electronic systems.

To make ICs operating under "normal" thermal conditions the choice between frequency or number of transistors had to be made: Frequency was the looser and has stalled at few GHz since.

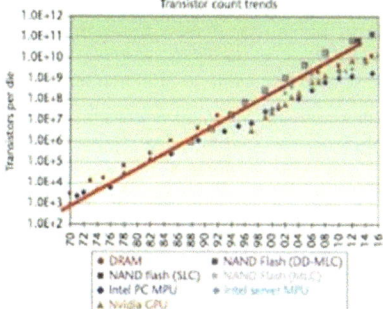

Processor performance does not have a first-order significance anymore. Future-range gains in processing performance may rather come from improvements in algorithms, memory, architecture, and interconnections.

We also have now reached many of the limits of human perception, so increases in requirements on display resolution and similar parameters will be limited in the future based on multimedia needs.

An emerging perspective in dealing with novel materials as III-V (GaN, InP, InGaP, etc.) or nano materials is the impact of their utilization. The utilization challenge as materials efficiency of incoming fab materials is <2%, or the treatment and abatement solutions will have to meet future regulatory requirements as well as increasing costs and restrictions on recycling, repurposing, and reuse.

Emerging research materials

As many novel materials are needed to satisfy in the long term the requirements for extending or even replacing CMOS, there still are substantial challenges for the development and integration of these alternative materials in the fields:

3D monolithic and vertical integration of high mobility and steep subthreshold transistors (III-V, Ge, 2D, carbon nanotube, complex metal oxides, etc.) for extending or replacing CMOS will be required.

We might see the emerging of non-charge-based memories and select devices (ferromagnetic, multiferroic, complex oxides, etc.) to replace present technologies and interconnects with improved reliability and electromagnetic performance at nanoscale as (CNT, novel interlayer dielectrics, metal organic framework and carbon organic framework) to replace copper, and integration on CMOS platforms, with flexible electronics or biocompatible functional materials will be required.

Beyond CMOS

The beyond CMOS era requests major research efforts. Nanoscale volatile and nonvolatile memory technologies to replace traditional SRAM, DRAM and FLASH in appropriate applications are necessary, for instance new types of resistive memories PCRAM (phase-change RAM), ReRAM (ResistiveRAM) or MRAM (magneticRAM).

Beyond MOORE

The scaling of information processing technology substantially beyond the ultimately scaled CMOS will oblige the search for of new ways of computing out of a plethora of options ranging from neuromorphic, approximating computing Graphene, CATOMs-(programmable matter, able to change physical properties between semiconductor and discrete molecules), molecular transistors (rotaxanes or Bencentenenthiole), Quantum dot, optical, QC computing to "Wet electronics" as DNA computing. Emerging is additionlly a new kind of computing using charges or even alternative state or hybrid state variables as spin, magnon, phonon, photon, or combination as electron-phonon, photon-superconducting qubit, photon-magnon.

This will be accompanied by the growing importance of packaging, due to the necessity to develop reliable interconnects, and substrates for wearable electronics (bendable, washable), bio compatible systems for miniaturized implants, efficient integration of electronic and optical components; and integration of cooling systems for quantum computing.

The end of Moore is not a dead-end but could rather can be the beginning of a golden age of architecture, software, and materials.

3. Applications

3.1. Artificial Intelligence

In 1956, first academic gathering on AI took place and thirty years later in Sept.1984, it made it already to the front-page front page of journals.

Sept.1984

The main difference enabling was the exponential development of hardware and storage cost and possibilities. While earlier generations of AI and Expert systems, were fed by human expertise, the new generation with algorithms starts ignorant at beginning, learns, consuming huge amounts of data, to function autonomously.

AI is an omnibus term for a salad bowl of different segment and disciplines reaching from robotics, computer vision, to identify persons to self-driving car technology.

AI is may have a greater impact than anything since the arrival of computers and Internet. Therefore it is supported by intense economic interests.

3.2. Robotics

Since this subject will be covered in a special session let us refrain to some notes:

Robotics has made tremendous progress in the last years, with impact mainly in developed economies and driven by demographic fact of aging skilled population (esp. in Japan), increasing salary levels and last but not least its military potential. (NZZ 14.11. 2018)

3.3. Nano Medicine (Applications on the horizon)

Medical Applications, one of the most desirable developments could be products as "smart pill" for e.g. coloscopy

- Trailing of bacteria (magnetic)
- Medical care by automated diagnosis of common ailments
- Bathrooms (toilets as health indicators).
- Cancer detection by blowing on a mirror
- Small MR machines

The tradeoff is giving data of your intimate life for the price of a reduction of your life or health insurance may lead to the question "what is the cost limit for your therapy"?

3.4. HR (Human Resources)

The application range from screening candidates, determine pay, when to give a salary based on performance etc.

Companies like Transparenca, US, offer programs to monitor that there is no discrimination in HR. Humanyze provides people analytics to track employees by "enhanced" badges (micros, MEMS, accelerometer, data from calendars, email contacts to other persons differentiated by sex and analyzing the duration of speaking vs. listening. Hitachi has a similar product (officially developed against "karishi" = overwork). It means that your company may know more about you than you and your family. "

Amazon, Google and Microsoft already offer pre-trained models that corporate clients can use to build AI enabled systems.

The future may extend the technology to Mind reading fMRI. AI makes workplaces more efficient and much creepier.

3.5. Retail and Logistic

Another attractive field of application of AI and RFID is retail automation. Promising no waiting at the checkout, but also automated 3D of customer tracking, instantaneous discounting if customer not sure to buy, data of customer, less personnel, and profiling every single customer form eating habits to diabetes or pregnancy are evaluated features. However it is presently still an expensive investment,, but Amazon, Google or Alibaba and Baidu would not be so successful without AI. Targeting advertising forecasting demand, guiding robots through warehouses, optimize packaging and delivery (Amazon). Another example is preventive maintenance combined with IoT Inventory optimizations (2015 cost to companies more than 1000b$), including appliations as smart placement boosting efficiency by 20% (IHL Group research firm).

3.6. Privacy and AI

Think of examples as China with 600 mio. cameras, social evaluation system of e.g. your visits to your old parents or pedestrian behavior, speed of bicycle. It records not just facts of your past life but affects your future behavior.

Another example is the US Home land security system AVATAR (Automated virtual agent for truth assessment in real time). Avatar monitoring pupils dilation, and other uncontrollable reactions, or the "Consensus eye detector" which achieves an accuracy of today 86% with a future target of 90%. This is raising "dystopian" fears.

3.7. Some developments to think about:

About 85% of companies think AI will offer a competitive advantage, (but presently only 1 in 20 are using it actively). Most are more interested in the potential labor and cost savings than in more complex opportunities, whereas non-tech companies get worried and buy promising young firms.

AI will effect competition in business giving big companies an advantage through lower costs and prices, but at the same time put small companies at the edge of business.

All algorithms are discriminating. The proliferation of dystopian applications is much easier than for weapons of mass destruction.

There are AI no regulatory standards neither an up to date antitrust law up to now, but we may witness the first attempts by the DoJ in the US in the impending Facebook case.

3.8. Digital Dementia

Every activity changes brain the structure of brain, as the permanent use of navigation systems deteriorates the sense of orientation, the overuse of Internet verbal communication capabilities as the development of speech, the use of mobile phones calculators the mental arithmetic a.s.o.. The use of an average of 3,75 h per day mobile phone and other media might show long range paraphernalia as well as an increasing "multitasking epidemics". Digital media per se is not the problem but adequate use. (M. Spitzer, and Chr. Egger). The time frame is still too short evaluate the effects.

That Janus duality characterizes AI, devastating and exhilarating at the same time.

Until now, there is no great political answer, knowing that in history transition have been very bumpy! These developments underline the necessity for regulations to navigate through the Janus headed scenario, and to develop algorithms to make life better, richer, and more interesting (Max Ridley Oxford Univ.).

The synthesis with other technologies as IoT & IoE has opened an additional dimension with promising perspectives. The advent of foundries, fabless companies can now cover all the aspects of IoE. It would be a mistake to assume that the semiconductor industry is by now a mature industry, the new fabless/foundry ecosystem has opened the door to a flow of innovation available at very reasonable and affordable costs. The advent of the third phase of device integration plus the new capabilities associated with the introduction of revolutionary materials in the semiconductor industry will revolutionize how computers are built.

4. IoT

IoT is one of the most important developments supported by high anticipations. Since an IDIMT session will be devoted to this subject, we will restrain us to few comments.

The development of IoT also faces significant long-term challenges as improvements in the areas as cost-efficient energy harvesting using multiple sources to develop autonomous systems, energy storage and management, low power sensing, computing and communication, automatic network configuration, and security.

Supercomputer (Summit The IBM Supercomputer)

The reputation of supercomputing stems not only from their prestige and military application potential but also because it shows new developments and features that will triple down. Today US Department of Energy's IBM supercomputer (143,5 petaflops) followed by another IBM supercomputer and two Chinese contesters is the fastest on earth (potential nonmilitary uses range from research on fusion energy, material science, AI, to weather forecast.)

IBM's Watson "The Debater"

A new feature of IBM's Watson is the "The Debate." It addresses the question: Can a computer with access to large bodies of information digest and reason on that information and understand the context and present it in natural language, with no human intervention?

In a public demonstration The Debater, speaking in nearly perfect English, replied on topics as shown.

IBM Debating Technologies

Topics

The sale of violent video games to minors should be banned >

The US and EU should re-engage with Myanmar >

The Keystone XL pipeline should be constructed >

Europe should weaken its austerity measures to guarantee greater social support for its citizens >

To put things into proportion, we should remember that the human brain has 100 trillion synapses, 100billion neurons, 20W in comparison with the lowest power supercomputer in the world 1,5 M processors it is 1500 times slower while using 8MW (Livermore Labs simulation).

5. QC

The idea of quantum computing appeared in 1980, when the Russian Yuri Manin, first put the notion forward. The concept really got on the map, the following year, when Richard Feynman independently proposed it, but it did not attract much attention until 1994, when Peter Shor proposed an algorithm that would allow very large numbers to be factored much faster than could be done on a conventional computer (QC threatening many crypto protocols as SSL, HTTPS, AES, DSA, RSA etc. This theoretical result and the temptation of computers one billion times faster than today's fastest supercomputer triggered an explosion of interest in quantum computing. Thousands of research papers, mostly theoretical, have since been and continue to be published on the subject, at an amazing rate.

We have reviewed the basics of quantum physics in IDIMT 2000 and 2014, so let's in this session only recap some of the phenomena as the famous two slit experiment, Superposition or Entanglement, which cannot be understood applying classical logic

Experts estimate that the number of qubits needed for a useful quantum computer, one that could compete with your laptop in solving certain kinds of interesting problems, is between 1,000 and 100,000. Thus the number of continuous parameters describing the state of such a useful quantum computer at must be at least 21,000, which is to say about 10300. That's a number, much greater than the number of subatomic particles in the observable universe.

Error correction is still a practical unresolved challenge. Yet quantum-computing theorists are claiming that this is feasible, that the threshold theorem proves it can be done. They point out that once the error per qubit per quantum gate is below a certain value, indefinitely long quantum computation becomes possible, at a cost of substantially increasing the number of qubits needed.

The huge amount of scholarly literature generated about quantum computing is notably light on experimental studies describing actual hardware. The relatively few experiments that have been reported were extremely difficult to conduct, but command respect and admiration for the physicist involved. There is a tremendous gap between the rudimentary but very difficult experiments that have been carried out with a few qubits and the extremely developed quantum-computing theory. That gap is not likely to be closed soon.

QC has become a kind of self-perpetuating arms race, with many organizations seemingly staying in the race to avoid being left behind. Some of the world's top technical talent, at places like Google, IBM, and Microsoft are working with lavish resources in state-of-the-art laboratories, to realize their vision of a quantum-computing future.

Many people overlook that top researches have been working decades on QC without any practical results and that various scientific and journalistic publications feel obliged to relate or justify their work by claiming some relation with QC.

The famous question remains unanswered: When will useful quantum computers be constructed? The most optimistic experts estimate it will take 5 to 10 years. Ones that are more cautious predict 20 to 30 years. Similar predictions have been voiced, for the last 20 years, but they have been moving targets.

6. Communications

We take it as granted that communication technology will provide the infrastructure as the horse pulling the chariot we are all sitting on for future developments. One of the pending implementations is 5G, so a short overview could be useful.

Pros are:

- Data rates up to 20 Gbps (about 100 times 4G).

- Latency below 1msec (30-70 msec at 4G).

- About 90% lower power consumption, so some IoT devices (one button cell for years).

Cons:

- Electromagnetic waves in the frequency range of 5G are more strongly absorbed by the atmosphere and have lower penetration, therefore, the network cells are smaller than at 4G which means many more stations are needed (about every 100 meters), making a nationwide coverage very expensive.

- There is also skepticism and ambiguity from an environmental and medical perspective, calling 5G the most serious intervention in nature in human history and the 5G risk greater than climate change. WHO classifies the cancer risk of cell phones as 2B (limited evidence of carcinogenicity,) whereas CDC, FDA, FC, NIH see no health risk from cell phone use.

The expected market of 33 B$ in 2026 is luring companies into this huge investment. (Leaders guide Oct 2018). Especially for applications as Industry 4.0, IoT, Factory Automation, Virtual / Augmented Reality, Autonomous Cars, Smart Homes, Smart Cities, Digital Healthcare, etc. the improved latency is essential.

The attitude of government is ambiguous. Some are pushing 5G not to fall back in the technology race. In June 2019 Germany has auctioned the frequencies 2GHz and 3GHz for 6,5B€ with a planned implementation in 2021 and 2026. In contrast, Australia twice banned Huawei's 5G, Brussels (city) and Geneva the expansion of 5G in April 2019. US bans Huawei to avoid dependence on a Chinese infrastructure network mainly for espionage exposure concerns.

While we discuss 5G, 6G is already in discussion at international congresses

7. Further "Lateral" Challenges

We may face substantial environmental, safety, health and sustainability challenges because of a possible impact on health and environment by emerging materials (III-V materials, perfluorooctanoic acid (PFOA). Driving green chemistry and engineering concepts considering their impact on sustainability can become a criteria for future technologies, and future regulations.

An international comparison of education and human resources shows future challenges heightened by increasing East-West competition. Points arising were:

Shortage of "hard core" students esp. in mathematics, physics (MINT) in Western countries. Other issues are days in school 178 vs 251, or Silicon Valley's universities having 50% foreign born students on H1B visa, and 50% of PhD students or at the East coast especially Univ. of NY up to 100%.

US is better in design and production of high-end chips, but China has launched an incentive program to attract top people from Taiwan.

What can the West offer to meet that challenge? Proposals reach from an improved education system that promotes excellence, the "appetite" for creativity to the famous "Ingenieurkunst" of Germany even missing in Silicon Valley.

8. Summary And Outlook

From the users perspective the outlook is very promising as he can expect continued progress for the next 5 to 10 years. However, intensive R&D activity behind the scene will be necessary to maintain more Moore and constitutes a big effort from the ICT industry.

In spite of the fact that a dependable weather forecast for three weeks is already impossible, we have tried to enumerate some of the emerging trends for the coming years:

- Continuing industry restructure
- New materials
- "Golden" age of architecture and software
- 3D technologies from chip to printer, production and medicine
- Interconnection and Communication improving dramatically
- First driverless cars (US)
- First city w/o traffic lights
- Robotic pharmacist or equivalent applications
- One trillion sensors
- Supercomputer in the pocket
- IoT pervasive into daily life
- 80% of population will have digital presence
- Start of brain wave communication

All this in the challenging scenario of:

- Population growth, predominantly in low education level areas, concurrent with increasingly difficult productivity increases in rich countries and a shortage of experts.
- Increasing influencibility by technology and impact on the political system
- Speed of adoption may be too fast for regulation and education system
- Protection of private sphere disappearing
- Cloud, AI and 5G/6G among the most important technologies
- No fundamentally new technology ready for mass production in sight
- A time window of 10-15 years of more Moore and beyond Moore full of improvement for the user implementing more scaling and parallelism.

We can look forward to fascinating but challenging times.

9. References

ALPHABET, 2018 Annual Report and SEC Report

ANDERSON M., (2019), Polarizing the Data Center, Spin lasers, IEEE Spectrum,

AMAZON, 2018 Annual Report, and SEC Report

APPLE, 2018, Annual Report and SEC Report

ARM, Techn. (2018), Moore´s law is dead, Republic

Desjardins J., (2019), How the tech giants make their billions,

Dyakonov M., (2018), the case against Quantum Computing

Economist, (2018), AI in business and (2018) Chip making

FACEBOOK, (2018) Annual Report and SEC Report,

IBM, (2018) IBM´s use of Samsung 7PP, Power10 and z15, Golem.de and The IBM Watson Debater,

INTEL´s (2017) "Next 50" study

IRDS (2017) International Roadmap for Devices and Systems

KAKU M., (2011) Physics of the future, Penguin Books, 978-0-141-04424-8.

Lain-Jing Li., How 2D semiconductors could extend Moore´s law

LOESCH Chr. IDIMT 2010 and 2014

MANJOO F. (2018) Para sobrevivir a la siguiente era de la technologia, frena y se consciente

MICROSOFT, (2018), Annual Report and SEC Report

PATERSEN D., (2018), Time for new computer architecture and software

RMIT Univ., Technical Breakthroughs allow 100-times faster internet

SPITZER M., (2015), Cyberkrank, ISBN 978-3-426.27008-2

WEF 2022, (2018), Mega trends which will shape the future, WEF

BRAVE NEW WORLD OF ICT

Christian W. Loesch

cwl0001@gmail.com

1. State of the ICT Industry

The ICT Industry is reaching never imaged heights, the demand for more and more complex chips in more and more newly created products with never before needed chips, led by an explosion of data, processing power requirement and further on to a server and storage explosion.

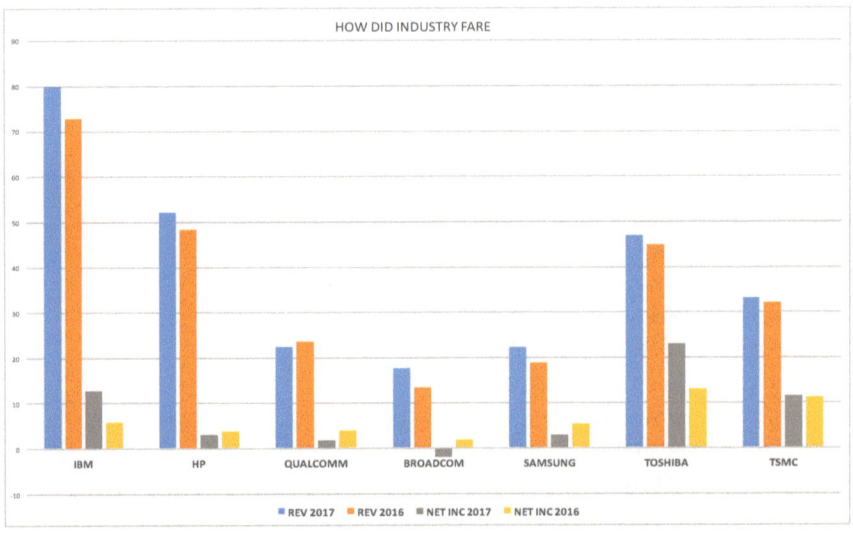

Differing reporting periods by country and exchange rate fluctuations are distorting the picture.

1.1. How did ICT Industry fare

Industry has found new ways to pack more power onto tinier chips but unfortunately it is not possible to cut costs on the same exponential curve, due to the increasingly complex and expensive manufacturing tools and processes. Its successful growth and the emphasis on R&D are shown below.

2017 Rank	2016 Rank	Vendor	2017 Revenue	2017 Market Share (%)	2016 Revenue	2016-2017 Growth (%)
1	2	Samsung Electronics	59,875	14.2	40,104	49.3
2	1	Intel	58,725	14.0	54,091	8.6
3	4	SK hynix	26,370	6.3	14,681	79.6
4	5	Micron Technology	22,895	5.4	13,381	71.1
5	3	Qualcomm	16,099	3.8	15,415	4.4
6	6	Broadcom	15,405	3.7	13,223	16.4
7	7	Texas Instruments	13,506	3.2	11,899	13.5
8	8	Toshiba	12,408	3.0	9,918	25.1
9	17	Western Digital	9,159	2.2	4,170	119.6
10	9	NXP	8,750	2.1	9,314	-6.1
		Others	177,201	42.2	159,655	11.0
		Total Market	**420,393**	**100.0**	**345,851**	**21.6**

Source: Gartner (April 2018)

Semiconductor Vendors 2016 - 2017 (by revenue in Mio US$)

2017 Rank	Company	R&D Exp ($M)	R&D/Sales (%)	17/16 % Chg in R&D
1	Intel	13,098	21.2%	3%
2	Qualcomm	3,450	20.2%	-4%
3	Broadcom*	3,423	19.2%	4%
4	Samsung	3,415	5.2%	19%
5	Toshiba	2,670	20.0%	-7%
6	TSMC	2,656	8.3%	20%
7	MediaTek*	1,881	24.0%	9%
8	Micron	1,802	7.5%	8%
9	Nvidia	1,797	19.1%	23%
10	SK Hynix	1,729	6.5%	14%
	Top 10 Total	**35,921**	**13.0%**	**6%**

Source: Company reports, IC Insights' *Strategic Reviews* database
*Sales and R&D spending of acquired semiconductor supplier are included.

R&D TOP 10 Semiconductor Companies

ICT became multidimensional and not constrained to computing and storage, this means equally impressive growth rates in fields as optoelectronics, sensors or discretes.

ICT industry is not only restructuring itself but also restructures other industries as the automotive industry i.e. profit shifts to electronics. Nvidia "Drive Xavier" and automotive firms want a piece of the cake or share of the market (producing SW) themselves.

The current assumption is that ICT industries R&D will run out of money before it runs out of physics.

Innovation will continue but it will be more nuanced and complex. The rise of Asian companies has continued and led to surpassing famous US companies. An example is the loss of density lead by INTEL. It's a six-transistor SRAM bit cell implemented in its 10-nanometer technology measures 0.0312 μm^2. Competing TSMCs (Taiwan Semiconductor Manufacturing Company) and

GlobalFoundries 7-nanometer technologies measure only 0.026 μm^2, 0.0272 μm^2, and 0.0269 μm^2, respectively.

2. Technology

We all know exponential growth cannot go on forever but the end may be much farther away in the future than many think.

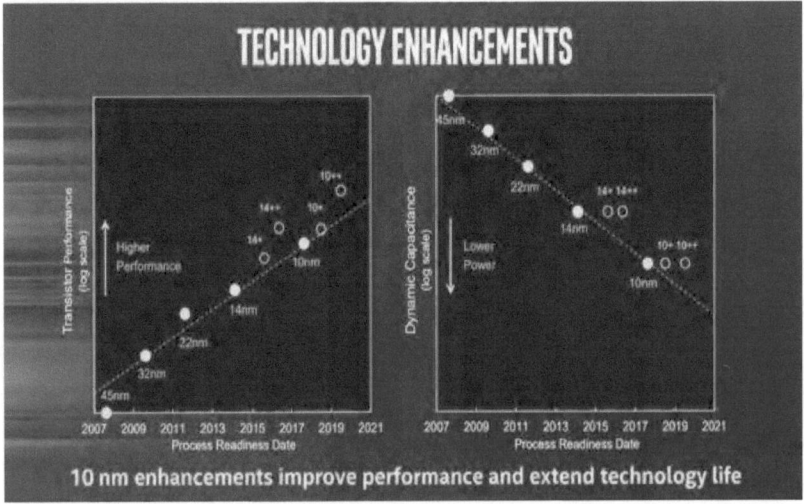

The master rule of the game is: the more we shrink it, the more it costs.

Every time the scale is halved, ICT manufacturers need a whole new generation of ever more precise photolithography machines. Building a new fab line today requires an investment typically measured in billions of dollars, something only a handful of companies can afford. Rising costs over the past decade have forced a massive consolidation and concentration process of the semiconductor industry; most of the world's production lines now belong to a handful of multinationals.

Additionally the fragmentation of the market triggered by mobile devices is making it harder to recuperate that money. When the cost per transistor at the next node exceeds the existing cost, scaling will stop.

This leads to multipronged R&D efforts and the search for new avenues and technologies.

3. Emerging technologies

3.1. Innovations that could shape the future of computing

- In-memory computing
- Super flat and 2D materials (TMDCs)
- Ultra-miniature computers
- Carbon Nano technology

- The 5nm transistor
- Advanced Memory Technology (as STT RAM)
- AI and Neuromorphic computing
- IoT
- QC

4. Architecture

4.1. In-Memory computing

As computation becomes increasingly data centric and the scalability limits are reached, alternative computing paradigms are sought. An approach is that of computational memory. The physics of nanoscale memory devices is used to perform certain computational tasks within the memory unit in a non-von Neumann manner. Computation and storage at the nanometer scale could enable ultra-dense, low-power, and massively-parallel computing systems.

IBM Research announced in Oct, 2017 it's first" "computational memory" computer system architecture, which is expected to yield a 200x improvements in computer speed and energy efficiency, enabling ultra-dense, low-power, massively parallel computing systems, 'in-memory' computing architecture.

Their concept is to use one device (such as phase change memory or PCM) for both storing and processing information. That design would replace the conventional "von Neumann" computer architecture, used in standard desktop computers, laptops, and cellphones, which splits computation and memory into two different devices. That requires moving data back and forth between memory and the computing unit, making them slower and less energy-efficient. (IBM, 2017)

5. Materials

5.1. New Super-flat materials TMDCs

Super-flat materials have been languishing in graphene's shadow. These materials named transition-metal dichalcogenides (TMDCs).

A single sheet of transition-metal atoms such as molybdenum or tungsten is sandwiched between equally thin layers of chalcogens: elements, such as sulfur and selenium that lie below oxygen in the periodic system of elements table. (KIS, 2018)

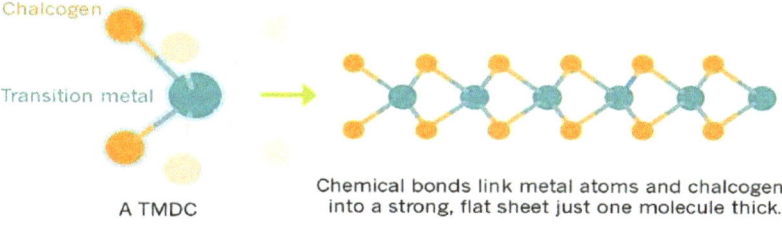

Chalcogen

Transition metal

A TMDC

Chemical bonds link metal atoms and chalcogens into a strong, flat sheet just one molecule thick.

TMDCs (transition metal dichalcogenides are made up of one transition metal atom for every two chalcogens atoms and can be split into 2D layers that are flexible, transparent and have high conductivity. One of the exciting possibilities of 2D materials is stacking them into structures that are very thin. Taking advantage of the vastly different properties of various super-flat materials, it should be possible to build entire digital circuits out of atomically thick components, creating previously unimagined devices. Building conventional silicon transistors involves high temperatures i.e. over 1,000°C. Putting a second layer of silicon circuits on top, at that high temperature will damage the bottom layer of circuits. Carbon nanotube circuits and RRAM memory can be fabricated at much lower temperatures: This means they can be built up in layers without harming the circuits beneath. More than 40 such TMDCs are under development and some are additionally semiconductors. (Shulake, 2017)

5.2. More Alternative Approaches in Computing

Ultraminiature Computer

Thin film surface structure of mono-layer iron (Fe) deposited on boron, gallium, aluminum or indium nitride substrate non-magnetic) could be the basis of another significant downsizing to a new dimension of computers and memories and having the advantage of being MRAM type. (Yu, 2018)

Hybrid architecture

At Stanford Univ. Cal. S. Mitra and colleagues have developed a hybrid architecture that stacks memory units together with transistors made from carbon nanotubes. This could reduce energy consumption to less than one-thousandth of standard chips.

Probabilistic Computing

Another interesting avenue is Probabilistic Computing. Turning from deterministic to probabilistic calculation allows for attractive trade-offs. For example, based on contemporary chip technology, a fourfold reduction in power can result in less than a 1% chance that a computational step will be incorrect.

5.3. Carbon Nano Technology

Carbon nanotubes is ready to take torch from Si according to Qing Cao of IBM Research. A future graphene-based transistor using spintronics could lead to tinier computers a thousand times faster and using a hundredth of the power of silicon-based computers. Especially Carbon-Nanosheets with their three-dimensional integration may lead to an intimate interweaving of memory and logic, featuring:

- Logic circuits made from carbon nanotubes an order of magnitude more energy-efficient compared to today's logic made from silicon.

- RRAM memory is denser, faster, and more energy-efficient than conventional DRAM devices.(Shulake, 2017)

- Dense through-chip vias (wires) that can enable vertical connectivity 1,000 times more dense than conventional packaging and chip-stacking solutions, dramatically improving the communication bandwidth between vertically stacked functional layers. Each sensor in the top layer can connect directly to its underlying memory cell. This enables the sensors to write at high speed their data in parallel directly into memory.

5.4. STT-MRAM

STT-MRAM technology may lead to the next big change in the evolution of computer memory. With this technology, traditional electrical currents can be used to change the magnetic state of the tunnel junction. Flowing electrical currents through the two ferromagnetic layers set the memory element into the parallel or antiparallel relative magnetic orientation without the use of an externally applied magnetic field.

5.5. The 5 nm Transistors

These dimensions mean signals are passing through a switch not larger than the width of two to three DNA strands. This is made especially attractive by the potential 75% power saving at a 40% performance improvement, and all this with standard tools and processes. But caution, may take 10 to 15 years of R&D before a groundbreaking new chip technology will be mature for the market.

The economy, measured in cost per transistor, is the only element of the "law" that's kept similar pace over the last 50 years. A future 5nm node chip with nanosheet transistors, and its scaled density, is to deliver the expected value of performance, power, and economy. We can potentially scale a CNT transistor further than silicon for the primary reason that they are only 1,2 nm thick. This reduces gate length to 10 nm, provides a better electrostatic control of the gate, and helps to minimize current leakage, and takes advantage of the fact that electrons travel faster in CNTs than in silicon, enhancing thus device performance.

But it needs new ways to connect CNTs to their source and drain, a mix of materials to "bake" these 10nm elements together at a manufacturable temperature. Previously contacts between source-and-drain required processing temperatures high, at around 850°C. Switching to a cobalt-molybdenum alloy for the wiring between the elements lowered the required temperature to an acceptable 650°C.

A new magnetism-control method could lead to ultrafast, energy-efficient computer memory. A cobalt layer on top of a gadolinium-iron alloy allows for switching memory with a single laser pulse in just 7 ps. This may lead to a computing processor with high-speed, non-volatile memory right on the chip. The researchers found a magnetic alloy made up of gadolinium and iron that could accomplish those higher speeds, switching the direction of the magnetism with a series of electrical pulses of about 10 ps, more than 10 times faster than MRAM. Another single femtosecond optical pulse can fully reverse the magnetization within picoseconds. (Gorchon, 2018)

6. Communications

The future dimension of information volume automatically creates the demand for a matching dimension of communication. In our session we will try to shortly peruse the upcoming era of 5G technology and the potential and practicability of the development towards a 6G technology.

7. AI

7.1. The renascence of AI

Following a period of exaggerated expectation AI disappeared from the stage for some years. The renascence of AI, becoming a household word in the last years, is paralleled by attracting worldwide investments and venture capital financed start-ups.

Top AI Investments Since 2013
Chinese startups lead the global pack with software and self-driving cars.

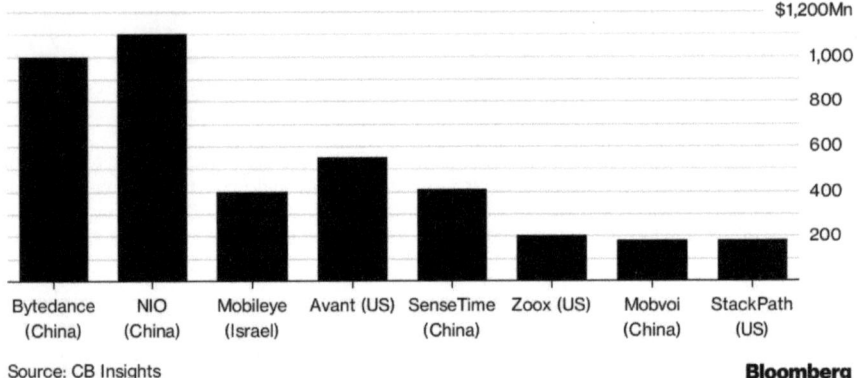

Source: CB Insights

Bloomberg

The first consumer AI offerings share a common trait: they enhance products but don't directly contribute to the bottom line. ? The future centers of application gravity may be

- Governments
- Banks and
- Retail.

Buyers are not interested in AI just because it is an exciting highly publicized technology, they want AI to generate a solid ROI (return on investment) by solving specific problems, saving them money, or increasing sales and profits. From where is it expected to come?

- 40-50% Services solution and user cases
- 40-50% HW
- 0-10% Training

Considering cost of ownership; every use case is having slightly different requirements, each one will need partially customized hardware rather than commodity hardware, such as general-purpose central processing units (CPUs). For instance, accelerators optimized for convolutional neural networks are best for image recognition and thus would be chosen by medical-device manufacturers. But accelerators optimized for memory networks are better suited to speech recognition and language translation and thus would appeal to makers of sophisticated virtual home assistants.

In the past 10 years, the best-performing AI systems, such as the speech recognizers on smartphones or automatic translators have resulted from a technique called "deep learning." Deep learning is a name for an approach to artificial intelligence called neural networks, going in and out of fashion for more than 70 years

The resurgence of neural networks, the deep-learning renaissance, comes courtesy of the computer-game industry. The complex imagery and rapid pace of today's video games require hardware that can keep up, and the result has been the graphics processing unit (GPU), which packs thousands of relatively simple processing cores on a single chip. It didn't take long for researchers to realize that the architecture of a GPU is remarkably like that of a neural net.

How does it work? To each of its incoming connections, a node will assign a number (value) known as a "weight". When the node receives different values over each of its connections and multiplies it by the associated weight. It then combines the resulting products, yielding a single value. If that value is below a threshold value, the node passes no data to the next layer. If the value exceeds the threshold value, the node "fires," which in today's neural nets generally means sending the value, the result of the weighted inputs, along all its outgoing connections.

AI needs big data. A vast quantity of examples is required for training neural networks, representing a valuable asset, e.g. millions of hours of annotated street driving videos are required for the training of basic autonomous driving skills.

Both approaches DL (deep learning) and ML (machine learning) are considered simultaneously because partially they are parallel, partially they are symbiotic. ML is preferred when only small amounts of data are available and the structures behind the data base is known. Neuronal methods need less knowledge and preparation to start with but much more data.

The approaches differ in practice: Deep Learning: first placing, testing afterwards vs. Science: first research and testing, then placement

Another aspect of AI stresses simulations, in which machines teach themselves using synthetic data or in virtual environments. An example has been demonstrated by the program to play Go, by DeepMind, a company acquired and now a unit of Alphabet. Computers were trained using data from actual games; the latest were simply given the rules and started playing Go against itself. Within three days it had surpassed its predecessor, which had itself beaten the best human player. If this approach proves widely applicable, future AI systems can be trained using sparser amounts of data.

The handling of personal data by all-too-human intelligence has turned into a big also ethical challenge of this new world.

Automation has in the long run not led job losses but to more employment. It has done so in every technological revolution since the threshing machine, and will this time too, though it may be now lawyers and medics who may have to readjust rather than farmhands and factory workers. Nothing is proving more egalitarian than the smartphone, and AI should likewise be mostly available to rich and poor alike. (Ridle, 2018)

Whereas the previous generation of AI was based on "expert systems" pre-loaded with human expertise, today's algorithms know almost nothing at the start, but crunch lots of data to learn how to do something. It is the access to deep draughts of data, and the ability to learn from them. In future 1 the decision "make or buy" might change to "teach or buy"? (Batra, 2018)

7.2. AI Technology and Neuromorphic Computing

Traditional workloads we have known for the last 40 years do not more apply. AI requires different capabilities from the machines we build.

There are well known companies to which we deliver our data free or even at our expense, and the volume of data will increase dramatically by IoT, and automation. Think of automated driving or Tesla recording the data of its cars automatically or the upcoming automated emergency call feature which send is also supposed to send selected data to the car manufacturer.

Our brains are much more efficient than computers for classifying unstructured data, like facial recognition and natural language processing, in part due to the reduced precision required for the brain to make a reasonable classification. By exploiting the reduced precision requirements for unstructured data workloads, the innate efficiency advantage of analog computing can be harnessed.

Intel's new 'Loihi' chip mimics neurons and synapses in the human brain and is getting automatically smarter over time.

As result of six years development efforts, the chip uses 130,000 "neurons" and 130 million "synapses" and learns in real time, based on feedback from the environment. Fabricated on Intel's 14 nm process technology, the chip is also up to 1,000 times more energy-efficient than general-purpose computing required for typical training systems.

For comparison, IBM's True North neuromorphic chip currently has 1 million neurons and 256 million synapses. (IBM, 2017)

The new NIST synapse has two unique features that researchers claims to outperform human synapses and other artificial synapses. Operating at 100 GHz, it can fire at a rate that is much faster than the human brain, 1 billion times per second, compared to a brain cell's rate of about 50 times per second, using only about one ten-thousandth as much energy as a human synapse. The spiking energy is less than 1 attojoule, compared to the roughly 10 femtojoules per synaptic event in the human brain... As NISTs M. Schneider stated, we do not know of any other artificial synapse that uses less energy.

Adding the advantages of super-conduction, a superconducting 'synapse' could enable powerful future neuromorphic supercomputers faster, lower-energy-required, compared to human synapses firing 200 million times faster than human brain, using only one ten-thousandth as much energy.

But overall current neuromorphic platforms are still orders of magnitude less efficient than the human brain

Nvidia's "Supercharged law". GPUs today are 25 times faster than five years ago. If they were advancing according to Moore's law, they only would have increased their speed "only" by a factor of 10 considering the increase in power of GPUs. Measured by another benchmark: the time to train AlexNet, a neural network on 15 million images. Five years ago, it took six days to go through the training process; with the latest hardware, it takes only18 minutes, a factor of 500. Development benefits from simultaneous advances on multiple fronts: architecture, interconnects, memory technology, algorithms, and more. The innovation is not just about chips, it is about the entire stack. (Huank, 2018)

Every year more than nine billion microcontrollers are shipped as part of goods ranging from mobile phones to computers, toasters or refrigerators and we want to connect all of them in the long run.

Technology does not just happen. It is based on deliberate human choices and decisions.

To ensure that these choices are based on general acceptable and ethical principles will be a key problem for the future.

7.2.1. The "Brave new world" of AI, examples and potential issues

Surveillance and spying especially electronically empowered spying by states and governmental agencies has been around and officially tolerated since years. Extending scenario from the well-known stories of Edward Snowden, Facebook, Amazon, Google or project Echelon etc., to some of the more recent AI applications.(Loesch, 2017)

The prognostic use of AI is another two-edged development. Models evaluating the probability of delinquents becoming retrograde based on the record of the parents (weight 50%) or personal interests as membership in a civil rights movement (weight 20%), with wide implications that may determine the future of the person.

At the Zhengzhou railway station (PRC) a test with robots has been successfully implemented. Robot police were rolling through the waiting halls and identified faces and aggressive behavior. Only for arresting people human police is still required.

As Bloomberg reports face recognition is already used to control said to be dangerous groups of people as in the region of the province Xinjiang the computer is alerting the police if certain target objects leave a certain area.

Sometimes the area of free movement is restricted to few blocks (Human Rights Watch criticizes the virtual fencing a serious offence against of human rights). It is called fight against crime and terrorism but is shifting to maintain stabilization and public security and even monitor so called inappropriate behavior. Amnesty International finds that all restraints to use these techniques seem to have vanished.

The new glasses for police officers are more than a gadget, they offer the identification of billion citizens (In many countries a biometric ID card or passport is obligatory and thus the government has already a powerful data base, faces included).

Similar models are available for evaluation and selection of applicants for jobs, or employee performance also.

A study of using automated language analysis, published in the renowned psychiatry journal World Psychiatry, was studying a larger patient cohort, based on a retrospective model of patient speech patterns that would have predicted with 83% accuracy whether a patient subsequently developed psychosis

Deep neural network models have already scored higher than humans in reading and comprehension test. Microsoft achieved 82.650 on the ExactMatch metric, and the Alibaba Group Holding Ltd. scored 82.44.0 The best human score so far is 82.304.(Yampolskiy, 2018)

8. Quantum Computers

The general idea for a quantum computer is often traced to the physicist Richard Feynman in 1981. An alternative starting point could be a paper by Peter Shor in1994, then of AT&T Bell Laboratories, outlining how a quantum computer could quickly find the prime factors of large numbers, thus defeating commonly used public-key encryption systems.

Many companies work to lead the Quantum Computers out of the laboratories. Technology giants and startups alike want to bring quantum computing into the mainstream and market. The list ranges from D-Wave, IBM, Microsoft, Intel, and Northrop Grumman to Google to many start-ups.

Scientists are cringing at press reports overstating progress. The algorithm Google is running to demonstrate quantum supremacy but does not do anything of practical importance yet. Building quantum computers that can solve real-world computing problems people actually care about will require many more years of research. Engineers working on quantum computing at both Google and IBM say that a quantum "dream machine" capable of solving computing's most vexing problems might still be *decades* away.

The picture below of the IBM 50-Qubit Processor may give you an impression of the state of technology of today's QCs.

Photo: IBM, Christopher Payne

The idea of a 50-qubit+ (or so) quantum computer outperforming a state-of-the-art supercomputer sounds alluring, but it leaves a lot of questions hanging. Outperforming for which problem? How do you know the quantum computer has got the right answer if you can't check it with a tried-and-tested classical device? And how can you be sure that the classical machine wouldn't do better if you could find the right algorithm?

All current designs for quantum computers involve pairing them with classical ones, which carry out myriad pre- and post- processing steps. Many everyday programming tasks that can now be executed quickly on traditional computers might actually run *slower* on a quantum one, given the hardware and software overhead associated with getting a quantum computer to work in the first place. IBM's new quantum computers, like those of Google, must be chilled to near absolute zero temperature to function.

Qubits must be kept isolated from even the minutest amount of outside interference, at least for as long as it takes for the computation to be completed.

Because of all the noise that surrounds them, qubits tend to be error prone. To deal with this problem, quantum computers need to have extra qubits standing by as backups to enable restoring the errant qubit to its proper state. Such error correction occurs in regular computers too, but the number of required backups is much greater in quantum systems i.e. for a reliable quantum computer, every qubit used might need 1,000 or more backups. Because many advanced algorithms require many qubits to begin with, the total number of qubits necessary for a useful quantum machine, including those involved with error correction, could run into *millions*.

Researchers have suggested to express the power of a quantum computation as "quantum volume," which bundles all the relevant factors: number and connectivity of qubits, depth of algorithm, and other measures as noisiness. It is this quantum volume that characterizes the power of quantum computation.

The emerging consensus seem to be, surprises are always possible, expect the progress to be gradual. While researchers warn against excessive optimism, also don't rule out the prospect of breakthroughs that will allow the machines to do much more with less.

Some researchers are pointing out that we are essentially at the point that classical computing was at 100 years ago, not even at vacuum tubes yet.(IEEE, 2018)

EU announced a flagship program on Quantum Computing (announced, but not yet agreed by council and parliament), expecting from this program:

- Prim number factoring very large numbers into prime numbers
- Precise sensors for solid state physics new materials
- GPS from meters to millimeters using entanglement
- Contributions to the „Human brain" project
- Secure "Quantum Internet"

But caution against overselling; neither computers nor the Internet will not be entirely quantum

9. IoT

Since it will be addressed in separate sessions, let us restrain ourselves to few selected points.

IoT's value, from the customer's perspective, is in Services and IoT analytics & applications. These two layers are expected by 2020 to have captured 60% of the growth. The rest of the technology are enabling components with lower growth potential.

9.1. IoT´s Market potential and Applications

Market potential (B$ 3 ys)
Discrete manufacturing B$ 40
Transportation B$ 40
Utilities B$ 40
B2C B$ 25
Health care B$ 15

Applications
Predictive Maintenance Self-Optimizing Production.
Automated Inventory Management
Remote Patient Monitoring
Smart Meters.

> Track and Trace.

10. Summary and Outlook

Summarizing the points covered and guessing how the new scenario may look:

- Industry reaching new heights,
- Shift in constituency and geography
- Concentration and Oligopoly
- A bouquet of fascinating technologies emerging
- Another period of quasi exponential growth ahead
- A plethora of promising competing ideas in the R&D pipeline

But principal questions may arise, since 90% of rare earth metals mines are in China and at current speed will run out in 20 years

Potential areas of impact and basic questions arising:

- Productivity gain (less jobs more profit)
- Which layer of society will benefit?
- Society reduced to statistics (loss of other dimensions)?
- Autopilotation: extended from car to autopiloted enterprise (Industry x.0)
- Transition of knowledge from state to private enterprise?
- AI ethics: Selection of samples and algorithms?
- Society of Prognostic and algorithmic controls ahead

Privacy, a new "quality" additional surveillance, control and user transparency

But there may also be significant social implications ahead:

Automation has led to more employment, not less, in every technological revolution since the threshing machine, and will continue to do so. (Though it may now affect lawyers and medics who may have to readjust rather than farmhands and factory workers.)

Nothing is proving more egalitarian than the smartphone, and AI should likewise be mostly available to rich and poor alike. A new egalitarianism with an invisible hand on the horizon?

The handling of personal data turned into one of the big challenges of this brave new world.

Society must grapple with the dilemma of preserving people's privacy and ownership of their data, while letting machine-learning algorithms harvest insights of value to everybody. The starry-eyed optimism that greeted, for example, the Obama campaign's use of Facebook data in 2012 has given way to rage at similar practices used by in the recent US election campaign. Is there a sensible compromise to be found?

The rise of AI will make life richer, better, more interesting, and then be taken for granted, as electricity and cars are. Yet the same old, all-too-human ethical and political dilemmas about how much power to allow the state, or private enterprise, will persist. (Ridle, 2018)

Transgressing the limits of human capabilities and act beyond the scope of proven human behavior and power and traditional ethics is a tricky endeavor, especially without ruling ethical democratic principles?

Technology has always assisted human endeavors but its use is up to us. We still have all the opportunities but should not be late.

11. References

ACCENTURE, Major Trends that will shape IT

AGERWALA T. Systems research challenges, IBM J. of R&D 2006

BBC, Fifty years of the Web, How the web went worldwide, BBC Archive 2006

Batra G., Queirolo A., and Santhanam N, What will IT look like in the age of cognitive workloads and deep learning?

CHROUST G., 15 years of IDIMT, Synergie, Emergenz und Innovation in der IKT Industrie, Univ. Linz, 2007

Huang and Clayton J., Nvidia's "Supercharged law"

IBM, Computational Memory IBM Research (Oct.2017) and IBM's True North neuromorphic chip

IEEE Spectrum, Quantum Computing: Both Here and Not Here, April 2018.

Isaac R.D, The future of CMOS technology, IBM J. R & D 44, No. 3, 2000

IWAI HIROSHI, The future of CMOS downscaling, Frontiers Collection 2004

Jie Xiang Yu and Jiadong Zang, Science advances, March 2018

Gorchon J. et al, Cobalt layer on top of a gadolinium-iron alloy allows for switching memory, Applied Physics Letter

KIS, Superflat Materials

KURZWEIL R. The Law of accelerating returns, 2001

LOESCH C.W. Trends in Technology, Proceedings of Euromicro, 2003,

LOESCH CHR., Trends and Scenarios, 2000-2017

RIDLE M., House of Lords report on the Opportunities of AI

ROWEN Chr., International Fabless 2005

SHULAKE M., MIT July, 2017, Nature.

WIKIPEDIA, Timeline of computing, 2007

YAMPOLSKIY R., Update your AGI predictions

IDIMT 2017

ICT Beyond the Red Brick Wall

Abstract and Introduction

It would be difficult to overstate the impact of Moore's Law. It is all around us, in the myriad gadgets, computers, and networks that power modern life. However, the winning streak cannot last forever. For all phenomena of exponential growth, the question is not whether, but only when and why they will end, more specifically: would it be physics or economics that raises the barrier to further scaling?

Physics has been our friend for decennia ("Dennards Law") has now become the foe of further downscaling. In spite of all doomsday prophesies since the '80s, we will reach, thanks to the ingenuity of physicists and engineers, the famous red wall only within the next five to ten years and it might be a second an economic wall. The third wall may be a "power" wall, not just for the well-known power problems also for a other reasons, as the proportionality of system failure and power consumption.

Some sort of "Moore's law" can also be found in the software area, as at operating systems doubling in size every new generation or as a law of diminishing returns or leading to the increasing reluctance to accept new hard and software generations?

On the request of many we look on the emerging long term options rather than at the immediate and mid-term scenario.

We will review how ICT Industry is performing and trying to meet these challenges and preparing adequate strategies. The variety of responses is stunning and ranges from Memristor, QC, cognitive computing systems, big data, to graphene and the abundance of emerging fascinating applications which will impact our life.

Processor productivity, bandwidth, number of transistors per chip, upgrades in architecture, continue to increase further causing increasing demand on processor communications, bandwidth and transmission speed on the chip and worldwide networks.

1. Economy

Will review how the industry fared. Since most 2016 results will be published too late for the printing press, we will to cover them in our session but based on latest results.

2017	Brand	Category	2017 ($M)	change	2016
1	Google	Technology	245,581	+7%	1
2	Apple	Technology	234,671	+3%	2
3	Microsoft	Technology	143,222	+18%	3
4	Amazon	Retail	139,286	+41%	7
5	Facebook	Technology	129,800	+27%	5
6	AT&T	Telecom providers	115,112	+7%	4
7	Visa	Payments	110,999	+10%	6

8	Tencent	Technology	108,292	+27%	11
9	IBM	Technology	102,088	+18%	10
10	McDonald's	Fast food	97,723	+10%	9

Source: Marketing BrandZ

Revenue and income can only give a very vague picture, but they are providing an overall impression how some key players of the industry performed in the 2016/2015 timeframe.

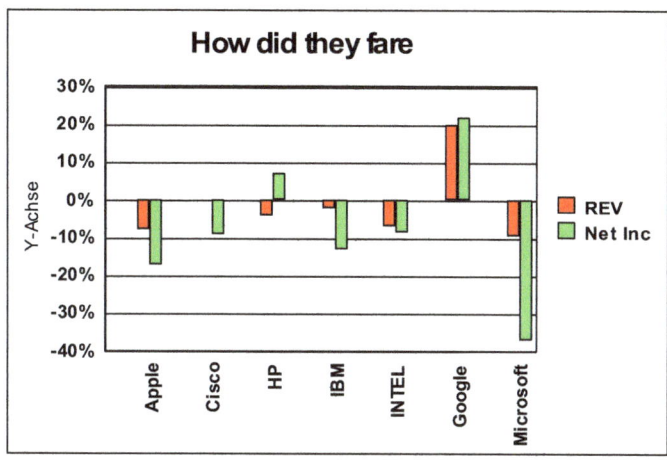

2. Technology

Moore's "Law" has been a synonym for faster cheaper processing power. Key contributors have been and are in a two to three years rhythm:

- Performance + 30% operating frequency at constant energy
- Power - 50% energy / switching process
- Area size reduction -50%,
- Cost -25% wafer and up to -40% scaled die

However since the end of Dennard scaling more than a decade ago, doubling transistor densities have not led to corresponding higher performance By 2020 feature size will be down to just a few nanometers leading to the transition to the economically more attractive vertical scaling

ITRS names three applications areas driving innovation:

- High performance computing
- Mobile computing
- Autonomous sensing & computing (e.g. IoT)

The quest for an alternate technology to replace CMOS has come up with no serious contenders in the near future. "Little room left at the bottom ".

STT technology is today's research focus. Advantages range from lower footprint, reduced writing current by one or two orders of magnitude and full scalability. STT MRAM may be the low hanging fruit we are waiting for, with spin orbit torque technology on the horizon

2.1 Nanotechnology, atomic and molecular

Nanotechnology breakthroughs pave the way for the ultra-small.

Recently published research papers highlight these as:

Single-molecule switching, which could lead to molecular computers, the discovery of two hydrogen atoms inside a naphthalocyanine molecule that can do switching, means storing enormous amounts of information and the idea of a computer comprised of just a few molecules may no longer be science fiction, but exploratory science. Such devices might be used as future computer chips, storage devices, and sensors for applications nobody has imagined yet. They may prove to be a step toward building computing elements at the molecular scale that are vastly smaller, faster and use less energy than today's computer chips and memory devices. The single-molecule switch could operate without disrupting the molecule's outer frame. In addition to switching within a single molecule, the researchers also demonstrated that atoms inside one molecule can be used to switch atoms in an adjacent molecule, representing a rudimentary logic element. [Meyer G., IBM Zurich Research Lab]

2.2 Graphene

Graphene has become one of the most shining materials for the scientific community and a popular candidate for IoT and flexible electronics;

At present information processing is split into three functions with different types of material:

- Information processing: Si- transistor based
- Communications: Compound semiconductor based, as InAs, GaAs, InP by photons
- Information storage: Ferromagnetic metals based.

Such a division is not very efficient. Graphene triangular quantum dots (GTQD) offer a potential alternative; there is a special class of nanoscale graphene, triangular with zigzag edges meeting all three functions.

One atom thin integrated graphene circuits pose many problems to be resolved as controlling size, shape and edges with atomic precision or that graphene FETs suffer from the lack of a large band gap, therefore generating a band gap without sacrificing the mobility remains the greatest challenge for graphene. [Technology Innovation, Kinam Kim and U-In Chung Samsung advanced Institute of Technology, Giheung, S. Korea], [A. Güclü, P.Potasz and P. Hawrylak, NRC of Ottawa, Canada]

These atom-thick 2D materials could lead to a new industrial revolution for the post Si era, atomically thin tunnel transistors offer transparency with comparable performance, 2D providing wider bandwidth and cheaper integration with Si for data communication but will take five to ten years to reach the marketplace due to problems of material quality and integration. [Sungwoo Hwang et alii, Graphene and Atom-thick 2D Materials, Samsung advanced institute of technology, Suwon, S. Korea]

In view of the fact that 38% of energy consumption in data centers (2009) copper interconnects of devices between and on chips. Substitute Cu by optical interconnects resulting in a 1000-times lower attenuation could be another promising technology. [D. Stange, Jülich, R. Geiger PSI Villingen et alii., Univ. Grenoble, Z. Ikonic, Univ. Leeds UK]

2.3 Racetrack

IBM claims that its racetrack storage technology to store data in magnetic domain walls is reaching market maturity within the next years. The expected performance is impressive:

- Data stored in magnetic domain walls

- 100 times more storage than on disk or flash

- Fast r/w in a nanosecond

2.4 The Memristor

According to the original 1971 definition, the Memristor was the fourth fundamental circuit element, forming a non-linear relationship between electric charge and magnetic flux linkage. In 2011 Chua argued for a broader definition that included all two-terminal non-volatile memory devices based on resistance switching. But broader definition of Memristor could be a scientific land grab that favors HP's Memristor patents. Back to the '60s date first description of Memristor, Today are many implementations under development.

Memristor change their resistance depending on the direction and amount of voltage applied, and they remember this resistance when the voltage is removed. Most memory types store data as charge, but Memristors would enable a resistive RAM, a nonvolatile memory that stores data as resistance instead of charge.

Memristors promise a new type of dense, cheap, and low-power memory.

What are the potential advantages of the Memristor?

- Density > hard drives

- $100GB/cm^2$ -> 3D 1000layers = $100TB/cm^3$

- 100x faster than flash memory (5/2012)

- 1% of energy and works up to 150 C (Ge_2Se version)

One Memristor has equivalent logic function to several connected transistors means higher density and uses up much less power.

In 2010, HP labs announced that they had practical Memristor working at 1ns (~1 GHz) switching times and 3 nm by 3 nm sizes. At these densities, it could easily rival the sub-25 nm flash memory technology.

A major problem is how to make large numbers of them reliable enough for commercial electronic devices. Researchers continue to puzzle over the best materials and way of manufacturing them.

Memory fabric (HPE Labs)

3. Future Generation Computing

3.1 "The Machine"

HPE is developing "The Machine", the largest R&D program in the company's history in three stages, of which it is unveiling the first. In the second and third phases the company plans to move beyond DRAM to test phase-change random access memory (PRAM) and memristors, over the next few years. HPE assigned 75% of its human R&D resources to this project. The Machine still has not arrived completely; HPE is providing a peek at progress so far.

A prototype has been on display at *The Atlantic*'s: Return to Deep Space conference in Washington, D.C., featuring 1,280 high-performance microprocessor cores, each of which reads and executes program instructions in unison with the others, with access to 160 terabytes (TB) of memory. Optical fibers pass information among the different components.

The Machine is defined by its memory centric computing memory driven architecture i.e. a single, huge pool of addressable memory." A computer assigns an address to the location of each byte of data stored in its memory. The Machine's processors can access and communicate with those addresses much the way high-performance computer nodes.

HPE's X1 photonics interconnect module laser technology replaces traditional copper wires with optical data transfer between electronic devices. [Hewlett Packard's Silicon Design Labs in Fort Collins, Colo. Enterprise].

3.2 Cognitive Computing, Neurocomputing and AI

IBM is taking a somewhat different track in its efforts to develop next-generation computing, focusing on neuromorphic systems that mimic the human brain's structure as well as quantum or another approach can be found in Microsoft's Cortana Intelligent suit.

Potential applications range from face detection, AI machine learning and reasoning, Natural language processing, predictive maintenance, to risk detection to Diagnostics or forecasting future sales (up to 90% correct).

The impossibility to maintain current knowledge is could be addressed by IBM's Watson.

Knowledge degrades so fast that Hi-Tecemployer as GooglespaceX etc are focusing less on qualification but on logic thinking, problem solving and creative thinking.

AI is not programming computers but training them.

What is a cognitive chip? The SyNAPSE chip, introduced in 2014, operates at very low power levels. IBM built a new chip with a brain-inspired computer architecture powered by 1 million neurons and 256 million synapses chip. It is the largest chip IBM has ever built at 5.4 billion transistors, and has an on-chip network of 4,096 neurosynaptic cores. It consumes 70mW during real-time operation, orders of magnitude less energy than traditional chips.

The TrueNorth Chip or the SpiNNaker chip of the Univ. of Manchester is comparable endeavors.

Below are some characteristics of cognitive systems aim to fulfil:

- Adaptive
- Interactive
- Iterative and helpful.
- Contextual

They may understand, identify, and extract contextual elements such as meaning, syntax, time, location, appropriate domain, regulations, user's profile, process, task and goal. They may draw on multiple sources of information, including both structured and unstructured digital information, as well as sensory inputs (visual, gesture, auditory, or sensor-provided).

Neurocomputing, often referred to as artificial neural networks (ANN), can be defined as information processing systems (computing devices) designed with inspiration taken from the nervous system, more specifically the brain, and with particular emphasis in problem solving.

"An artificial neural network is a massively parallel distributed processor made up of simple processing units, which has a natural propensity for storing experiential knowledge and making it available for use." [Haykin S., Neural Networks and Learning Machines, 1999.]

The first neural networks were already presented in 1964, attempting to mimic the logic process of the brain. Brains are good at performing functions like pattern recognition, perception, flexible inference, intuition, and guessing, but also slow, imprecise, make erroneous generalizations, prejudiced, and are sometimes incapable of explaining their own actions. Cognitive Computing is progressing impressivly. Deep learning, pattern recognition, matching photos (97,5 %) or language translation may be found everywhere in five years.

Four areas expect to benefit especially:

- Nanotechnology (Biotechnology)
- AI
- Genetics
- Robotics

3.3 A short Introduction to the Quantum World

Quantum physics is with us in our everyday life. No transistor would work without it.

Erwin Schrödinger, who developed quantum theory's defining equation, once warned a lecture audience that what he was about to say might be considered insane.

The famous double slit experiment should serve as an introductory first step into this world. Will discuss these two phenomena to give a first clue to the world of quantum physics:

- Superposition
- Entanglement

From a physical point of view, entangled particles form only one entity (one single waveform instead of two) and locality of a particle is an illusion. These particles have a probability of presence that stretches out infinitely, with their local position of very high probability of presence as "particles". Entangling means merging different waveforms into a single one, but which has several local positions of very high probability instead of one, like having a single particle (one single waveform), but with several centres of mass instead of one.

"Observing" one of the high-probability locations of entangled particles modifies this single probability cloud, which also determines the "state" of the second high-probability location of the other entangled particles).

Entanglement and Superposition cause qubits to behave very differently from bits. A two-bit circuit in a conventional computer can be in only one of four possible states (0 and 0, 0 and 1, 1 and 0, or 1 and 1), a pair of qubits can be in combination of all four. As the number of qubits in the circuit increases, the number of possible states, and thus the amount of information contained in the system increases exponentially.

Many various approaches are currently under development. Researchers favor currently qubit design, based on superconductors microchip-scale circuits made of materials that lose all electrical resistance at very low temperatures. Thanks to the Josephson effect, electric currents flowing around tiny loops in such circuits can circle both clockwise and counter clockwise at once, so they are perfect for representing a qubit. Within few years R&D efforts have increased Qubit lifetimes by a factor of 10,000, that is maintaining their state for around 50 - 100 µsecs, and reducing the error rate. [Martinis]

3.4 The Quantum Computer (QC)

The idea of QC is to store values of 2^N complex amplitudes describing the wavefunction of N two-level systems (qubits) complex amplitudes and process this information by applying unitary in formations (quantum gates), that change these amplitudes in a precise and controlled manner.

Building the first real QC is an estimated to be a 10 B$ project. What could be the "killer applications" justifying this effort?

Scientists spent already several years looking for an answer, an application for quantum computing that would justify the development costs. The two classic examples, code-cracking and searching databases, seem not to be sufficient. QCs may search databases faster, but they are still limited by the time it takes to feed the data into the circuit, which would not change.

A much more promising application for the near future could be modelling of electrons in materials and molecules, something too difficult even for today's supercomputers. With around 400 encoded qubits, it might be possible to analyse ways to improve industrial nitrogen fixation, the energy-intensive process that turning unreactive molecules in air into fertilizer. This is now carried out on an industrial scale using the 120 years old Haber process, that uses up to about 5% of the natural gas produced worldwide. A quantum computer could help to design a much more energy-efficient catalyst. Another "killer application" might be searching for new high-temperature superconductors, or improving the catalysts used to capture carbon from the air or from industrial exhaust streams. "Progress there could easily substantiate the 10 billion." [Troyer].

Which will be potential QC areas?

- Design of drugs

- Supply chain logistics
- Material science (properties, as melting point etc. design of new metals)
- Financial services
- Cryptanalysis

However, veterans of the field caution that quantum computing is still in the early stages. The QC will rather appear as coprocessor than as stand alone computer. The development is in a phase that compare to Zuse in 1938. In 5 years special application superior to today's computers with TP access may appear. [R. Blatt]

3.5 IoT

Market potential estimations range wide between: Cisco 20 -50 billion or IBM 20 bio devices.

Optimists have reason to be encouraged. More than 120 new devices connect to the Internet every second. McKinsey Global Institute estimates IoT could have an annual economic impact of $3,9 trillion to $11,1 trillion by 2025.

However, several short term obstacles to be fixed:

- Missing Standards

- Speed requirements to be resolves by transition from 4G to 5G (license auction 2017/18)

- Address space (transition from IP4 to IP6 on its way)

The growth of the IoT, combined with the exponential development of sensors and connectivity, will make it more challenging to provide power to untethered devices and sending nodes. Even with long-life battery technology, many of these devices can only function for a few months without a recharge.

The arrival of the quest for an electric car has is additionally emphasizing the problem, but the 800 km reach may not come before 2020.

Energy harvesting increasing performance of energy transducers and the decreasing power requirements of ICs may bridge the gap. [A. Romani et alii, Nanopower Integrated Electronics for Energy harvesting, conversion and management, Univ. of Bologna, Italy]

Both consumers and the media are fascinated by IoT innovations that have already hit the market. With short time, some IoT devices have become standard, including thermostats that automatically adjust the temperature and production-line sensors that inform workshop supervisors of machine condition. Now innovators target more sophisticated IoT technologies as self-driving cars, drone-delivery services, and other applications as:

- Large structures (bridges, buildings roads)
- Adv. personal sensors (breath analysis)
- Logistics
- Crop monitoring
- Pollution
- Tracking from kids to dogs and shoes etc.

Up to now the adoption of IoT is proceeding more slowly than expected, but semiconductor companies through new technologies and business models will try to accelerate growth.

3.6 Fiber

Replacing copper by optical connections within and outside the computer, increasing connectivity and the exponential growth of information will put further emphasize the development of data transmission.

The longer the light travels, the more photons will scatter off atoms and leak into the surrounding layers of cladding and protective coating. After 50 km, about 90% of the light will be lost. To keep the signal going after the first 50 km, repeaters were then used to convert light pulses into electronic signals, clean and amplify them, and then retransmit them.

The British physicist D. Payne opened a new avenue, by adding and exciting erbium atoms with a laser; he could amplify incoming light with a wavelength of 1.55 μm, where optical fibers are most transparent. The erbium-fiber amplifier enabled another way to boost data rates: multiple-wavelength communication. Erbium atoms amplify light across a range of wavelengths, a band wide enough for multiple signals in the same fiber, each with its own much narrower band of wavelengths.

The classical way to pack more bits per second is to shorten the length of pulses. Unfortunately, the shorter the pulses, the more vulnerable they become to dispersion and will stretch out traveling through a fiber and interfere with one another. Techniques previously developed, dubbed wavelength-division multiplexing, along with further improvements in the switching frequency of fast laser signals, led to an explosion in capacity.

Together, quadrature coding and coherent detection, with the ability to transmit in two different polarizations of light, have carried optical fibers to allowing a single optical channel to carry 100Gb/s over long distances, in fibers designed to carry only 10 Gb/s. Since a typical fiber can accommodate roughly 100 channels, the total capacity of the fiber can approach 10 Tb/s.

4. Redirection: Applications and Lateral Developments

The plethora some of these developments rising on the horizon stretch from

- Photovoltaic with 500% of today's capacity and 1/100 thickness
- Water-purification
- Medicine:

   Some facts and figures:

   - 14000 illnesses and 5000 publications/week.
   - Improved scanning can achieve 80%-90% hit rate in mammography.
   - "Chirurgical Intelligent Knife" (distinguishing malign from non malign areas)
   - Improved diagnostics: "The first time right" envisions future medicine to be predictive, personalized and precise [Zerhouni E., US NIH, 2006]

- Intelligent prosthetics
- 3D printing of drugs or simple organs
- Lab on a chip (biofluid evaluate plasma and bio markers)
- Anti-bacteria nanoparticles.

We mentioned the information avalanche. Watson, as covered previously is a possible answer and avenue to be followed, as learning machine, without internet connection, trained to understand meaning of words, "Super Google "may answer questions before you realize you have it".

5. Summary

We have been perusing the scenario in view of approaching the red brick wall and beyond we found a plethora of developments and emerging technologies and applications.

- In spite of longstanding doomsday prophesies since the ´80s, thanks to the ingenuity of physicists and engineers, we will reach the red wall only within the next five to ten years. There may be a second wall an economic wall due to unjustifiable investments reached earlier. Many believe a third wall may be a "power" wall, not just for the well-known power problems but for the proportionality of system failure and power consumption.

- Future technologies ranging from STT to graphite and future computing from "The Machine" to Quantum Computers, Cognitive Computing, Neurocomputing , AI and Watson.

- The effects of "getting physical" by direct connecting computers increasingly to the physical world around, integrating all types of devices from keys to sensors, tags etc.

- The evolution of human knowledge has been accelerated by storing and sharing information. The amount of data will reach 44 ZB in 2020, the number of Internet-connected devices 50 B in 2020 (doubling every two years). Handling these is by far exceeding the human capabilities, so we have to entrust them to automated systems, thus raising questions about the future ethical, security or privacy concerns.

- The social impact of Industry 4.0 is estimated to create two million jobs, although it might destroy seven million jobs (in Germany) and by 2030 will affect up to 50% jobs as well as job and skill requirements worldwide.

- The trend of shifting emphasis to applications and designing for people (not enterprises)

The impact of these developments and its lateral ramifications on the business environment, on future products and their investment priorities cannot be underestimated. Politics is evaluating perusing ideas as basic income or machine tax to avoid loss of elections by angry voters. These developments will not only model the future scientific scenario but even more the future economic development, education requirements, social evolution and thus our lives.

The outlook is exciting; the rate of progress will continue to provide better tools that will enable the development of even exponential better tools.

6. Literature and References:

Banine V.Y., EUV Lithography Today and tomorrow ASML Inc.

Blatt R., Univ. of Innsbruck, Austria.

Deutsch D.,(2014) Deeper Than Quantum Mechanics, Univ. of Oxford.

Haykin S., (1999) Neural Networks and Learning Machines,

HP Silicon Design Labs in Fort Collins, Colo. Enterprise.

HPE 2017Atlantic 's: Return to Deep Space conference in Washington, D.C..

HPlabs April, 2010.

IBM, (2014). SYNAPSE chip,

ITRS, (2016), Final ITRS report.

Kim Kinam and U-In Chung, Technology Innovation, Samsung advanced Institute of Technology, Giheung, S. Korea, and A. Güclü, P.Potasz and P. Hawrylak, NRC of Ottawa, Canada.

Kurzweil R., (2014). The singularity is near.

Ledentsov N. et alii, VI Systems S. Burger and F Schmidt, Zuse Institute Berlin, New generation of vertical cavity surface emitting lasers for optical interconnects.

Loesch, C. (2015). ICT Trends and Scenarios, IDIMT 2015, Trauner Verlag Universität, Linz, Doucek P., Chroust G., Oskrdal V. (Editors).

Martinis J., (2014). Design of a Superconducting Quantum Computer" Google TechTalks,

Meyer G., IBM Zurich Research Lab.

Nokia (Bell Labs) and TU Munich

Payne D., Imperial College London U.K.

Romani A. et alii, Nanopower Integrated Electronics for Energy harvesting, conversion and management, Univ. of Bologna, Italy.

Stange D., Jülich, Geiger R., Villingen et alii. PSI, Univ. Grenoble, Z. Ikonic Univ. Leeds UK.

Sungwoo Hwang et alii,, Graphene and Atom-thick 2D Materials, Samsung advanced institute of technology Suwon, S. Korea.

Troyer.M., Institute for Theoretical Physics, ETH Zurich.

Wikipedia (2017), english version.

Zerhouni E.. The first time right, US NIH.

IDIMT 2016

DIGITALIZATION

HARDWARE - SOFTWARE – SOCIETY

Abstract:

Passing through a period of paradigm change, it is advisable to take stock and see where we stand and peruse state and outlook of ICT and the options available regarding hardware, software and the interdependent societal development. We shall examine how some of these developments are affecting both the technological, economic and societal scenario and look at the reactions and preventive actions by the key players to meet the upcoming scenario.

1. ICT some business aspects

1.1 Key players in 2015

Revenue and Net Income 2014/15

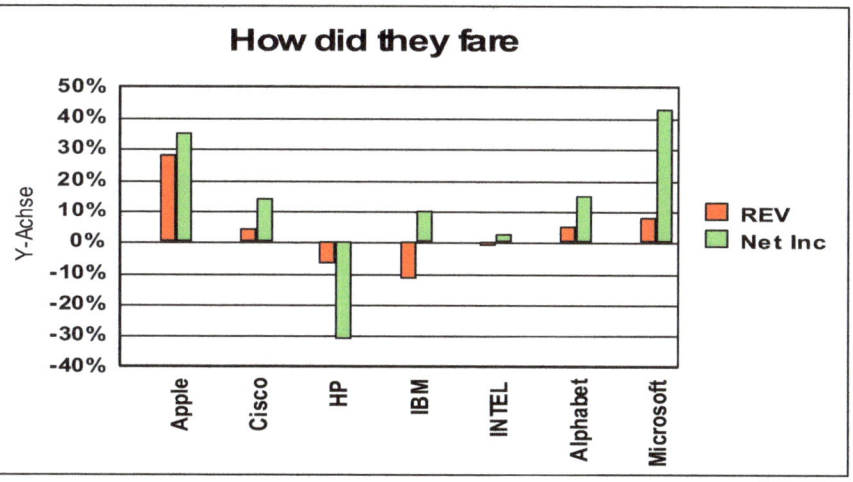

Annual Reports

The prevailing phenomenon seems to be the paradigm change from the previous concentration on the core business to diversification and buying all missing expertise, accompanied by actions to meet future profit and dividend exposures.
We will discuss how the key players are meeting these challenges and their results.

1.2 Is the success story of mobile repeating?

- Smartphones and tablets are getting faster and more capable
- Smartphones and tablets have taken over many of the PC tasks
- The symbiosis of smartphones and AI is showing the future direction
- The demand on communications exploding

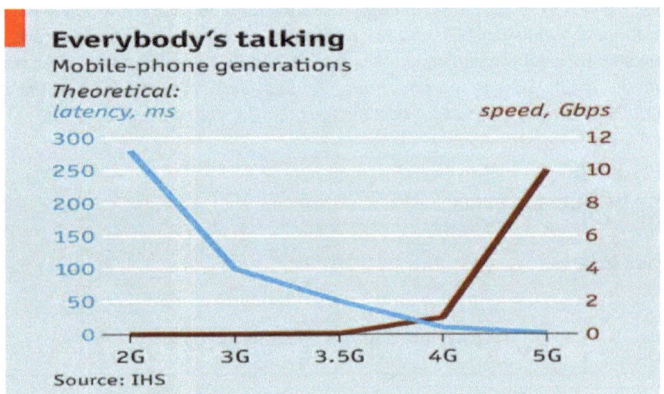

2. Software

2.1 The state of the industry

Rank	Company	Country HQ	2014 Software revenue (US$M)	2014 Total revenue (US$M)	Software revenue as % of total
1	Microsoft	USA	$62,014	$93,456	66.4%
2	Oracle	USA	$29,881	$38,828	77.0%
3	IBM	USA	$29,286	$92,793	31.6%
4	SAP	Germany	$18,777	$23,289	80.6%
5	Symantec	USA	$6,138	$6,615	92.8%
6	EMC	USA	$5,844	$24,439	23.9%
7	VMware	USA	$5,520	$6,035	91.5%
8	Hewlett Packard	USA	$5,082	$110,577	4.6%
9	Salesforce.com	USA	$4,820	$5,274	91.4%
10	Intuit	USA	$4,324	$4,573	94.6%

PwC Global 100 Study

2.2 Operating systems market share (PC)

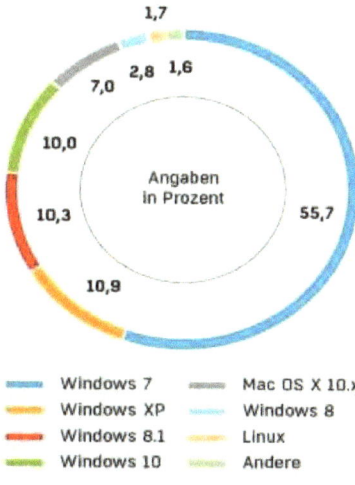

NetMarketShare, Dec 2015

- Windows 10 usage has doubled in six months, reflecting marketing efforts of Microsoft.
- The lifespan of PCs are going to lasting a long time as SSDs replace hard drives.
- New releases of Windows are not driving sales anymore
- The coming back of powerful mainframes/servers
- Applications will increasingly need to be concurrent to exploit exponential CPU gains.
- Windows and Android dominating (exp. splitting)

3. PC use - how is the time spent?

Games 32%
Entertainment 8%   together 60%
Facebook 18%
News 2%

Source: FLURRY analytics, Comscore, NetMarketshare

The fact that nearly 60% are spent on games, Facebook, entertainment and news may cause the rise of some eyebrows.

4. Semiconductor industry

4.1 Semiconductor and semiconductor equipment revenues

It is indicative to evaluate not only semiconductor industry but as well especially the semiconductor equipment industry, which is watching the ICT developments based on an intrinsic knowledge of technological developments is an excellent indicator.

4.2 Technology

Many technological developments as shown below have enabled and enable the extension of Moore's law. Increased complexity must be offset by improved density, making the heat problem becoming again a central issue as Moore asked decennia ago „will it be possible to remove the heat"

To enable more function, power reduction is critical and will cause the shift of the R&D focus from speed to power, further on, to the quest the quest for cost reduction.

Approaching the end of the Moore laws final phase we encounter the shift that future developments will depend more and more on financial rather than on technological aspects. The question is whether we can afford to continue. According to Intel, the maximal extension of the law, in which transistor densities continue doubling every 18-24 months, will be reached in 2020 or 2022, around 7nm or 5nm.

Technologies in the pipeline are continuing to improve; a foreseen 30-fold advance in the future years is still significant. Nevertheless, the old way a perpetually improving technology is gone. Nobody thinks graphene, III-V semiconductors, or carbon nanotubes are going to bring it back. Further gains will be incremental, with performance edging up perhaps thirty fold in the future years. DARPA has investigated 30+ alternatives to CMOS, but only 2 or 3 of them show long-term potentia. The decline of Moore strengthens the emphasis on high performance computing and developments like cloud computing and AI. (Google bought Deep mining not just for AlphaGo). The scenario for storage is different (Source: ISSCC 2016)

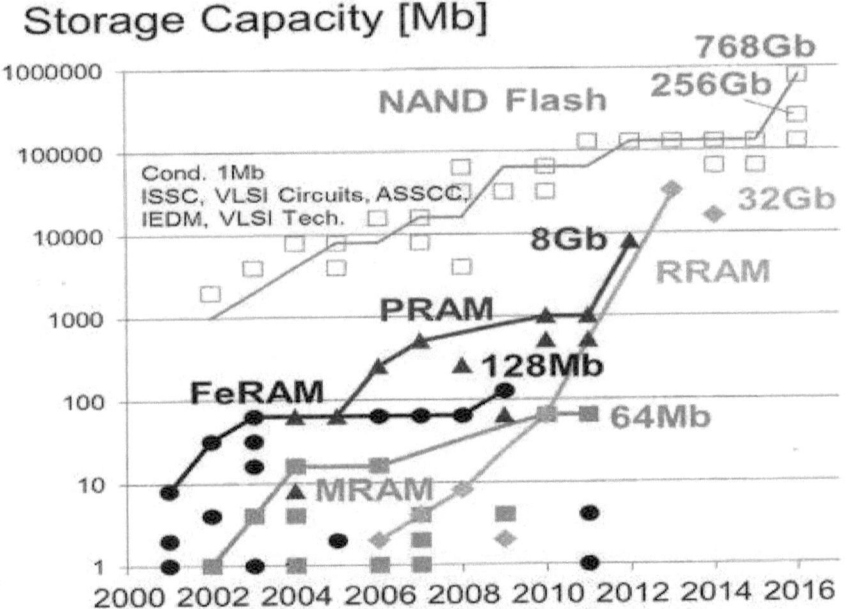

NAND flash memory continues to advance to higher density and lower power with still scaling down 2D technology. Recently 3b/cell NAND with up to 768 Gb have been reported extending the number of layers from 32 to 48.

Let us look at some further potentially influential developments.

4.3 Supercomputing

We can observe astounding progress and strategic competition in the field of Supercomputing. Chinas latest supercomputer, a monolithic system with 10,65 million cores is built entirely with Chinese microprocessors. No U.S.-made system comes close to that performance of China's new system, the Sunway TaihuLight with a theoretical peak performance of 124,5 petaflops.

4.4 KiloCore

Researchers at the University of California, have created a new processor with 1000 CPU cores. The "KiloCore" processors can be independently clocked to a maximum of 1,78 GHz, and shut down independently when not used. The 1000 processors can execute 115 billion instructions per second while dissipating only 0,7 watts, making the KiloCore 100 times more power-efficient than a laptop despite being built on old 32nm CMOS processor technology of IBM. By contrast, current Intel chips are much higher-clocked and built using a 14nm process, which achieve millions, not billions, of instructions per second.

What would be the use a chip with 1,000 cores? The same way as any other modern multi-core chip, i.e. video processing, encryption and decryption, and scientific tasks.

4.5 IoT

NZZ estimates the no. of connected units to increase from 2015 to 2020 by 200% –4500%.

However, it is not an easy and clear win, as the width of the forecasts show. A survey by Gartner shows that 39 % of companies do not intend to implement IoT in the next future and 9% have no intention to implement IoT at all. There are significant variations between different industries. Leading are asset-intensive industries as gas, oil and utilities as well as manufacturing, while less asset intensive industries and service industries as insurance or media show less interest. Gartner estimates that until the end of next year 56% of the first group will have projects implemented, where as light industries group will be in the range of a third only.

Crucial for the implementation of IoT is the solution of the energy supply. There are many ideas around but a newly emerging idea is energy from TV emitters, according to Kurzweil they could deliver 10-100s μW.

The widening of the thrust from vertical to lateral developments will bring additional sensors and new features as for vibration, drift, pressure, ultrasonic transducers, highly precise temperature measurement using the spectral information of radiation (change of resonance frequency with temperature of MEMS), displays as LCO panels and touch screens with thinner layers and higher sensitivity at lower cost.

4.6 Cognitive Computing (combining digital 'neurons' and 'synapses')

IBM research presented a new generation of experimental computer chips designed to emulate the brain's abilities for perception, action and cognition. This is moving beyond the von Neumann architecture that has been ruling computer architecture for more than half a century. Neurosynaptic computing chips try to recreate the phenomena between spiking neurons and synapses in biological systems, through advanced algorithms and silicon circuitry. The technology should yield orders of magnitude less power consumption and space than today's computers. Its first two prototype chips are currently undergoing testing.

Cognitive computers will not be programmed the same way as traditional computers today, they are expected to learn through experience, find correlations, create hypotheses, and remember and learn from the outcomes, mimicking the brains structural and synaptic plasticity.

4.6.1 Neurosynaptic chips

The ambitious long-term goal is a chip system with ten billion neurons and hundred trillion synapses consuming merely one kW of power and occupying less than two liters of volume. While they contain no biological elements, these cognitive computing prototype chips use digital silicon circuits to make up a "Neurosynaptic core" with integrated memory (replicated synapses), computation (replicated neurons) and communication (replicated axons).

IBM has two working prototype designs. Both cores were fabricated in 45 nm SOICMOS and contain 256 neurons. One core contains 262,144 programmable synapses and the other contains 65,536 learning synapses. The IBM team has successfully demonstrated simple applications like navigation, machine vision, pattern recognition, associative memory and classification.

4.7 Hewlett-Packard's futuristic 'Machine'

HP claims that a prototype of the futuristic „Machine" computer should be ready for partners to develop software on by next year, though the finished product is still half a decade away. HP is placing a huge bet on a new type of computer that stores all data in vast pools of non-volatile memory. HP says the Machine will be superior to any computer today and claims system the size of a refrigerator will be able to do the work of a whole data center. The single-rack prototype will have 2,500 CPU cores and an impressive 320TB of main memory; this is more than 20 times the amount of any server on the market today.

4.8 AI (artificial intelligence or cognitive computing)

4.8.1 AI and the Future of Business

The symbiosis of microelectronic, sensoric and AI is enabling a leap in the development of robotics.

After many false dawns, AI has made extraordinary progress in the past few years, thanks to the technique of "deep learning". Given enough data, large (or "deep") neural networks, modeled on the brain's architecture, can be trained to do a range of things from search engine, to automatic photo tagging, voice assistant, shopping recommendations or Tesla's self-driving cars. However, this progress has also led to concerns about safety and job losses. Many wonder whether AI could get out of control, precipitating a conflict between people and machines. Some worry that AI will cause widespread unemployment, by automating cognitive tasks previously be done by people. After 200 years, the machinery question is back and needs to be answered. John Stuart Mill wrote in the 1840s "there cannot be a more legitimate object of the legislator's care" than looking after those whose livelihoods are disrupted by technology. That was true in the era of the steam engine, and it remains true in the era of artificial intelligence.

Google's concept of the 'device' to fade away, will lead the computer, whatever its form factor, to be an intelligent assistant helping through the day. We will move from mobile-first to an AI-first world your phone should proactively bring up the right documents, schedule and map your meetings etc. Google by its investments in AI is preparing itself for such a world, aiming to be there, offering "assistance" to their users so they do not have to type anything into a device.

5. Fiber Optics

Moore's Law gets all the attention, but it is the combination of fast electronics and fast fiber-optic communications, that has created "the magic of the network" of today.

Since 1980, the number of bits per second sent in an optical fiber has increased 10 million fold. That is remarkable even by the standards of 20th century electronics. It is more than the jump in the number of transistors on chips during that same period, as described by Moore's law. Electronics has enormous challenges to keep Moore's Law alive; fiber optics is also struggling to sustain its momentum. The past few decades, a series of new developments and break-throughs have allowed communications engineers to push more and more bits down fiber-optic networks. However, the easy gains are history. After decades of exponential growth, fiber-optic capacity may face a plateau.

5.1 The Fiber Optic Exponential

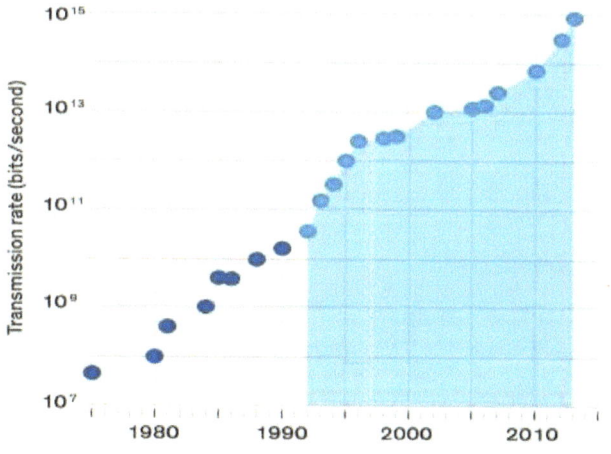

Data source: Keck INTEL

Fiber-optic capacity has made exponential gains over the years. The data in this chart show the improvement in fiber capacity by the introduction of wavelength-division multiplexing.

The heart of today's fiber-optic connections is the core: a 9-micrometer-wide strand of glass that is almost perfectly transparent to 1.55-μm, infrared light surrounded by more than 50 μm of cladding glass with a lower refractive index. Laser signals are trapped inside by the cladding and guided along by internal reflection a rate of about 200000 km/s. The fiber is almost perfectly clear, but every now and then, a photon will bounce off an atom inside the core. The longer the light travels, the more photons will scatter off atoms and leak into the surrounding layers. After 50 km, about 90% of the light will be lost, mostly due to this scattering. To keep the signal going, repeaters were used to convert light pulses into electronic signals, clean and amplify them, and then retransmit them down the next length of fiber.

The physicist D. Payne opened a new avenue. By adding and exciting erbium atoms with a laser, he could amplify incoming light with a wavelength of 1.55 μm, where optical fibers are most transparent. Today, chains of erbium-fiber amplifiers extend fiber connections across continents or oceans.

The erbium-fiber amplifier enabled another way to boost data rates: multiple-wavelength communication. Erbium atoms amplify light across a range of wavelengths, a band wide enough for multiple signals in the same fiber, each with its own much narrower band of wavelengths.

This multi-wavelength approach, dubbed wavelength-division multiplexing, along with further improvements in the switching frequency of fast laser signals, led to an explosion in capacity. The classical way to pack more bits/s is to shorten the length of pulses or lack of pulse. Unfortunately, the shorter the pulses, the more vulnerable they become to dispersion, and will stretch out traveling through a fiber and interfere with one another. Fortunately, scientists had two techniques previously used to squeeze more wireless and radio signals into narrow slices of the radio spectrum.

Together, quadrature coding and coherent detection, with the ability to transmit in two different polarizations of light, have carried optical fibers to allowing a single optical channel to carry 100Gb/s over long distances, in fibers designed to carry only 10 Gb/s. Since a typical fiber can accommodate roughly 100 channels, the total capacity of the fiber can approach 10 Tb/s.

Global Internet traffic increased fivefold from 2010 to 2015. The trend is likely to continue with the growth of streaming video and the Internet of Things.

6. 3D Printing has arrived

During the past years in several IDIMT´s we have been discussing the coming potential of 3D printing. Now let us look at results that surpassed expectations. This does not include the potential by extending its use to organic or other new fields of applications.

Morris Technologies had been experimenting with metal sintering and super alloys for several years. In 2011, the firm zeroed in on the fuel nozzle as the part most appropriate for a makeover.

The result is a monolithic piece, which has replicated the complex interior passageways and chambers of the nozzle down to every twist and turn. Direct metal laser melting where alloy powder is sprayed onto a platform in a printer and then heated by a laser, and repeated 3,000 times until the part is formed converting a many-steps engineering and manufacturing process into just one.

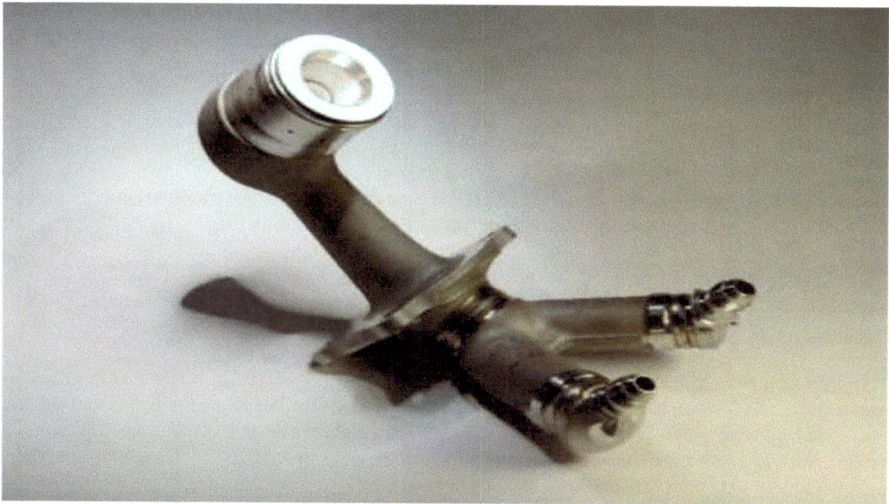

Image: GE

Before 3D printing and modeling, this fuel nozzle had 20 different pieces. Now, just one part, the nozzle is 25% lighter and five times more durable all of which translates to a savings of around US $3 million per aircraft, per year for any airline flying a plane equipped with GE's LEAP engine. Finally, it took three to five months to produce; now it is about a week.

7. Society and Digitalization

There are some things that machines are simply better at doing than humans are, but humans still have plenty going for them.

Machine learning, AI, task automation and robotics are already widely used. These technologies are about to multiply, and companies study how they can best take advantage of them.

Google's CEO Pichai believes that devices will completely vanish, to be replaced by omnipresent AI. "Looking to the future, the next big step will be the concept of the 'device' to fade away,"

Most of us know and use positive effects of ICT ranging from social networking to participating in a wider, even worldwide, society, increasing opportunities for education, real-time information sharing and free promulgation of ideas, a development enjoying unparalleled acceptance.

7.1 Personal Impact of ICT

In spite of the plethora of positive effects of the use of ICT and networks, there is also another side of these developments. As Marcus Aurelius wrote: "The brain takes in the long run the color of the thoughts". We should not only enjoy the benefits but also monitor the negative effects of social networking, ranging from neuro-physical effects to loss of privacy.

Social networks (SNW) pretend to an individual to have thousands of "friends." However, these supposed "friends" are no more than strangers. SNW became the market place ("Bassena") of today and watching the mobile phone a substitute for searching rewards. Research has also proven deteriorating influence on:

- Storage capabilities in the working memory
- Capability of multitasking
- Judgments of order of magnitude (Columbia disaster, financial products, mm/inch)
- Differentiation between important and unimportant information

This is not just speculation; it can be measured and is related to the volume of the amygdale or the size of the prefrontal cortex as it relates to the size of social group. Is there Digital Dementia on the horizon?

Healthy men have a sound warning; you may call it feeling for saturation. Men as "Informavoris rex" as carnivores successor, shows a kind of digital Darwinism based on the belief that the best informed survives and SNW brings advantages. Because many think that, the exchange of information brings additional value and it facilitates their participation and social acceptance. Being afraid to miss something, compulsion to consume and swallow every information, leads without any inhibitors or a saturation point to the loss of the capability to distinguish between import and unimportant information (Paris Hilton, Boris Becker) and thus independent thinking. We do not even apply the rational animals apply. Animals do not use more energy than prey will bring (Lions are not hunting mice, but buffaloes), but we are hunting information without evaluation and we do not know what is hiding behind information. We seem to follow an "All you can eat to all you can read" trend.

Network structure is not accidental; it follows "laws". Search machines are rank high if a page is read/consumed by many people and creates much traffic (is this comparable to the idea that a species is important if it eats many different things and is eaten by many different species.). The number of links not content gives importance, not quality but number. Google page ranking has implications called Mathew effect (MT.25, 29).
In addition, the selection of content is shifting from established journalists, newspapers, and TV- and radio stations to uncontrolled secret search algorithms and private companies.

With ICT, many new legal issues arise ranging from copyright to personal privacy. Major technological evolutions triggered an adequate legal framework, as the industrial revolution led to labor law, motorization to traffic law, and the Digital Revolution to...? (see a special session).

7.2 Privacy

IC-Technology should be used to create social mobility, productivity and improve the lives of citizens. However, it added also new dimensions of surveillance.

In the wake of the Snowden revelations, the question was repeatedly asked: Why would governments wiretap its population? One of the answers may be: it is very cheap. Many people have compared today's mass spying to the surveillance of East Germany's Stasi. An important difference is dimension. Stasi employed one snitch for every 50 or 60 people it watched. Today a million-ish person workforce could keep six or seven billion people under surveillance, a ratio approaching 1:10,000. Thus, ICT has been responsible for the two to three order of magnitude "productivity gains" in surveillance efficiency.

Many companies try to profit from diminishing privacy and lure people into giving away their privacy for short-term financial benefits as price difference in medical cost or insurance, discounts for disclosure as of personal health data, living or driving habits.

7.3 ICT and Society

There have been an increasing number of studies on the impact of ICT on the present and future job market predicting that up to 45% of German employment being exposed within the next two decades. Many major companies reacted to economic challenges in the last decennia by personnel reduction, statistics show 44% of firms reduced H/C by automation. It is a worldwide phenomenon Foxcomm replaced recently 60 000 jobs with robots. Are we prepared for this?

John Stuart Mill wrote in the 1840s "there cannot be a more legitimate object of the legislator's care" than looking after those whose livelihoods are disrupted by technology. That was true in the era of the steam engine, and it remains true in the era of artificial intelligence.

8. Outlook

Having pursued some parts of the prevailing and future scenario, let us combine it with an outlook on some options arising. The continuation of Moore's law is not over, the extension of the law, in which transistor densities continue doubling every 18-24 months, will be hit in 2020 or 2022, around 7nm or 5nm.

We have entered a phase of further improvement of present technologies and fascinating lateral developments. We may expect not only 30 to 50 fold improvements of present technologies but also new technologies beyond CMOS and lateral amplifications based on developments being already integrated or as entering in the test phase, and there is already a beyond CMOS scenario visible.

BEYOND CMOS COMPUTING (present and future technology)

Material	Si	III-V, correlated oxides, High-Z metals
Devise	MOSFET	Tunneling FET, MESO (mag-electr/spin orbit torque)
Circuits	CMOS	Electronic, Spintronic
Memory	SRAM/DRAM	Electronic, Spintronic

Innovation is continuing. With many technologies in the pipeline, potential advance in future years could be significant, but it will depend more on financial rather than on technological aspects, but in all that excitement let us not overlook the societal effects.

Beyond CMOS ICT will not be the same but again, offering an outlook full of opportunity, a different question is whether we can afford to continue.

9. Literatur

Investors relations (2015) https://investor.shareholder.com/alphabet/investorkit.cfm

Apple – Investors relations -Financial Information (2016), www.investor.apple.com/financials.cfm

Brzeski, C. (2015). Die Roboter kommen, Die Welt, ING-Diba Economic Research 03.04.2015.

Cisco Systems, Inc. Investor relations – Overwiew (2015); www.cisco.com
Alphabet (2016) Annual report, Investors relation

Cowell, B. (2013).The Chip Design Game at the End of Moore's Law, http://www.hotchips.org/wp-content/uploads/hc_archives/hc25/HC25.15-keynote1-Chipdesign-epub/HC25.26.190-Keynote1-ChipDesignGame-Colwell-DARPA.pdf

Davis, J. (2011) SCM Global Semiconductor Business, www.mckinsey.com/.../semiconductors/.../mosc_1_r...

Demkov, A. (2014) EE TimesInternational, (ITRS)_https://web2.ph.utexas.edu/~aadg/

Fink, M. (2016) HP Labs at the HP Discover conference.

Hecht, J. (2016) Fiber Optics Keck's Law

HP Investor Relations (2015) - 2015 HP Annual Reports,10ks, & Proxies www3.hp.com/financial/annual-reports-and...2015.aspx

IBM Investor relations (2016) www.ibm.com/investor/

INTEL Corporation (2016) Annual report 2015, www.intc.com/results.cfm

Hruska, J. (2013) ReRAM, the memory technology that will eventually replace NAND flash, finally comes to market, https://www.extremetech.com/computing/163058-reram-the-new-the-memory-tech-that-will-eventually-replace-NAND-flash- finally-comes-to-market

ITRS (2013 and update 2014) Edition and update, http://www.itrs2.net/

Loesch, C. (2015) ICT Trends and Scenarios, IDIMT 2015, Trauner Verlag - Universität, Linz, Doucek P., Chroust G., Oskrdal V. (Editors)

Johnson, R. Colin (2015) FeFET to Extend Moore's Law, Advanced Technology, EE Times (Source: Univ. of Texas) www.eetimes.co./document.asp?doc_id=1325307

Jung, B. (2016) The Negative Effect of Social Media on Society and Individuals, smalllbusiness.chron.com>…>Media, Chron.

Kaiser, T. (2015) Maschienen könnten 18 Millionen Arbeitnehmer verdrängen, Die Welt 02.05.2015 Hamburg

Mack, C. (2015) The multiple lives of Moore's law, IEEE Spectrum, spectrum.ieee.org/.../processors/the-multiple-lives-of-Moore's-law

Metz, C., (2002) Learn the Difference between urgent and important, lifehacker.com/.../learn-the-difference-between-urge... and The Meaning of Life (Stanford Encyclopaedia of Philosophy)

Microsoft Investor Relations – Annual Reports (2015) https://www.microsoft.com/en-us/investor/annual-reports.aspx

Nass, C. (2009) Media multitasker pay mental price https://news.stanford.edu/2009/.../multitask-research-study-0824

Niccolai, J. (2015) IDG News Service

Pichai, S. (2016) Google, Letter to the Shareholders

Prabhjot , S. (2013) Peek into GE's Global Research and GE Additive Manufacturing Lab's, 3dprintingindustry.com/.../a-peek-into-ges-additive-...

Rastl, P. (2015) Letter to Pioneer Members of the Internet Society

Roseburg, A. (2013) The Effects of Social Networking upon Society, www.teenink.com<nonfiction>academic

Schirrmacher, F. (2011) Payback, Pantheon Random House, München

Spitzer, M. (2012), Digital Dementia, Broemer, München

Strogatz ,S. (2016) False Sense of Connection, Cornell University, smallbusiness.chron.com%2negative-effect-social-media-society-individuals-27617.html

The Economist(2016) March of the machines (June 2016)

Turkle, S. (2011) Alone together (MIT) Basic Books

Weizenbaum, J. (2002) Cognitive Change, Persönliche Mitteilung, Europ.Forum Alpbach and Wr .Vorlesung

WE AND ICT

INTERACTION AND INTERDEPENDENCE

Abstract:

ICT has been all-pervasive, fertilizing and empowering nearly all areas of our life creating interaction and interdependence. We will examine some of the developments, starting with the state of the industry economically and technologically, the transition from mM to MtM and its impacts on us as individual and society. Additionally we will render tribute to the two anniversaries meriting special attention: 50 Years of "Moore's Law"and 25 Years of Public Internet.

1. ICT some business aspects

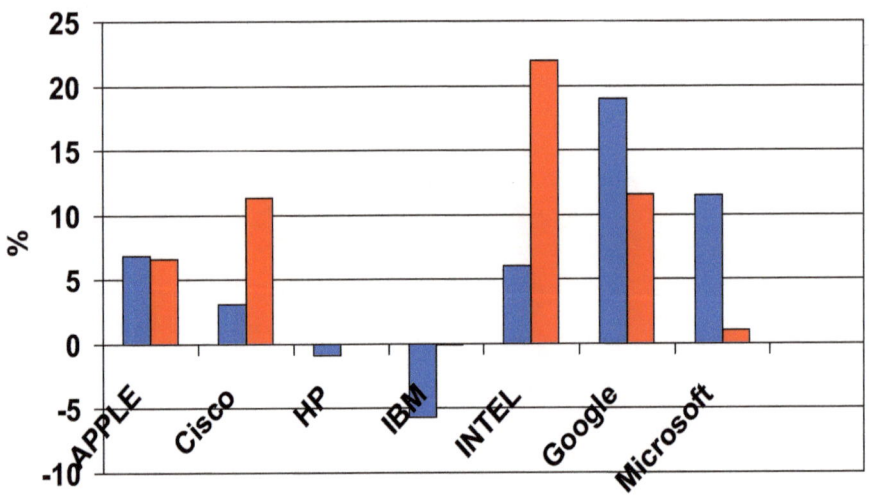

How did they fare in 2014 ?
Revenue and Net Income 2013 to 2014

The major common denominators are change and restructure, characterize also by developments as tablets reaching 50% market share making it one of most disruptive devices ever, the cycles for wearables now averaging two years, and for smart TV's six years only. Or other emerging phenomena are Android surpassing iOS, US adults spending more time on smartphones than on

PCs (34 vs. 27h/month) and the growth of health and fitness apps by 62% last year (female use is three times higher than male).

The shift of the centre of economic gravity from the "saturated" West to East as the market of future is making China for 2016 the largest smart phone market of the world.

For the user it does not matter who is on top but that there is a variety to choose and competition.

2. IC Technology

2.1 50 Years of "Moore's Law"

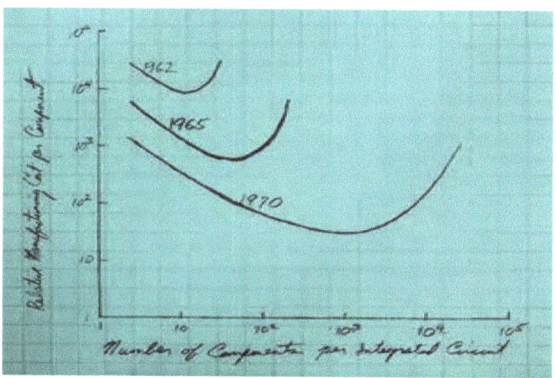

Intel (Moore's original picture)

Economics was at the core of Moore's 1965 paper. He argued that, there is a cost curve of manufacturing technology. The cost of making a component declines the more you pack onto an integrated circuit, but past a certain point, yields decline and costs rise. The sweet spot, where the cost per component is at a minimum, moves to more and more complex integrated circuits over time. Ten years later, Moore revised his prediction. In an analysis for the 1975 IEEE Meeting, he argued that three factors contributed to the trend:

- decreasing component size,
- increasing chip area, and
- "device cleverness, " how much engineers could reduce the unused area between transistors.

Of the three technology drivers Moore identified, one turned out to be special: decreasing the dimensions of the transistor. For decennia, shrinking transistors offered something that rare in the world of engineering: no trade-offs. The scaling rule named for IBM engineer Robert Dennard, says every successive transistor generation is better than the last, faster and less power hungry. This single factor has been responsible for much of the staying power of Moore's Law, and it lasted several decennia.

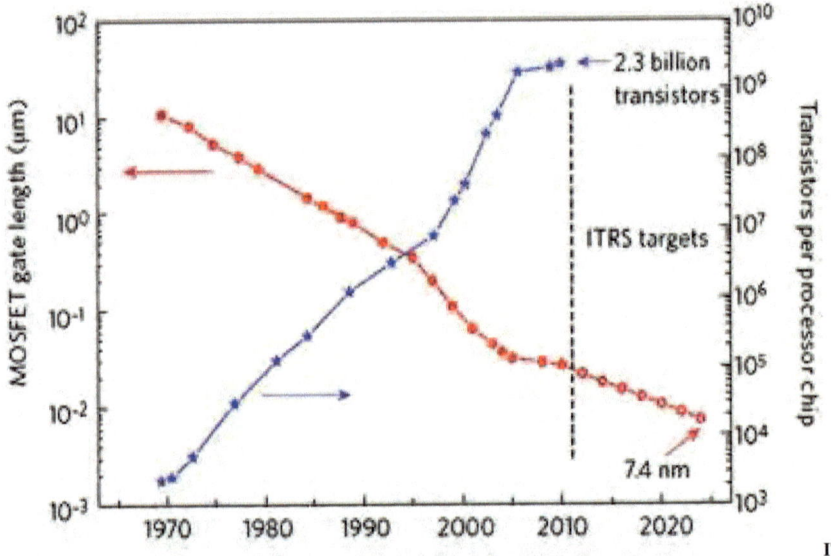

ITRS

In the early 2000s, transistor sizes began to creep down below 100 nanometres, and Dennard's scaling rule hit its limit. Transistors became so small that it was quite easy for electrons to sneak through them even when the devices were supposed to be off, leaking energy, and lowering device reliability.

For the last decade, Moore's Law has been more about cost than performance, making transistors smaller to make them cheaper. There have been design improvements, but much of the gains have come from the integration of multiple cores enabled by cheaper transistors. Today's smartphones has three times the computing power of yesterday's Cray's supercomputer and without the progress we would not enjoy mobile computing, GPS in the car or HD video.

The steady work also improved yield, starting in the 1970s at around 20% and now at 80 to 90 %. The tools employed in lithography cost 100 times as much today as they did 35 years ago. However, these tools pattern wafers 100 times as fast, making up the cost increase while delivering far better resolution. This trend may be ending largely because lithography has gotten expensive.

Over the last decade, the manufacturing cost per unit area of finished silicon raised about 10% p.a. Since the area per transistor shrank by about 25% p.a. over the same period, the cost of each transistor kept going down. If lithography costs rise fast, Moore's Law as we know it will come to a quick halt. Innovations in semiconductors will continue. Instead, new forms of integration will define progress, gathering disparate capabilities on a single chip to lower the system cost. We are talking about uniting the non-logic functions that have historically stayed separate from our silicon chips.

An example of this is the modern cell-phone camera, which incorporates an image sensor directly onto a digital signal processor using large vertical lines of copper wiring. Chip designers are integrating micro-electromechanical systems, as accelerometers, gyroscopes, relay logic, or micro-fluidic sensors.

However, this new phase of Moore's Law also called "more than Moore" (MtM) may not make always economic sense. Instead of a regular, predictable road map for continued success, the path forward will be much murkier and Moore's Law as we know it ending. However, new options emerge:

2. 2 Overall characteristics of the Roadmap

- DRAM   Half pitch 2013 28nm, 4-years cycle, formerly before 3-years cycle
- MPU   For faster MPU/ASIC the 3-years cycle will continue until 2026.
- FLASH   Four years cycle until 2018 (0,5 per 8 years)

The Increasing role of non-traditional scaling

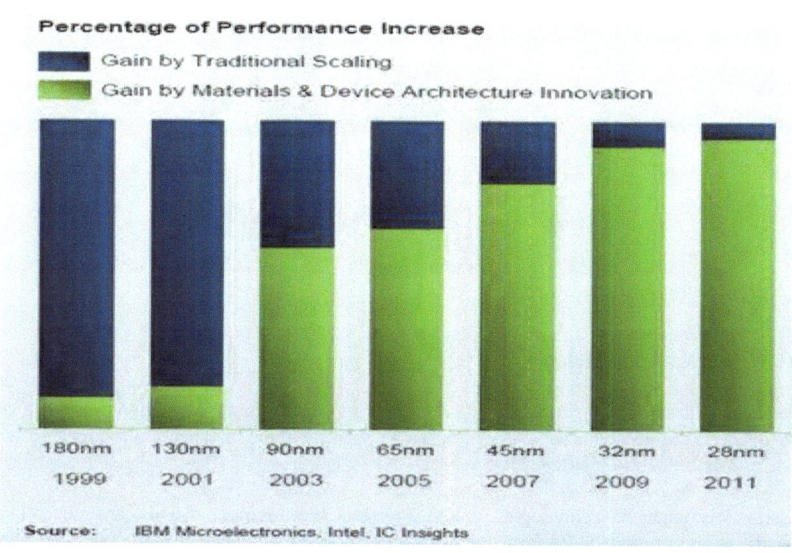

2.3 Devices

The era until the beginning of last decade classical geometric scaling has been followed by the era of equivalent scaling, strained silicon, high k/metal gate, and multi-gate transistors integration of Ge and compound transistors.

The new era of scaling is characterized by features as 3D, reducing interconnect resistance by increasing the vertical conductor cross section and reducing the length of each interconnect, new materials to improve performance by III-V materials and Ge (higher e-mobility than Si)

2.4 MtM and mM

MtM encompasses the incorporation of functionalities that do not scale with Moore's law but provide additional value to migrate from system board level to SiP and SoC, provide functional diversification, interaction with outside world and the subsystem for powering the product included.

This implies analogue and digital signal processing, the incorporation of passive components, high voltage components micromechanical devices, sensors, actuators, micro-fluid devices enabling biological functionalities, as well as an increased role of software.

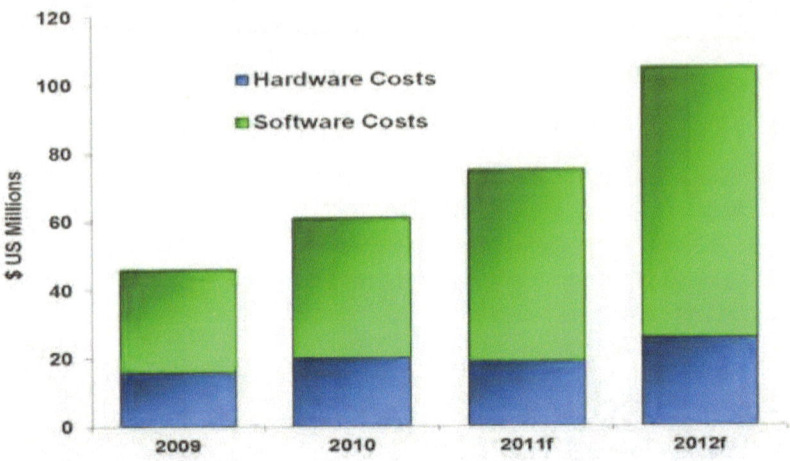

2.5 SCM (Storage Class Memory)

The specialists describe the situation with a term called "Pentalemma" - which represents a conflict in five different requirements such as write current, stability of the bits, readability, read/write speed and the process integration with CMOS.

Approximately ten new technologies, called Storage Class Memory (SCM), are currently under development and promise to be fast, inexpensive, and power efficient, showing potential of a 100- to 1,000-fold improvement for SCM in terms of the space and power required examples are:

- MRAM (stored by magnetic storage)
- SRAM (Static random-access memory)
- Universal memory (ferroelectric gate over Ge channel material)
- FeFET (faster semiconductors for channels either Ge or GaAs)
- STT (spin transfer torque) spin-aligned "polarized" electrons)
- ReRAM (resistance)
- TAS-MRAM (Thermal Assisted Switching)

2.6 Transistors Emerging Alternatives

- Graphene
- Ge (Germanium)
- InAs/Si Nanotube Tunnel Transistors
- Spin-based computing schemes

2.7 The 450 mm Wafer Transition

The transition of leading-edge semiconductor manufacturing to 450mm wafers is a complex and challenging issue. Improved silicon productivity is the primary argument for wafer size transitions leading to a theoretical reduction in die cost of approximately 30% (all other costs constant). Even after two years of analysis, the 450 mm wafer scale-up still represents a low-return, high-risk investment opportunity. Advocates claim larger wafers are necessary to keep pace with Moore's Law cost targets and that there are no technical showstoppers. Opponents claim it will negatively affect profitability, and drain precious R&D funding away from essential innovations in scaling, cycle time improvements, and manufacturing.

2.8 Quantum Computation

The idea sounds promising, but there are tremendous obstacles to overcome as:

De-coherence:
During the computation phase of a quantum calculation, the slightest disturbance in a quantum system (a stray photon or wave of EM radiation) causes the quantum computation to collapse.

Error correction:
Because isolating a quantum system has proven so difficult, error correction systems for quantum computations have been developed. Qubits cannot use conventional error correction. Error correction is critical - a single error can cause the validity of the entire computation to collapse.

Output observance:
Closely related to the above, retrieving output data after a quantum calculation is risking corrupting the data.

Even though there are many problems to overcome, the advances in the last years, have made some form of practical quantum computing not unfeasible, but there is much debate as to whether this is a decade away or a hundred years into the future; remains an open question.

2.9 Neuromorphic Chips

The idea of neuromorphic chips dates back decades. In a 1990 paper Carver Mead, the Caltech professor emeritus coined the term. A neuromorphic processor, a noise suppression chip developed by Audience sold in the hundreds of millions. The chip, which based on the human cochlea, has been used in phones from Apple, Samsung, and others.

Neuromorphic chips	Detect and predict patterns in complex data, using relatively little electricity	Applications that are rich in visual or auditory data and that require a machine to adjust its behavior as it interacts with the world

These "neuromorphic" chips will be designed to process sensory data such as images and sound and to respond to changes in that data in ways not specifically programmed. They promise to accelerate progress in artificial intelligence and lead to machines that are able to understand and interact with the world in humanlike ways. Neurons also change how they connect with each other in response to changing images, sounds, and the like. A process we call learning; chips do the same. Especially of interest is the possibility that neuromorphic chips could transform smartphones and other mobile devices into cognitive companions.

2.10 ICT, Robots and their Impact

The driving force is costs (salaries) increasing faster than productivity in industrial countries, thus promoting the development in the areas of robotics and software to replace expensive human work by cheaper machines. Four companies, i.e. Fanuc, Yaskava, ABB and Kuka are sharing 2/3 of the world industry automation market of 122 billion US$ p.a.

According to several studies, the impact can be dramatically, potentially replacing (in the German labor market only) 18 million jobs. Especially administrative and accounting jobs are highly exposed (up to 86%), as well as delivery, sales, and secretarial jobs. The less qualified the more exposed. Nevertheless, there are areas less impacted as healthcare, chemists, or physicists.

The experience of preceding technological developments shows that it is not realistic to assume that people losing jobs by these changes will be easily absorbed in other fields.

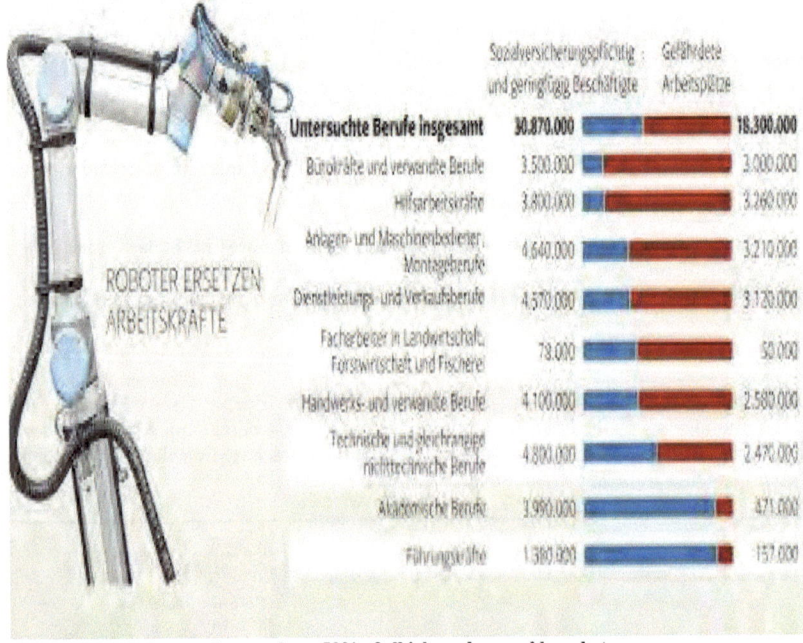

Die Welt, Robots replace workers, 59% of all jobs endangered by robots

Two of the most disruptive technological innovations of the recent decennia came from Mobility and Communication

4.   25 Years of Internet

A fundamental development in communication, if not the most important and disruptive was and is Internet. Its idea and potential fascinated brilliant people around the world, who contributed an abundance of enthusiasm and personal dedication to its success.
The enthusiasm and joy of the early years faded, as today it has become an integral part of our life. However, this was not an easily achieved breakthrough. The worldwide enthusiastic appreciation in and success is beyond discussion and nobody wants to be remembered as having been on the other side of the fence. Adversaries were ranging from national telecommunication administrations to the department manager of Tim Berners-Lee at CERN were not very helpful. In Austria, the famous 64k-backbone connection from Vienna to CERN had to be financed by a department of a private company for a year because the responsible Ministry claimed to have no money for this. So only based on our contribution of 1,000.000 ATS and the efforts of the Supercomputer Centre of the Univ. of Vienna this endeavor could take off.
In many countries, predominantly the enthusiasm and ingenuity of individuals enabled this key project of the 20th century to lift off, while most of these people remained unrewarded, many latecomers are striving today for the glory.

5. We and ICT

Some of the well-known positive effects of ICT on Social Media, Society, and us as Individuals are

- Facilitating to meet, communicate and organize
- Making researching information easier
- Communicating 24/7 to and from anywhere.

Bringing many benefits to organizations, such as cost and productivity improvements as VoIP, email, messaging, video conferencing, e-commerce, access to worldwide markets and to process financial and other transactions 24/7.

- Social networking allowing people to participate in a wider, even worldwide, society.
- Increasing opportunities for education.
- Real-Time Information Sharing and Increased News Cycle Speed.
- Free promulgation of ideas and advertising.

5.1 Personal Impact of ICT

There is a plethora of phenomena arising in the context of personal use of ICT and the rise of social networks and there is another side of these developments.
As Marcus Aurelius wrote: The brain takes in the long run the color of the thoughts, we should not only enjoy the benefits but also monitor the negative effects as effects of social networking , neuro-physical effects or loss of privacy .
Social networks allow an individual to have thousands of "friends." However, these supposed "friends" are no more than strangers. Many of those people will "know what fifteen of their friends had for breakfast, but don't know of their struggle with major life issues" Social networks became the market place ("Bassena") of the 20th century and watching the mobile phone is a substitute for searching rewards. Research has proven deteriorating influence on the:

- storage capabilities in the working memory
- reaction to false alarms
- capability of multitasking
- judgment of order of magnitude (Columbia disaster, financial products, mm/inch)
- differentiation between important and unimportant information

This is not just speculation; it can be measured and related to the volume of the amygdala (and the size of the prefrontal cortex relates to the size of social group).
Is there a Digital Dementia on the horizon?
There exist correlations between:

- Poor and low IQ parents correlate with higher use of screen
- TV use as child is inverse proportional to education level in future
- Videogames alter programming of brain by using and activating different regions as reading

Network (NW) structure is not accidental; it follows "power laws". Search machines are rank high if a page is read/consumed by many people and creates much traffic (comparable to the idea that a species is important if it eats many different things and is eaten by many different species). The number of links not content gives importance, not quality but number (Paris Hilton, Boris Becker). Also the selection of content is shifting from established journalists, newspapers, and TV- and radio stations to uncontrolled secret search algorithms and private companies.

Men as "Informavoris rex" as carnivores successor, with Digital Darwinism is based on the belief that the best informed survives and NW brings advantages. Being afraid to miss something, compulsion to consume and swallow every information leads to neglecting independent thinking and loosing the distinction between import and unimportant information.

With ICT, many new legal issues arise ranging from copyright to personal privacy. All major technological evolutions triggered an adequate legal framework:

The Industrial Revolution led to labor law, Motorization to traffic law and the Digital Revolution...?

5.2 Privacy

Technology should be used to create social mobility and improve the lives of citizens.
However, it added also new dimensions of surveillance.

The company Cataphora offers tools to identify people in companies who contribute more than others in new ideas etc. thus estimating the value of employees (and may in future include their medical/genetic data) to the company.

In the wake of the Snowden revelations, the question was asked repeatedly: Why would the US continue to wiretap its entire population, given that the only "terrorism" they caught with it was a single attempt to send a small amount of money to Al Shabab?

One of the obvious answers may be: it is very cheap. Spying is cheap and becomes cheaper every day. Many people have compared today's mass spying to the surveillance programme of East Germany's notorious Stasi.

An important difference is dimension. Stasi employed one snitch for every 50 or 60 people it watched. Today a million-ish person workforce keeps six or seven billion people under surveillance, a ratio approaching 1:10,000. Thus, ICT has been responsible for the two to three order of magnitude "productivity gains" in surveillance efficiency. Stasi used an army to survey a nation; today secret services use a battalion only to survey a planet.

Technology also brings productivity gains to social programmes. Basic sanitation, green revolution crops, cheap material production, and access to vaccines and mobile internet devices allow states to lift the desperately poor into a more sustainable existence for less than ever, affording stability to wealth gaps that might have invoked the guillotine in previous centuries. The mobile phone is important example, since it is both a means of raising quality of life, through access to information and markets, and keeping its users under close, cheap surveillance ironically paid by the user.

6. Summary

We have discussed how the famous Moore's Law is approaching its end, but we can look forward to a decade of further device improvements. We have perused the challenges ranging from lithography costs, interconnect resistance and capacitance slowing performance, to connectivity problems and seen that the historical cost trends that we have been enjoying are fading out. We have shown that Dennard type scaling has already reached diminishing returns and looks like going to 'hit the wall'. Since atoms do not scale, and it is hard to imagine good devices smaller than ten lattices across - reached in 2020.

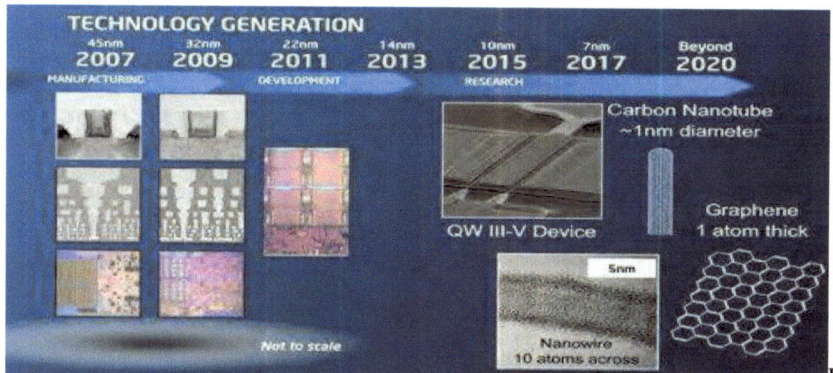

Intel

The question remains: Do you have you an urgent need and are you prepared to use efficiently the still coming 100-fold improvements?
For SCM the result of an extrapolation is even more impressive showing a 100- to 1,000-fold improvement potential.

Extrapolations of the next ten years may be technically viable but the question remains, will carbon nano-tubes, graphene, nanowires, InGaAs, Spintronics, etc. save Moore's law in time? Not likely, and most probably not by 2020.

We are witnessing the fascinating developments facilitated by ICT, especially the effects of Moore's law, Communication and Internet and many phenomena which we did not foresee, some very inspiring and innovative, some less so. Having to concede that it saddens that the proliferation of the Internet for many years involuntarily also contributed to the implementation of a dangerous global surveillance and repression tool.

ICT is not only an unprecedented technological advancement and cultural asset for all humanity; it is also a turnkey infrastructure on the verge of being abused.

7. Literature:

Brzeski, C. (2014). 59% of all jobs endangered by robots, ING-Diba

Cowell, B. (2013). Intel microprocessor fame and End of Moore's law, DARPA's MTO,

Davis, J. SCM, Global Semiconductor Business

Demkov, A.. (2014). EE TimesInternational, Technology Roadmap for Semiconductors (ITRS)

Hruska, J.. (2013). ReRAM, the memory technology that will eventually replace NAND flash, comes to market,

ITRS. (2013 and update 2014). Edition and update,

Loesch, C. (2013). ICT Trends and Scenarios, IDIMT

Mack, C. (2015). The multiple lives of Moore's law IEEE Spectrum

Johnson R. Colin, Advanced Technology , EE Times (Source: University of Texas)

Jung, B. Demand Media The Negative Effect of Social Media on Society and Individualy

Kaiser, T. (2014). 18 Millionen Jobs in Gefahr, Die Welt

Nass, C. (2009). MultitaskingS negative effects

Mack,C. (2015): The Multiple lives of Moore´s law

Metz, C., (2002). Less differencing less differing between important and unimportant

Rastl, P. (2015). Letter to Pioneer Members of the Internet Society

Roseburg , A. The Effects of Social Networking upon Society

SEMATECH International Manufacturing Initiative (ISMI) 450 mm Wafer Transition

SEMI White Paper, Equipment Suppliers' Productivity Working Group 450 mm Economic

Schirrmacher, F. (2011). Payback.

Spitzer, M. (2013). Digital Dementia

Strogatz ,S. False Sense of Connection, Cornell University

Times (2014), Higher Education World University Rankings

Turkle S. (2011). Alone together MIT

Weizenbaum J. Cognitive change

Wikipedia (rev. April 2015)

IDIMT 2014

THE STATE OF ICT

SOME ECO -TECHNOLOGICAL ASPECTS AND TRENDS

Abstract:

We are witnessing and benefiting of advantages of the remarkable ICT evolution. A development hardly matched by any other technological advance both in depths as well as in the lateral dimension.

In spite of all doomsday prophesies and prognosis ICT is moving ahead. Just over the last 20 years only, CPUs improved by a factor 2400, DRAM's by 1000 and NAND Flash by 32000, paralleled by an increase in network speed by a factor of 840 and Internet traffic by a an annual CGR of more than 30 %. Can this continue?

We shall review the status of R&D in its quest for solutions, some of the challenges ahead, the desired innovations, and the economic consequences of this drive. Will future investments into technology be sufficiently rewarding and economically feasible?

The advancements mentioned are inseparably from the R&D efforts of the key players and their strategy, we will look at the changes now reshaping the scenario.

A new generation of consumers and the first generation of digital natives has arrived and shaping future markets, applications, and reciprocally being shaped by them.

ICT is penetrating, fertilizing and empowering new areas as energy, photonics, health, and medical applications which by their weight are creating future markets and R&D directions.

Finally we will complete our review be perusing the status of the development of "more than Moore (MtM)" as well long range options.

1. The ECO -TECHNOLOGICAL SCENARIO

A new ecosystem has emerged during the past decade:

- the aggressive bi-annual introduction of new semiconductor technologies allowed ICs to be produced cost efficiently, to integrate extremely complex systems on a single die or in a single package at very attractive prices,
- Manufacturer of ICs offering foundry services were able to provide new ASIC's at attractive cost leading to the emergence of the profitable new businesses as "design only" houses.
- The development of sophisticated equipment for advanced ICs proliferated to adjacent technology fields and thus enabling the realization of flat displays, MEMS sensors, radios, and areas as medicine, energy etc.

- Internet and the rise of mobiles led to extensive deployment of fiber cables and multiple wireless technologies ranging from communication satellites to thousands of repeater stations.
- Internet of things inspires many innovative product houses, ITC companies, data- and information distributors, battling now for dominant position in this newly created market.
- All this facilitated the creation of unexpected markets as the social NWs.
- Up to 40% of the global productivity growth of the last two decades has been attributed to the impact of ICT.

From a technological point of view, the scenario looks as below:

The first era, until the last decade was the era of classical geometry driven scaling.

The second era, the era of equivalent scaling, supported the growth of the semiconductor industry in the past decade, and will continue to do so until the end of the present decade and beyond.

Significant R&D efforts are concentrated on improving device performance by use of III-V materials and Ge (higher mobility than Si).

2D scaling will reach its limits very soon, but both logic and memory devices are entering the third era, the era of 3D scaling.

SOC and SIP products have become main drivers and the total volume of smart phones and tablets surpassed production volume of microprocessors in the past years thus shifting dramatically the emphasis of the industry.

MEMS have become an indispensable part of cars, smart phones, and video projectors, tablets, games platforms, inkjet printers.

These advances are shifting in sight advances ranging from robots (from household assistance to personal care and prosthetics) to the futuristic enhancement to the muscle memory by wearable computers.

1.1 How did the ICT Industry fare

We shall review the situation of some key players based on the recent facts and figures as the 2Q14 results, their 2013 annual and the SEC reports.
We see a Janus-headed picture, the contribution of ICT to growth and GDP and the rising question:

Will economics doom Moore's law?

While many trends appear positive for the continued applicability of Moore's law from a technological perspective, economics could prove its undoing. Recent developments indicate that the economics of continued miniaturization could break down as cost-per-transistor reductions flatten for nodes with feature sizes below 28nm, because of the rapidly rising costs of technology development and capital equipment needed to produce next-generation nodes. The extreme investments required for leading-edge lithography technologies and the process complexities required for nodes at 32nm and 28nm and below, drive these cost increases.

Moving from 32nm to 22nm nodes causes typical fabrication costs to grow by roughly 40 percent. It also boosts the costs of process development by about 45 percent and chip design by up to 50 percent. These dramatic increases will lead to process-development costs that exceed $1 billion for nodes below 20nm. In addition, the state-of-the art fabs needed to produce them will likely cost $10 billion or more. As a result, the number of companies capable of financing next-generation technology will likely dwindle.

~

2. Technology

Heterogeneous system integration of multiple technologies in limited space (GPS, phone, tablet, Mobil etc.) has revolutionized the semiconductor industry shifting the emphasis from performance driven to reduced power.

Since most of energy is lost in metal interconnects, photonics may offer the solution.

Not only the internal but also the macro-power consumption becomes a challenge. In 2008 1.1Petaflops (10^{15}) computing consumed 2,8MW power, extrapolating to Exascale (1018) might dissipate 2,3GW (~ two nuclear plants).

2.1 Logic

To maintain the dynamic performance increases in the last decade innovation in device structures and new materials had to be invented as Cu/low-k dielectric at the 120nm technology node, SiGe source/drain for the 65nm node and metal electrode/high-k dielectric gate stacks replacing poly-Si/SiO_2 gate stacks at the 45nm node. However, the node name is losing its previous significance as shown below.

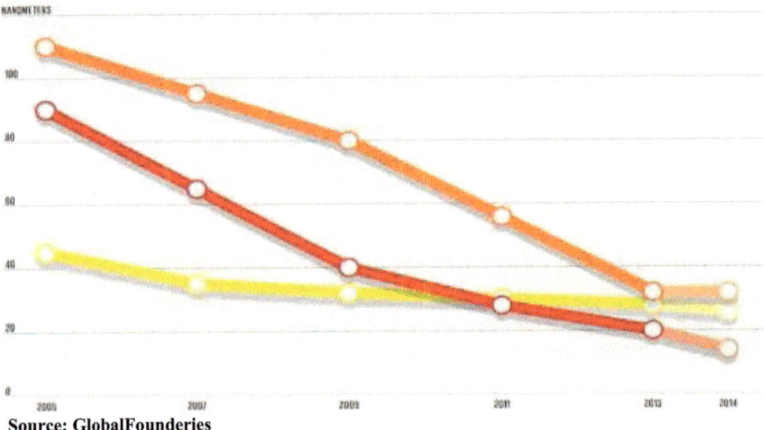

Source: GlobalFounderies

Key chip dimensions, such as the transistor gate length (low, yellow) and the metal one half pitch (top, orange) have decreased but not strictly tracked the node name (middle, red).

The performance of an MPU executing program is limited by the interaction between processor and memory - the current approach to increase the MPU cache is increasing the floor space that the SRAM occupies on an MPU chip. However, this leads to a decrease of the net information throughput. CMOS logic beyond 2018 will replace strained Si MOSFET channel with an alternate material with higher mobility as Ge, SiGe a variety of III-V compound semiconductors and graphene.

This leads R&D efforts to the areas of high mobility III-V materials or Ge channel materials to enhance the electron/hole mobility and enable power reduction. A few materials have emerged as front-runners for the two kinds of transistors needed for logic circuits. For the positive-channel field-effect transistor (pFET), the leading candidate is germanium, which can transport charge four times as fast. For the negative-channel FET, or nFET, which depends on the movement of electrons, engineers are considering a mix of elements from groups III and V of the periodic table. One of the most promising is indium gallium arsenide (InGaAs), with an electron mobility of more than six times that of silicon.

Emerging research materials include memory and logic devices, as the mentioned planar p-III-V, n-Ge, nanowires, graphene, and other 2D materials, complex metal oxides as well as emerging lithography and approaches novel molecules to enable ultimate pattering and DSA (Directed Self Assembly).

2.2 Memory

DRAM density has doubled every 18 month but downscaling to the sub10nm will represent a major challenge. Downscaling from 90 to 20 nm was possible by structural changes. It is crucial to maintain important criteria of minimum cell capacitance to have an adequate signal for sensing and reasonable retention times.

2.3 Architectural Concepts

Future 3D technology architectural concepts encompass 3D dense packing for interconnects, fluid cooling, and power delivery of energetic chemical compounds transported in the same fluid with little power for pumping.

Interlayer cooled 3D chips could thus solve the cooling bottleneck thereby allowing stacking of several stacks, but are still limited by power delivery and communication. Electromechanical power delivery would eliminate the electrical power supply network thus freeing valuable space for communication. By 2025, chip stacks with embedded liquid cooling are expected. In the future by 3D and minimal power consumption supercomputers may shrink to the size of a sugar cube.

Today supercomputers use 10000 times more energy than brain with 20W. Some optimists infer by scaling up chips stacks even biological efficiencies can be reached by 2060. For sub-10 nm structural innovation this may not help due to the physical limitations for complex 3D structures (the distance between electrodes becomes 10nm or less, which means thinness of 5nm or less for storage electrode and dielectrics). With the optimization of the 3D cell storage capacitor and array transistor DRAM, downscaling to the sub-10nm regime is anticipated, nevertheless patterning technology as etching, and lithography will become critical and the productivity of these technologies remains a major concern.

Chipmakers are in the process of moving from traditional planar transistors. Intel introduced these 3D transistors and is now shipping them widely. Leading foundries, such as GlobalFoundries, Samsung, and Taiwan Semiconductor Manufacturing will switch to 3D with the next generation.

The chip industry has made it a priority to keep up the pace ensuring that manufacturers can continue to build and release new product families using a new process every 18 to 24 months, thus leaving no time to explore design optimization to cut down on power or boost performance.

PLANAR   **3-D**

Planar and 3D Source: (Intel)

In few years, chipmakers may face a struggle with wiring as they attempt to push chip density down past the 10-nm generation. Each copper wire requires a sheath containing barrier material to prevent the metal from leaching into surrounding material, as well as thick insulation to prevent it from interacting with neighboring wires. This thickness limits. The thrust for smaller DRAM cells will faces great technological and economical challenges because of severe charge leakage and calls for non-charge-based memory devices.

2.3 Emerging computing devices

The basic architecture has remained unchanged for decennia. With the introduction of multi-core systems, redesign became inevitable leading to reduced power consumption, the minimization of wasted cycles, and bandwidth.

The rapid evaluation of emerging memory technologies as MRAM and ReRAM in combination with logic devices would allow more flexibility in circuit design, and faster revision and product cycles. Post NAND devices are studied using the technology of ReRAM a resistive material acting as the memory element and with a control element acting as the switch, Ta_2O_5/TaO_x bi-layer structure offering 10^{12} cycles of endurance and a 10 years retention time with fast program and erase pulses in the order of 10ns are promising R&D targets.

One of those promising devices is the STT-RAM (spin transfer torque magnetoresistive random access memory). This promising technology uses the MTJ (magnetic tunnel junction) tunneling for resistive storage and MgO as tunnel barriers. MRAM means that the devices change resistance under magnetic influence built of ultra small magnetic sandwiches of magnetic and non-magnetic materials; they are very dense, very cheap, and durable requesting no permanence power on. It is likely that we will see Spin Transfer Torque Magnetostatics (STT MRAM) and ReRAM in next 5-10 years period.

A further prospect is that PCM (Phase Change Memory) memory will replace flash storage, because PCM chips are fast (1-2 nsec respond times) and low cost in production.

2.4 Lithography

Whether Moore's law will continue depends on technological developments, especially in the critical areas of innovation lithography tools, especially for extreme-ultraviolet (EUV) lithography technology, using short-wavelength light sources to scale feature sizes below 10nm.

Lithography is an important potential source of productivity improvements in semiconductor manufacturing. An opportunity to improve is to increase the wafer size. This explains why several companies are working toward semiconductor wafer sizes of 450mm wafers.

However, complex lithography approaches like multipatterning carry a high price. As a result, the percentage of corporate capital spending allocated to lithography rose to an estimated 24% for 2010–15 from less than 20 % in 2000–05. Per-layer costs and accompanying complexity levels are exploding for double and multipatterning. For instance, moving to 22nm with double patterning, from 32nm ArF immersion, could double the number of process steps per layer, depending on the product, and raise costs per layer by 50 percent. This could lead to a breakdown of Moore's law as the cost advantages of scaling disappear.

A technological innovation that could overcome these challenges is extreme-ultraviolet (EUV) lithography. This technology uses new light sources with a wavelength of 13.5nm. The industry expects EUV to reduce per-layer costs because fewer steps will be needed. Double patterning, for example, can require more than 30 patterning steps per layer, but EUV will likely need just 10, with resulting cost-per-layer advantages estimated to be as high as 35 percent. In addition, EUV promises to deliver node sizes of 10nm and below.

EUVL is not production ready because of unsolved technical issues, as the lack of a light source with sufficient power and stability, fast resists, defect-free and high flatness masks. However, recent developments suggest the industry is moving to make EUV commercially feasible.

Scalability of the power efficiency is a crucial feature. The picture below shows that computation/kW follow a pattern similar to Moore's law hand with the decrease of the printed feature size.

Another technical option DSA (Directed self-assembly) has shown progress but defectivity and positional accuracy still needs to be improved considerably but seems to be possible.

3. Technological cross fertilization and lateral empowerment

Advanced materials will allow spintronics, III-V and even graphene based integration into Si devices and also integrating Si into electro photonic ICs, enabling energy saving devices, solid state lightning, and power electrics and on-chip optical connections among others.

This technology transfer will insert new power and opportunities collaterally into areas as health, energy and medical applications ranging from ultra fast DNA sequencing, medical imaging devices, low cost - high efficiency light sources etc. These applications may conquest a significant part of the future semiconductor market and change the market in the coming decade, as not long ago the portable devices did.

3.1 Solar cells

This industry has grown over 25% in recent years with crystalline Si solar cells are holding 90% of the market. The current efficiency for cells and modules is in the range of 13- 21 % (presently the

~

highest cell efficiency demonstrated is 24,7% at Univ. of NSW) but this could not be commercialized due to the high wafer and process cost.
The most urgent task is resolving economic i.e. issues lowering investment cost and reaching grid parity.

3.2 Silicon technology and photonics

Future Exascale systems, as multicore systems, will require high speed and energy efficiency. This means extending optical interconnects from rack to rack of today to tomorrows board to board and further to chip-to-chip interconnects i.e. enabling Si photonics integration for Exascale computing, realistic 3D and holographic images.

Since the computational power of processors continuously nearly doubles every year, Ultra fast Nanophotonics Devices for Optical Interconnects have become an intensive research target. To match the power of processors, the related bandwidth demand the single channel bit rate must increase 20 fold every decade in all major electrical and optical interconnects and interfaces. The core networking speed must increase 100-fold in the same period, which requires a five-fold increase in the number of channels per link.

Even the modern 10GB/s copper based links become too bulky and power consuming thus making a shift towards optical interconnect necessary. Modern supercomputers as the IBM blue Gene Power 7 systems and others employ about 5 million optical links each operating at 10Gb/s to reach 10 petaflop. The number of optical links/per supercomputer increases hundredfold every 3 years, so its performance will be defined by optical interconnects.

3.3 Advanced Si based image sensors
Another trend is the 3D image capturing capability, providing depth information along with the image by time-of-flight technology. IR emitted by a camera and reflects back; by measuring light travel time, it is possible to calculate depth information. Unfortunately, the trend for as many pixels as possible means smaller pixels and therefore more cross talk and a signal to noise ratio decrease.

3.4 Si technology and health

Healthcare has benefited immensely from Si technology in the past years. The current line of thinking in medicine is called 4Ps (predictive, preventive, personalized and participatory). Here does ICT again come in. Examples are devices monitoring potential of health risks or improving medical diagnostic imaging. A key requirement is ultra low power vital signal sensing for ECG, blood pressure, glucose level etc. The discussed ICT developments would support improved medical imaging, ultrasound on Si, X ray detectors on Si, direct conversion of X rays into electrical signals, needing less radiation or third generation DNA sequencing.

3.5 The Mobile Optical communication

Optical NW delivers today 98% of telecommunication traffic today, in the last 20 years transmission capacity increased by a factor 1000, but to meet the future demand another thousand-fold increase over the next 20 years will be required. Transmission speed defines NW transmission capacity, the NWs bandwidth requirements are determined by its load architecture and protocols. The development of intelligent NWs might help to reduce the NW s traffic load but the demand for NW capacity will soar further. Nevertheless, projections promise that optical communications could to meet the challenge.

3.6 Neuromorphic devices

The expression Neuromorphic devices refers to analog/digital VLSI devices and programs that allow mimicking neural system for perception, control sensory processing and decision-making. Neuromorphic VLSI chips mostly use an integrate and fire spiking neuron model, computing from inputs in the sub-threshold area and emit sparse high voltage pulses for cell-to-cell communication. Problems are still the unavoidable transistor variability due to fabrication process, wiring large numbers of neurons a N neuron chip requires N^2 wires for independent paths to be fully connected, or the implementation of synapse (biological structure passing signal from one neuron to another) and its updating. A special feature is that the "synapses weight" can change over time so that the brain learns.

4. NANOTECHNOLOGY from Nanotubes to Graphene

As discussed in preceding sessions, nanotubes have a plethora of outstanding properties ranging from less energy needed to change the state, to its superiority in dissipating heat due to its higher thermal conductivity, leading to more and denser chips.

However, there are other materials comparable even more attractive as graphene.

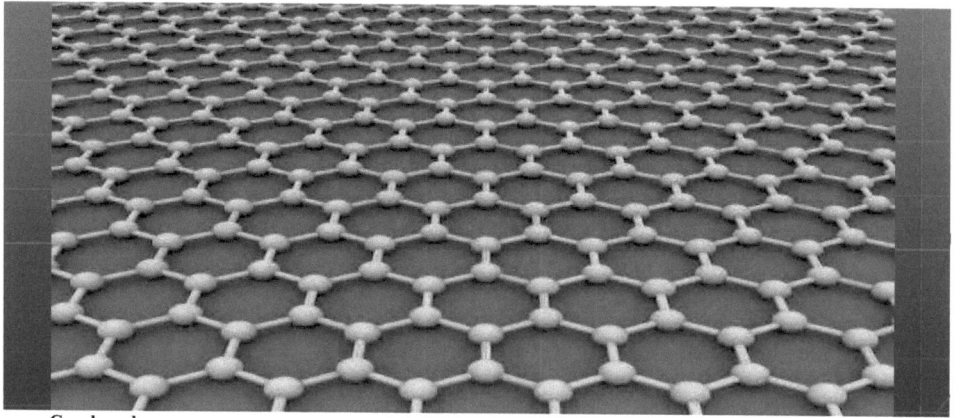

Graphene layer

4.1 Graphene

Information processing consists of three functions, realized with three classes of material: processing with Si transistors, communication with photons using compound semiconductors (mainly InAs, InP and GaAs) and storage with ferro-metals. Such a subdivision is inefficient and by the dependency on some rare materials as In exposed in the long range. Graphene and in particular graphene dots may offer an alternative. There exists a special class of graphene triangular quantum dots with zigzag edges, which fulfill all three functions, needed.

Graphene can be used as an improved but already existing device, but with the additional properties of graphene triangular quantum dots and the possibility of integrating electronic, optical and magnetic functionalities at a single platform thus creating a carbon only IC. Again developing control over size, shape and edges with atomic precision will be a challenging task.

Graphene well known for its strength and conductivity can also convert IR into electrical signals (photodetectors). Conventional photodetectors on Ge convert only a limited range of wavelengths according to their energy band but graphene has no bandgap this means that all wavelength are suitable, additionally it is cheaper as Ge and easier to incorporate into chips. However, today it is not very efficient needing a 50-100 fold improvement.

Another graphene-based application emerging is the graphene-based wireless transmission module.

IBM created a wireless module out of graphene which could transmit on a 4,3 GHz frequency.

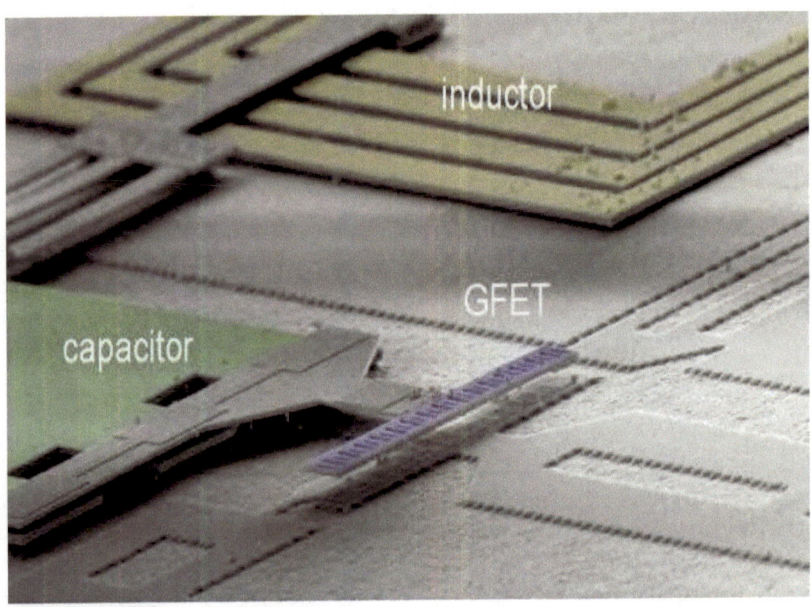

GFET, Source IBM

IBM added a GFET onto an integrated circuit thus enabling this circuit to transmit. This could by a prototype of a high performance, ultra-compact and cheap communication system.

5. Further Trends - a Scenario

5.1 Consumerization of business technology (Megatrends at CES 2014)
  - Wearable computing
  - Seamingless integration into daily life
  - Moving away from wrist and face
  - Health and fitness gain popularity
  - Increased focus on design for better user appeal

- Contextual computing (predictive computing) Technologies Changing Our World
- Mobile as high priority and wearables as next phase
- IoT (Internet of Things)

5.2 Quantum Computing

Responding to many questions and after many years of hope and promises, a review of the state of QC (quantum computing) may be appropriate. The idea of QC is to store information in the values of 2^N complex amplitudes describing the wave function of N two-level systems (qubits) and process this information by applying unitary transformations (quantum gates), that change these amplitudes in a precise and controlled manner.

The value of N for a useful machine is estimated to be in the order of 10^3 or more. ($2^{1000} \sim 10^{300} >>$ number of protons in the universe). This means that 10^{300} continuously changing quantum amplitudes must be followed closely and the random drift caused by noise, gate inaccuracies, and unwanted interactions etc. suppressed. Fault tolerant computation using error-correction may provide the solution to the problem.

The "threshold theorem" says that once the error/qubit/gate rate falls below a certain value ($\sim 10^{-6}$ to 10^{-4}) indefinitely long quantum computation becomes feasible. Theorists claim that the problem of quantum computing error correction can be solved, at least in principle, and physicists and engineers need only find good candidates for qubits and an approach to achieve the accuracy required by the threshold theorem so all hopes rely on the threshold theorem.

Another question is the applicability of quantum information processing. Large QCs may be able to address special tasks only as factoring cryptographic system (but cryptography that not depending on factoring cannot be broken). It appears that the simulation of strongly interacting quantum system is the meaningful application of QC systems.

During the last 20 years, many unfounded promises have been made and people became saturated by frequent announcement of "breakthroughs", all the tenure positions in QC are already occupied, the proponents are getting old and less zealous but literature activity remains very high.

5.3 AI - the Era of Modesty?

Since 1952 when Turing asked the his famous question, new slogans as formal logic, connectionism, neuronal NW, genetic programming, statistical interference, fuzzy logic etc. came up but hopes were disappointed. The expectation level may have been too high.

It would be misleading to expect a big AI moment in history, rather it may rather become gradually a part of everyday life (appliances, devices, transport and will become connected to the internet).

However, investments as Google acquisition of Deep Mind for 400 mio BP or IBM's 1Bio$ Watson efforts prove the ongoing attention and determination to pursue this R&D direction further.

5.4 Cognitive Computing

Cognitive computers have a number of characteristics different from today's computers. One is that they learn patterns and trends. They no longer require reprogramming by humans for all the tasks we want them to do. Secondly, cognitive systems interact with people in a much more natural way. They understand our human language, recognize our behaviours, and fit more seamlessly into our work–life balance - and that will change how humans and computers interact. Will IBM's Watson usher in as a platform to help with decision-making? Watson has a lot to learn, this may be exactly the point. The system learns patterns, learns outcomes, and learns what sources to trust. Some journals, some doctors, are more accurate than others are.

How does the latest Watson compare to its predecessor? Three times as fast and about a quarter the size of the original system. Some through hardware optimization but as well the underlying learning algorithms became more efficient. However, compared to the human brain there is still a long way to go: The *Jeopardy!*-version of Watson utilized 85,000 W of power to compete with two humans, but the human brain uses about 20 W of power for much more. Computer chips inspired by human neurons can do more with less power. This leads to field of Neuroelectronics, the quest to make smarter computer chips.

In the 1990s, Mead and his colleagues had shown that it is possible to build a realistic silicon neuron. That device could accept outside electrical input through junctions that performed the role of synapses. It allowed the incoming signals to build up voltage in the circuit's interior, much as they do in real neurons. If the accumulated voltage passed a certain threshold, the silicon neuron 'fired', producing a series of voltage spikes that traveled along a wire playing the part of an axon, the neuron's communication cable. Although the spikes were 'digital' in the sense that they were either on or off, the body of the silicon neuron operated in a non-digital way, meaning that the voltages and currents were not restricted to few discrete values as they are in conventional chips. The project used "Spaun", a design for a computer model of the brain that includes the parts responsible for vision, movement, and decision-making. Spaun relies on a programming language for neural circuitry developed at the University of Waterloo in Ontario, Canada. A user just has to specify a desired neural function for example, the generation of an instruction to move an arm, and the system will automatically design a network of spiking neurons to carry out that function.

6. Some Social Impacts - Digital Dementia

Apart from the impressive developments of ICT and social NW there do neurologists as M. Spitzer highlight some phenomena worth attention:

Many of us have witnessed indicators as:

- People calculating 2+8 with a pocket calculator,
- NASA's "inch vs. cm disaster", leading to the loss of a satellite,
- News speakers short of distinguishing between mixing of Mio and Bio,
- Time spent on PC at home vs. reading and calculation skills.
- Performance in spatial orientation and social response.

The average "Digital Native" of today (with an average of 21 years) has

-      sent & received 250.000 emails and SMS's
-      spent 10.000 hours on mobile phones
-      spent 5000 hours with video games and
-      spent 3500 hours in social NW's

Generally speaking, many young people spend more time consuming digital media than in school.

The picture below shows recent studies proving correlation between times spent watching TV and education level:

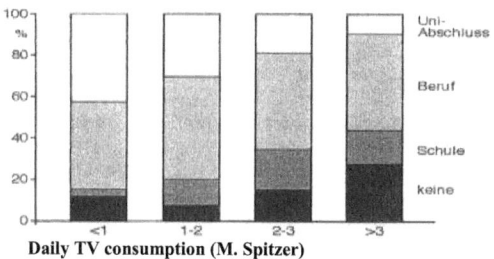

Daily TV consumption (M. Spitzer)

Neurologists warn of these developments as detrimental for the establishment of the cognitive reserve capacity of the brain.

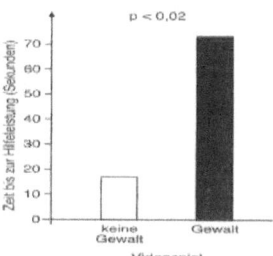

Videogames (M. Spitzer)

There are also indications of the impact of videogames on behavior, as the graphic above shows the impact of videos on the reaction time to help other people.

As Huxley remarked in Brave New World Revisited, the civil libertarians and rationalists who are ever on the alert to oppose tyranny "failed to take into account man's almost infinite appetite for

In the beginning, the PC user was intelligent, avant-garde, and curious; the picture has changed to a different a game- and social NW oriented clientele.

A key issue remains the influence on the development of the human brains prefrontal cortex.

"The Dose makes the Poison" (Paracelsus 1493-1541)

7. From lessons learned in the past to beyond 2020

A fundamental lessons derived from the past of the semiconductor industry is that most of the innovations of the past ten years revolutionizing the technology were initiated 10–15 years before they were incorporated into the CMOS process. Strained silicon research began in the early 90s, high-κ/metal-gate initiated in the mid-90s and multiple-gate transistors were pioneered in the late 90s. This observation generates a simple but fundamental question: "How to identify now what the ICT industry will need 10–15 years from now?"

In the years 2020–2025, we may expect many physical dimensions to cross the 10nm threshold, and when dimensions approach the 5–7nm range, fundamental limits will be reached. We expect new devices like the tunnel transistors, allowing a smooth transition from traditional CMOS to this new class of devices to reach these new levels of miniaturization. By fully utilizing the vertical dimension, and stacking layers of transistors on top of each other and this 3D approach will continue to increase the number of components per mm^2 even when horizontal physical dimensions will no longer be amenable to further reduction.

The "More than Moore" (MtM) concept addresses an emerging category of devices that incorporate functionalities that do not necessarily scale according to "Moore's Law," but provide additional value to the user. The MtM approach allows non-digital functionalities (e.g. RF-communication, power control, passive components, sensors, actuators, MEMS) to migrate from the system board-level to a particular package-level (SiP) or chip-level (SoC) system solution. By the end of this decade, it might become possible to augment the capabilities of CMOS by introducing new devices to realize some "beyond CMOS" capabilities, without replacing the CMOS functionality totally.

We have tried to re-evaluate the increasing dilemma between technological progress, economic feasibility and the tremendous potential created by ICT's further proliferation into many other fields that may lead to a systemic evolution.

Another R&D avenue would be to re-examine how to get more information into a finite amount of space. The semiconductor industry has thrived on Boolean logic; after all, for most applications, the CMOS devices are just than "on-off" switches. It becomes tempting to investigate new techniques that allow the use of multiple (i.e.> 2) logic states. However, short of reaching the ultimate goal of quantum computing it may be possible to increase the number of states to a moderate level, as 4–10 states as an example, and perhaps, increase the number of "virtual transistors" by two every two years.

During the progress of semiconductor logic and storage products, many other technologies have progressed as well, even though at a slower pace and thus many new capabilities are now available because of these "complementary" technologies. A variety of wireless devices contains examples of this confluence of technologies mentioned above, thus enabling the megatrends as: mobile, sensors, robotics, cloud, and big data etc.

Consumers have become the drivers of the proliferation of products that are "pliable" in the sense of being molded into unique individual applications for consumers as "Custom Functionality".

We can look forward to be witnesses to these plethora of fascinating developments or even to be part of it.

8. References and Literature

Banine V., EUV Lithography today and tomorrow, ASML Inc, The Hague (2013)

Betschon St., Das Ende der Bescheidenheit, NZZ (2014)

Bauer H.. Veira J. and Weig F., Insights and publications, (2013)

Cave K., Where is AI heading, Technology planning and analysis, (2014)

Computerworld, Replacing Si by nanotubes, (2013)

Courtland R., EUV Chipmaking inches forward and The End of the Shrink, IEEE (2013)

Chroust Gerhard, Personal Discussions and Intervention, (2014)

Dyakonov M., QC State of the Art and Prospects for quantum computing, (2013)

Eliasmith C., Brainpower for neural circuitry, Univ. Waterloo CDA, Nature (2013)

Falk T., 15 predictions for the digital future, The Bulletin, (2014)

Gerecke K., STT-MRAM Spin Storage für big data, Storage technology conference (2014)

Gilpin L., CES 2014 Wearable computing, Tech republic (1/2014)

GlobalFoundries, (2013)

Greenmeier L., Will IBM's Watson Usher in a new era of Cognitive Computing, SciAm (2013)

Güclü A., Potasz P. and Hawrylak P., Graphene based Integrated Electronic, Photonic and Spintronic circuit, (2013)

Hiner J., Watch for the megatrends at CES 2014

Huxley Aldous, Brave new world revisited, Harper & Brothers, US, (1958)

ITRS 2013 Edition and update, (2013 and update 2014)

Kalenda F., Graphene-based wireless transmission module, ZDNet mobile (2014)

Kim K. and Chung U., Technology Innovation Reshaping the Microelectronic Industry (2013)

Ledentsov et alii, Ultrafast Nanophotonics Devices for Optical Interconnects VI Systems (2013)

Loesch C., ICT Trends and Scenarios, IDIMT (2013)

Malik O., The coming era of magical computing, Fast Company Magazine (2014)

McKinsey, The Internet users (2014)

McKinsey research perspective, Moore's law Repeal or Renewal, (2014)

Peplow M., Graphene makes light work of Optical Signals, SciAm and Nature (2013)

Pinto M., Silicon Photovoltaics, Accelerating to grid parity; Appl. Mat. Science (2013)

Postman Neil, Amusing ourselves to death, Penguin Books, 2006

Spitzer M., Digital Dementia, Droemer München (2012)

Status of Moore's law, IEEE spectrum (2013)

Stevenson R., Changing the channel, IEEE spectrum (2013)

IDIMT 2013

ICT TODAY & TOMORROW

SOME ECO -TECHNOLOGICAL ASPECTS AND TRENDS

Abstract:

Evaluating status and future of ICT, means evaluating the technological and the economic aspects, and discuss some of the emerging options.

This perusal of the economic–technological scenario will demonstrate structural dynamics, emerging future developments and strategies for the scaling with and beyond Moore's law.

Complimenting this by the economic perspective is of importance since it is not only determining the financial feasibility of current projects but through the direction of investments into R&D, marketing and manufacturing furthermore the direction of future developments. This approach should result in a vision of future options for ICT arising over the horizon.

1. Economic Overview

1.1 Eco -Technological Aspects and Trends

The semiconductor industry has been an amazing source of industrial innovation in recent history. Starting with the discovery of the transistor in Bell Labs in the 1940s, the development of the integrated circuit in the 1960s, the semiconductor industry has grown into a $300 billion giant and supports the even-larger ~$1.2 trillion electronic systems industry. It has driven incredible innovations from decoding the human genome, to enabling people to communicate verbally, in pictures, and in video almost anytime, anywhere. For the first few decades, the industry relied primarily on geometric scaling - making stuff smaller. The new millennium brought a millennial shift, requiring many more innovations such as the shift to high-k dielectric materials and the move from aluminium to copper for on-chip interconnects. However, this is just the beginning - future innovations in materials and device structures will be even more exotic, involving fundamental shifts like using photons to exchange information instead of electrons, and perhaps new substrates like graphene, instead of the old warhorse silicon. [Pushkar P. Apte , Pravishyati Inc.]

Semiconductor technology and electronics are embedded in almost every aspect of our life. The semiconductor industry spends more on R&D than almost any other industry, and its spending is increasing rapidly, outpacing revenue growth.

But disruptive transitions as e.g. the advent of nanotechnology and the rise of the global consumer as the main end-user – are reshaping the industry.

How are some of the leading companies performing in this race?

INTEL once holding a quasi-monopolistic position, has been confronted with new markets and business directions, which Intel left without any fight to its competitors. Up to now there is practically no tablet or smart phone with an Intel processor.

Trying to regain leadership Intel expects contribution from its Ivy bridge processors with only 25% energy consumption. It is working on near threshold Technology which would enable a reduction of energy by another 80% and a variation of the working frequency by a factor of 10. Extrapolating these figures would result in a smart phone by 2017 with the computing power of a server rack of today. Some estimate Intel's advance in processor development up to three years.

Intel PC-processor revenue sank by 6%. But the second may market chips for storage systems and corporate customers grow by 4 percent.. The market research company Gartner estimates a shrinking of the revenue by 4,9 percent encompassing 90,3 mio notebooks und desktops. Its competitor IDC corresponding figures are shrinking of the revenue by 6,4 percent encompassing 89,3 mio notebooks und desktops.

Actually, INTEL is building its Processors Ivy Bridge and Haswell with a 22 nm process and to introduce its next generation in 14nm technology soon. However, intensive research efforts are going to find a way for a 10nm technology.

IBM is continuing to shift its emphasis to services and software climbing from 68% of its revenue in 2000 to 86% in 2012. Additionally since the beginning of 2000, IBM acquired more than 140 companies in strategic areas including analytics, cloud, security, and Smarter Commerce, and it expects to spend $20 billion in acquisitions over the 2015 Road Map period. IBM invests a billion$ in the development of new flash technologies. It claims that SSD will drive down cost and maintenance in advantage of Flash-based Computer-centres equipped with SSD of 30%.

ARM has been the newly rising star, it is licensing its processor designs to be manufactured by companies as Samsung, TSMC and Globalfoundries. The power-saving chip architecture of the British development company ARM has gained the leadership ánd maintains a 95% market share of smart phones and tablets. It has licensed its 64-bit processor technology to 15 companies as AMD, NVIDIA or Samsung.

1.2 Productivity paradox

Innovation has never been faster. In fact, if you look at the underlying statistics, productivity growth is doing pretty well. Productivity levels are at an all-time high, and in the 2000s, productivity growth was faster than it was in the 1990s, which was a great decade.

On the other hand, the median worker is doing worse. U.S- Median households and workers in the have lower incomes today than in 1997 and the employment-to-population ratio has fallen. Similar developments are visible in the worldwide OECD statistics. That is the paradox of our era.

However, there is no economic law that says that technological progress needs to benefit everybody, or even a majority of people. It is entirely possible for technology to advance, to make the pie bigger and yet for some people to get a smaller share of that pie.

As you are well aware approximately every two years, circuit line widths are driven smaller, device performance is improved and cost is reduced, putting more processing power into a handheld smart phone than all of the Apollo space missions combined. Many are predicting that CMOS will soon reach the proverbial "red brick wall" of the laws of physics, where conventional scaling becomes impossible (or at least impractical). If this does happen, the results will not only be felt in the fab, but will also negatively impact global economies that are influenced by demand for the latest and greatest technologies.

2. Technology

2.1 Potential Technology developments

Since its inception in 1992, a basic premise of the Roadmap has been that continued scaling of electronics would further reduce the cost per function (historically~25 -29% per year) and promote market growth for integrated circuits (historically averaging ~17% per year, but maturing to slower growth in more recent history).

One of the fundamental lessons derived for the past successes of the semiconductor industry comes for the observation that most of the innovations of the past ten years, which have revolutionized the way CMOS transistors are manufactured nowadays, were initiated 10–15 years before they were incorporated into the CMOS process. Strained silicon research began in the early 90s, high-κ/metal-gate initiated in the mid-90s and multiple-gate transistors were pioneered in the late 90s.

Looking at the timeframe 2020–2025, we can see that many physical dimensions are expected to be crossing the 10nm threshold. It is expected that as dimensions approach the 5–7nm range it will be difficult to operate any transistor structure that is utilizing the MOS physics. Naturally, we expect that new devices, like the promising tunnel transistors, will allow a smooth transition from traditional CMOS to this new class of device miniaturization. However, the fundamental geometrical limits will be reached in the above timeframe. By utilizing the vertical dimension, it will be possible to stack layers of transistors on top of each other and this 3D approach will continue to increase the number of components per mm^2 when horizontal physical dimensions will no longer be amenable to any further reduction.

It seems then important to ask the fundamental question: "How will we be able to increase the computation and memory capacity when the device physical limits will be reached? " It becomes necessary to reexamine how to can get more information into a finite amount of space. The semiconductor industry has thrived on Boolean logic; after all, for most applications, the CMOS devices have been used as nothing more than an "on-off" switch. One way out of this dilemma would be to develop new techniques that allow the use of multiple (i.e. > 2) logic states in any given and finite location. This evokes the "magic of quantum computing" looming in the distance. However, short of reaching this ultimate goal, it may be possible to increase the number of states to a moderate level as e.g. 4–10 states and increase the number of "virtual transistors" by 2 every 2 years ("Multiple States Law").

2.1.1 RF and A/MS Technologies

RF and A/MS Technologies for Wireless Radio frequency and analog mixed-signal technologies serve the very rapidly growing wireless communications market and represent essential and critical technologies for the success of many semiconductor manufacturers. Communications products are becoming key drivers of volume manufacturing. Consumer products now account for over half of the demand for semiconductors. For example, 3G cellular phones now have a much higher semiconductor content and now comprise 50 percent of the cellular phone market compared to only 5 percent of the market a few years ago. The consumer portions of wireless communications markets are very sensitive to cost. With different technologies capable of meeting technical requirements, time-to-market and overall system cost will govern technology selection. [Herbert S. Bennett, National Institute of Standards and Technology, John J. Pekarik, IBM, Margaret Huang, Freescale Semiconductor Communications Future Fab, Intl. Volume 36, January11,2011]

2.2 The race for the 450 mm wafer

The rationale for a transition to 450mm diameter wafer is productivity. This is the ability to decrease the manufacturing cost of each mm^2 of IC by the use of larger diameter wafers. Based on economic considerations, that to stay on this productivity curve, the industry needed to achieve 30% cost reduction and 50% cycle time improvement in manufacturing.

The European EEMI 450mm consortium initiative continued to make progress and report of their plans for targets for 450mm development in new facilities in IMEC in Belgium

The private consortium initiative, the Global 450mm Consortium (G450C), among five major industry players—Intel, Samsung, TSMC, GLOBALFOUNDRIES, and IBM—in cooperation with the state of New York, has begun to invest $4.4B to advance 450mm manufacturing and technology development.

At the SEMI Industry Strategy Symposium (ISS) this week, Intel demonstrated a fully patterned 450mm wafer. This wafer was created after intense collaboration Intel and various suppliers.

This "triumvirate" of functionality, higher performance, and lower power market benefits to consumers continued into the early 2000's; when, passing through nano-scale dimensions, the shrinking of technology began to approach molecular and atomic levels (in the case of gate and channel thickness and length)

As a result the usual dimensional reduction of the scaling of printed and physical gate length of transistors had to slow, compensated by a tradeoff with what became known as "Equivalent Scaling"—the inclusion of process techniques such as gate strain in the channel, HiK-metal gate materials in the transistor gate; and more recently, transistor 3D architecture called multiple gate FET (MugFET) or FinFET.

On the near horizon, new channel materials, such as III/V Germanium, will also enter into manufacturing to benefit performance and power of devices. Additional chip and system-level architectural and software design "Equivalent Scaling" such as SRAM memory architecture, CPU multiple-core, and power software management enabled the chips, limited by slower voltage decreases and slower speed of operation, to still achieve the needed market low powernd high performance requirements of the latest centralized Communications and Cloud Computing high performance and also the Portability and Mobility low power of the latest and future market applications.[Updates to 2012 ITRS roadmap (ORTC)]

2.3 Lithography

Lithography being a key technology for further implantation of the ambitions targerts merits some attention.

Single optical exposure has reached its limit at roughly 40 nm half-pitch (hp) using 193nm wavelength (ArF) exposure tools. Flash devices with 32nm hp are being manufactured today using double patterning (DP) to reduce half-pitch while keeping the existing exposure NA and wavelength.

For even smaller dimensions, extreme ultraviolet lithography (EUVL), multiple patterning (MP) or some non-optical lithography must be introduced. EUVL, which uses light with a wavelength of 13.5nm, is the clear preference of the semiconductor industry for patterning smaller dimensions. EUVL has been gaining significant momentum with several manufacturers running early EUV pilot lines and some manufacturers have announced plans to purchase production tools to be delivered in 2013. The key technical issue gating is whether power EUVL will be ready on time..

Higher NAs will require more mirrors or constrained optical design. A new wavelength would have fewer photons and resist sensitivity issues.

2.4 Directed Self-Assembly ("DSA").

As the costs of lithography continue to escalate, a viable and complementary alternative is emerging in the form of directed self-assembly ("DSA"). In lithography, all the information for the patterning is transmitted "top down" from the mask, but cost scales with complexity. The DSA approach uses a "bottom up" chemical approach, similar to that used in nature, to drive complexity with a potentially compelling cost of ownership. [Geoff Wild, AZ Electronic Materials]

Nano-imprint and e-beam direct write.

Alternative emerging patterning technologies are nano-imprint and e-beam direct write. Nano-imprint is a technique like embossing. It is also in development for other industries such as hard disk drive patterning as well as for the semiconductor lithography. It requires 1×masks and has stringent defectivity needs since it is a contact printing technique.

There are prototype tools available, but so far the semiconductor industry hasn't bought many of them. The key issue seems to be defects, especially defects after using a patterning template for many wafers.

Direct write e-beam is a mask less lithography (ML) technique. Since masks can be quite expensive, direct write is especially appealing for prototyping and for small production volume parts. The biggest challenge is achieving sufficient throughput. They are under development, but none are yet available for use [ITRS 2012 update].

Development potential of Logic

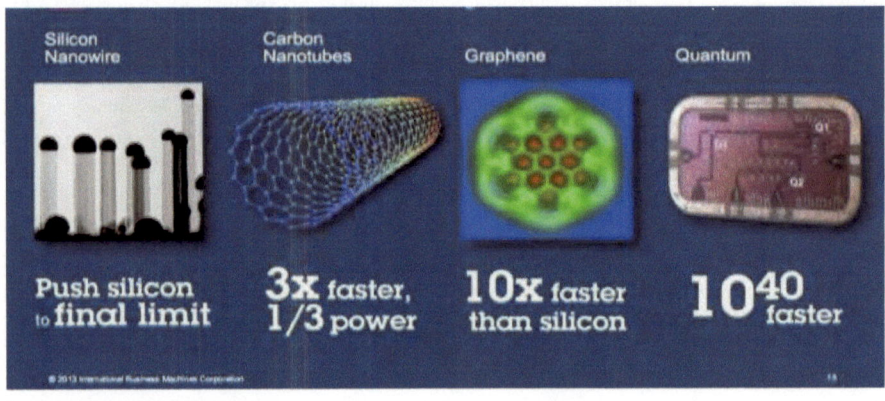

Source: IBM Investor Briefing

2.5 Disruptive Technologies

- Mobile Internet
- Automation, Robotics
- IoT
- AI
- Cloud
- Next generation medicine and genetics
- Energy storage
- 3D printing

There were other technologies on the radar ranging from nuclear fission, fusion power, quantum computing to candidates far out as OLED/LED lightning, to wireless charging and 3D and volumetric displays. It would exceed the frame to discuss all of them. Much of what we call innovation is routine and essentially evolutionary innovation. Cloud computing is an example, it has been around for a long time and is just mainframe computing in a different mode. [McKinsey Global Institute May 2013]

2.6 Big Data

The exponentially increasing amount of data over the last decade made memory technology emerging as key to future developments.

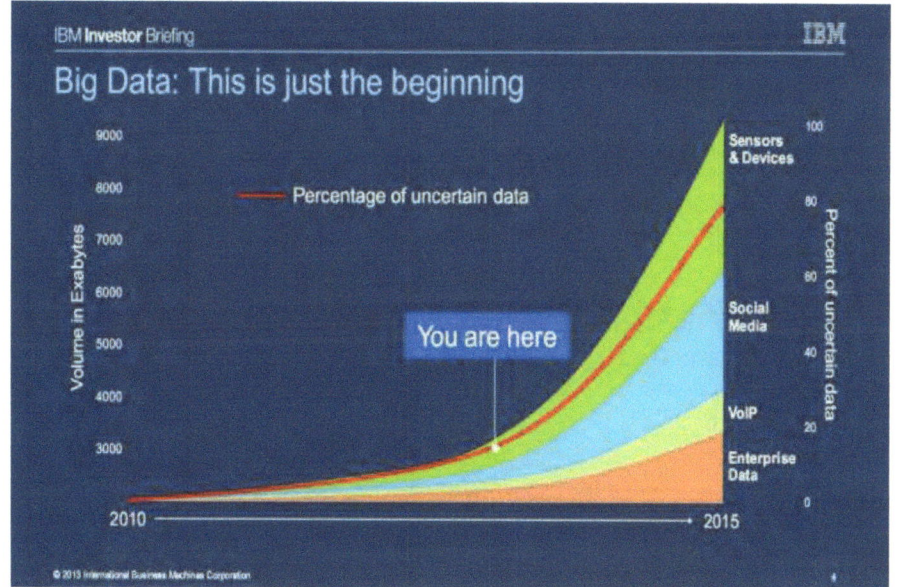

2.7. Technology outlook

2.7.1 Phase-Change Memory (PCM)

IBM's research division has announced a huge step forward in memory technology that could make existing Flash technology redundant. (2011). A PCM system is able to write and read data 100 times faster than Flash memory, and can carry out at least 10 million write cycles, compared with the 3-30,000 cycles available today

The PCM technology uses precise measurements in electrical resistance across materials to store and process multiple data points within a single memory cell, as opposed to single unit storage in use today. It is capable of storing four-bit combinations in this way: 00, 01, 10, and 11.

The announcement comes at a good time, as many analysts are worried that current memory technology is running out of steam on an engineering front. Architecture sizes are approaching as low as they can go, and the PCM system could offer a way forward.

2.7.2 Nanowire transistor

But in parallel efforts as Nanowire transistors are made to keep Moore's Law alive. Researchers are trying to develop ways to produce gate-all-around devices.

It consists of an array of 225 doped-silicon nanowires, each 30 nm wide and 200 nm tall, vertically linking the two platinum contact planes that form the source and drain of the transistor. Besides their narrowness, what's new is the gate: A single 14-nm-thick chromium layer surrounds each nanowire midway up its length. [Alexander Hellemans Apr 2013]

2.7.3 Mobile hologram display

HP Labs in Palo Alto, California is currently working on a new type of three-dimensional display technology that is capable of displaying hologram-like images and videos using a modified LCD. The technology could make it possible for phones, laptops, tablets, and other mobile devices to display hologram-like still images with 200 viewpoints and videos with 64 viewpoints and 30 frames per second. The new technology does not require any moving parts or glasses. Videos and images that are displayed using this technology hover above the screen and viewers are able to walk around them and experience them just as you would a real object.

2.7.4 DNA storage

There was a successful attempt by researchers some years ago. They started with two kinds of information. They had the 0s and 1s that composed the digital version of the book. They also had the four chemicals in which DNA codes its genetic instructions: adenine (A), guanine (G), cytosine (C) and thymine (T).

Next, they translated the zeros into either the A or C of the DNA base pairs, and changed the ones into either the G or T. Then, using now-standard laboratory techniques, they created short strands of actual DNA that held the coded sequence, almost 55,000 strands in all. Each strand contained a portion of the text and an address that indicated where it occurred in the flow of the book. What they ended up with was a viscous liquid that held a billion copies of the book, could comfortably fit into test tube and could last for centuries without requiring, say, extreme cold or tremendous energy to preserve it, unlike some other experimental forms of storage. You can drop it wherever you want, in the desert or your backyard, and it will be there 400,000 years later. [Church, The Wall Street Journal]

Souce:IBM

Having perused one of the newest developments in the area of technologies let us return to the recently emerging

3. Cognitive Computing

The example of IBM´s WATSON

- Jeopardy Quizshow in the US
- Capability to answer questions in natural language
- 4 years research project
- Human contestants were the two top Jeopardy winners

- 90 P570 systems
- DeepQA with 2880 processors
- 16 TB of memory
- No Internet connection allowed
- 200 mio pages scanned in
- Price money:

Winner: $1 mio, 2nd: $300K, 3rd: $200

Contestants give 50%, IBM 100% to charity

Jeopardy! was selected as the ultimate test of the machine's capabilities because it relied on many human cognitive abilities traditionally seen beyond the capability of computers, such as: The ability to discern double meanings of words, puns, rhymes, and inferred hints. Extremely rapid responses. The ability to process vast amounts of information to make complex and subtle logical connections

To meet this grand challenge, the Watson team focused on three key capabilities: Natural language processing, Hypothesis generation, and Evidence-based learning.

The technology behind Watson relies on analytics to understand what is asked, to crunch through massive amounts of data and provide the best answer based on the evidence it finds.

After the success in Jeopardy search for application in many fields is going on:

- Finance
- Healthcare
- Legal
- Telemarketing

5. Summary

As a picture says more than thousand words

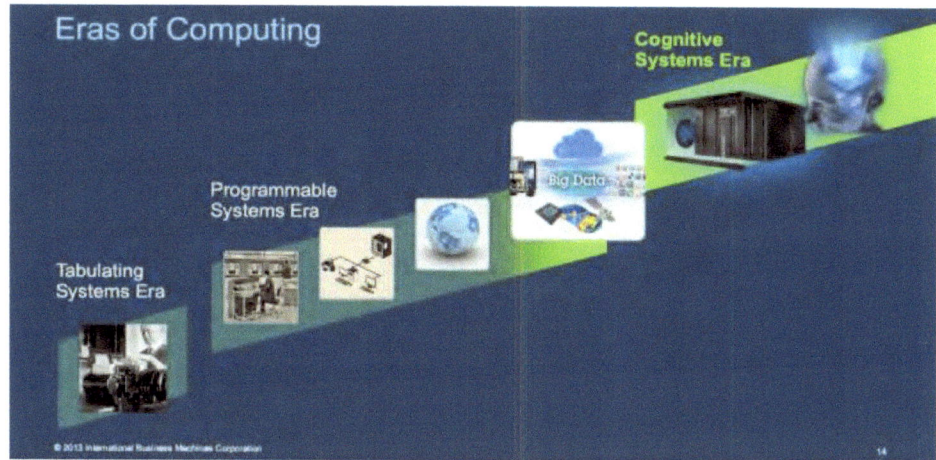

We are entering a new era: Computing will be Everywhere, Unnoticeable and more Intelligent.

6. Literature:

[1]   ARM Annual Report, 2012, may 2013

[2]   Herbert S. Bennett, National Institute of Standards and Technology, John J. Pekarik, IBM, Margaret Huang, Freescale Semiconductor Communications Future Fab Intl. Volume 36, January11,2011

[3]   FUTURE FAB 2010 and 2012

[4]   A. Hellemans, Apr 2013.

[5]   P.A. Gargini ITRS Issue 44

[6]   IDG Connct 2012

[7]   INTEL Annual report 2012

[8]   IBM Annual report 2012

[9]   IBM Investors briefing 2013

[10]   Global Technology Outlook IBM May 2012

[11]   ITRS ROADMAP (ORTC) 2012, updates 2013

[12]   McKinsey Global Institute May 2013

~

[13]   McKinsey Global Institute analysis 2012

[14]   Pushkar P. Apte , Pravishyati Inc.

[15]   Geoff Wild, AZ Electronic Materials

[16]   ZDNet 8815952 April 2013-04

~

IDIMT 2012

20 YEARS IDIMT

ITC TRENDS AND SCENARIOS REFLECTED BY IDIMT

Abstract

The continuous series of contributions to this subject offers the prospect to review and analyse emerging trends and developments of ITC and microelectronics. We will revisit scenarios of past years and pursue the opportunity to balance the promises of the once newly emerging trends and ideas to their realization and impact, as well as failures, impasses or ideas that never made it to the market.

> 2011   *ICT Trends, Scenarios in Microelectronics and their Impact*
>
> 2010   *Some Eco-Technological Aspects of the Future of Information Technology*
>
> 2009   *Technological Outlook: The Future of Information Technology*
>
> 2008   *Technological Forecasts in Perspective*
>
> 2007   *15 Years moving in Fascinating Scenarios*
>
> 2006   *Do we need a new Information Technology?*
>
> 2005   *Future Trends and Scenarios of Information Technology*
>
> 2004.   *Information Technology: From Trends to Horizons*
>
> 2003   *Trends in Information Technology*
>
> 2002   *Safety, Security and Privacy in IS/ IT*
>
> 2001   *Trends in Business, Technology, and R & D*
>
> 2000   *Ethics, Enforcement and Information Technology*

Having reviewed success and failure of once praised achievements in today's light, the shifting priorities both scientifically and economically, we will attempt to gain some insight into future developments and options and emerging phenomena (as e.g. nanotechnology, MtM, Exascale, Cognitive computing etc.)

At IDIMT 2012, under a separate cover the above listed overview and appraisal of the past as well as an outlook on future scenarios will be presented.

1. Retrospectives

1.1 Scenario

~

Let us look at the year 1993 the year IDIMT started. It was a period of optimisms, the fall of the iron curtain had initiated a wave of positive enthusiastic mood and the mood of a new exciting plethora of opportunities, and improvement both generally and personally persisted.
It was the feeling of tremendous personal and economic potential at the doorstep and the dedication to peruse it prevailed and concurring with the feeling of a final arrival of democracy.

Historians as F. Fukuyama published successful books as "End of history and the last man" and the world was looking at Japan a leading industrial nation and trying to learn from Japanese techniques installing quality circles and studying W.G. Ouchi´s book "Theory Z".

Europe was fully engaged in the enormous tasks ranging from German reunification to rearranging itself after the dissolution of the former COMECON and Yugoslavian structures, and all that in the after waves of the transition of the UdSSR from the Gorbatchov to Jelzin era of the restructuring.

Civil rights and the right for privacy were highly valued; fingerprints had the connotation of criminal investigations and the legality on fingerprints on ID cards etc was disputed.

 This paralleled by an unprecedented revolution in the fields of telecommunication ranging from the transition from A- and B- net to mobile phones, to the liberalization of the telecom industry thus supporting the cost decrease and new applications.

SMS, blog, surfing, outsourcing etc as well as terrorist were no household words and airlines changed to low cost mass transportation.

The scenario started to change by the arrival of CD and DVD, two events the cheap laser, the advances in compression technology enabled music, and movies on small portable devices as the MP3 player started their worldwide success.

However, it was not a scenario of unspoiled peace and happiness if you think of events as

1992 Kuwait invasion

1994 NATO war in Serbia and the first Gulf war

2001 Sep 11 and the invasion of Afghanistan

2003 invasion of Iraq

2005 increasing inter-religious tensions (cartoon crisis)

2006 Israel Lebanon conflict (the use of phosphorus shells cluster bombs) or

- Threats as SARS, Aids, Ebola virus, or avian influenza
- The Euro zone expansion on fake data etc. or
- a new dimension of financial, political and debt scandals, as ENRON, WorldCom, AIG, Lehman, PIIGS and many more.

1.2 Science and Technology

An outstanding example of both high quality forecasting as well as of exponential growth is microelectronics and communication technology. These achievements were not realized by the normal research and developments and seemingly final borders had to be overcome. To achieve these improvements and preserve the improvement speed several technological breakthroughs have been necessary.

The combination of a high-k technology and metal gates are improves the drive current by 20% (by use of high k gate dielectric) and five times the source drain leakage. Hf-based material reduced leakage by the factor of more than the 10 times, reduced switching power by approximately 30% and improved transistor density approximately two times over the previous generation.[7

1.2.1 Developments meeting forecasts

The quality and accuracy of technological forecasts is impressive as:

- THE CONTINUATION OF MOORE'S LAW
- TRANSISTOR TECHNOLOGY AS ROADMAP
- STORAGE TECHNOLOGY ITS RISE AND ROLE
- LITHOGRAPHY
- DESIGN, INTERCON'S, & ARCHITECTURE
- OPTICAL CONNECTIONS
- MEMS AND RFIDS
- SPINTRONICS GMR '97
- PARALLEL PROCESSING
- GLOBAL COMMUNICATION SKIN
- INTEGRATION OF TECHNOLOGIES
  (DP -> IT->MICRO->NANO)
- PERVASIVENESS
- INTERNET OF PEOPLE AND THINGS

What we take as granted parts of everyday life also stems from this period, as e.g.

89	Google online, satellite TV
93	WWW access for CEE
94	Sony Playstation
95	Amazon, Windows 95
99	DVD
04	Facebook
07	iPod
08	Google earth

As well as developments as the

- Start of dot.com
- The shift from assets to expenses (Saas business, cloud)
- Role of rare earth elements
- New business models as global foundries etc.
- Outsourcing (India outsourcing today >160 B$ p.a.) were envisaged.

1.2.2 What did not meet expectations and forecasts or came as a surprise

- SOCIAL NETWORKS AND THE WILLINGNESS TO SACRIFICE PRIVACY (FACEBOOK, TWITTER, GOOGLE STREET, CAMERA SURVEILLANCE ETC.)

- SUPERCOMPUTING REVIVAL FROM (DEEP BLUE TO WATSON)

- VIRUS RESISTANT SW

- SELF-REPAIRING AND FAIL-SOFT SW

- CONTRIBUTION OF SW VS HW TO PERFORMANCE ENHANCEMENT

- NO REPLACEMENT TECHNOLOGY FOR CMOS FOR IN SIGHT

- HOLOGRAPHIC STORAGE

- CANTILEVERS / MILLIPEDE

- MOLECULAR ORGANIC COMPUTING / STORAGE

- IMPACT OF AI / QC / CHAOS THEORY

- RISE OF THE MASS MARKET (CONCORDE TO AIRBUS/ 767 OR iPXX EFFECT)

1.3   Communication Technology

Some of the most dramatic developments influencing the way we live may have come from ICT. The dramatic improvement of price/performance in ICT especially enabled today's applications.

1.3.1   The Internet

Many people regard Internet and WWW as the overwhelming success story of this timeframe. Starting from the US Defence Department's ARPA net it finally merged into Internet, which it has helped to create.

1.3.2   The WEB

At CERN in Switzerland Tim Berners-Lee addressed the issue of the constant change in the currency of information and the turnover of people on projects. Instead of a hierarchical or keyword organization, he proposed a hypertext system that will run across the Internet on different operating systems. This was the World Wide Web unveiled in August 1991 for the scientific community of physicists, and in April 1993 CERN made WWW technology and code free for everyone. It was not as easy as it might look today. He had to defend this idea against uninterested superiors at CERN, Internet-organisations like IETF and later against commercial covetousness of companies like Microsoft and Netscape.

But nothing succeeds as success.

> 1991 100 documents were retrieved per day at CERN,
> 1992 1000
> 1993 10 000
> Today more than a billion pages are retrieved p.d. in the US only (Media Matrix).

Soon after the scientific the commercial use started to boom when in August 95 Microsoft released Internet Explorer as part of Windows 95, followed 1996 by Hotmail.

In our European neighbourhood, events were the 64k line connecting the University of Vienna with CERN or the pioneering role of Academia in establishing the European Internet network via the Vienna node, with CS leading as the first of the former COMECON countries connected in 1993.

The success story of Internet remains a story of idealistic, dedicated engaged individuals who were interested in the progress and the plethora of new possibilities this tool made available for their communities. Czechoslovakia, Hungary and Poland established centres and connected via Vienna to the world. They overcame numerous problems ranging from space to finance and the availability of lines and personnel, the absence of legal frameworks and responsible persons not to mention obstacles like the regulatory environment prevailing at this time. Outstanding devoted personalities (as P. Rastl and others) engaged themselves without consideration for fame, financial or carrier advantages made it possible that e.g. the University of Vienna becoming the hub node of the Ebone-net the backbone of Internet which meant also the start of the commercial internet. This node became Supercomputing Centre connected to CERN and the hub of the first nationwide system library system BIBOS, and many other applications. Internet/WWW remained a field of individual creativity and endeavour. This applies as well to PGP, released in 1991, Linus Torvald's release of the free kernel for LINUX V1.0 in 1996 or of Wikipedia founded by Jimmy Wales in 2001. None of them was making money from it.

Worldwide this looked a little bit like Eden not a snake in sight, but soon afterwards were we mired in problems caused by things like online scams viruses and traps aimed at your computer and sometimes even your identity, making mischief on the Web, stalkers, predators, identity thieves, aso. Picture 8 attributes the sizing and sourcing of some these troublemakers.

1.3.3 How Internet/WWW transformed business

E-business (dot.com)
Internet has not only transformed business but also transformed the way we do business.

~

cover story

The rise of
e-business

Number 1, 1999

IBM Think research

1.1   IT community's perception

ITC is not science and technology but daily life. Many people turn off their PCs, HDTV's plasma screens and grab their cell phones and their laptop computers as they leave their homes, some use GPS to plan their route and bring along their digital cameras.

Laser technology already patented in the 1960s took years before it found practical applications, but when it arrived and merged with Internet/WWW it changed the way music industry does business, changed the photo- and music industry, as Wikipedia changed the world of encyclopaedia and the new compression techniques gave birth to the present dimension of downloading, MP3 players etc.

The enabling technology is taken for granted by the average consumer, like ATM's or MEMS (Micro-Electro-Mechanical System). Few people surviving a car accident walking will say, "Thanks goodness for the advent of nanotechnology and MEMS...." but without these technologies, the airbag would not have deployed in time.

 The groundwork for many of these innovations mentioned is fibre optics which has helped to turn the world into a global village. The change of the scenario literally reaches from the bottom of the sea to the sky. A key innovation, which laid the groundwork for the advancement in many fields, can be found on the bottom of the sea where fibre optics has improved communications up to satellites, which have helped to turn the world into a global village. It might be worth to remember that all this first criticised as overinvestment served as basis of broadband and the .com revolution.

The general users perceptions of the top technical breakthroughs reflects a survey CNN made in celebration of its 25th anniversary asking for

Top Technological breakthroughs

        1 INTERNET
        2 CELL PHONE
        3 PC
        4 FIBRE OPTICS
        5 E-MAIL
        6 GPS
        7 LAPTOP COMPUTER
        8 CD DVD
        9 DIGITAL CAMERAS
       10 RFID

11 MEMS
12 DNA FINGERPRINTING
13 AIRBAGS
14 ATM
15 ADVANCED BATTERIES

[10]

Having perused the past 20 years, let us now look at future trends and perspectives.

2. Perspectives

4]

ITRS confirms the continuation of the exponential trends for key features as

- MPU/ASIC Metal ½ pitch (trailing at 2 years cycle extended to 2013, then 3 years cycle);
- the MPU printed gate length will follow a 3 years cycle from 2011 and
- the MPU physical gate length (nm) begin 3,8 years cycle from 2009

2.1 Technology

Looking at the patentees is an indicator wher R&D is promoted. Among the 10 top patentees 2011 are only two US companies, while five years ago there were still five US companies, and especially disquieting is the absence of European companies.

2.2 Communication

2.2.1   Internet of Things

Let us look at some features of future examples of this as:

- 2015 many new cars will start to have internet connection
- The congruence of applications will result in a sevenfold (up to twelve fold) traffic of today
- 2016 people who cannot read and write will use it
- 2020 nine of ten people will be permanently online

We have only few years to make the right choices.

If we make the right choices, we will have 100 times more applications
If we blow it Internet becomes a controlled cable TV with little innovation and charge []

2.3 Storage Class Memory

The area with outstanding growth even in a field used to grow exponentially is storage. This explains the concentration of research efforts in this field, resulting in newly arising technologies.

Larger installation can have up to 1 Mio disk drives and are therefore exposed to MTBF problems. This is compellingly increasing the importance of secure storage to diminish the technologically vulnerability of storage farms, special architecture (e.g. XiP) have been developed,

One of the promising technological endeavours as mentioned in previous IDIMT is the Racetrack technology. There are several other promising research fields, but it would exceed the given framework permit to describe them in more depth, therefore let us just name some few of them:

- Atomic scale magnetism

- Battery technology

-Homomorphic encryption

2.4 Watson Jeopardy Challenge

After Deep Blue defeated the world champion chess Kasparow, IBM developed further supercomputers mainly for scientific applications as e.g. BlueGene. With the development of the WATSON project supercomputing entered a new territory.

IBM Research   IBM

IBM Jeopardy Challenge

- Jeopardy Quizshow in the US
- Capability to answer questions in natural language
- 4 years research project
- Human contestants were the two top Jeopardy winners

- 90 P570 systems
- DeepQA with 2880 processors
- 16 TB of memory
- No Internet connection allowed
- 200 mio pages scanned in
- Price money:

Winner: $1 mio, 2nd: $300K, 3rd: $200

Contestants give 50%, IBM 100% to charity

© 2012 IBM Corporation

The requirements were demanding:

- Three seconds answer time,
- Unstructured Data entry
- Understand the complexity of natural language incl. daily newspapers or jokes.
- Analysis without programming and reprogramming means the system must learn autodidact

To understand better some of the questions correctly answered:

✓ It is a poor workman who blames these

✓ Even a broken one on your wall is right twice a day

✓ William Wilkinson's "an account of the principalities of Walachia and Moldavia" inspired this author's most famous novel

2.5 Upcoming Technologies

6]

2.5.1 From Programming to Cognitive Computing

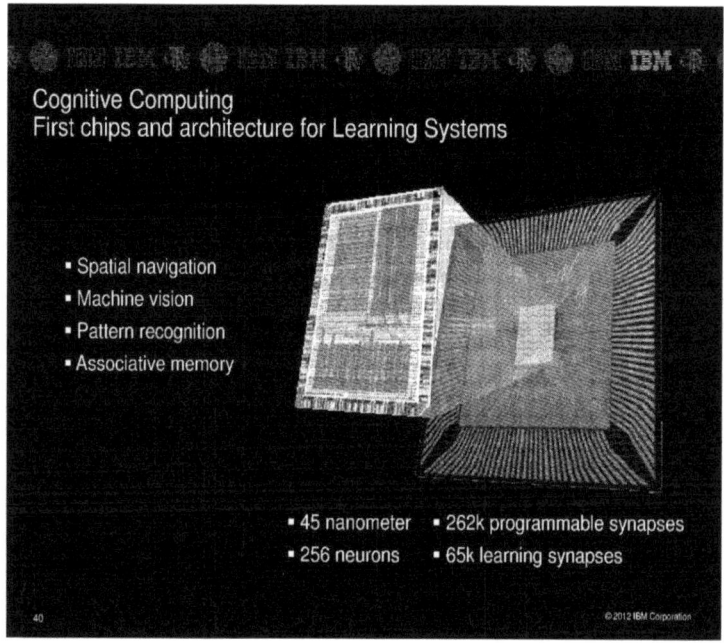

[6]

DARPA recently gave IBM a contract for cognitive computing development, to simulate brain functions now in its early phase of this project named SyNAPSE.

2.5.2. Data

The data explosion will be triggered by the "Smarter Planet and the Internet of people and things" producing Exa- and Zetabytes of data. This needs big/ fast data processing. Additionally Data will have a different structure, with uncertain data on the rise. [2]

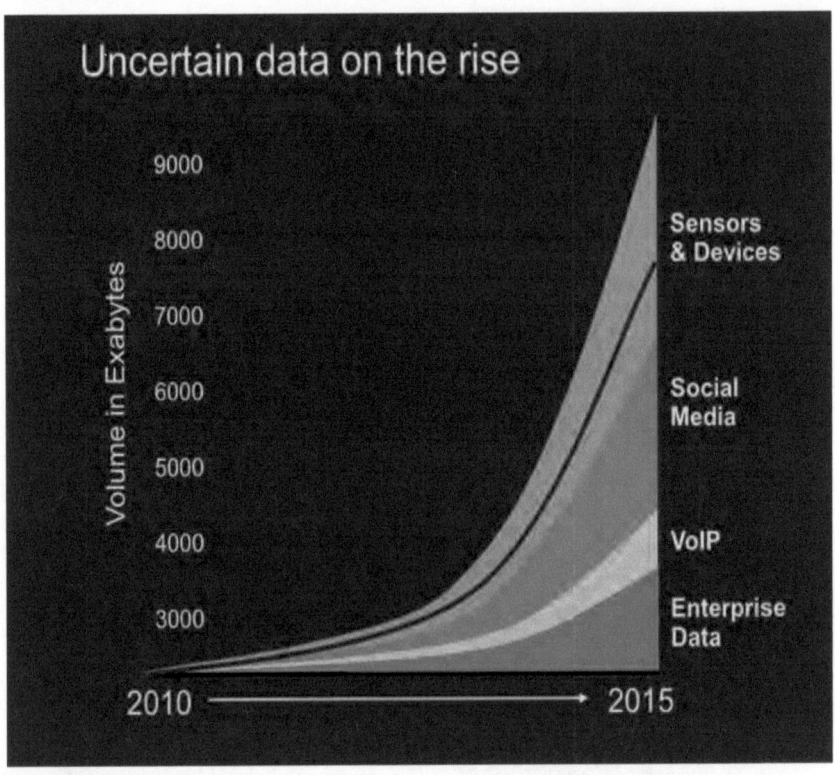

2.5.3   Nanotechnology

[6]

- o   Medicine
- o   Scarch resistive lacquer
- o   DNA sequencing
- o   Photovoltaics
- o   Self-cleaning surfaces
- o   Purifcation and Antibiotics

Applications reach as shown in the below from Nano medicine a fast cheap way to use genetics (DNA Transistor under development with ROCHE), to antibacterial nanoparticles to detect and destroy antibiotic-resistance bacteria.

3. Summary and Outlook

Great expectations and optimism characterised the beginning of the time period perused. The symbiosis of computer and communications lead to a further acceleration of the development and the convergence of technology, physics, and biology improved human performance and enabled new research areas from the way we conduct our life from banking to shopping and entertainment to DNA testing.

We have also perused stagnant fields of science where expectations were not met, or the expectation level was just too high realistic or the results not economically feasible.

Forecasts have shown some weakness in non-technological areas as forecasting computer networks developing into social networks and profiting from the readiness of crowds to give personal information and identity and join into a collective. People pay for the values they provide instant of being paid for.

Every year manufacturers put out a new line of more powerful products – twice as powerful, in fact, every 18 months.

This is not far-out futurism. Intel designed its new D1X Oregon research facility to be ready next year. It will start work when Intel is beginning shift to 15 nm circuitry. Manufacturers are trying new UV tools for chip manufacturing and new materials. Intel wants to move from 300 mm Si wafer to 450 mm Si- wafers an increase of surface area of 2,5 times and an estimate of a 30 to 40% cost reduction.[1]

If we can believe well-known physicists, this exponential development has to end. The laws of physics are to blame. Eventually, or about 2020, transistors will become so small that quantum theory or atomic physics will take over and electrons will begin to leak out of the wires. Around 2020 we could get to the point where we have the ability to create transistors that are 5 atoms wide. At this juncture the well-known Heisenberg uncertainty principle $\Delta x \cdot \Delta p_x \geq \frac{\hbar}{2}$ comes into play, (which states that one cannot know both the position and velocity of any particle), which means we cannot know exactly where an electron is, and therefore it cannot be confined to a wire. But there is more on the horizon. As we transition to atomic-scale devices, we are entering a paradigm where quantum mechanics promises a technological disruption. It is the promise of this future technology that makes this present development so exciting. [5]

Using a pair of impurities in ultra-pure, laboratory-grown diamonds, the researchers were able to create quantum bits and store information in them for nearly two seconds, an increase of nearly six orders of magnitude over the life span of earlier systems. [8]

The single-atom transistor could lead the way to building a quantum computer that works by controlling the electrons and thereby the quantum information, or qubits. Such a device was build by a team of researchers at the Univ. of SW and Melbourne. The single-atom transistor does have serious limitations, one of them: It must be kept cold, at least – 196° C.

Some scientists, however, have doubts that such a device can ever be built. Whilst the above-mentioned result is a milestone in quantum computing, it does not answer the question whether quantum computing is possible or not.

Given the lack of any other low-power and high-volume technology than CMOS, the frequency of microprocessors will grow at a much lower rate than in the past. Even with advances in base silicon, on-chip interconnects, and cooling technologies, microprocessor performance growth rates have slowed. However, higher levels of on-chip functional integration will sustain chip-level performance growth. The fundamental reason for this is the nonlinear relationship between power and performance. It may be possible, to decrease the power of a system tenfold with only a threefold reduction in performance

Thus for the next ten years, industry expects further dramatic improvements in performance, technologically, economically and ecologically.

To summarize

"The end of Moore's Law is always 10 years away, and yes it is still 10 years away!" [1]

4.

5. References

[1]   BOHR M., Intel Processor Research

[2]   GTO Global Technology Outlook

[3]   IBM Think research 1999

[4]   ITRS, Technology Trends 2011

[5]   KAKU M., Science June 8, 2012

[6]   KELLY J., IBM Investors briefing Research 2011 and 2012

[7]   LOESCH Chr. W., IDIMT Contributions 2000 – 2011 and references

[8]   LUKIN M. et alli, Univ. Harvard, MPI f. Quantenoptik and CalTec 2012

[9]   SINGER W. IBM Technology leadership 2012

[10] TIMES CNN Top 25 Innovations, Technological breakthroughs and Business feels technology's influence, 20051

[11] ZAKON R.H., Hobbes Internet Timeline 2011

IDIMT 2011

ICT Trends

Scenarios in Microelectronics and their Impact

Abstract

Reviewing the state of the ICT industry and its impressive capability to overcome economic turbulences will lead us to investigate trends, scenarios, and R&D strategies for the medium and long term. In the 90s, two inventions were shifting the final goalposts further away, rescued Moore's law, but the end of the CMOS evolutionary path comes nearer, and thus a plethora of alternatives is being proposed for the MtM (more than Moore) era. We are witnessing the transition from classical to equivalent scaling. The long-range quest is to replace charge by other variables as polarization, spin, phase etc.

We will discuss some of these options and some emerging developments ranging from the interdependence of technological and social development to an increased emphasis on memory as well as some newly emerging technologies as photonics, nanotechnology or plasmonics and their potential contributions.

Continuing the central theme of focusing on future scenarios, we will peruse how the ICT Industry is extending its footprint to new opportunities. Some of the most exciting trends in electronics today are not defined by computers but by macro electronics as flat panel displays, solar cells or bioelectronic sensors or three-dimensional printing technology, providing properties that broaden the reach of electronics in life further. For such systems: Big is beautiful!

On the other end of the scale, we find Exascale Systems as RSFQ systems (rapid single flux quantum circuit technology) or Terascale Computing, a development noteworthy by the capability of the devices and applications it could enable.

Key words:

ICT, Information Technology, Communication Techology, Microelectronics, Future trends.

1. State of Microelectronics industry

Based on current technology trends, the scaling limits to planar CMOS are clear. Though simple scaling of planar CMOS is ending, the technology will continue approximately on Moore's historical performance trend for another decade.

Moore's law is not a physical law but a law about economics. Consumer products and emerging markets have become the dominate end markets for semiconductors and will continue to be so for the next decade (versus the military in the 1960s-70s). A key attribute in these markets is price and power consumption. Silicium technology is on course to offer a billion transistor chips for less than $1, which will be very difficult to displace. (Thompson, 2010)

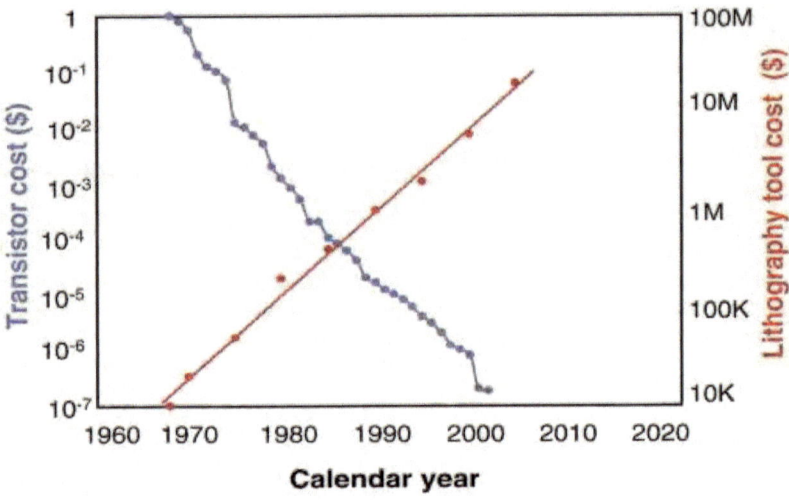

Moore's law and the future of Si-microelectronics [20]

2.   The Future of Si-Microelectronics – Beyond Si CMOS

Technologies are developed in response to economic drivers and technological requirements arise for given product classes application driven.

Semiconductor industry has become more complicated with each passing decade, having been driven by the mainframe, then the PC, expanding to portable devices microprocessors and memory business, gradually stretching out its application footprint and hence its technology footprint.

Processing complexity, applications as networking are likely to feature larger number of cores earlier in the technology cycle. Power consumption has become the quintessential requirement for all applications, not only for wired but increasingly for wireless as well.

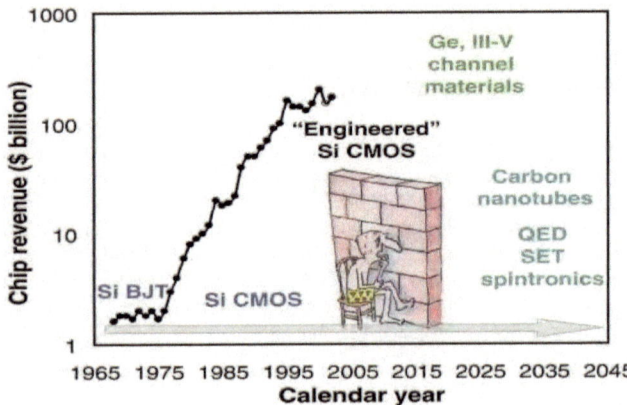

Moore's law: the future of Si-microelectronics, [20]

2.1 From classical to equivalent scaling

In the 90s, two inventions came to rescue to prolong the development along Moore's logarithmic scale: Strained silicon and high-k metal gate replacement of conventional gate dielectric by Hf-compounds.

Since speed and clock-frequency increases became no longer feasible, since power and thermal requirements begin to outstrip the benefits, results in reorienting the thrust towards parallel execution in multicore designs.

As the end of the Silicon evolutionary path nears paradigm changes are proposed as Ge, carbon, III-V semiconductors etc, different geometries as nanotubes, nanowires, grapheniod sheets and different operating principles.

However, new paradigms create new challenges. Nanotechnological challenges are to grow semiconductor CNT's in desired location in a defined direction or to deposit graphene on desirable surfaces. [8]

Growing nanowires on both III/V and silicon substrates may allow future integration of optoelectronics on Silicon as well as beyond CMOS devices exploring spin as fundamental carrier of logic information [19]

Scaling for frequency and power efficiency has unfortunately not kept up with expectations in part due to the limitations of interconnect materials and the lack of scaling advantages in packing technology.

Emerging research devices encompass a large variety of potential devices ranging from Ferroelectric gate FET (FeFET), STT MRAM (Spin transfer torque memory) resistive random access memory (RRAM), phase change RRAM to polymer and molecular memory devices. [15]

This weird device menagerie needs some sorting/weeding out.

A medium to long-range objective appears to replace charge by other variables as polarization, spin, phase etc. leading to smaller switching energies (avoidance of charging the gate capacitance of an FET). We see Spintronics features prominently, setting aside QC as the proposed solution fits poorly into the Neumann type architecture, thus research in compatible architectures will be integral to future developments.

2.2 Nanowire-based one-dimensional electronics

The roadmap for downscaling and introducing new technologies in the semiconductor industry is well laid out for the next ten years, one-dimensional structures, such as carbon nanotubes and semiconductor nanowires, are explicitly mentioned as realistic additions. Devices based on such materials are, however, still in an embryonic stage from an industrial point of view. Whether they will have an impact on future post-CMOS technology depends on more factors than just superior single-device performance. The history of the semiconductor industry shows that only those technologies will survive and have impact that can be integrated and scaled up for large hierarchical systems.

2.3 Graphene single-electron transistors

Research on graphene nanostructures started a few years ago, but it seems to be only the very beginning of research of quantum transport in graphene, and of graphene electronics for applications. Graphene, a single layer of carbon atoms forming a perfectly stable and clean two-dimensional crystal with very few defects, has been proclaimed a new revolutionary material for electronics. These hopes rest mainly on the unique band structure properties of graphene. Although living essentially on the surface, electron mobility in this material does not suffer extensively from surface contaminations and is surprisingly high even at room temperature even in comparison to high quality semiconducting materials such as silicon. The understanding of electronic transport in graphene is still in its infancy. [18]

Two daunting problems preventing significant increases in processor speed are thermal and signal delay issues associated with electronic interconnection. Optical interconnects, on the other hand, possess an extremely large data carrying capacity, and may offer new solutions for circumventing these problems. Optical alternatives may be particularly attractive for future chips with more distributed architectures in which a multitude of fast electronic computing units (cores) need to be connected by high-speed links. Unfortunately, the large size mismatch between electronic and dielectric photonic components of at least one or two orders of magnitude is hampering their implementation.

2.4 Photonics

Modern photonics will potentially contribute significantly to optical communication technology. The performance of CPUs increases much faster than the transmission speed of the links between of the links between the modules. Leading to interconnects problems as delay, crosstalk, general noise, high power consumption i.e. heat dissipation. With data range changes from 10 Gb/s to 40 Gb/s and 100Gb/s technology changes will become inevitable. Future architecture and the transition from multicore to many-core architectures will require bandwidth of 200GB/s to 1TB/s. [18]

Main advantage of optical communication is speed, i.e. greater bandwidth (transmission capacity).

Photonic crystals consist of thin layers of two dielectric materials with different refraction indices, these layers reflect radiation within a resonant band and transmit other wavelengths. Main application for photonic crystals in optical communication is associated with photonic crystal fibres which can be used as amplifiers, building fibre lasers etc. and could lead to integrated optical devices on the silicon-on isolator platform [12, 18]

Engineers growing lasers on Silicon pave way for on-chip-photonics overcoming the communication bottleneck between computer chips marrying III-V with Silicon, forcing two incongruent puzzle pieces together. There is still the temperature problem that III-V growth at high temperatures 700°C destroys the electronics, but now the possibility to grow nanopillars of indium gallium arsenide on a Silicon surface at 400°C has been developed (already used to produce thin solar cells and LEDs). [2]

2.5 Plasmonics: the next chip-scale technology?

An exciting new device technology that has recently emerged is Plasmonics. It exploits the unique optical properties of metallic nanostructures to enable routing and manipulation of light at the nanoscale. Plasmonics may bridge microscale photonics and nanoscale electronics A tremendous synergy can be attained by integrating plasmonic, electronic, and conventional dielectric photonic devices on the same chip and taking advantage of the strengths of each technology.

Imagine a cube of metal placed in an external electric field pointing to the right. Electrons will move to the left side (uncovering positive ions on the right side) until they cancel the field inside the metal. If we switch the electric field off, the electrons move to the right, repelled by each other and attracted to the positive ions left bare on the right side. They oscillate back and forth at the plasma frequency until the energy is lost. Plasmons are a quantization of this kind of oscillation. [22]

Plasmonics has the potential to play a unique and important role in enhancing the processing speed of future integrated circuits. The semiconductor industry has performed an incredible job in scaling electronic devices to nanoscale dimensions. Interconnect delay time issues provide significant challenges toward the realization of purely electronic circuits operating above ~10 GHz. However, photonic devices have an enormous data-carrying capacity (bandwidth). Dielectric photonic components are limited in their size by the laws of diffraction, preventing the same scaling as in electronics. Plasmonics offers precisely what electronics and photonics do not have: the size of electronics and the speed of photonics. Plasmonics may well serve as the missing link between the two device technologies that currently have a difficult time communicating. By the synergy between these technologies, plasmonics may be able to unleash the full potential of Nanoscale functionality and become the next wave of chip-scale technology. [23]

2.6 Exascale Systems, Terascale Computing, RSFQ,

2.6.1 Terascale computing.

"Tera" means 1 trillion, or 1,000,000,000,000. Intel's vision is to create platforms capable of performing trillions of calculations per second (teraflops) on trillions of bytes of data (terabytes).By scaling multi-core architectures from 10s to 100s of cores and embracing a shift to parallel programming, R&D aims to improve performance and increase energy-efficiency.
Terascale computing is a twofold revolution through the capability of devices and application it facilitates. Terabytes of data must be handled by platforms capable of teraflops to handle applications like AI, virtual reality, modelling, visualization, physics simulation, training, studio quality photorealistic graphics in real time or even Supercomputing for everyday devices. [14]

2.6.2 RSFQ

Another high performance technology is RFSQ based on Rapid Single Flux Quantum circuits' technology exceed 100 GHz while keeping processor power consumption low. Investment in R&D has increased sharply and produced result as FLUX-1 (2002), based on chips with 63107 JJ's (Josephson Junctions) on a 10x10 mm die with a power consumption of only 9,5mW at 4,5°K or in 2009 several bit serial floating point units with up to11k JJ operating at 22-25 GHz clock frequency in Japan . Challenges are design and synchronization at 50-100 GHz wide data path RSFQ processors, latency tolerance, memory, CAD tools for VLSI superconductor circuit design, cooling costs from room temperature as well as the lack of a cryogenic RAM. The new 1,0μm 10kA/cm2 Nb eight metal layer technology developed in Japan chips with 10^5 JJs may become competitors. The technological success has been notably for the RSFQ prototypes have been working but the commercial market has not materialized up to now. [8,17]

3. Technological and Social Interdependence

Push-pull effect of technology:

Modern technologies have strong interactions and with many domains of the human society. After initially pushing technology into a human domain, the perceived advantages and the newly created need and market demand an even more advanced technology. After a short delay with respect to technology adoption, these domains will create a pull-situation for more technology to fullfil even better the promises made by technology as e.g. mobile electronics, games or social networks.

The classical old approach was based on technology deployment by separate disciplines developing their own approaches and solutions, interfaces between technologies not lending themselves for integration or synergy.

To overcome this system development should become more interdisciplinary and integrative, calling for holistic approaches to new systems, especially for embedded system encompassing all aspects of life and society in an ubiquitous and pervasive way. The development of memory technology would be a matching example of the above. [5, 6]

4. Memory

In a world overflowing with increasing amounts of information, memory performance is becoming a key bottleneck limiting overall system performance. The lack of instant-on capability is a hindrance for many users, as in data centre applications, the time to read and write large sets of data is becoming more of an issue than raw processor speed. Critical applications become more data-centric and less compute-centric, and as power consumption becomes an ever-more-important factor in all systems, existing memory technologies cannot deliver the performance required in the future.

The exponential market growth of the ubiquitous portable and mobile electronics, USB, Memory cards etc. push the need for non-volatile memory (NVM). In the later half of 90s, mobile devices as MP3 players, digital still cameras, PDA, cell phones were making flash memory the most widely used form of memory. Market acceptance and its integration into daily life, have made memory technology a key technology driver.

Present technology largely depends on lithography, but in spite of the fact that optical lithography has surpassed all expectations it will reach its limits. Therefore, intensive research for alternatives is ongoing. The recent ITRS study (2009 and update 2010) has identified eight candidates to review in depth. [15]

Out of the plethora of opportunities, let us review selected technologies worth attention as:

4.1 STT-RAM

STT-RAM (spin-transfer torque random access memory) is a new memory technology offering a solution to many critical issues. Of all the major existing and prototype memory technologies, it is unique in capacity, endurance, and speed of working memory in addition to being non-volatile and requiring low write-power. As a magnetic random access memory (MRAM) technology that is scalable to future technology nodes, it offers the perspective to develop new products with new architectures, high performance, and low power consumption. It has the potential to revolutionize the performance of electronic products in many areas, create new sectors in the semiconductor industry, and give rise to entirely new products not yet envisaged.

An STT-RAM memory cell consists of an access transistor and a magnetic tunnel junction (MTJ) storage element). Unlike most other memory technologies, STT-RAM is easily embedded in standard CMOS processes with the addition of just two extra masks. It is worth emphasizing that, the extra cost associated with adding the STT-RAM process and equipment to a standard DRAM process is estimated to be minimal. Furthermore STT-RAM write-energy scales down with technology node, but also it is also smaller than the write energy of any other non-volatile memory technology.

STT-RAM is accepted by major semiconductor manufacturers as the leading next-generation memory solution. As STT-RAM chips begin to become available in the next one to two years, they will enable revolutionary advances in latency, bandwidth, reliability and power efficiency, and its wide range of applicability and will usher in a new era of instant-on computers and high-speed portable devices with extended battery life.

4.2 Phase-change random access memory (PRAM)

Phase change memory based on the crystal-glass phase transition is known since the mid-60s, discovered 1955 at Ioffe Institute (UdSSR). Phase-change random access memory (PRAM) is a non-volatile memory technology that has a number of advantages over flash memory technology. PRAM uses heat-induced changes of state (between crystalline and amorphous) in a chalcogenide glass to store information. The state changes accompany changes in resistivity, which provide the electrical mechanism for data storage and retrieval. Chalcogenide glass is already found in optical storage media (CD/DVD), though in these applications changes in refractive index are used to store information. Recent developments have demonstrated the ability to double PRAM storage density by incorporating two additional intermediate states (for a total of four) to store two bits of information per cell. The most commonly used Chalcogenide glass, known as GST, is composed of germanium, antimony and tellurium (Ge2Sb2Te5). Modern cell Ge2Sb2Te5 feature attractive properties as 10^{12} cycles endurance, simple production, and fast set and reset times. [17, 21]

4.3 Race track memories

IBM's race track technology is based on using the boundaries of magnetic domains a information carrier. Thus single domains are only 10-100 bits small, with very high speed movable domain boundaries, having no moving parts and thus a high density of data even compared to flash memories (100x data on same surface i.e. 500000 music titles or 3500 films) combined with low power consumption (MP3 player several weeks with one battery). [13]

4.4 Memristance

As the name "memory resistor" implies, it is a type of non-volatile random access memory. Such a memory would have useful properties, as it would not 'forget' the data that it stored when the power is turned off.

Memristance is a property of an electronic component known at least since the early 1960's. If charge flows in one direction through a circuit, the resistance of that component of the circuit will increase, and if charge flows in the opposite direction in the circuit, the resistance will decrease. If the flow of charge is stopped, the applied voltage the component will 'remember' the last resistance that it had, and when the flow of charge starts again the resistance of the circuit will be what it was when it was last active. Various metal oxides that have been identified are highly compatible with present chip fabrication facilities, so they can be made in existing foundries without requiring major changes. [11]

4.5 Holographics

Holographic storage is already around for some decennia but is still holding promises in applications as versatile disc HVD, with transfer rates of 1Gbis/sec vs. 36 or 72Mbit/s for blue ray disc 3,9Tbytes vs. blue ray disc with 200GB storage capacity. In 2004 of 20 companies HVD Alliance was founded a cooperation to instigate further R&D.

Under laser light Photopolymer material changes. Radiated locations change the direction of light stronger than non-radiated spots. A special feature of high attraction would be that it could enhance single bit read to bit-pattern reading meaning reading with one light flash up to several hundred thousands of bits.

5. The Future of Microelectronics is Macroelectronics

Even as the microelectronics technology slides into a more mature phase it continues to impress and amaze. However, some of the most exciting trends in electronics today are not defined by computers but by flat panel displays solar cells, bioelectronic sensors aso. [4]

Macroelctronics encompasses large area devices with low to moderate performance as polysilicon transistors for displays, carbon nanonets for TFTs, mesoporous electrodes for supercapacitors, donor-acceptor blends for solar cells. A distinguishing attribute of macroelectronics is that the economics of material/energy dictate that these devices use thin films processed at the lowest possible temperature, optimization of amorphous/roughened/gyriod materials (solar cells and thermoelectric) and mesoporous structures.[1]

For such systems: the bigger the better!

The materials should not be considered the poor cousin of the single crystalline silicon but rather a new system with unique properties that can broaden the reach of electronics in life. It is a different new dimension where Ohms law does not apply but nonlinear percolation theory.

The malleability of many macroelectronic devices offers new opportunities of device optimization i.e. improvement of material performance through application specific tailoring of the nanomaterial. In this sense macroelctronic material is biometric.

Let us continue the central theme of focusing on future trends, but venturing beyond the current main path of the ICT to other fields of microelectronics that may affect the future.

5.1 The printed world

The development of three dimensional printer technologies enables the building complex structures at costs never achieved before, and may lead to a plethora of applications and the digital production plant with potentially less capital tied up, less work in progress and less material wasted. The race for this cheaper and less risky way to the market success has already started and it is no preserve of west. It would enable building prototypes at costs never achieved before or allowing producing small and medium sized components, and changing them easily. Concept to production time could drop by 50-80%.

The production process would be reduced to powder being spread onto tray and solidified with a squirt or liquid binder or by sintering it with electron beam or deposit of filaments of molten plastic

Already today applications range from aerospace companies (EADS) producing parts lighter but as sturdy as machined parts to medical-implants made to measure with features that resemble bone strong lattice structure to encourage growth of bone to implant or measure dental crowns at a rate of 450 per day on a single machine. Since there are only few limits in sight for application and complexity the well renowned Economist called the technology "Print your Stradivarius". [9]

5.2 Biosensing

Acquiring information is an essential part of ICT. The development of microelectronics has extended the acquisition of information to new fields. By combining the unique electrical properties of nanoscale gaps, electrical detection systems supply excellent prospects for the design of biomolecular detection devices.

A major goal is the efficient detection of molecular binding events of very small quantities of biomolecules, such as the binding (hybridization) between two strands of DNA. Many other kinds of molecules, including antibodies, enzymes or proteins, can be identified by specific binding reactions. When many different events occur in a single sample, distinguishing between them becomes crucial. Combination with advanced nanotechnology such as dip-pen nanolithography or bar-coded molecules offers a label-free alternative for biosensing. Finally, the 'lab-on-a-chip' community is constantly progressing towards the development of fully electronic multifunctional devices that can channel fluids and sort and detect cells or biomolecules. [4]

5.3 Third-generation Photovoltaics (PV)

Classical solar cells are made of simple single crystalline junctions in whom the incident sunlight separates the electron-hole pair to drive an output load. The efficiency limit of ca. 30% and the high cost of the single crystalline silicon and the high installation cost of bulky panels make them still significant more expensive than competing sources. The alternative technology of lower efficiency of polymer cells (typically PCBM and P3HT dual polymer structures) are counterbalanced by low-cost production, ease of installation of lightweight panels

Third-generation approaches to PV aim to decrease costs to below the $1/W level of second-generation PV to $0.50/W or even to $0.20/W or better, by significantly increasing efficiencies but maintaining the cost advantages of thin-film deposition techniques. Increasing efficiency means also smaller areas required for a given power, such that efficiency values well above 30% could decrease these costs per Watt. This requires multiple energy threshold devices. There are several approaches to achieve such multiple energy threshold devices. Cost and efficiency projections are

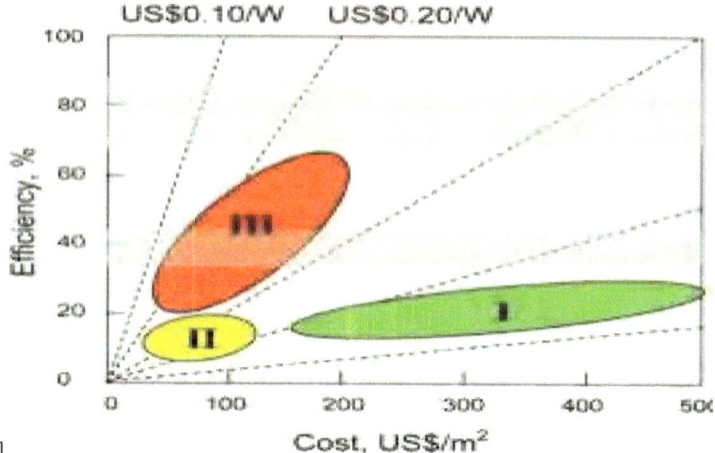

shown below [7]

5.4 Silicon based Solid Ox Fuel Cell (SOFCs)

Fuel cells convert chemical energy from hydrogen or hydrocarbons into electrical energy with high power density high-energy efficiency and low carbon footprint- Potential applications reach from large-scale power plants to portable electronics.

The primary physical structure of a TF(thin film) SOFC is a membrane consisting at least three layers cathode, electrolyte and anode. During operation, oxygen molecules are reduced to ions on cathode surface or triple phase boundaries. The O-ions are than transported through electrolyte and anode to combine with hydrogen as exploratory studies on SOFCs by B. Lai, A. Johnson, H. Xiong, C.KO, S. Ramanathan at Havard Univ. Cambridge show.

5.5 Semiconductors for Organic transistors

Organic molecules/polymers with a π-conjugated (hetero)-aromatic backbones are capable of transporting charge and interact efficiently with light. Therefore, these systems can act as semiconductors in opto-electronic devices similar to inorganic materials. However, organic chemistry offers tools for tailoring materials' functional properties via modifications of the molecular/monomeric units, opening new possibilities for inexpensive device manufacturing.

Although organic semiconductors offer significant potential for inexpensive electronic device fabrication, there are key requirements where existing materials fall short. These include realization of high carrier mobility and environmentally stable semiconductors; if the above conditions are met, will offer significant promise for the establishment of a new electronic technology. [4]

5.6 Cloak of Invisibility

The range of new application and ideas to expand microelectronic technologies seem to be expanding at a surprising rate. An example is the an optical cloak of invisibility for three-dimensional objects presented recently in Science journal by Scientists of the Karlsruhe Institute of Technology (KIT) and the Imperial College, London, [Science Express Reports, DOI 10.1126].

6. Summary

Implementing the shift from classical to equivalent scaling the exponential development with MtM will most continue successfully for the near future.

Furthermore, radically new device types will require changes along many research and development levels from materials to software. Since the time frame to implement a radically new device is estimated to be about 30 years Silicon CMOS will remain the dominant form of technology for the foreseeable future.

In spite of the continuing trend in the industry to migrate to tertiary areas of higher profitability the backbone of the industry remains technology dependent.

Important obstacles have still to be overcome and improvements in several orders of magnitude to be achieved but the creativity and genius of physicists and engineers have proven in the past to overcome apparently insurmountable barriers, giving us at the outlook on a scenario of fascinating developments and opportunities.

7. References

[1]   Alam M.A., Pimparak N., and Ray B. Purdue Univ. West Lafayette IN USA (2010) Elec. Nanogap devices for Biosensing, Materials today

[2]   Berkley UC (2011) eurekAlert! 6.2.11

[3]   Chen An (2009) Global Foundries Memory taxonomy, Memory technology review

[4]   Chen Xing, Zheng Guo, Gui-Mei Yang, Jie Li, Min-Qiang Li, Jin-Huai Liu and Xing-Jiu Huang The future of Microelectronics is… , MatScience Kyushu Univ, Japan

[5]   Chroust G., J. Kepler Univ. Linz, Mutually Reinforcing Innovations in ICT, Business and Society, IFSR 2005

[6]   Chroust G. Mutual Influences of Society's Paradigm, Information, and Communication Technologies, 2005

[7]   Conibeer Gavin, Third-generation Photovoltaics, ARC Photovoltaics Ctre of Excellence, School of Photovoltaic&Renewable Energy Engineering, University of New South Wales, Sydney NSW 2052, Australia

[8]   Dorojevets M. (2009) Current Status and Recent Dev. In RSFQ Processor Design SUNY, NY, USA

[9]   Economist,Printing a Stradivary, Feb.2011

[10]   Grützemacher D. et alii (2010), Nanowires Technology, Physics and Perspectives. Institute for Semiconductor Nanoelectronics Jülich, Germany

[11]   HP, HP Labs News April / June 2010

[12]   Hutchby J.A., Garne C. Michael (2010). Emerging Research Devices Technology overview INTEL Corp

[13]   IBM, IBM Research Almaden Lab, Spintronic Devices Reasearch, April 2008

[14]   INTEL Corp. From a few cores to many more, White paper 2005 and Terascale Computing 2011

[15]   ITRS (2009 Edition) Executive Summary and 2010 Update.

[16]   Loesch Chr. W., (2010) Some eco-technological aspects of the future of Information Technology, IDIMT 2010.

[17]   Luryi S., Xu J. Zaslavsky (2010). Future Trends in Microelectronics, Wiley IEEE Press.

[18]   Mynbaev Djafar Moore's law: the future of Si microelectronics CUNY, NY USA

[19]   Salomon P.M., Device Proposals Beyond Silicon CMOS 2010 IBM T-J. Watson Research CENTER, NY

[20]   Thompson Scott E., Parthasarathya Srivatsan, SWAMP Centre, the future of Si microelectronics, University of Florida, Gainesville, FL USA.

[21]   Tsedin K.D., Chalconide glassy semiconductors, Ioffe Inst. Russian Acad. of Sc., St. Petersburg Russia.

[22]   Wikipedia

[23]   Zia Rashid, Schuller Jon A, Chandran Anu and Brongersma Mark L., Geballe Laboratory for Advanced Materials, Stanford University, Stanford, CA.

IDIMT 2010

SOME ECO-TECHNOLOGICAL ASPECTS OF

THE FUTURE OF INFORMATION TECHNOLOGY

Abstract:

The financial crisis is shifting the centre of attention from technological and scientific brilliance of IT- and especially semiconductor industry's developments also to its economic feasibility and business strategies to cope with the approaching scaling limits of Si-technology.

First, we will peruse the economic–technological scenario, its structural dynamics, emerging business models, future development of the technological platform and the strategies for continuing improvement of the cost per function subsequent to the scaling with and beyond Moore's law.

Second we will endeavour to look ahead and discuss some of the emerging technological options ranging from New Materials and Devices, Nanotechnology & Nanoscience, Molecular electronics, Spintronics, Optoelectronics, Photonics and Quantum Computing.

In spite of its speculative character will we attempt to gain an overview of the fascinating plethora of future options for Information Technology arising over the horizon.

1. The Economic-Technological Scenario

The normal way to look at the future of information technology is to present status and extrapolate future developments.

We would like to compliment this by including the economic perspective not only determining the financial feasibility and its strategic direction and thus the direction of investment into R&D, marketing and manufacturing.

Let us first recap how the semiconductor industry faired during the crisis of the recent months and years and review some of the major trends shaping the industry.

The semiconductor industry has not only been much less impacted by the recent economic recession than by the recession of 2001 and additionally the speed of recovery has been significantly faster than in the previous recession.

Nevertheless, the recent economic development impacted the business thinking of the industry and triggered major restructuring and productivity enhancements and significant headcount reductions made by many companies.

The structural dynamics of the industry continued further but was showing some restraint in investment for hardware while the service industry continued its booming. During the recession worldwide hardware industry continued to grow by 1,6 % while the service sector even continued to grow by six percent.

The first quarter results of 2010 confirm not only these developments but exceed these developments by far.

1Q10 REV (Bio $) 1Q10 Net Earnings (Bio $)

AMD	1,6	+30%	0,26 (0,33)	
IBM	22,9	+5%	2,6	+13 %
HP	31,2	+8%	2,6	+8,3%
INTEL	10,3	+44%	2,4	+400%
SAMSUNG	31,2	+21%	3,6	+600%

[1, 2, 8 -14, 26, 27]

In parallel the restructuring of the industry progressed further, companies like IBM attribute only few percent of its revenue to hardware. The use of products has been continuously shifting to consumer electronics, wireless communications, mobility, sensors and related applications. The emphasis shifted to enhancing the present technological level.

The worldwide semiconductor market is expected to grow by 27 percent according to an estimate of the market research company Gartner.

Structural dynamics is the continuous shift to software and service and enlarging the scope of business.

Another phenomenon is the continuing tendency of big companies to acquire smaller complimentary companies that is expanding into software, service and application oriented fields rather by purchase as shown below.

2002	IBM	3,5 Mia $	PWC
2008	HP	18 Mia $	EDS
2009	DELL	4 Mia $	Perot
2010	HP	1,2 Mia $	Palm

IBM bought 75 smaller companies in recent years, and during the recent weeks as e.g. Coremetrics, Storwise, BigFix and Cast Iron Systems.

This while investment in research and development has remained flat which means in inflation adjusted terms a reduction, but continues at a level unimaginable for many industries.

Additionally we see a continuous high level of patents registrations, which also illustrate the shift to SW and Services.

The reasons for this development are shifting market opportunities, the trend to areas of higher profitability and the rising CAPEX challenge. The increasing size of capital investment needed for next generation manufacturing capacities led to the restructuring of the production, the foundry model, light-out manufacturing facilities, fabless companies, EDA´s, pre-competitive cooperation aso.

As shown below Asian companies have taken the lead, but recently IBM, SAMSUNG, Toshiba, NEC, Infineon, ST etc. established a company called Global Foundries to participate in the above development.

Rank	Company	Country	Revenue (million $) 2008	2007	2006
1	TSMC_	Taiwan	10,556	9,813	9,748
2	UMC_	Taiwan	3,400	3,755	3,670
3	Chartered	Singapore	1,743	1,458	1,527
4	SMIC_	China	1,354	1,550	1,465
5	Vanguard	Taiwan	511	486	398
6	Dongbu	South Korea	490	510	456
7	X-Fab	Germany	400	410	290
8	HHNEC_	China	350	335	315
9	He Jian_	China	345	330	290
10	SSMC	Singapore	340	350	325

[32]

Having reviewed some aspects of the economic scenario, let us turn to some of the arising technological challenges ranging from lithography, interconnections, new materials, power dissipation, to cost of manufacturing, design and verification.

We are right now witnessing the successfully coping with these challenges by extending the present technologies through improvement ranging from power reduction to performance enhancing measures, multi-core processors, further integration, optical connections, 3D Chips and new materials (High-k, HfO_2, TiN, TaN), thus extending the present technological platform.

These trends affect both hard- and software as the shift of 3000 Microsoft software engineers to parallel programming tasks demonstrates.

2. The Roadmap for Semiconductors

The ITRS (international technology roadmap for semiconductors) a prestigious organization assessing present and future developments forecasts an optimistic picture for that coming decade and beyond.

Key messages of the ITRS ROADMAP 2009 forecasts are for

- MPU until 2013   2 years cycle
       from 2014   3 years cycle
- DRAM $6F^2$ design -> $4F^2$ design
- WAFER 2014 -2016 the transition to 450 mm.

Looking at the longer-term future means looking beyond silicon technology. The Post-Silicon area holds a fascinating plethora for of options. New materials are improving and extending the present technology and offer options for an evolutionary improvement of Si technology and are complimenting and substituting Si for special applications.

Considering key properties as e-mobility, we see a theoretical improvement potential through III –
V materials as GaAs of 600% or InSb of 5000% or energy consumption improvement by use of
InSb of 1000% at 0,5V. However, at present the costs of these technologies preclude their use
except for special applications.

Due to the strategic importance and the fact that the US is importing 90% of its rare earth
requirements, a critical view on the global supply situation should speak for itself.

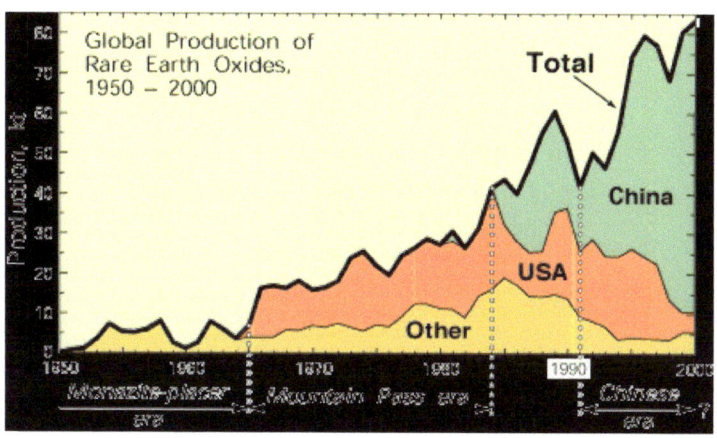

[31]

3. Emerging Research Devices

However, nothing should obscure the view on ultimate physical limits we are approaching as the
wavelength of the electron 10nm, direct tunnelling limit in SiO_2 of 3nm or the distance between Si-
atoms of 0,3nm.

These are not a pie in the sky speculations but potential studies based on systematic analysis as
prerequisite for R&D investments into ERD (Emerging Research Devices) as

ATOMIC SWITCHES

SPIN TRANSISTORS

NEMS DEVICES

PSEUDOSPINTRONIC DEVICES

SETS

MOLECULAR SWITCHES

SPIN WAVE DEVICES

NANOMAGNETIC DEVICES

MOVING WALL DEVICES aso.

The potential is not judged by its intellectual attraction, but each single field of ERD is evaluated against a series of criteria:

CRITERIA FOR LONG TERM POTENTIAL OF DEVICES

- PERFORMANCE
- ENERGY EFFICENCY
- ON/OFF RATIO
- OPERATIONAL RELIABILITY
- OPERATIONAL TEMPERATURE
- CMOS TECHNOLOGY COMPATIBILITY
- CMOS ARCHITECTURE COMPATIBILITY
- SCALABILITY

Each criteria is assessed for its potential and rated from one to three indicating

1 Substantially inferior to the ultimately scaled technology

2 Comparable to the ultimately scaled technology

3 Substantially exceeding the ultimately scaled technology

As an example of emerging research device studies Moving Domain Wall devices are shown selected out of more than a dozen different studies

[14]

4. Beyond Silicon

The table below shows some of the potential research and development areas both in near and long-term as

MOLECULAR (NANO) ELECTRONICS
OPTOELECTRONICS
SPINTRONICS
LONG TERM

QUANTUM COMPUTING

ORGANIC COMPUTING

(DNA, PROTEINS)

[17]

5. Molecular electronics

The outstanding properties of some the nanoelectronic devices make nanotechnology extremely attractive, we covered already in previous IDIMT sessions.

Turning to Molecular Electronics we see a series of outstanding properties of potential molecular electronic devices as low power consumption, high storage density (10^5 times), potentially cheap (manufacturing by self-organization) and long-term stability.

Molecular Computing holds the promise of being fast in spite of low e-mobility (the electron being part of the orbit of a molecular chain). But massively parallel operations could easily counterbalance this and enable theoretically 10^{23}ops/s vs. today's supercomputers 10^{17}ops/s. But Cost of Mfg & Assembly, (defect correction), Interconnection & logic remain problems to be solved. [7]

6. Optoelectronics

Here we are not at the beginning we are already in the middle of an exciting development.

Photonics and especially glass fibre connections have enabled the exponential development of communication, the Internet, wide area networks and locate area networks etc., but short distance connections are hampered by the fact that it takes more energy to send a signal over short distances then with current technologies and the conversion of optical to electrical signals is expensive. Nevertheless, research is ongoing to empower rack-rack card-to-card and even on-card optical connections. The drive to convert from electrons to photons as close as possible to the source of the signal is continuing.

Photonics is another promising field. What makes photonics attractive? It holds the potential of being smaller, cooler, and faster (up to 1000 times!) and may be even cheaper. For the problem of storage, encouraging experiments are showing up with as echo chamber storage in an Yttriumvanate orthosilicate crystal and praseodymium ions to trap photons.

The all optical computer remains far away in the future but optical components and interconnections are continuing to penetrate the computer.

7. Spintronics

Turning to spintronics means turning to a different kind of physics, we are not anymore looking at streams of electrons but at the physics of individual electrons.

Instead of looking at the mass and charge, we are looking at the spin, the angular momentum of an electron.

What are the promises of spintronics, they are significant improvement in data storage, something we are already enjoying based on that GMR effect, non-volatile memory chips, instant-on capabilities and higher speed at less energy.

8. Quantum Physics and the Quantum Computer

Quantum physics the ICT of the 21th century? Quantum physics is already around since the past century and we use it since more than half a century. Its phenomena as superposition or entanglement are still hardly comprehensible and compatible with our daily experience, but Quantum Physics is proven and has not failed a single test in these hundred years.

1900	Plank
1913	Bohr
1926	Schrödinger
1935	„Cat"and EPR
1982	QC
1994	Shor

QC (quantum computing) represents a very different approach, a paradigm change and it is no Turing machine anymore.

In view of the fact that we have covered the principles of QC in previous IDIMT´s, let us rather discuss where QC stands today and what are the achievements needed for the timeframe of the next 5 -10 years are:

- Cryptography available with restrictions
- Qubits   today tens, needed   1000-10000
- Gates   today tens, needed   > 100000
- Applications (with few Qubits)
- Many-qubits specialized applications
- Quantum interface
- Quantum repeaters
- Quantum error correction & purification
- Multi-particle entanglement & applications

- Larger quantum memory
- Quantum algorithm with up to 50 qubits
- Longer distance quantum cryptography and Satellite quantum communication
- Multi-node Quantum networks   [33]

There is still a long way to go to the quantum computer; it is a tremendous challenge but also there is no fundamental roadblock in sight.

We should not review far out technologies without devote some words to organic computing

9. Organic Computing (DNA)

Even far out, the prospect of integrating the fascinating properties of DNA, make it so appealing both for computing and storage:

- Slow but fast by parallel 10^{14} ops/sec
- Energy effizient 10^9
- Enormous quantities i.e. memory capacity
- Durability
- Dense 10^8 x Si + 3D
- Cheap?

Organic computing represents again a very different approach. Hardware and software are mixed in a solution, an unprecedented density of data storage – in 1 m^3 of water with the addition of 0,5 kg of DNA all data in all computers worldwide could be stored. Again, as in the case of Quantum Computers, Organic Computers may be programmable but not universally.

10. Organic Computing (Proteins)

Protein-based Organic Computing would mean additional fascinating new paradigms and features as

- Dynamically reprogrammable
  (Nervous system, genome)
- Senses state and responds appropriately
- Network can be „rewired"
- Bistability and apoptosis
- Memory

- Oscillations
- Pattern selection (preferences, tuned responses)

[23]

It might appear as pie in the sky research projects but it is theoretically feasible and may have an impact far beyond IT.

11. Summary

Forecasts indicate an evolutionary development, a continuation of Moore's law for the next decennium and beyond with impressive cost/benefit achievements, attractive both by its scientific and even more by its economic aspect with the inherent shift to higher profitability areas as software and services.

All this should be observed in front of the CAPEX perspective, taking into consideration, that the necessary CAPEX for a plant in 2020 may reach 1 T\$. Such an investment can only be afforded if supporting volumes can be reached. This explains the drive for horizontal expansion and use of all evolutionary approaches to prolong the lifetime of the prevailing Si-technologies before entering new endeavours. It will ensure that the industry will not leave silicon until the last drop of performance is squeezed out it.

"The race goes on", this excellent outlook combines with a plethora of options on the horizon, an outlook that only few fields of science and industry can match, with the caveat that extrapolations are to some extend predictable while paradigm shift and revolutionary developments remain unknowable.

12. References:

[1]   AMD, Quarterly Report 1Q 2010

[2]   AMD, Annual Report 2009, 2010

[3]   DYAKONOV, M.I., Spintronics, Univ. Montpellier, 2004

[4]   EAGELSHAM, D.J., Issues in Scale for Semiconductors 2003

[5]   GERSHENFELD, N., KRIKORIAN R., COHEN D., The Internet of Thinks, SciAm 10/2004

[6]   GOROKIN, H., TSUI, R.K., Molecular Electronics a proposed roadmap to commercialisation, Motorola Labs, 2001

[7]   HP, Annual report 2009 and Quarterly Report 2010, 2010

[8]   HIRAMOTO, Toshiro Extreme Future CMOS Devices using SOI Technology, IIS Tokyo 2004

[9]   IBM Corp, Annual and Investors Report 2009, 2010

[10]   IBM Corp, Quarterly Report 1Q2010

[11]   IBM Corp, Investor Report, 2010

[12]   INTEL Annual Report 2009, 2010

[13]   INTEL Quarterly Report 1Q 2010

[14]   ITRS, International Roadmap for Semiconductors 2009

[15]   IWAI, HIROSHI, The future of CMOS downscaling, Frontiers Collection 2004

[16]   LOESCH Chr. W., Trends in Technology, Proceedings of Euromicro 2003.

[17]   LOESCH Chr. W., Information Technology from Trend to Horizons IDIMT 2009

[18]   MILLER, D. A. B., Silicon Photonics Stanford Univ. 2008

[19]   KIM, K., Koh, G., Future Trend in Memory Development, Challenges and Perspectives, Samsung, 2004

[20]   MagiQ Technologies, NYC 5/2004 , Sci Am, Dec 04

[21]   MOORE, G., Moore's vision, Intel Corp., 2003

[22]   NISHI, Yoshio Future Challenges and Needs for Nanoelectronic from a Manufacturing Viewpoint, Stanford Univ.2004

[23]   RAMAKRISHNAN N., BHALLA U.S., TYSON J., Computing with Proteins, Nat. Centre for Biol. Sciences, India

[24]   M. ROUKES, Plenty of room indeed, SciAm, 9, 2001.

[25]   SMITH III, T.P., Wireless Sensor Networks and the Sensor Revolution, Mc Lean,   2004

[26]   SAMSUNG, Quarterly Report 2010

[27]   SAMSUNG, Annual Report 2009, 2010

[28]   SciAm, Diamond Age of Spintronics 10/2007

[29]   SCIENCE News, May 2008

[30]   THEIS, Th., IBM Research T .J. Watson Res. Centre 3/2003

[31]   USGS, US DOI, US Geologic Survey, Critical Resources for High Technology 2002

[32]   Wikipedia 2010

[33]   ZOLLER Peter, Univ. of Innsbruck, Lecture 2010, 2010

[34]   ZUGIC I., and FABIAN, Towards spin based logic, SUNY, N.Y. 2007

IDIMT 2009

THE FUTURE OF INFORMATION TECHNOLOGY

BEYOND MOORE'S LAW - BEYOND CMOS - POST SILICON

Abstract

Approaching the limits of CMOS scaling – sometimes called "the end of the reign of Moore's Law" – necessitates to consider both, the possibilities to prolong the present successful avenue and shift these limits further as well as look for promising technological alternatives.

Firstly this means perusing technologies to reduce design and manufacturing costs and continue the improvements of cost per function of integrated circuits extending the scaling economically further.

Secondly the endeavour to look two, three or more generations ahead and discuss some of the emerging technological options ranging from New Materials and Devices, Nanotechnology, Molecular electronics to Spintronics, Optoelectronics, Photonics and Quantum Computing.

In spite of its speculative character will we try to gain an overview of some of the fascinating future technological options arising over the horizon.

1. Where do we stand

Discussing the future of information technology means discussing two different scenarios. Information technology industry represents enormous industrial investments therefore everything will be done to keep these investments as long as possible viable i.e. profitable.

Keeping in mind that the time span from laboratory to the marketplace can be 10 years or more in parallel intensive research efforts are devoted to technologies beyond CMOS and Post-Silicon.

Main challenges for future CMOS devices are increasing leakage currents causing high power dissipation and increasing device variability, but new materials (high-κ/metal gate, low-κ dielectrics, and strained silicon), new device structures, interfaces and tailored layouts will assist to increase performance further.

Some key areas and the scientific options to overcome the challenges are shown below:

- LITHOGRAPHY

- NEW MATERIALS

- POWER DISSIPATION

- INTERCONNECTION

- ECONOMICS

1.1 Lithography

Lithography has played and plays a key role in the success story ICs (Integrated Circuits), creating the image of the features that will be etched into a chip by imaging a negative mask, but every change means a new expensive effort.
Pattern assisted self-assembly and placement may eventually replace optical and even extreme UV lithography in the next decade. [20] Mask-less lithography circumvents this problem by writing directly on the chip with a beam of electrons or ions, but this method is slow and parallel multibeam is difficult. Another alternative could come from the applications of nanophotonics by plasmon and plasmon lenses.[10]

1.2 Interconnection

Interconnects are becoming essential. A microprocessor running at 3.6 GHz can execute several instructions each time its clock ticks, but the system typically takes about 400 times as long to fetch data from the main memory keeping the processor waiting [12]. Interconnectors are replacing transistors as the main determinants of chip performance. This "tyranny of interconnectors" will escalate in the future, and thus nanoelectronics that follow silicon must be interconnect-centric. Consequently, mainstream electronics will have an interconnect era - even beyond Moore's law.

1.3 New Materials

The gate stack used in current-generation, metal-oxide semiconductor field-effect transistors (MOSFET) is running out of steam because the insulating silicon dioxide in current device generations has arrived at about five atomic layers only. Thus the operating frequency of transistors can no longer be scaled more and future performance enhancements will result from materials innovation instead of pure scaling

New materials range from HfO_2 (high-κ material) as SiO_2 replacement as isolator for gates to solve the leakage problem to gates TiN, TaN metallic layers.

A great step could be replacing silicon by a material with higher carrier mobility such as Ge or III-V materials (GaAs, InAs). But GaAs may be an option for the middle of the next decade since it has about six times higher mobility, InSb (Indium Antimonide) has even a mobility 50 times higher, in addition one can achieve a more than 10 times improvement in power for InSb operating at 0.5 V compared to the equivalent common devices. [6] But production yield will be affected as GaAs Wafers are typically 150 mm wide versus 300 mm in silicon.

1.4 Power dissipation

One sentence describes the challenge. If the current trend in clock frequency and number of transistors per chip would continue power consumption of a high performance microprocessor would reach $1kW/cm^2$ within the near future.

But not all prevailing technologies areas are reaching a maturity stage where the speed of innovation is slowing down, there may be exceptions as multi-core processors, optical data connections, 3D chips and accelerators. [1].

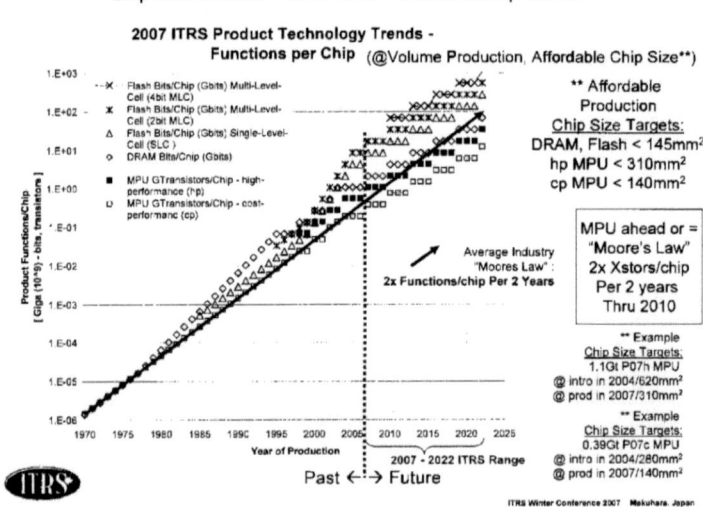

Chip Size Trends – 2007 ITRS Functions/Chip Model

ITRS 2007 Product Technology Trends update 2008

The ITRS chart shows the expected trend of the available technologies up to 2025.

1.5 Some Economic Aspects

Just as in agriculture governments fuels the tendency to oversupply. Asian governments have been especially active and today more than half of the world chips are produced there.

Costs per transistor are halving with every doubling of the number per unit, but as costs of transistors come down the cost of fabs goes up. Investment costs exceed six billion $ for leading edge fabs; TSMC (Taiwan Semiconductor Mfg Co.) built two fabs for eight to 10 billion $ each.

Since established chipmakers will not longer afford to develop their own manufacturing processes or even run their own fabs, so companies have teamed up to chip making technology jointly, as in the precompetitive cooperation in the 3D Integration Initiative between Amkor, Infineon, Micron, NEC, NXP,Panasonic, Qimondo, Samsung, ST Microelectronics, TI and TSMC. The past years have seen the rise of fab-less firms merely designing integrated circuits. [17].

Another phenomenon is the rise of "foundries". These are essentially contract manufacturers; the biggest TSMC has a manufacturing capacity greater that INTEL. Decent profitability will be limited only to firms with unique intellectual property, to those who make commodity chips and to those who dispose of enough cash to achieve unprecedented scale

When industry goes to 450 mm at 22 nm or even 11 nm it is conceivable to have one fab handling all demand, the rest could be nationalistic motivated ventures or never-put-all-eggs-into-one-basket strategies or niche-operators. [3, 5]

There are corresponding developments on the consumer side; supplemental to the well-known trends comes the rise of "good enough computing", OSS far beyond Linux, or Cloud computing allowing smaller companies to outsource rather than doing all themselves. Thus SaaS and other online computing services, have become better, more widespread and report steeply growing revenues and profits and show no signs of an "economic crisis".[3]

2. Beyond Silicon - Post Moore

In the second part we will try to peruse some of the upcoming technological opportunities as

```
          MOLECULAR ELECTRONICS

          OPTO ELECTRONICS

          SPINTRONICS

          QUANTUM COMPUTATION
```

2.1 Nanotechnology and Molecular Electronics

Nanotechnology is not an industry but rather an interdisciplinary enabling technology. To visualize the proportions: a nano-meter to a meter is as a soccer ball to the earth. It is more an evolution than a revolution. The use of nanotechnology is not a privilege of IT, shoe polishes, golf balls, toilet seats, paint, sun milk to mention a few, are nano-technologically enhanced products.[12]
Carbon nanotubes have been around since 1991, exciting by their unique qualities, their astonishing physical properties,

Property	Single wall Nanotubes	Comparison / Sizing
Tensile strength	45 bi Pa	Special steel alloys 2 bio Pa
Current carrying capacity	Ca. $10^{**}6$ A/cm2	Cu wires would burn
Temperature stability	Up to 2800°C in vacuum, 750°C in air	Metal wires 600 –1000°C
Cost	~500 $ /g	Au ~10 $ /g

Source: Scientific American

Applied to IT this could result in RAM's with 1 trillion bit/cm^2, which could read 100 times faster than silicon and conduct electricity extremely well.

A major problem is still to make nanotubes uniformly, reliable and in quantity, since structural differences can change a conductor to a semiconductor. Building molecular and Nanoscale devices is a first step, but interconnecting these devices seems to be the even greater challenge. [7, 23]. Intel hinted that Carbon and Nanotubes hold much promise for logic applications in the post CMOS era. It has already manufactured a 22-50 GHz Carbon Nanotube device with geometries from 2-5 nm; but to put millions of them on a wafer looks like a big task. [19]

2.1 Photonic computing

This is also an evolutionary development and much photonic has already arrives years ago.

	Internet, Wide Area Network	Local Area Network	Rack-to-Rack	Card-to-Card	On-Card	On- MCM	On-Chip
Distance	multi-km	10 - 2000 m	30+ m	1 m	0.1 - 0.3 m	5 - 100 mm	0.1 - 10 mm
Number of lines	1	1 - 10	~100	~100-1000	~1000	~10'000	~100'000
Use of optics	Since the 80s and the early 90s	Since the late 90s	Now	2010+	2010-2015	Probably after 2015	Later, if ever

Optical Interconnects[8]

Photons of light have a potential for manipulating information that surpasses electronics. Photons can move faster than electrons especially in semiconductors carry many orders of magnitude more information, and in addition, the photonic transistors have the ability to switch within one cycle. The structure of light is quite different from the electron. Each photon, being quantum, provides an independent information-carrying variable for each independent photonic frequency or colour e.g. each colour in theory can carry over 200 Tbits/sec.

Optical computers would produce substantially less heat, and are not subject to the restrictions caused by capacitance, inductance, resistance, and reluctance, have no interference among the beams. Thus, an optical computer, besides being much faster than an electronic one, might also be smaller. [3]

Recent research shows promise in temporarily trapping light in crystals a necessary element in replacing electron storage for logic devices.

Optical switching, while not all-optical, has already become important in networking environments. 100 Tbit/sec data handling is expected within a decade. Technologies range from micro-electro-mechanical systems to photonic integrated circuits and use of non-linear optical effects. A completely optical computer requires that one light beam can turn another on and off. This was first achieved with the photonic transistor, realized in 1989 at the RMRC (Rocky Mountain Research Centre). The samples developed are switching light in 1.5 femtoseconds (fs is 10^{-15} sec.) i.e. switching light with light at the full speed of light.

2.2 Molecular electronics and Organic Computing

A quarter century ago scientists of Bell Labs suggested the use of molecules for electronics. Single-molecule devices appear to be ideal candidates for future nano-electronics; they hold the potential of creating high-density devices with low power consumption in combination with high speed. But reproducible fabrication at the molecular scale presents a challenge. If molecular devices can take advantage of self-assembly processes, however, molecular devices may also feature low manufacturing costs.

Molecular memories could have a million times the storage density of today's chips. If molecular computing on its own becomes feasible, it would mark a leap beyond silicon. Engineers could pack more circuitry onto a microchip than silicon ever dreamed of, and even much more cheaply. This would translate into small devices with supercomputer capabilities on your wrist or within your shirt. The first molecular electronic devices will probably not compete with silicon devices and they are more likely to be sensors rather than logic devices. [12]

Potential applications are in large area electronics (e.g. electronic paper, print circuitry, displays, bulletin boards and smart cards etc.). They could be fabricated on flexible substrates at low cost, as 100 millions transistors in postage stamp size, or as large flexible plastic displays driven by plastic transistors or in futuristic sounding applications like a wall or car that change color upon request. These outlooks would comprise equally futuristic manufacturing outlooks like inkjet printer or "stamping" technologies replacing the clean room fabrication or a "fab-in-a-box" or chemical factory on a chip. [11]

Another approach is the development of new conducting polymers which create transistor-like switches smaller, and theoretically up to 1000 times faster than silicon transistors.

2.3 Organic Computing

Adelman's demonstration of the solution of the "traveling salesmen problem" by organic processes created a worldwide response and interest.

Special attractiveness results from the storage capabilities e.g. DNS is 100 billion times denser than Si and potential parallelism enabling theoretically 10^{20} simultaneous processes/calculations. A tank with 0,5 kg DNS diluted in 1 m^3 of water would have more storage capacity than all computers at present in use.[10]

Disadvantages are it is slower than Si-based computing, and it is voluminous, sticky and liquid technology. Additionally chemical reactions always have and nonzero probability of going backward.

A first step in this direction may be a hybrid heterogeneous technology. As shown below, a voltage applied to the substrate increases the conductance between source and drain, demonstrating that highly ordered monolayers of conjugated polymer, can act as the channel for a FET.

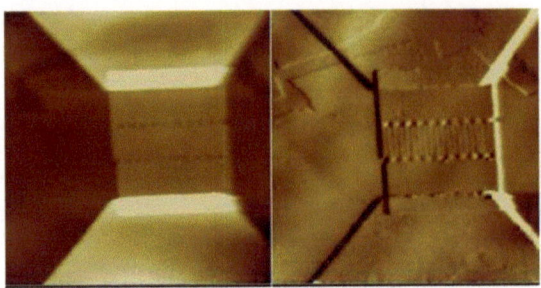

PDA acid multilayer on electrode pattern [IBM Almaden Research Centre]

Even with pure organic computing still being far away, a mixture of organic and anorganic layers patterned to form the channels of thin-film FETs may appear earlier. The question arises which architecture these forms of computing will require. Nature provides us with many examples of the use of physically processes for information processing as neural network models of computation, excitable media, and molecular regulatory circuit in cells, cellular DNA/RNA computing and pattern formation, and morphogenesis or computing with proteins.

Computing with proteins in information processing is still beyond our reach and rather a speculative option for the future. The complex intracellular molecular reaction networks that control the nervous system which is dynamically programmed during use by continually revising the strength of synaptic connections between neurons are not yet well understood.

Akin the genome's output is dynamically reprogrammed during development by switching on or off whole suites of genes to adopt and maintain their unique role within the body. Living organisms have an information processing system based on complex protein signaling networks that sense a cell's chemical state and respond appropriately. All these need intensive research to be understood [15]

2.4 Spintronics

The word "spintronics" (short for "spin electronics") refers to the electrons quantum property called spin.

Spintronics describes a technology using of the spin state of electrons. It can provide an extension to electronics. When the intrinsic spin of an electron is measured, it is found in one of two spin states. The Pauli Principle dictates that the quantum-mechanical wave function of two paired fermions must be antisymmetric, no two electrons can occupy the same quantum state, and an entangled pair of electrons cannot have the same spin.

Spintronics´ promise is very fast switching, reduced power consumption, as well logic gates with fewer element than for their charge-based counterparts. [18]

The most widely used Spintronic device is the Giant Magnetoresistive (GMR) spin-valve head for magnetic hard-disk drives with a spacer layer only 2-3 atoms thick. When their orientations are "parallel", electrons with one type of spin pass freely while those with the opposite spin meet greater resistance. The GMR, pioneered by IBM in 1997, enabled a more than 40-fold increase in data-storage density over few years.

Promising potential of spintronics lies in embedded memories. Non-volatile memory devices such as magneto resistive random access memory (MRAM) may revolutionize the memory market and contribute to the development of sophisticated and versatile computing and personal devices and innovations such as instantly bootable computers.

2.5 Emerging storage technologies

The expected growing need for more and more storage led to a plethora of R&D efforts; while flash-memory can offer little in the way of write speed over hard drives, alternative technologies could potentially offer access times nearly five orders of magnitude faster (<100 nanoseconds). Storage technologies coming in the pipeline range from Resistive RAM (RRAM), Phase Change RAM (PRAM) to array based memory to name a few. In addition, there are new data storage concepts upcoming using metal oxygen compounds that change their conductivity under the external influence of magnetic fields or light up to the 10th power or resistance change memory a magnetic random access memory (MRAM) based on magnetic tunnel junctions. [15]

2.5.1 Racetrack Memory

IBM works on a next-generation non-volatile memory dubbed "RaceTrack" which is expected to replace flash memory and may be even conventional hard-disk drives. The prototype encodes bits into the magnetic domain walls along the length of a silicon nanowire. This method allows "massless motion" i.e. moving the magnetic domain walls along the silicon nanowire for the storage and retrieval of information. Such drives would be able to store data up to 1 Tbits on a 3.5 inch drive with an access time 1 million times faster than conventional disk drives

Further away is another type of spintronics: quantum spintronics, i.e. the individual manipulation of electrons to exploit the quantum properties of spin. Quantum spintronics could provide a practical way to quantum information processing.

2.6 Quantum Computing

Let shortly recall some basics and shortly explore two key phenomena of the quantum world for computing and communication.

The first is the notion of quantum "state" as exhibited by the spins of atomic particles. Atomic particles are also spinning clockwise or counter clockwise - but until that spin is observed, the direction is unknown and is a probability of one direction versus the other. Thus, a particle can be in two states at once; these particles are called qubits (quantum bits). In quantum mechanics, the state of a system composed of a number of electrons and nuclei is described by a superposition of electronic configurations. Two qubits can therefore be in four states and 20 particles in a million states. Such devices could solve arithmetic problems as factoring numbers and search problems much faster than conventional computers by exploiting the properties of being in many states at once. A silicon computer uses to seek a single solution for a complex problem; a quantum computer can potentially explore all the solutions at once.

The second phenomenon is entanglement. Two particles can have linked spins even though they are at a distance. This has been demonstrated in laboratory conditions and is quoted to be a way to distribute securely cryptographic keys over distances. The quantum key distribution systems employed in quantum cryptography is an example of a few-bit system and one can already find commercial quantum cryptography systems on the market. Manipulating one particle and then reading the spin of the other linked particle is the basis of quantum information teleportation.

The advantages are counterbalanced by many unresolved problems as decoherescence, connection and signal input/output, while error correction first thought impossible seems possible but with an enormous increase in complexity.

The research challenges of quantum computing are enormous. Just to mention a few general ones: the quantum computer would not be a Turing machines, it has simultaneous read, write, and calculate capability, requiring new types of algorithms that utilize being in multiple states a.s.o.

3. Summary

We tried to pursue the present scenario of R & D and potential developments. Technological forecasting for ICs shows that the present technologies are promising progress for at least another decade, may be, even keeping the trend on track through 2020.

Nevertheless R & D for new physics replacing or complementing "charge-based physics'" that does not require the movement of an electronic charge is a fascinating option.

Nobody can forecast completely new technologies for which there are no existing paradigms.

The future is to be invented not predicted.

4. References:

[1]   ANDERSON Carl, IBM, EE Times 04-08-2009

[2]   CHROUST G.,15 years of IDIMT, 15 years of change, Univ. Linz 2007

[3]   FORBES Magazine. 2009

[4]   GIBBS W.W., A Split at the Core, SciAm 11/2004

[5]   ECONOMIST, Here we go again, Jan. 2009

[6]   KOEHL S., Enforcing Moore's Law through Technology Research Intel

[7]   IBM Research, Nanotechnology, 2004.

[8]   IBM Research, Physics 2009

[9]   J. JAFFE, Bell Labs perspective 2003

[10]   LEE Chris (Nature 2008)

[11]   LOESCH Chr., Trends in Information Technology,   Proc. of the IDIMT 2004 and 2007.

[12]   MEINDL, J.D. Computing in Science & Engineering

[13]   G. MOORE, Moore's vision, Intel Corp., 2003

[14]   NAIR R., Effect of increasing chip density on the evolution of computer architectures, IBM J. Res. Develop. 46, No 2/3, 2002

[15]   RAMAKRISHNAN N., BHALLA U, and. TYSON J., IEEE Comp Soc 2009.

[16]   ROUKES M., Plenty of room indeed, SciAm, 9, 2001.

[17]   SCALISE G., ITRS Pres. SIA 2008.

[18]   SCIENTIFIC AMERICAN, Spintronics basics, 73/02 et alii

[19]   WIKIPEDIA

[20]   UNIV. of WISCONSIN, Research Reports

[21]   WONG S., Beyond the conventional transistor, IBM J. Res. Dev. 46, No 2/3, 2002

[22]   ZUGIC I., and FABIAN, Towards spin based logic, SUNY, N.Y. 2007

IDIMT 2009

OPENS SOURCE SOFTWARE AND IBM

SOME COMMENTS:

Abstract

Coming from differing reasons and fundamental decisions, IBM also accepted after some reservation the fact that Open Source Software is a feasible and often very successful business model.

To get a deeper understanding of the ideas, intentions and the environment lets recall the period when IBM's System /360 [1] and later /370 revolutionized the field of data processing.
Suddenly IBM offered a range of machines (a 'system family') of different performance (small to large), but all having the same interface for programs. This meant that a program could run on any member of this family. Changing the hardware did not any more imply the need to reprogram the software. This was a tremendous success for software use. This success was creating problems, too. At the last day of the outgoing US administration in 1968 it filed an Anti-trust suit against IBM, implying that IBM was monopolizing the software market.

At this time, customers did not generally pay for software or services; software was provided at no additional charge, generally in source code form; services (systems engineering, education and training, system installation) were provided free of charge at the discretion of the IBM Branch office. Similarly, IBM services were divided into two categories 'free', provided at the discretion of IBM, and 'for fee' open to non-IBM customers.
In 1969, IBM decided to "unbundle" software, services, and education from hardware sales, this meant to price its software, services, and education separately. It was an incentive for other independent companies to offer software and services on the market and this initiated the creation of a software industry (see also [2] and [5]). This decision vastly expanded the market for independent computing services companies.
Many regard this as the birth of the business software, service, and education market.

Before 1999, IBM's involvement in OSS (Open Source Software) was on a case-by-case basis. A change happened in spite of many concerns in the late '90's, taking an alternative view on OSS as an alternative business model providing different types of flexibility, opportunity, and benefits than those provided by the conventional proprietary business model. IBM was among the earliest of the major computer companies to embrace OSS as consistent with its business goals, e.g. by accepting Linux as the possibility of a unified operating system on its platforms in a way that has been realized since, or granting a licence for 500 patents to any OSS effort).
Since then IBM has contributed to many OSS initiatives [4, 5]

References:

[1]   Amdahl, Gene. M., Blaauw, G.A. and Brooks, F.P.J: Architecture of the IBM System/360, IBM Journal of R & D,   vol.8, No. 2, 1964

[2]   Campbell-Kelly, Martin: Historical reflections - Will the future of software be open source? J. Comm. ACM, vol 51, no. 10, 1996

[3]   Weber, Steven The Success of Open Source, Harvard Univ. Press, Cambridge/London, 2004, ISBN 0-674-01858-3

[4]   IBM: Open Source and Standards, http://www-03.ibm.com/linux/ossstds

[5]   Open Source Software, IBM Systems Journal vol. 44, no 2. 2005

IDIMT 2008

TECHNOLOGICAL FORECAST IN PERSPECTIVE(S)

Abstract

The desire for understanding the present and divining the future has always been inherent in human nature to cope with the future and its risks. Nevertheless, we have to keep in mind that all forecasts (FC) are opinions on the future, more or less profound, responsible or futile. K. Popper argues that it is for strictly logic reasons impossible predict the future course of history and C. v. Clausewitz writes that the volume of relevant factors to be considered surpasses human capabilities. FC are becoming even more complex evolving from static structural thinking models to dynamic process thinking, self-organization, order through fluctuation and dissipative structures.

The increasing leverage of mankind on its future and the development of science have instigated the development to enrich non-scientific approaches by scientific methods. Technology FC as e.g. the Delphi method, brainstorming, regression analysis, scenario planning or technology road mapping can be defined as the methodology and practice of predicting the future state of technology.

We will examine examples from business and the factors impacting the implementation. The increasing risk of FC based decisions in industries resulted in high quality technology FC. Reviewing some of it findings, technologies that may forge the future as Nanotechnology, Fabricators, Spintronics, Quantum computing, Medico-electronics or Photonics will complement our session.

1. Introduction

" God does not throw dices"
A. Einstein

1.1 Philosophy and FC Limits of Forecasting

The search for causality accompanied human thinking probably because without causality a disquieting feeling of helplessness can arise and it seems to be a better feeling to be responsible having thus the illusion or possibility of influence.

The principle of causality is already appearing at Democritus, at the Stoics and Epicure; the scientific causal concept has been introduced by G. Galilee and J. Kepler.

I. Kant regarded the principle of causality as a priori condition to the possibility of experience. The question of causality and determinism has been discussed since centuries and is actually discussed on the background of the free will by neurophysiology.

The paradigm of determinism can be understood as the success story of science since P. S. Laplace, But the development and achievements of modern physics changed the prevailing paradigm.

K. Popper understands himself as representative of the physical indeterminism, and argues that it is for purely logic reasons impossible to predict the future course of history because it is strongly influenced by the growth of human knowledge. Since we cannot predict the future growth of our scientific knowledge, it means that no society can scientifically predict its own future states of knowledge. Therefore, we cannot predict the future [14]

1.2   From Philosophy to Physics

Limits to Forecasting

The belief in a well-understood statically clear picture of the world in science has been shattered at the end of the 19th century. The 20th century brought several breakthroughs in physics revolutioning the 19th century understanding of the world. It is connected with names as Heisenberg, Schrödinger, Boltzmann, Plank or subjects as Quantum physics and uncertainty relation; also the concept of Entropy creating a direction of time is incompatible with the consequences of Laplace, even before it was even more extended by the introduction of self-organization, dissipative structures, bifurcation or order through fluctuation as heralded by I. Prigogine [12, 19] and others.

2. Technological Forecasting (TFC)

TFC can be defined as the methodology and practice of predicting the future state of technology and extend of its use.
Early TFC as developed in the 40′s through the 60′s and effectively captured in monographs by Jantsch, Ayres, Martino etc, has not flourished. The concept of TFC had its core in the application of mathematical tools of modest sophistication and the analysis of historic trends in order to forecast future developments. By the end of 60′s interest dropped, society was stable and the economy booming. But technological forecasting emerged as a recognized management discipline around 1960. With the increase of risk associated with wrong decisions, forecasting has become increasingly important. In order to prepare effectively business strategies in the technologically fast-paced world it has become imperative for companies and policymakers to apply more sophisticated models and techniques. The development of the Delphi Method by the Rand Corporation (Ted Gordon and his associates) looked like a potential shortcut. Normative FC became popular in WWII and the post-war period of the Cold War and space age (man on the moon). In the civil sector the PERT charts became a forecast.
It took not long to the rise an increasing interest in the future and consequently in TFC. Governments and many organizations moved into forecasting as Japan in the 1970, the OECD, UN, Fraunhofer Institute.
Times have never been better for forecasting. Today there are myriads of forecasting techniques on the market, ranging from simple extrapolations to Delphi techniques TRIZ, corporate models and OR applications. An additional trend in FC over the last decennium has been the shift from acute attention to technical astuteness to a growing consideration of how to deliver the message, a shift from correctness and analytic elegance to emphasis on the communication of results. [5]

A recent study of the Economist Intelligence Unit [6] shows the present use of FC status in industry:

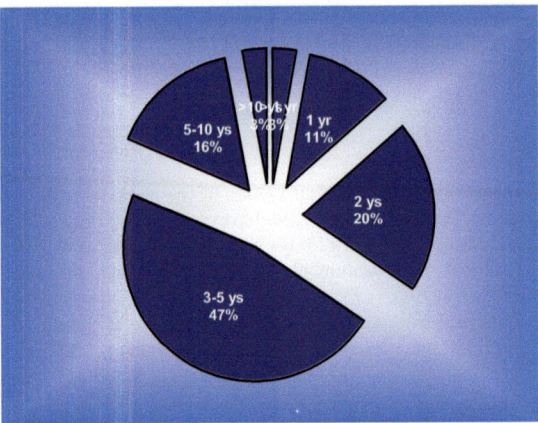

Study Risk 2018 "How far into the future does your company plan"

It smacks of hubris to say that one can predict the future, but much benefit can be gained from considering what the coming years might hold. To check the quality of forecasts the highly reputed journal Scientific American compared the forecasts of an article in October 1920 aiming 75 years into the future in 1936 as follows:

38 %	already verified
30 %	nearly certain to be verified
8 %	proven wrong
3 %	probably be proven wrong
22 %	uncertain

Steinmetz (Chief scientists of GE Corp) made 25 predictions relating to housekeeping in 1915 by 1936 their status was as the following:

28 %	fulfilled
48 %	destined to be fulfilled
24 %	doubtful
0 %	proven wrong

2.1   Limits to technological FC

No matter all the industrial companies are in the business of forecasting the future: what a customer will buy, how a product can be made more attractive, how competitive it will stay or how new laws will affect profit margins. The company that forecast the future is the company that is going to lead the market. In addition to the arguments stated above, we cannot forecast completely new technologies for which there are no existing paradigms.

2.2   The Human Factor

Nevertheless having good forecasts does not mean you can implement them without problems. There are potential sociological and psychological barriers of technology transfer both in interfacing the user as well by the prevailing organization culture, some of these we will address below. [6] Internal psychological barriers have to be overcome; we are prisoners of our basic images of reality. The influence and bias of personal or vested interests on forecast results both intentional and unintentional should not be underestimated. Ethical, gender and other factors can be of importance but can be integrated into the planning process. We will discuss in the context of the ITRS and IBM where examples the integration of personal interest and responsibility is a crucial factor to make these forecasts successful.

The "Stock option model" approach is another approach mobilizing the hidden knowledge and attitudes of employees to contribute to corporate forecasting.

Famous predictions show that the human factor is not always very helpful, (in spite of assuming that the present population is the result of f selection of the better forecasters throughout millennia).

- "640k are enough" Bill Gates, Microsoft,
- "Five Computer will be enough", Watson, IBM
- TV (Darryl F. Zanuck, 20th Century Fox) "TV wont be able to hold on to any market",
- Motion Pictures – "books will be obsolete" Thomas A. Edison,
- Telephone (US Pres .R. Hayes)"an amazing invention but who would ever want one?"
- William Orton (Pres. of Western Union) rejects telephone patents for 100 00 $ "what use can this company make of an electrical toy",
- McKinsey (1981) less than 1 mio mobile phones in US by 2001 (YTD > 130 mio users)
- "Two years from now spam will be resolved", Bill Gates 2004.

3.   From Theory to Business

Due to the high if not existential risk of decisions in industry forecasting has reached special importance and quality, especially in fast developing industries as IT, aerospace aso.

3.1   ITRS

The International Technology Roadmap for Semiconductors, known throughout the world as ITRS, is the fifteen-year assessment of the semiconductor industry's future technology requirements. It constitutes worldwide organizations with participants reflecting the structure of the IT world in its composition as shown below:

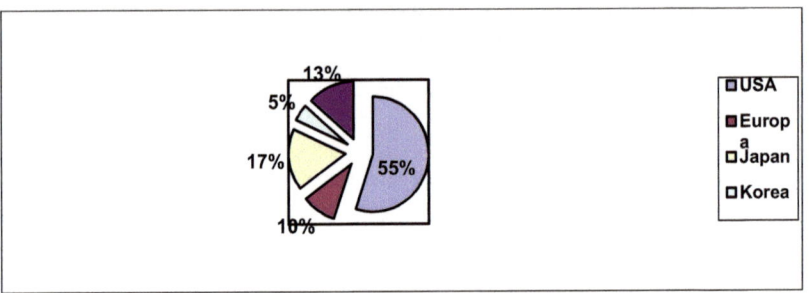

ITRS representation [10]

The picture below compares the forecasts of a key feature of ICT technology DRAM (half pitch) by ITRS and the achievements of three leading companies, showing an impressive quality of the forecasts. [10]

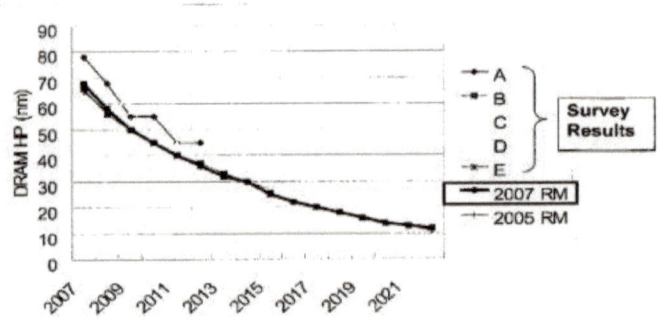

Scaling of DRAM (half pitch) [10]

The quality of the planning process is enhanced by the knowledge of the participants that the forecast can become a practical commitment to achieve it in competition with other companies participating and thus a self-fulfilling prophecy.

3.2   IBM Planning & FC System

The IBM planning system is an example of a combination of rational data based research, business cases and human assessments. It consists of several strings of inputs consolidated into a plan in a bottom-up and top-down process. A key feature is the regular review and updating process leading to a revolving planning system. The inputs of different plans are interacting with the strategic plan which has a revolving two years operating plan at its front-end.

```
Strategic Plan
Operating plan
Marketing plan
Sales plan
```

Since the quality of the plan and its achievement is a personal responsibility and implies consequences reaching from personal targets to budget, manpower, income and career, forecasting is regarded as an important personal responsibility and not just a theoretical exercise.
There are few major trends developing over years that cannot be identified by systematic research. Nevertheless new revolutionary technologies sometimes appear from nowhere others are heralded by such long fanfares that it seems they will never arrive. The problem is both the detection and the selection; let us look at some of these forecasts especially relevant o ICT.

4. Forecast for IT

Each of the following subjects would well merit a monograph or dedicated session but we have to restrain ourselves to the timeframe of our IDIMT 2008 session.

4.1 The future of CMOS

The current ITRS Model 2007 confirms the extension of the exponential CMOS improvements for more than another decade

The continued exponential increase will facilitate and is facilitated by developments, some of which are highlighted below:

The Tera-scale Computing is one of the efforts for the next decade. . "Tera" means 10^{12} or performing trillions of calculations per second (teraflops) on trillions of bytes of data (terabytes). By scaling multicore architectures to 10s to 100s of cores and embracing a shift to parallel programming, it aims to enable applications and capabilities only dreamt of today [9] This may mean hardware features as:

*   Scalable multi-core architectures with 10-100s integrated processor cores,

*   Memory sharing and stacking.

*   High Bandwidth I/O and Communications.

- Software supporting model-based applications, make decisions, and synthesize virtual possibilities like ray tracing, physical modelling, visualization, computation, management of massive amounts of data as media mining [6]

4.2 Hafnium and Chips

The ongoing efforts for a continuation of "Moore's law" are still the main thrust in IT. One consequence of these efforts has been the explorations of the periodic table of elements – similar to European navigators search for Spice Islands half a millennium ago. Discoveries range from Indium-tin oxide for transparent and electrically conductive liquid crystal displays; Tantalum with luck unlike spice, the quantities required will not be worth fighting a war for it, to Hafnium a SiO_2 replacement as isolator for gates to solve the leakage problem. Penryn chips having twice as many transistors as their predecessors (a billion) use only one fifth of power.

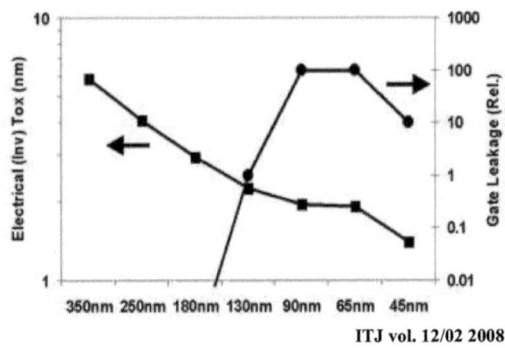

ITJ vol. 12/02 2008

4.3 Scale out systems
Since system-level performance though power dissipation is threatening to create a discontinuity in the development of microprocessor technology, scale out systems may be a solution in some areas. A scale out system is a collection of interconnected, modular low-cost computers that work as a single entity. However, system management, reliability and Amdahl's law are challenges to scale-out systems. [1, 8] Applications range from life sciences: protein folding, climate modelling, digital entertainment, data analytics to military applications.

4.4 Cloud computing

Some experts as N. Carr have caught wide attention forecasting that the majority of business-IT will go to the width of Internet. An indication for this may be that in spite of the fact that SW is not ready for utility computing, but storage on demand is growing 33% pa. Users may be afraid of security lacks but data might be more secure in the net than on the computer of the user.

4.5 Rewritable holographic storage

Holographic systems having been announced since many years might finally become ready for sale.

Starting with 12 times blue ray or 60 times DVD i.e. 300 GB, improving in few years to 1, 6 TB storage capacity. They can store multiple pages of digital data at slightly different angles in the material at a read/write speed of 160 Mb/sec.

4.6 Software

Software will trend to become more complex as needs become more complex, Limitations such as computing power and infrastructure will not longer be concerns. The unprecedented growth in data, brought about by the Internet, will also influence the way in which programmers design future software. The human side of programming will remain an issue, noting that factors such as huge computing power and the right infrastructure will not be a guarantee that software engineers will come up with the "right" software. [23]

With increasing needs and costs the pressure to improve SW will rise. Better software tools promise to produce better and low-defect software; this will help but not solve the SW productivity problem. There is plenty of room for improvement as two examples may show.

A recent IBM study tracked 50 developers and found that, 30% of their time was spent coding the rest talking to other members of the team.

The CHAOS Report of the Standish Group reports an improvement from 35% of SW projects on time and on budget in 2006 vs. 16% in 1994 or a project failure rate 19% vs. 31% .in the same timeframe. [24]

4.7 Fabricators

Knowledge intensive manufacturing is coming. Desktop manufacturing or personal fabrication is the use of a personal computer to drive a special printer that deposits (or catalyses) material in layers to form three-dimensional objects. It can be used for making prototypes or objects that have limited demand.

For example, a designer may load a digital design into a Fused Deposition Modelling (FDM) machine. The FDM then extrudes thin beads of ABS plastic in thin layers. That is where organic electronics comes into play. Organic electronics were born in the 1970s when researchers discovered that chemically doping organic polymers, or plastics, increases their electrical conductivity. Since then, researchers have worked to develop effective and inexpensive organic compounds that can be patterned on flexible substrates to create useful circuits. In the private sector, companies ranging from Bell Labs or IBM to the UK start-up Plastic Logic are also working on the development of quality organic transistors that are fabricated far more cheaply than silicon circuits.

Another proposal is nanofactories also called fabbers that employ arrays of nanoscale machines to assemble macroscopic products from molecular feedstock. This level of control would enable production of high-performance materials that form structures of nearly perfect precision.
The term "fabber" is also used to refer to hypothetical devices that would be capable of Universal Fabrication. Given a sufficiently detailed set of plans, power and the correct raw feedstock, a universal fabber could produce any manufacturable item, including a copy of itself.

4.8 Nanotechnology

Nanotechnology can be viewed as an evolution from the micro- to the nano regime. To visualize the proportions: a nano-meter to a meter is as a soccer ball to the earth. It has entered microelectronics over a decade ago, so it is more an evolution than a revolution. The use of nanotechnology is not a privilege of IT, shoe polishes, golf balls, toilet seats, paint, sun milk to mention a few, are already nanotechnologically enhanced products.

Carbon Nano Tube (CNT) is a revolutionary device, because for the first time dimension of the conducting Channel are controlled by chemically bond lengths and not by some manufacturing process; its electrical and mechanical properties are extraordinary; making the nanotube a contender for the post CMOS arena.

The ideal picture would be equally shaped properly ordered tubes but the real picture of nanotubes shows the picture below.

10mm = ca. 1µm

Many challenges have to be overcome as the integration on a chip or the contacting of the CNTs. Additionally the expected ballistic nature of transport at sub micrometer dimensions opens a plateau for high frequency applications in the THz regime.

IBM "RaceTrack" memory

Recently IBM announced next-generation non-volatile memory dubbed "RaceTrack" which is expected to initially replace flash memory and eventually mechanical magnetic hard disk drives. The prototype encodes bits into the magnetic domain walls along the length of a silicon nanowire, also known as RaceTrack. This method allows "mass less motion" to move the magnetic domain walls along the silicon nanowire for the storage and retrieval of information. Such drives would be able to store data nearing one Terabytes on a single 3.5-inch (8.9cm) drive.

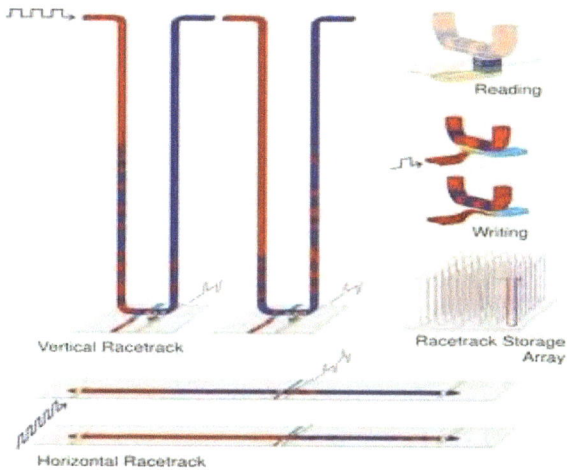

"RaceTrack "memory [IBM Almaden Research Centre]

4.9 Medico Electronics

Here we are entering a field of symbiosis of IT, physics, biology and medicine and encounter a plethora of potential new IT enabled applications.

The general vision is that IT enabled genetic predisposition testing and early diagnoses using molecular tests and more personalized treatment will lead to improved patient outcomes. Aspects of this vision are referred to as evidence based personalized medicine, or nano-medicine and bioinformatics. It might mean curing diseases before symptoms become apparent! Molecular diagnosis, molecular imaging, are based on microelectronics elements like biosensors, gene chips or may change the current practice of health care. This sector of the economy is projected to grow to 25% of the GDP of industrialized countries in the next the decade and could displace information in technology as a dominant sector of economy.

The promise of molecular medicine is earlier and faster diagnosis, better prognosis and tailored therapy with higher efficiency and reduced side effects, as compared to the present state of art, which is based on trial, and error basis after serious symptoms have developed. [7]

Synthetic biology is another newly emerging scientific discipline compressing the knowledge of many disciplines to create novel biological systems with functions that do not exist in nature like derivatives of existing organism (bacteria, yeast, and viruses), designing novel building blocks for engineering biological systems like viruses. One of the fundamental requirements is the computer-assisted ability for large scale DNA analysis, sequencing and synthesis.

For example viruses can be described in chemical terms; the empirical formula of the organic matter of poliovirus being $C_{332,652}$ $H_{492,388}$ $N_{98,245}$ $O_{131,196}$ $P_{7,501}$ $S_{2,340}$ or as computer model of the virus.

The intriguing dual nature of a poliovirus as an inanimate entity and a replicating organism has led to the question whether the virus can be synthesized in a test tube. Nuclear acid synthesis is already developed at a stage where individual genes can be assembled from their known sequence. [18]

Even more futuristic is the vision that engineered bacteria could become "living computers", since DNA molecules have the natural ability to store and process information, which would mean the parallel processing power of a million computers all in the space of a water drop.

4.10 Photonics

Optics been around for several decades in many applications ranging from fibre to CD and DVDs and dominates long-range communications since years. Basic issues of physics as shown in the picture below make optics attractive for communication of higher density of information over longer distances.
Apart from the advantages in power consumption there is a difference in the capacity for transmission of signals. Wires perform increasingly poorly at higher frequencies, showing signal attenuation and distortion. Scaling a wire in all three dimensions leaves its information capacity the same, through scaling transistors in the same way makes them faster. For many reasons now is optics increasingly considered for communication and interconnect now possible all the way to silicon chips. The implementation is challenging, but recent breakthroughs are promising for the ultimate construction of an integrated low-cost, low-power technology.

4.11 Spintronics

Spintronics describes a technology that makes use of the spin state of electrons. It can provide an extension to electronics. When the intrinsic spin of an electron is measured, it is found in one of two spin states. The Pauli Exclusion Principle dictates that the quantum-mechanical wave function of two paired fermions must be antisymmetric, no two electrons can occupy the same quantum state, implying that an entangled pair of electrons cannot have the same spin.

The most widespread application, the overwhelming majority of hard disk heads use it, is based on the giant magnetoresistance (GMR) effect. A typical GMR device consists of at least two layers of ferromagnetic materials separated by a spacer layer. When the two magnetization vectors of the ferromagnetic layers are aligned, an electrical current will flow freely, whereas if the magnetization vectors are antiparallel then the resistance of the system is higher.

Perhaps spintronics' biggest potential lies in embedded memories. Non-volatile memory devices such as magneto-resistive random access memory (MRAM) will revolutionize the memory market and contribute to the development of sophisticated and versatile computing and personal devices. Promising to introduce innovations such as instantly bootable computers, MRAM looks poised for success.
Spintronics' promise is very fast switching, reduced power consumption, as well logic gates with fewer element than needed for their charge based counterparts. [24]

The understanding of spin transport is yet not sufficient for digital logic and signal processing. Spin transport differs also from charge transport in that spin orientation is a non-conserved quantity due to spin-orbit and hyperfine coupling.

Future applications may include a spin-based transistor, which requires the development of magnetic semiconductors exhibiting room temperature ferromagnetism. One possible material candidate is manganese-doped gallium arsenide GaAsMn.

Much further away is another type of spintronics: quantum spintronics, i.e. the individual manipulation of electrons to exploit the quantum properties of spin. Quantum spintronics could provide a practical way to quantum information processing.

4.12   Quantum Computing

We will shortly explore two key phenomena of the quantum world for computing and communication.

The first is the notion of quantum "state" as exhibited by the spins of atomic particles. Atomic particles are also spinning clockwise or counter clockwise - but until that spin is observed, the direction is a probability of one direction versus the other. Thus, a particle can be in two states at once; these particles re called qubits (quantum bits). In quantum mechanics the state of a system composed of a number of electrons and nuclei is described by a superposition of electronic configurations such as e.g. a configuration $|1,1,0,0,1,0,0,1,0,1,0,0>$ where 5 electrons are distributed on 12 possible states. The state could be atomic orbital of the quantum material or we can think of them as quantum registers. The number of possible configuration for $N_s =12$ and $N_e=5$ is $12![5!(12-5)!]=792$ however for only the double number if states and electrons $N_s=24$ and $N_e= 10$ gives rise to over a million configurations and rising it to the tenfold leads to $10**70$ a number comparable to the number of all atoms on earth. Two qubits can be in four states and 20 particles in a million states.

The new field of quantum algorithms has demonstrated that such devices can solve arithmetic problems (factoring numbers) and search problems much faster than conventional computers by exploiting these properties of devices being in many states at once. During the steps a silicon computer uses to seek a single solution for a complex problem, a quantum computer can potentially explore all the solutions at once.

The second phenomenon is entanglement. Two particles can have linked spins even though they are at a distance. Manipulating one particle and then reading the spin of the other, linked particle is the basis of quantum information teleportation. This has been demonstrated in laboratory conditions and is quoted to be a feasible way to securely distribute cryptographic keys over distances.

The research challenges of quantum computing are enormous. Just to mention a few general ones: the quantum computer would not be a Turing machines, it has simultaneous read, write, and calculate capability, new types of algorithms are needed that utilize being in multiple states, and new devices that have coherent spin states immune to environmental hazards are still to be invented. The advantages are counterbalanced by the unresolved problems of decoherescence and signal input/output. Error correction first thought impossible seems possible but with an enormous increase in complexity hence it seems only feasible to start with few-bit systems.
The quantum key distribution systems employed in quantum cryptography is an example of a few-bit system and one can already find commercial quantum cryptography systems on the market.
Some compare the status of quantum computing today resembling the state before the Abacus, but only future will show if quantum computing will be able to assume a major role.

5.   Summary

We perused the world of forecasting from the philosophical, physical and industry point of view and discussed some scenarios. Times have never been better for forecasting making FC an indispensable tool. In FC happened a shift from acute attention to technical astuteness to a growing awareness how to deliver and implement the message, a shift from analytic elegance to emphasis on the communication of results.

Technological forecasting for IC shows Moore's Law looking healthy for at least another decade. INTEL expects at least another 10 years of biannual doubling, while AMD sees innovations on the horizon that could keep the trend on track through 2020 and is already developing new technology needed for 16 nm transistors, which is on the road map for 2014.

The industry is already looking for some new physics replacing or complementing "charge-based physics"' by some new physical-switching mechanisms that do not require the movement of an electronic charge. It is too soon to tell, but this is the kind of work that could allow Moore's Law to continue well beyond 2020."

Thus there is no reason not to be optimistic in spite of problems to be overcome; but it is also wise not to be too optimistic, since some projects may prove to be just hype, and nobody could ever forecast completely new technologies for which there are no existing paradigms. The future is invented not predicted.

6. References

[1]   AGERWALA T. and GUPTA M. IBM J.of R&D 2007

[2]   R. BAJCSY, Quantum and molecular Computing, Comm. on Science U.S. House of Representatives, 2000.

[3]   CASLON, Analytics digital environment 2008

[4]   CHROUST G. and SCHOITSCH E., Choosing Basic Architectural Alternatives 2008

[5]   COATES J., Technological forecasting and social change North Holland

[6]   Economist Intelligence Unit 2008

[7]   HOUTEN, H. van, et alli, PhilipsResearch 2008

[8]   IBM Journal of R&D 50, 2/3

[9]   INTEL, Techn. Journal Aug 2007

[10]   ITRS International Technical Roadmap for Semiconductors, 2007

[11]   HOFSTEDE, G., Cultures and Organizations. McGraw Hill 2005

[11]   JANTSCH E., Technological Forecasting in Perspective, OECD 1966
            Die Selbstorganization des Universums, Hanser 1979

[13]   KARGER A., Leitidee des Determinismus in Wissenschaft, Philosophie und Gesellschaft

[14]   KRINGS H., System und Freiheit, 1980

[15]   LOESCH Chr., Do we need a new Information Technology, IDIMT 2006
            Information Technology Quo vadis? OCG 2007

[16]   MILLER, D. A. B., Silicon Photonics Stanford Univ. 2008

[17]   MITROFF I. and TUROFF M., Technological Forecasting and social change, American Elsevier 1973.

[18]   MUELLER S. et alii and D. PAPAMICHAIL, SUNY NY 2007

[19]   PRIGOGINE, I., Order out of Chaos, Bantam 1984
        and Nobel Price speech

[20]   Scientific American, Diamond Age of Spintronics 10/ 2007

[21]   Science Technology Quarterly 7/2007

[22]   Science News, May 2008

[23]   ZDNet Asia, Speech of G.Booch IBM Rational Software Conference, 2008

[24]   ZUGIC I., and FABIAN, Towards spin based logic, SUNY, N.Y. 2007

IDIMT 2007

15 YEARS IDIMT

15 YEARS MOVING IN FASCINATING SCENARIOS

Abstract

Discussing the scenario of the last 15 years, we have the privilege of the presence of eyewitnesses and even of contributors to these developments.

In 1992 when IDIMT started, an advanced PC ran on a processor like i486 with 0,8 μm technology and 1,2 mio transistors, today's processors will use 45 nm technology packing more than 400 mio transistors into a chip of size of half a postage stamp, and come in dual- and quad- core versions.

Rarely a single technology like information technology has been the driving force for such dramatic technological, economic, social, and scientific developments. We look at intertwined developments as e.g. the computer becoming a network and the network becoming social network or how information technology is even changing the way the world changes.

Many life-altering innovations were made in these years with information technology enabling advances from decoding the genome to the Internet or WWW. Two figures may characterize the dynamics of the scenario. October 1994 when the W3W (WWW consortium) was founded the number of web sites was approx.3000, ten years later it surpassed 50 million.

The change of the scenario literally reaches from the bottom of the sea to the sky. Innovations that laid the groundwork can be found on the bottom of the sea where fibre optics has improved communications up to satellites that have helped to turn the world into a global village.

We also look onto developments close to us, as the closing-up-race of Central and Eastern Europe, with a leading role of academia, to which personalities participating in the IDIMT contributed personally.

1. Scenario

Complementing the specific history and development of IDIMT which will be addressed in a special paper we will restrain us to spotlights on selected global political, technological, and economic scenarios.

1.1 General scenario

When IDIMT started in 1993, the prevailing mood was positive to enthusiastic, full of hope, energy and dedication to realize the tremendous potential and opportunities at our doorstep. The feeling of final victory of democracy persisted.

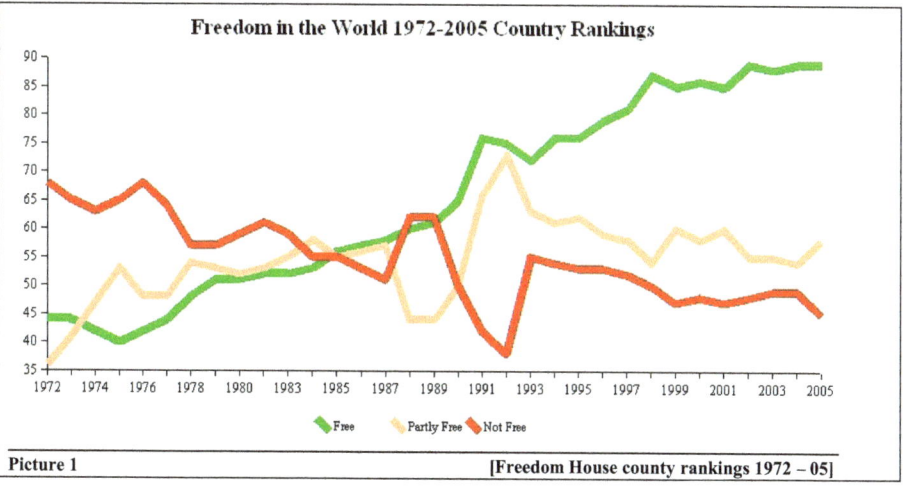

| Picture 1 | [Freedom House county rankings 1972 – 05] |

Francis Fukuyama wrote his famous book "End of history and the last man" in 1992 (based on his article published in 1989).

Japan was the admired example of a leading industrial nation, with everybody looking at it and trying to learn from Japan. A book as "Theory Z" by W.G. Ouchi sold more than 130 000 hardcover copies in the US alone, quality circles where established around the world a.s.o...

Europe was busy with reshaping itself with major challenges as German reunification, the re-establishing of the former COMECON and Yugoslavia to Glasnost and Perestroika and Yelzin taking over from Gorbatchov to mention some processes.

It was a period of liberalization and significant decreases in prices ranging from airfares to communication cost, TV sets and mobile phones; it was also the period of changing paradigms from Concord and TU 144 to Airbus and 767.

Expressions like SMS, blog, surfing or outsourcing were unknown to the public. Nor was "terrorist" a household word.

Civil rights and freedom were highly valued. Strong protests were questioning censuses or fingerprints on ID cards as intrusion into the private sphere.

The euphoric atmosphere was supported by the progress in technology. The ITRS (International Technology Roadmap for Semiconductors) roadmaps as shown below were improving from review to review accelerating the exponential growth even further.

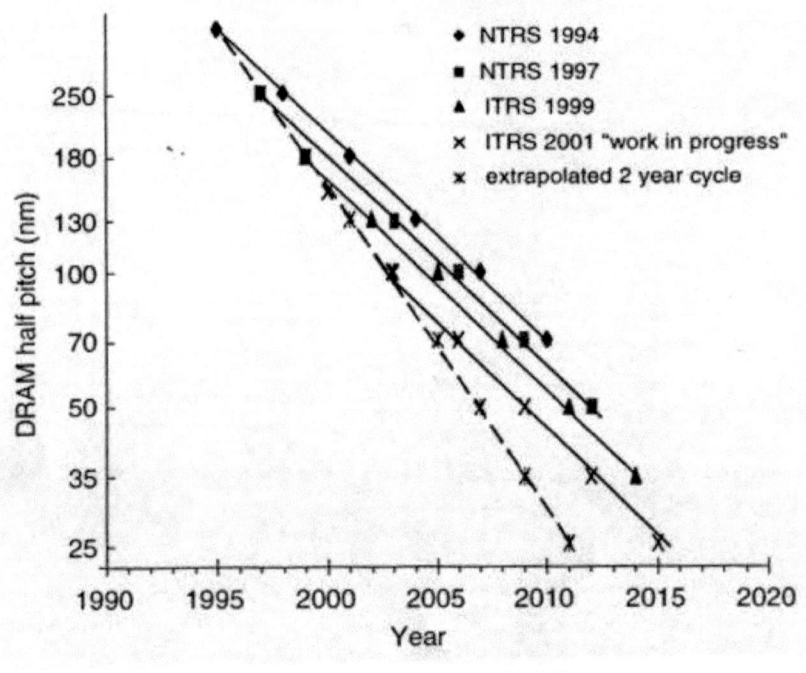

ITRS roadmaps 1994 -2003

In our part of Europe, to mention few examples, we were proud of events as

- the new 64k line connecting the University of Vienna with CERN,
- the impressive and successful closing-up race of Central and Eastern Europe countries with a leading role of the academia and universities (CS being the first former COMECON country becoming 1993 attached), or
- the start of Supercomputing and the transition from EARN to Internet (or PROFS to e-mail).

We were happy users of PCs with 386 or even 486 chips, running as main application writing documents and spreadsheet calculations. The migration of the C-net to the D-net using first mobile phones (price about thousand Euros) and was a privilege for few. The upcoming CDs or even DVDs were praised as latest technology. It has been a time of over-confident political statements like that the EU will overtake the USA in few years.

However, it was not a world of unspoiled peace and happiness. Just recall events as the

1992 Kuwait invasion

1994 NATO war in Serbia and the first Gulf war

2001 Sep 11 and the invasion of Afghanistan

2003 invasion of Iraq

2005 increasing inter-religious tensions (cartoon crisis)

2006 Israel Lebanon conflict (with use of phosphorus shells cluster bombs) or threats as SARS, Aids, Ebola virus or avian influenza,

to mention a few.

We would transgress the framework of this short paper to comment in detail on social developments as the weakening of family structure, changing to patchwork families, the decreasing role of trade unions, the increasing re-awareness of well-known ecological and environmental, worldwide weather and climate change problems, the public attentiveness to generation/social security problems, increasing criminality or rising inequality in the distribution of wealth etc.

1.2 Economy

The development with the largest long-range impact might be the rise of BRIC (Brasilia, Russia, India and China).
The period was also the timeframe of the boom and bust of the ".com bubble". Peaking in sky rocking investments as e.g., a billion $ flowing a week into Silicon Valley, this bubble burst in 2000 with a historic point loss in US stock market and the disappearance of many companies.

We have also seen deregulation from airline industry, financial service industry to telephone industry and we are going to see it in utilities.
It has also been a period of M&A's (mergers and acquisitions); many of them failing. Among the biggest flops was AOL (American Online) acquisition of Time Warner. The stock price of Time Warner fell to about one fourth of what it was in early 2000. Daimler Chrysler has lost half of its value since the automakers combined in 1998. And it's continuing, in the first half of 2007 M&A's reached according to UBS a record level of 2,5 Bio $.

We have seen the rise of globalization and some of the most extraordinary financial scandals of all times in the history of business. Enron collapsed WorldCom or Tyco and CEO's enriching themselves and ending up in court.

3. Science and technology

Even for those of us who have been around long enough to experience how the pace increases over time, our intuition nonetheless provides the impression that progress changes at the rate that we have experienced recently. A reason for this may be that a curve can be approximated by a straight line or tangent when viewed for a short interval. Nevertheless, exponential growth is a feature of any evolutionary process, of which technology is a primary example. One can examine the data for a wide variety of technologies ranging from electronic to biological, and the acceleration of progress and growth applies. We find not exponential growth, but "enhanced" exponential growth, meaning that the rate of exponential growth is itself growing. These observations do not rely merely on an assumption of the continuation of Moore's law (i.e., the exponential shrinking of transistor sizes on an integrated circuit), but is based on a rich model of diverse technological processes. What it clearly shows is that technology, particularly the pace of technological change, advances (at least) exponentially, and has been doing so since the advent of technology. It also shows the acceleration of the process the shortening of the doubling time from 20 to 18 month from the post-war period 1945 -1975 to the period 1975 -2000. [14]

2. C & C (computer and communications)

Dr. Koji Kabayashi, President of NEC Corp. coined the term and wrote the book "A Vision of C&C" in 1977 foreseeing the convergence of computer and communication technology.

4.1 Computer technology

We have covered the impressive developments of computer technology in previous IDIMT sessions and other papers in more detail; therefore let us mention here only some key facts and figures.

The table illustrates the increase in function, density and features of integrated circuits by some facts and figures for key INTEL products

	80486	PENTIUM	ITANIUM
MIPS	20	112	>10000
TRANSISTORS (MIO)	1,2	3,1	410
CYCLE (MHZ)	16 -50	60 -200	1000 - 1600
WIDTH	32	32	64
CACHE	8	16	256 KB 3/6 MB

[INTEL, Technology today]

To achieve these improvements and preserve the improvement speed several technological breakthroughs have been necessary. Let us recall some of them.
Silicon dioxide has been used to make the transistor gate dielectric for more than 40 years, it has been made even thinner and thinner and has been shrunk to a little as 1,2 nm. This thickness is equal to five atomic layers on the previous 65 nm process technology. Transistor gate leakage associated is one of the most formidable challenges we are facing. The combination of a high-k technology and metal gates are improves the drive current by 20% (because high k gate dielectric) and five times the source drain leakage.

Hf-based material reduces leakage by the factor of more than the 10 times (1970), reduces switching power by approximately 30 % and improves transistor density approximately two times over the previous generation.
Innovative design rules expand the use of 193 nm dry lithography to manufacture its 45 nm process because of its cost advantages.

INTEL (Penryn) and IBM have developed new processes with more than 400 million transistors in the chip of the size of a postage stamp. The recipe used by Intel and IBM has not been disclosed but importantly both companies have said they could incorporate them into cutting production technology with minimum effort. [11]

The picture below illustrates an IBM's view of major breakthroughs of the last ten years.

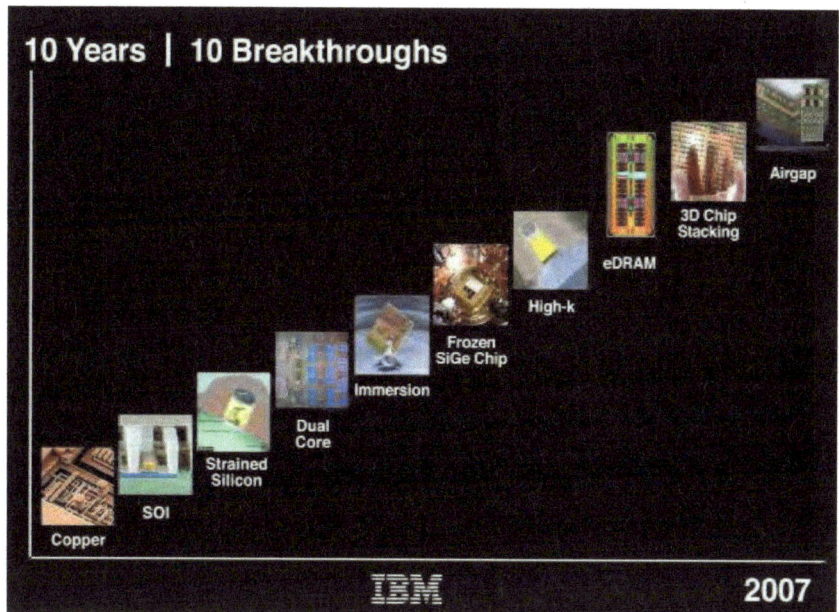

4.2   Communication Technology

Some of the most dramatic developments impacting the way we live may have come from C&C. It was the dramatic improvement of price/performance in ICT that enabled todays range of applications..

Electronic Mail was not really created in the year when IDMDT started. An IBM system named PROFS (for PRofessional OFfice System) was already in use in 1981. You might remember the e-mail aspect of the application, known colloquially PROFS notes, featuring prominently in the investigation of the Iran-Contra scandal, examined by US Congress [21].

4.2.1   THE INTERNET

Many people regard Internet and WWW as the overwhelming success story of this timeframe. Starting from the US Defence Department's ARPA net it finally merged into Internet, which it has helped to create. [19] The acceptance of this development is one of the most outstanding examples in the history of technology.

4.2.2   The WEB

In Switzerland at CERN Tim Berners-Lee addressed the issue of the constant change in the currency of information and the turnover of people on projects. Instead of a hierarchical or keyword organization, he proposed a hypertext system that will run across the Internet on different operating systems. This was the World Wide Web.

Tim Berners Lee created HTML, http://and unveiled the World Wide Web in August 1991 for the scientific community of physicists, and in April 1993 CERN made WWW technology and code free for everyone. It was not as easy as it might look today. He had to defend this idea against uninterested superiors at CERN, Internet-organisations like IETF and later against commercial covetousness of companies like Microsoft and Netscape. [4]

Nothing succeeds as success.

> 1991 100 documents were retrieved per day at CERN,
> 1992 1000
> 1993 10 000
> Today more than a billion pages are retrieved per day just in the US alone (Media Matrix).

Soon after the scientific commercial use started to boom when in August 95 Microsoft released Internet Explorer as part of Windows 95, followed 1996 by Hotmail.

The success story of Internet remained a story of idealistic, dedicated engaged individuals who were interested in the progress and the plethora of the new possibilities made this tool available for their communities and brought Internet to their countries. Czechoslovakia, Hungary and Poland established centres connected via Vienna to the world. They overcame numerous problems ranging from space to finance and the availability of lines and personnel, the absence of legal frameworks and responsible persons not to mention obstacles like telephone regulations prevailing at this time. Outstanding personalities (as P. Rastl and others) engaged themselves without consideration for fame, financial or carrier advantages made it possible that e.g. the University of Vienna becoming the hub node of the Ebone-net the backbone of Internet which meant also the start of the commercial internet (providers did not need to establish expensive leased lines to connect to Internet but could connect via this hub. This node became the hub of the first nationwide system library system BIBOS, and a supercomputing Centre connected to CERN and many others.

None of them was making any money from it. Internet/WWW remained a field of individual creativity and endeavour. Think of PGP, released in 1991, Linus Torvald's release of the free kernel for LINUX V1.0 in 1996 or of Wikipedia founded by Jimmy Wales in 2001. [21]

Worldwide this looked a little bit like Eden not a snake in sight, but soon afterwards were we mired in problems caused by things like online scams viruses and traps aimed at your computer and sometimes even your identity, making mischief on the Web, stalkers, predators, identity thieves,

4.2.3 How Internet/WWW transformed business

Internet has not only transformed business but also transformed the way we do business. For a long time people have thought of information as being a destination, you had to go to a book, you had to go to a library you had to go to a specialist or an office. But now the new mobile and wireless technologies are turning information into a companion.

Surfing the net on your PC has become as commonplace as making a phone call used for everyday purchases from buying a car to ordering a book or a pizza,

Number 1, 1999

IBM Think research

However, not everything emerging successfully in the 15 years of IDMDT has been invented in this timeframe.

Laser technology was patented in the 1960s but it took years before it found practical applications as in medicine, CDs, DVD's etc., but when it arrived and merged with Internet/WWW it changed the way music industry does business, gave birth to new dimension of downloading, MP3 players facilitated by new compression techniques etc.

Increased competition leads to lower prices, larger ranges of goods and lowering costs of transactions especially in the service sector and creating an online market of 170 bio $ in 2006. In addition, developments like globalization and outsourcing were facilitated by Internet and its growth enhanced. [3]

It might be worth to remember that overinvestment served as basis of broadband and .com revolution.

Simultaneously we are witnessing a massive M&A process. The process is ongoing is not finished; with a potential Internet superpower or powers emerging. GOOGLE which started its first office in a garage in California in1998, has in US 63 % market share (measured in requests) versus YAHOO's 21 %; and continues to grow by ventures like buying for 3,1 Bio $ DoubleClick - the largest independent broker between online publisher and advertisers in the market and also YouTube. Google forecasts operating profits of almost 5 Bio $ this year and a growing rate of 36 % for the next three years (while Microsoft's online business may loose 2 Bio $ this year and even more the next two years).

Google is already starting to offer processing and spreadsheets as free online services and will soon offer presentation software to rival Microsoft's PowerPoint. Microsoft itself bought for 6Bio $ aQuantive.

4. Perspectives

4.1   IT community's perception

What were the best Tech Products the IT community remembers?

What were the qualification criteria for the "best" tech product to come out of the digital age or what qualified a product as being "best"? First it must be a product, that means a piece of hardware or software that has changed our lives and that we can't live without (or couldn't at the time it debuted). Beyond that, a product should have attained a certain level of market acceptance, staying power, and perhaps made some sort of breakthrough or paradigm change, influencing the development of later products of its like. [18]

PC World survey ranks the best tech products. This ranking shows the outstanding creativity and fertility of the period we peruse. Fifty percent of the 10 best-ranked products and 56% of the 25 best ranked products are stemming from this timeframe.

4.2   Users Perception and Role

 C & C is not science and technology but daily life. Many people turn off their PCs, HDTV's plasma screens and grab their cell phones and their laptop computers as they leave their homes, some use GPS to plan their route and bring along their digital cameras.
Technology that makes this possible is taken for granted by the average consumer, like ATM's or MEMS (Micro-Electro-Mechanical System). Its safe to say that few people surviving a car accident walking a way unharmed will say "thanks goodness for the advent of nanotechnology and MEMS...." but without these technologies the airbag would not have deployed in time.

 It is interesting that the groundwork for many of these innovations mentioned above can be found underground where fibre optics has helped to turn the world into a global village. The change of the scenario literally reaches from the bottom of the sea to the sky. A key innovation, which laid the groundwork for the advancement in many fields, can be found on the bottom of the sea where fibre optics has improved communications up to satellites, which have helped to turn the world into a global village.

The general users perceptions of the top technical breakthroughs are reflected in a general survey CNN made in celebration of its 25th anniversary asking for

1 INTERNET
2 CELL PHONE
3 PC
4 FIBRE OPTICS
5 E-MAIL
6 GPS
7 LAPTOP COMPUTER
8 CD DVD
9 DIGITAL CAMERAS
10 RFID
11 MEMS
12 DNA FINGERPRINTING
13 AIR BAGS
14 ATM
15 ADVANCED BATTERIES   [6]

5. Summary and Outlook

Great expectations and optimism characterised the beginning of the time period perused. Unfortunately, some of these hopes have been in vain, especially those in the geopolitical and humanitarian area. We were fortunate having had the chance to witness or even participate in of one of the most fulfilling parts of Information Technology.

This period might be once seen as one of the most dynamic and fascinating periods in the history of Information technology. The symbiosis of computer and communications lead to a further acceleration of the exponential development and further on to an unprecedented rise of complexity. The convergence of technology, physics, and biology improves thus human performance and by cross-fertilization of many fields enables decoding and manipulation the genetic makeup of many organisms, DNA testing to the way we conduct our life from banking to shopping and entertainment.

Computer networks develop to social networks (10% of US marriages first contact happened over Internet). It is as well a story of community and collaboration on a scale never seen before. IT did not only change the world, but also change the way the world changes. People are developing themselves, reaching out to others, become more creative better educated and even richer than they otherwise would have been. [10]

It is also about the power from the few and helping one another for nothing. The tool that made this possible is not the world wide net as a way for scientists to share research. The new Web is a very different thing it is a tool for bringing together smaller contributions of millions of people and making them matter. It is about compendia of knowledge like Wikipedia or the million channel people's network YouTube.

It changed the way business operates and from a users perspective it lead to increasing competition, cheaper services and cheaper goods. [5]

For the sake of objectivity, we have to look at the other sides of the coin too. Not all effects have been exclusively. We mentioned above the dot.com boom. Now we seem to have the Web 2.0 boom. However, there are differences. The first dot.com boom was public, funded by Wall Street, now we see a private one funded by venture-capital networks.

The Web 2.0 harnesses also the stupidity of crowds as well as its wisdom and constitutes a massive social experiment and like zillions of people willing to give up personal identity and join into a collective (historically that propensity has usually been bad news [10]. People pay for the values they provide instant of being paid for.

Nevertheless, there are also stagnant fields of science where expectations were not met, or the expectation level was just too high as AI, Neural networks, Chaos theory or Fractals.

It was a period of outstanding economic growth and increase of wealth but also of increasing unequal distribution of and a widening wealth gap in 80 % of countries. Opening brought improving health, life expectancy and economic conditions to many, but also increasing inequality of distribution of income and wealth. It brought lower income groups decreasing economic influence – does this mean less democratic influence?

In Information technology, there are no "good old times." The outlook shows that systems-level performance must meet the demands of applications, even though power dissipation is creating a fundamental problem in the development of microprocessor technology. While technology scaling has allowed us to continue to increase the number of transistors on a chip, power densities have grown with every CMOS generation as designers have pursued higher operating frequencies. Given the lack of any other low-power and high-volume technology than CMOS, in the future, the frequency of microprocessors must grow at a much lower rate than in the past decade. Even with advances in base silicon, on-chip interconnects, and cooling technologies, microprocessor performance growth rates have slowed.

However, chip-level performance growth can still and will be sustained through higher levels of on-chip functional integration. The fundamental reason for this is the nonlinear relationship between power and performance. It may be possible, to decrease the power of a system tenfold with only a threefold reduction in performance. Higher performance at the chip level would then be obtained through higher levels of on-chip functional integration and multiple processor chips.

The disruption caused by power dissipation may affect all forms of computing systems. Scale-out systems represent a natural initial target for exploring solutions to this problem, given the high computational needs and the use of parallelism in their workloads. Systems management, reliability, and Amdahl's law[⊥] are challenges for scale-out systems. We require a holistic approach that considers all aspects of system design such as architecture, operating systems, compilers, and runtime systems, as well as workload characteristics and programming methodologies, in order to develop breakthrough solutions.

There is a dormant improvement potential in design changes as well in the software and application area. The movement from 180 to 90 nm technology hardware has grown by a factor of five while the software overhead has grown by a factor of twenty times e.g. options like Linux allow for much less overhead resulting in faster and more optimized systems. Thus SOC will provide an opportunity to overlap software, hardware and relatively small development teams resulting in 18 months time to bring new chips to the market. [17]

Many of these issues have been recognized as research problems since long time. The development of the current microprocessor technology will require us to address these problems and in a holistic manner by considering all aspects of systems design before turning to fundamentally new technologies.

6. References

[1]   ACCENTURE   Major Trends that will shape IT

[2]   AGERWALA T. Systems research challenges: A scale-out perspective, IBM Journal of R&D 2006

[3]   BBC   Fifty years of the Web, BBC 08/2006
                    How the web went worldwide, BBC Archive 2006

[4]   BERNERS-LEE Weaving the Web, Harper Collins (with Mark Fisher) 1999
[5]   CHROUST G.   15 years of IDIMT, 15 years of change, 2007
                    Synergie, Emergenz und Innovation in der IKT Industrie, SEA Univ. Linz, 2007.

[6]   CNN   Top 25 Innovations, Technological Breakthroughs and Business feels technology's influence, 2005
[7]   EAGELSHAM, D.J., Issues in Scale for Semiconductors, 2003

[8]   FAWKES M.   Highlights of the past ten years in Technology 2006

[9]   GASMAN L.   Foresight Nanotech Institute 2005

[10]   GROSSMAN L. The Person of the year: You
                   Making mischief on the Web and the Web Boom TIME 2.0 2006
[11]   HAENSCH W, Advanced Silicon Technology, IBM Journal of R & D

[12] ISAAC R.D,   The future of CMOS technology, IBM J. R & D 44, No. 3, 2000
[13]   IWAI HIROSHI The future of CMOS downscaling, Frontiers Collection 2004
[14]   KURZWEIL R. The Law of accelerating returns, 2001

[15]   LOESCH CHR. Trends in Technology, Proceedings of Euromicro 2003.

[16]   LOESCH CHR . Information Technology from Trend to Horizons IDIMT 2005
[17]   MAGEE M.   Clock speed will only double triple in 15 years

[18]   PC World   The 50 best products of all Time

[19]   PLASSER E.   What made the Internet work (with I. Haussteiner) SEA Univ. Linz Publ. SEA-SR-08

[20]   ROWEN Chr.   International Fabless 2005

[21]   WIKIPEDIA   Timeline of computing, 2007

[22]   ZEMANEK H.   Philosophie der Technik (with R. Knoll) 2007

IDIMT 2006

DO WE NEED A NEW INFORMATION TECHNOLOGY?

"All men by nature desire to know"
Aristotle

Abstract

Having discussed the physical and technological aspects at recent IDIMT's, let us this time devote some emphasis to a complimentary, potentially systemic viewpoint by looking at the general future scenario. The second word of the title already rises the question "who is we," and what kind of scenario do we have to expect at the time when new information technology could be implemented.

1. Demographic - Economic - Scenario

We will consider the demographic and economic scenarios and key players and then take some guesses at the scenario we might expect to consume and use the future information technology.

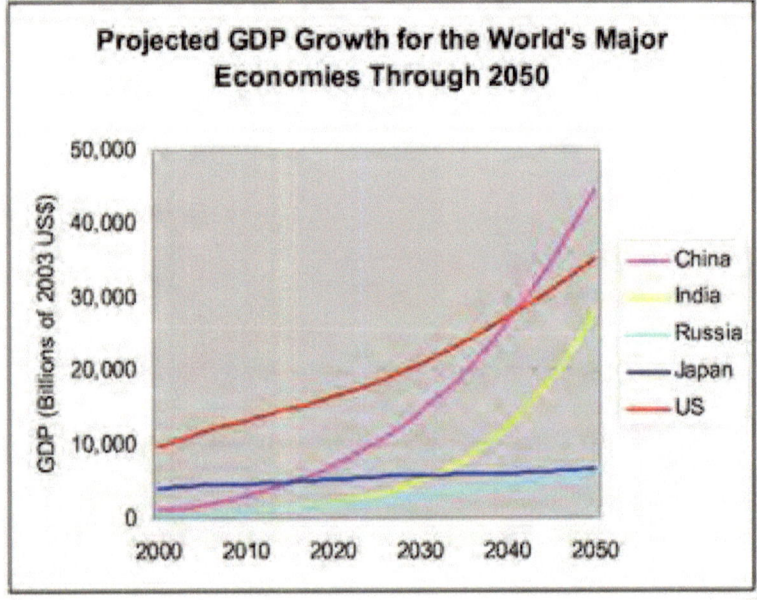

Source [3]

The GDP comparison between the US, China and India (figure 1) illustrates the potential shift of the centre of gravity from the so-called Western Hemisphere to Asia. This move is strongly supported by the heavy influx of Western investment and technology into this area. We see more and more R&D performed in this area, developing from the prolonged working bench to new centres of information technology. Government policies enforce these developments by requesting local participation in business ventures. Combined with the increasing local market potential for products developed based on these local joint ventures R&D for the large local and unsaturated market will enhance the thrust to satisfy these needs. Since leadership tends to gravitate where competence lies, leads us to consider future demographic and educational/skill developments. Even more so since markets in Western Hemisphere show signs of market saturation, e.g. the mobile telephone market.

Additional effects will arise from the different demographic structures in the Afro-Asian area and Western Europe and US. This means that the number of people in the most creative phase of their life we shall be most probably find in Asia and later on in Africa.

This quantitative shift will only have a lasting impact if education facilities and appropriate standards are developing accordingly.

2. Market Developments

2.1   Millions New Customers

In 2005 estimated 13,9% of the world's population had Internet access. If you ask them, which improvements they would like to see over the next years you will not be surprised that reliability and user friendliness will come up.

Research suggests that users of the next wave of computing users will look very different from the first. They will be less affluent and more heterogeneous, live in more challenging environments in the developing world, and in many cases have very different daily lives and abiding concerns. New users will come from the growing metropolis in Asia, Africa, and America. Mobile telephony promises to reach some two billion subscribers soon. As cost of computing continue to speed downwards new forms will appear that better fit the daily lives of more people, and new forms of wireless connectivity will be needed enable communities to "leapfrog" to high bandwidth connectivity, and become a new population of computing users. How do these changes affect us?

2.2   Some indicators

- In 2004, China graduated about 500,000 engineers, India 200,000 and the US 70,000.

- For the cost of one chemist or one engineer in the United States, a company can hire about five chemists in China or eleven engineers in India.

- The United States has become a net importer of high-technology products. Its share of global high- technology exports has fallen in the last 2 decades from 30% to 17%, and its trade balance in high-technology manufactured goods shifted from plus $33 billion in 1990 to a negative $24 billion in 2004.

- In 2004, chemical companies closed 70 facilities in the United States and tagged 40 more for shutdown. Of 120 major chemical plants built around the world with price tags of $1 billion or more, one is in the United States and 50 in China.

- In the recent period, low-wage employers, created 44% of the new jobs, while high-wage employers created only 29% of the new jobs.

- The United States is said to have 10,5 million illegal immigrants, but under the law the number of visas set aside for "highly qualified foreign workers" dropped to 65 000 a year from its 195 000 peak. Nor could Germany achieve an overwhelming success with its recent "green card program."

This may indicate that only high quality in all aspects ranging from education to innovation and R&D can support a continuation of the present role of the Western world. These figures also point out that we enter the period with the largest number of university graduates in R&D ever in history.

These data have to be weighted against the fact that many Chinese degrees are completed it in two or three years only. Some educators are concerned that the message that our engineering students will soon compete with one million graduates from India and China could create a sense of uncertainty and doubt and might scare many away turning them into lawyers, accountants or medical doctors. [24, 25]

Some more indicators from the legal scenario

- In 2001 US, industry spends more on tort litigation than on research and development. [26]

- No European and only three US companies rank among the top 10 recipients of patents granted by the US Patent and Trademark Office. The highest-ranking European company is Philips on rank 12.

Preliminary Rank (2004)	Preliminary no. of patents (2004)	Organization	Final Rank (2003)	Final number of patents (2003)
1	3,248	International Business Machines Corporation	(1)	(3,415)
2	1,934	Matsushita Electric Industrial Co., Ltd.	(4)	(1,774)
3	1,805	Canon Kabushiki Kaisha	(2)	(1,992)
4	1,775	Hewlett-Packard Development Company, L.P.	(5)	(1,759)
5	1,760	Micron Technology, Inc.	(6)	(1,707)
6	1,604	Samsung Electronics Co., Ltd.	(9)	(1,313)
7	1,601	Intel Corporation	(7)	(1,592)
8	1,514	Hitachi, Ltd	(3)	(1,893)
9	1,310	Toshiba Corporation	(13)	(1,184)
10	1,305	Sony Corporation	(10)	(1,311)

Table 2 [US Patent and Trademark Office]

3. Intellectual Property

Intellectual property represents the result of the intellectual effort and can be viewed as the legal embodiment of that effort, needed by companies in order to do business. Information and especially software technology is an area strongly affected by intellectual property and vice versa, requiring a balance between vested industry (e.g. prevention of illegal copying) and user interests. Restrictive terms imposed by large software vendors supersede the tradition and some licenses even make it difficult to examine material before purchasing it. It is not clear yet if the traditional "fair use" exceptions to intellectual property rights for education will be protected under the emerging copyright regime. [4]

4. Information Technology Industry Developments

In spite of the phenomenal success of the information technology industry linger pessimism and doubt since more than a dozen years on the continuation of this unprecedented growth.

BW, March 1, 1989

We can assume that the ingenuity of the researchers and engineers will continue to assure technological progress and a prolongation of the exponential improvement rally for the next decennium. Some authors see three growth cycles for the technology economy, defining growths periods as such when the growth of the ratio of information technology investment to GDP was greater than 5%. [20]

Digestive phases seem to follow growth periods where companies slowed their information technology spending, rationalized their infrastructure, and focused on the ROI of their technology investments. The focus in these periods is on changing business processes to take advantage of the capabilities of new technologies, which were often bought on faith during the boom times. According to this theory, we can ask what is next: another period in of accelerated growth. The chart suggests a takeoff around 2007 or 2008 based on a new set of technologies. The seeds of these technologies of the next growth phase are already around. [1]

Some more trends and innovations are

- Distance no subject

- Towards consumer electronics, visible and invisible.

- Shift towards services

- Outsourcing

- From assets to expenses

Anything with a chip in it may become a platform for service.

There are advocates that businesses should handover the key to their business systems because the technology is too complex and information technology services should be used and paid like a utility as gas or lightning bills. However, the competitive advantage to be realized from information technology by the individual company should not be overlooked.

This is not the end, call-centres work currently being outsourced to India may be automated by further advanced natural language recognition.

2.1 Internet of Things

There are trends showing very different technical characteristics since they ask for slower, simpler, and low energy technologies contrary to the ongoing pursuit along the exponential racetrack of Moore's law. They will lead to a different class of products and applications, which will be much simpler. A study entitled the "Internet of things" prophesises that the demands of multinational businesses would be forcing the adoption of these new technologies. This is not only a forecast of future development, it is happening already as shown by the RFID explosion, with production growing from 10 Bio pieces p.a. to 100 Bio pieces p.a. within few years and becoming a global standard.

Further trends point to ubiquitous flexible and reflective displays, extreme miniaturization, the integration of new functions such as sensors and actuators with silicon logic, textile electronics, and solid state lightning technologies.

The key bottleneck in the development of autonomous devices and ubiquitous computing the energy supply of distributed device nodes will be addressed later.

Wireless and sensor networks are emerging as the next technological thrust. These sensors will be imbedded in both ad-hoc and static networks that in turn exploit the Internet. They are technologically moving in the opposite direction to Moore's law, planning for lower power with fewer transistors even less input/output capacity then the semi conductor chips of the 1960s.

If the energy supply problem is adequately resolved will these sensors shrink to the size of a sand corn scattered across farms, industrial parks or battlefields, or attached to containers, trains cars, trucks and all kind of goods become an invisible extension of Internet. They will coupled with distributed or grid computing, handle the enormous data flood and with most traffic flowing from machine to machine.

We are reaching the point where the average quality of the display and audio system or a digital recorder, mobile phone or a PC is so high that quality is no longer a discriminating factor. Whenever such a point has been reached, appliances tend to become commodities and appliance makers find it more difficult to operate profitable.

Also interfacing the physical world will be a challenge in the pursuit for these microsystems. Autonomous systems should be battery less, taking their energy from the environment a technique known as energy scavenging. We may expect that energy supply will be the key limiting factor in the realization of ambient intelligent environments.

1. Energy scavenging

Vibration energy scavenging	$0,05\text{-}0,5$ mW/cm^3
Acoustic energy conversion	1μ W/cm^2
Thermoelectric energy conversion	$1\text{-}10\mu$W/cm^2
Photovoltaic energy conversion direct sun, light	10mW/cm^2

[10]

What can be done with that limited power?

Computation: the power range of $10 - 1000\mu$W/cm^2 would enable 100 Ops/sec for the 0,18 μm CMOS technology node (neglecting leakage power), enough for a low date rate application. Communication: For short range based on the available technologies as Bluetooth (1Mbit/sec) or Zigbee (80kbits/s) or PicoRadio (1kbits/sec), only PicoRadio falls into the $10 - 1000$ μW/cm^2 range. To transmit a single bit the energy required would be in the order of $10 - 30$ nJ. Standby power can be a limiting factor (~ 50μW), but a lot can be gained by proper system organization with e.g. a "sleep mode."
Another potential solution may come from the concept of nano-batteries now pursue, after a dormant period of 15 years, by Bell Laboratories and mPhase who showed their first samples last October.
Textile electronics will require the development of some special features as soft controls, wiring interconnect solutions, flexible displays, and integrated sensors; one may also think of apparel woven from light emitting or colour changing fibres. These applications are not limited to personal apparel. Electronics can be in furniture, soft furnishings (curtains, carpets, wallpaper) as well with chips forming a self-organizing network that can be cut into any shape. These devices are thought to become increasingly self-aware, space and location conscious, able to interact with the surrounding environment and exhibiting introspective behaviour. The size of the network and the complexity of the interactions within it demand that they are capable of cooperation, self-organization, self-diagnosis and self-repair. Finally, trust, privacy, security, and dependability must be assured. [10]
The march of electronics into the nano-cosm will make it economically feasible to fit all the signal processing and sophisticated traffic management and the high-speed fiber optics required onto a single chip, making powerful information technology available everywhere. We see hints that this might start to happen in a processor from Intel (incorporating with 90nm technique sophisticated features as firewalls or traffic management at a very low price). [4]

3. Technology

Since the 19th century electronic information technology has spread in waves. The first wave was the telegraph, then the telephone and than the PC, the Internet, fiber optic networks and mobile phones. Each wave made a new powerful information technology available to new groups and regions. However, each wave was as well based on additional technological breakthroughs. The idea of cell phone technology was ready in the 40´s, but it needed the computerized switching system and other technological breakthroughs to make it feasible.

Generally, we can be confident for the next decennium, since as discussed in previous IDIMT sessions, for the timeframe for the next 10 years the prolongation of Moore's law seems to be assured.

Asking for future technology needs, means asking for future applications. There is well-founded expectation for an accelerated growing demand for data storage and retrieval, enhanced visualization both static and dynamic and leisure applications as home entertainment, computer games etc. Techniques as ray tracing are a potential future image application (photo realistic graphics requires about one billion polygons p.u.), handling volumes of machine or sensor generated data, concepts like life long data storage, pattern, mode and speech recognition and the resulting data mining tasks will require significantly increased algorithmic processing power and storage.

In the past, as the graph shows, improvements have been driven in the past by frequency increases giving now room to other improvement strategy summarized as architecture.

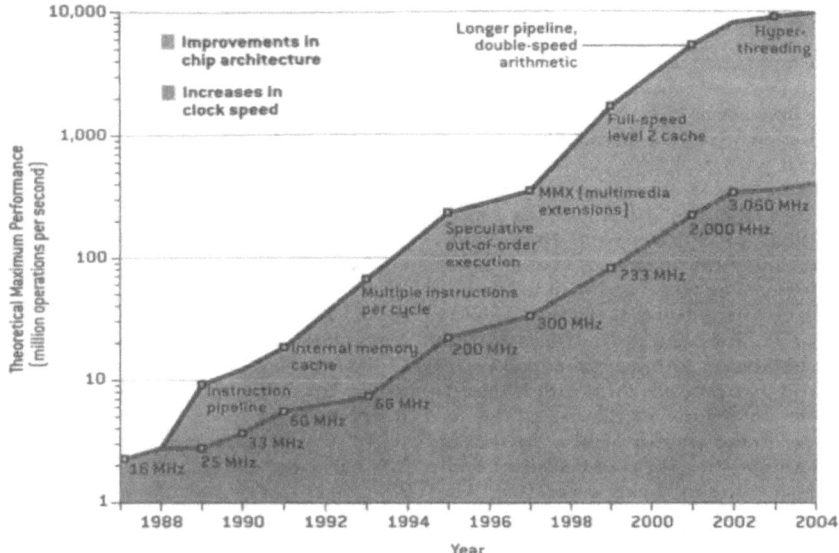

Source: INTEL. The upper curve shows the improvent by chip architecture, the lower by clockspeed

Some of the impediments to continue the exponential path further are:

Power density: If increasing at a rate as in the past years it will reach several thousand watts $/cm^2$ that are more than the surface of the sun.
Memory latency: The imbalance between memory and processor performance is detrimental to use the technological achievements. Memory speeds are not increasing at the rate of processor speeds:

today Pentium processors require 224 clock cycles to access memory these wasted clock cycles can nullify the benefits of frequency increases of the processor and this tends to be worsening.

RC delay: The delay caused by fact that a 1mm RC delay takes longer than a clock cycle, for typical chips in the 10 –12 mm range it takes about 15 clock cycles to go from one corner of the die to the other.

Physics our friend in the past is now becoming our foe, setting principal boundaries. E.g. the insulator thickness of 2-3 nm in present-day chips cannot be less than about 1,5nm because if the silicon dioxide layer is made thinner electron can tunnel through. Channel length, the distance between source and drain of a transistor, can due to the so-called short channel effects not be shorter than 25nm. It is not just physics as in the past, key criteria determining future will come from economics.

Even if for the first time no immediate accelerations of clock cycles are predicted, the breath of technology is increasing. This means while the growth rate of on-chip functionality would slow, the amount of functions per chip will continue grow exponentially. While the present CMOS technology is not nearly stretched to its limits fascinating technologies are emerging over-the-horizon. We are enjoying rather an abundance of new ideas for future technologies. Some of these technologies research are.

NANOTECHNOLOGIES & ELECTRONICS

MOLECULAR ELECTRONICS

OPTOELCTRONICS

ORGANIC COMPUTING

SPINTRONICS

QUANTUM COMPUTATION

These technologies have been covered in preceding presentation, to refresh memories just some keywords:

3.1 Technology and Molecular Electronics

Nanotechnology is not an industry but rather an interdisciplinary enabling technology.

The use of nanotechnology will improve memories, displays, processors, solar power elements, embedded systems, and enable self-configuring networks and thus help to create a pervasive computing environment. The uses are not restricted to information technology; possible applications can as well be in chemical and genetic probes, hydrogen and ion storage, super-strong materials, coatings, catalysts, fuel cells, batteries, filters lubricants or solid state lightening. Still many problems as large-scale processing with predictive capacities remain to be resolved, a potential solution might come by self-assembly, supported by defect tolerant architecture. This is not far stretched futurism. Nantero will soon begin sampling a memory chip based on carbon nanotubes and so will Honeywell and Freescale.

Molecular electronics was already proposed in 1974 but it took until 1997 to build a diode. Today carbon nanotubes are best researched and depending on their structure, carbon nanotubes can be semiconductors or metals.

4.2 Optoelectronics

Optical computing technology is not only attractive because it would break the rocky union of fiber optics, laser technology and electronic switching, but also because it would solve power, interconnections and cross talk problems and additionally need no cooling.

4.3 Single Spin Electronics

Spintronics can be described as electronics that takes advantage not only of the electron's charge but also the electron's spin (a quantum mechanical property considered to be either "up" or "down"). Spin processes have the advantage of lower energy consumption combined with higher speed compared to conventional electron processes.
Spintronic structures are also playing an important role in the development of the MRAM (magnetic Random Access Memory) devices already under development by IBM, Infineon and other companies.

4.4 Organic computing

The famous demonstration of the solution of "travelling salesmen problem" by organic processes created a worldwide response and interest.
Special attractiveness results from the storage capabilities e.g. DNS is 100 Bio times denser than Si and potential parallelism enabling theoretically 10^{20} simultaneous processes/calculations. A tank with 0,5 kg DNS diluted in 1 m^3 of water would have more storage capacity than all computers at present in use.
Disadvantages are that it is slower than Si-based computing, and a voluminous, sticky, and liquid technology. Even with pure organic computing still far away, a mixture of organic and inorganic layers patterned to form the channels of thin-film FETs may appear.

4.5 Quantum computing

Some call quantum computing the ultimate way of computing. This may be exaggerated in view of the limited scope of applications as factoring large numbers or searching huge databases. The first practical application is most probable in cryptography, assuming the problems as de-coherence, signal I/O, error correction will be resolved in technically and economically feasible ways.

5. Summary

In the pursuit to gain a view on some aspects of the future scenario of information technology we looked at selected demographic, economic, geographical, and technologic aspects.
  While present users hope for improved reliability, more user-friendliness and engineering-like quality and other standards especially in the software area, the priorities for new users will be different. They will be less affluent, more heterogeneous, living in more challenging environments in the developing world, and in many cases have very different daily lives and abiding concerns. Their hopes in the future of information technology will focus on finding economically feasible ways to catch up with the benefits the Western world by using information technology to improve their daily lives as e.g. medical or social uses.

The future of information technology will continue to be characterized by the exponential decrease of cost per function as long as it is economically advantageous, but the exponential development is not restricted to performance of integrated circuits, it has its antagonism in the equally exponential increase of cost for new production technologies and facilities. However, every future new technology faces a formidable competitor in the prevailing silicon technology. None of the newly emerging technologies can today successfully compete with the prevailing silicon technology. We may even not find anything able to compete successfully and replace silicon in the next years unless there are significant breakthroughs. Even so, some unique capabilities of other technologies based and integrated on top of silicon may add great value as e.g. non-volatile memory sensors, photo electronic conversion devices or nano-mechanically devices.

The unprecedented success and efficiency of the IT industry allowed compensating for shortcomings and imbalances in the past and including the lack of a "grand design" or engineering standard. The IT industry can be optimistic about technology but not so much about profits, therefore the emphasized service part of information technology became a growing alternative endeavour.

The broadening application of information technology will need additional developments. Expectations range from broadening the scope of use and user friendliness, better interfaces, to develop additional areas of applications by percolating into everything from biology, medicine to textiles to the pursuit of new user strata as sensor and network based applications, thus bringing improvement and enrichment of the quality of live of millions.

In spite of our efforts to cover potentially important aspects of future problems and developments, we know from the history of information technology that revolutionary breakthroughs have never been forecasted, so that the future may have surprises in petto for us.

6.   References

[1]   Carr, Nicolas, End of Corporate Computing, Sloan Mgt Rev., MIT Spring 2005

[2]   Colvin, Geoffrey. 2005. "America Isn't Ready." Fortune Magazine, July 25

[3]   Eagelsham, D.J., Issues in Scale for Semiconductors 2003

[4]   Gasman, Lawrence, Foresight Nanotech institute 2005

[5]   Gelsinger, P., Intel Corp., 2002

[6]   Gershenfeld , N., Krikorian R., Cohen D., The Internet of Thinks, SciAm 10/2004

[7]   Goldman Sachs, The path to 2050, 2003

[8]   Gorokin, H. and Tsui, R.K., Molecular Electronics a proposed roadmap to commercialization, Motorola Labs, 2001

[9]   Ron Hira, of Rochester Institute of Technology, 2005

[10]   Houten, Henk van, The physical Layer of Ambient Intelligence, Philips Res. Labs, 2004

[11]   Hoare, T., Milner, Robin, Grand Challenges in Computing, Brit. Comp. Society 2004

[12]   Iwai, Hiroshi, The future of CMOS downscaling, Frontiers Collection 2004

[13]   IBM Research, Nanotechnology, 2004

[14]   Isaac, R.D., The future of CMOS technology, IBM J. Res. Develop. 44, No. 3, 2000

[15]   Katz Stanley, In Information Technology, The chronicle of higher education, June 2001

[16]   Kwiatkowska Marta, Sassone Vladimir, Science for global ubiquitous computing 2005

[17]   Loesch, Chr. W., Trends in Technology, Proceedings of Euromicro 2003.

[18]   Loesch, Chr. W. Information Technology from Trend to Horizons IDIMT 2005

[19]   McKinsey Global research Institute, the emerging global market, New York 2002.

[20]   Mines Christopher, Forrester Research, June 200504

[21   Ministry of Science and Technology (MOST). 2004. Chinese Statistical Yearbook 2004. PRC.

[22]   Moore, G., Moore's vision, Intel Corp., 2003

[23]   Nishi, Yoshio Future Challenges and Needs for Nanoelectronics from a Manufacturing Viewpoint, Stanford Univ.2004

[24]   National Association of Software and Service Companies, India, NASSCOM. 2005.

[25]   National Center for Education Statistics, Trends in International Mathematics and Science, 2003

[26]   National Science Board's Science and Engineering Indicators 2004.

[27]   Roach, Steve. More Jobs, Worse Work. NYT July 22, 2004.

[28]   Roukes M. ., Plenty of room indeed, SciAm, 9, 2001.

[29]   Smith III, T.P., Wireless Sensor Networks and the Sensor Revolution, Mc Lean, 2004

[30]   Theis, Th., IBM Research T .J. Watson Res. Center 3 / 2003

[31]   US Patent and Trademark Office, 2003.

IDIMT 2005

FUTURE TRENDS AND SCENARIOS OF INFORMATION TECHNOLOGY

Abstract

We are enjoying the benefits of a period of unprecedented advancement of information technology stimulating similar advancements in many other fields. As for all phenomena of exponential growth the question is not whether, but only when and why this would come to an end, more specifically: would it be physics or economics that raises the barrier to further scaling?
As the end of CMOS-scaling is approaching, it will be advisable to review what research efforts could extend it, but even more, what the post-silicon future and scenario could be.
Is there practicality in the research results of such topics as Nanoelectronics, Molecular Computing, Silicon-Photonics, Spintronics and Quantum Computing? What are their implications? But there are other aspects worth discussion as:

- The effects of "getting physical" by direct connecting computers increasingly to the physical world around them, creating and networking billions of nodes with a new role of Internet as a seamless whole of networks integrating all types of devices from keys to sensors, tags etc.
- The future role and weight of ethical, security or privacy concerns. How far will the framework of ethics and law interact with these developments and technologies on a planetary scale?
- What will be the impact of human factors? Do we need a different, may be more disciplined or more engineer-quality-ethics like approach e.g. to software and applications?
- Shall we come to a systemic-thinking-type approach to meet these challenges?

Many are already trying to understand the impact of these developments on the business environment, on future products and their investment priorities. These developments will not only model the future scientific scenario but even more the future economic development, education requirements, social evolution and thus last but not least people's lives.

1.   Introduction

Before looking at future trends and scenarios it might be advisable to take stock where we stand today and which developments are already visible on the horizon emerging from the pipeline of research and development. We will try to review the key developments, its challenges, and the countermeasures. Since the physical and technological aspects were predominantly covered at IDIMT 2004 more room will be given to non -technical and human aspects today.
We will approach the subject by considering different points of view as seen from the public the user, professional societies and of course from that point of technology reflected in current research and development and its interaction with our life.
A recent CNN survey asking worldwide for the 25 top innovations people think affecting their life resulted in the enumeration shown below:

1.The Internet

2. Cell phone

3. Personal computers

4. Fiber optics

5. E-mail

6. Commercialized GPS

7. Portable computers

8. Memory storage discs

9. Consumer level digital camera

10. Radio frequency ID tags

11. MEMS

12. DNA fingerprinting

13. Air bags

14. ATM

15. Advanced batteries

16. Hybrid car

17. OLEDs

18. Display panels

19. HDTV

20. Space shuttle

21. Nanotechnology

22. Flash memory

23. Voice mail

24. Modern hearing aids

25. Short Range, HF Radio

Source: [2]

This shows the extent Information Technology has left the area of physics and mathematics and has become an integral part of our lives.

2. Scaling to Nanoscale

A "smaller–cheaper, cheaper-better" synergy model drove the semiconductor industry into nanotechnology by aggressive scaling, "Moore's Law" is an integral part of the semiconductor success story. It was, is and will be a success story for the next decennium of the years to come. This success story has not yet ended but we are approaching increasing challenges to be overcome both scientifically and economically as:

- Lithography
- Interconnection
- Power dissipation
- Cost

2.1 Limits for Downscaling and Integration

2.1 .1 Lithography and Integration

Photolithography is a combination of optical, chemical, and micro mechanical processes to transfer geometric shapes onto the surface of silicon wafer. This technology is successfully used for more than a billion transistors per second, but it approaches principal limits.
Optical lithography – the current workhorse of semiconductor industry – the minimum feature size is closely related to the wavelength of light, and since we are already approaching the short wave edge of conventional optics even shorter wavelengths are necessary, but sub-100 nm patterns can only be made by x-rays and electron beam or E(xtreme)UV.
This explains the efforts to extend the familiar technologies to advanced UV or EUV lithography to its limits and explore alternatives as described later. [18]
As IC's (Integrated circuits) are downscaled total performance of the IC is not automatically guaranteed to improve. Increase in the resistance and capacity of narrow and dense interconnect metal lines are obstacles.

When transistors on opposite corners of the chip send a signal from one to the other, those electrons have to flow through a wire. The resistance and capacitance of that wire limit the speed at which the electrons can flow and while most wires are getting shorter, wires are also getting thinner which increases the delay caused by a resistance and capacitance. Further effects as leakage currents, fluctuation, and thickness of films, line edge roughness and dopant distribution are resulting in performance decreases. So interconnects are becoming more and more of a bottleneck. That applies double for the connection between the processor and the main memory. A microprocessor running at 3.6 GHz can execute several instructions each time its clock ticks, 277 trillionths of a second. But the system typically takes about 400 times as long to fetch information from the main memory the processor is just sitting their waiting for each piece of data to come from memory.

Cost reduction measured in cost per bit or cost per microprocessor operation is the biggest driving force for downscaling. However, this is not the only positive effect of downscaling. Downscaling also opened new fields of applications, attractiveness and added value as image processing capacity, portability etc.

The problem ahead as the example from lithography (mask set costs) shows, is the exponential increase of costs.

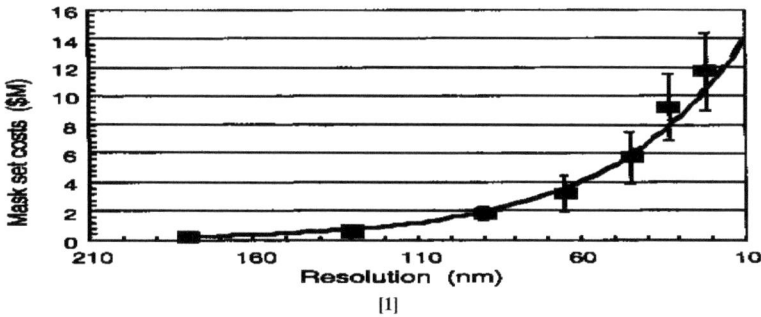

[1]

Or as another example, the tools to produce chips with features under 100 nm will cost up to hundred millions of dollars each.
Industry is trying to cope with this by technological, business and structural measures. The recent growth of strategic alliances between competing companies reflects the magnitude of necessary investments, as well as outsourcing and cooperation with universities and research institutions.

2.1.2 Power dissipation

If the current trend in clock frequency and number of transistors per chip would continue power consumption of a high performance microprocessor would reach 1kW/cm2 the near future. To counter this a plethora of developments reaching from new architecture, new devices, special heat sinks, trade offs with performance, multiprocessors, supply voltage adjustments to the duty of the chip has been advanced. [7]

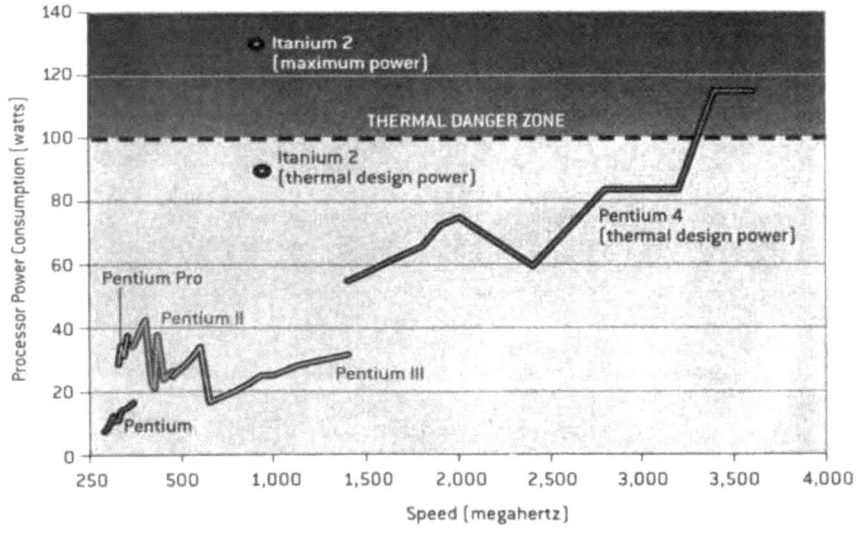

Source INTEL

icles and more complicated device
structures, which are obviously detrimental to reliability. To counter this error correction and fail
save structures will have to be increasingly incorporated.
One solution for continuing progress in IC performance, even before the downsizing limit is
reached is the integration of different functional chips on the silicon main chip as hybrid technology
thus reducing parasitic capacitances, saving power and increasing performance.

2.1.4 Architecture and others

The challenges mentioned above have been recognized and the quest for cost efficient solutions has
led to a systematic broadening of the research for sources of additional performance into all
directions, thus and related advances have become significant contributors to the total performance.

- Architecture

- Instruction pipelining

- Multiple instructions per cycle

- MMX (multimedia extensions) and Hyperthreading

We are already encountering the first-time effects of reaching limits when Intel in May 2004
decided to hold work on its next generation of processors. It meant that the micro architecture the
central engine of Intel's business and about three quarters of the world's computers have reached the
end of its life earlier than planned.

Beginning next year all new Intel microprocessors designed for desktop use will not have one but
two cores working side-by-side on the same chip (some high-end processors already have two or
more microprocessors as separate chips on circuit boards).

Integrating multiple processors into one multicore chip involves more than a dramatic design
change. It implies the reduction of their interaction time to fractions of nanoseconds. The shift to
multicore processing might also have significant ramifications how computers are sold, how they
are upgraded, and most significantly how they are programmed.

The first dual core chips will probably work at lower frequencies than the fast chips we are using
today. INTEL predicts that from now on 70% of performance gains will come from architecture
improvements mainly from parallelism rather than from additional megahertz. A notebook
processor might have eight cores; a program customized for such chips could divide itself into
many threats each running simultaneously on different cores. The operating system might turn off
some of the cores. Since most of the software has no idea how to exploit a multicore processor, it
would take the software community a long time to rework that.

A parallel processor deprives the programmer of one of the most valuable tools for debugging: the
repeatability. A threaded parallel program is not a deterministic thing. There are some applications
where you won't get any boost from multi-core. However, certainly they are many kinds of tasks
could run dramatically faster when redesigned for multicore chips. A few special tasks could exploit
as many cores as chipmaker can throw on them, but for general-purpose computing there is a point
of diminishing returns, 16 cores are certainly not better than eight are. The most worrisome
questions for the microprocessor industry may be whether the shift to multi core processors will

discourage customers from upgrading to new computers especially since today's computers are more than fast enough to handle most of the popular software.

Major design changes add uncertainty to apathy as reason that computer owners might postpone an upgrade. It questionable whether customers who buy the first dual core machines and replace much of their software to suit the new architecture will have to repeat the process few years later to take advantage of quad-core machine. Faced with that prospect many users could decide that the new architecture is not worth the hassle.

2.1.5 Summary of challenges and potential solutions

Performance	New device/process technologies
	New materials
	Chip integration
	New architecture, algorithms
Cost	Slower downsizing
	Cooperation, Alliances, Outsourcing
Power	Trade offs with performance
	New device/process technologies
	New architecture, algorithms
	Cooling technology
Reliability / Yield	New device/process technologies
	Fail-safe design

[8]

2.1.6 Memories

The development of classical memory devices is not only paralleling, if not surpassing the processor scenario.
Promising developments as FRAM (ferromagnetic RAM), MRAM (magnetic RAM), or PRAM (phase change RAM) have entered the research scene enriching already presently researched options as holographic, millipede or organic memories. While the search for next technology materials is on, it is reassuring to know that these developments will be supplemental since conventional memories will remain the key players down to the 30-50 nm technologies for the next future. [4, 11, 13]

Figure below is summing up the potential future development of the downscaling of processors and storage devices and their physical limits

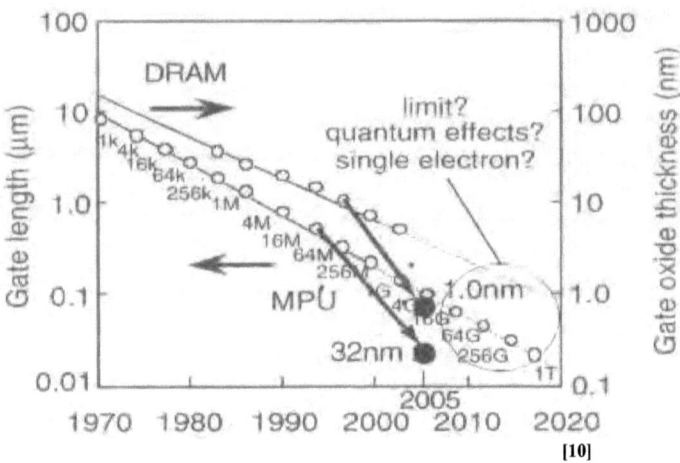

[10]

2.2 Long term future CMOS Devices

For the benefit of those who have attended IDIMT 2004, where we reviewed some these technologies, we will restrain to a short summary.
Let us look beyond the present horizon at some potentially supplemental or alternative technologies for the long range:

> NANOELECTRONICS
>
> MOLECULAR TRANSISTOR
>
> ORGANIC MATERIALS
>
> SPINTRONICS
>
> QUANTUM COMPUTATION

2.2.1 Nanoelectronics
We can certainly say that silicon based electronics has reached the scope of nanoelectronics and is therefore nanoelectronics. However, this does not encompass the full range of potential and some of the nano materials and their impressive properties that make this field so attractive.
A basic breakthrough was the Buckyball and its derivatives the nanotubes. A Buckyball or fullerene is a carbon molecule composed of at least 60 atoms of carbon arranged in a ball-like structure.

Nanotubes are long drawn fullerenes. The carbon nanotube is the best-known example of inorganic wires, functioning both as interconnections and as components.

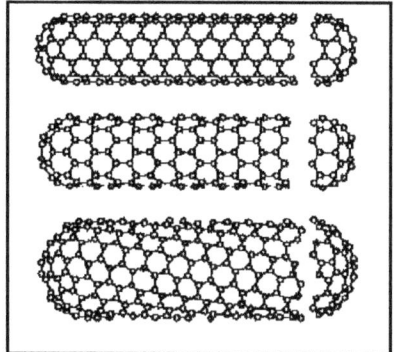

Different structures of nanotubes, Veld, TU Eindhoven.

Carbon nanotubes have been around since 1991. Scientists were excited about their unique qualities, their astonishing physical properties as 100 times the strength of steel but only of 1/60 weight, their outstanding electrical properties, their as potential use as RAM's with 1 trillion bit/cm^2, which could be read 100 times faster than silicon and conduct electricity well.
A major problem with nanotubes is still to make them uniformly, reliable and in quantity, since structural differences can make a conductor to a semiconductor. Building molecular and nanoscale devices is a first step, but interconnecting these devices might be the even greater challenge. [7, 23]

Recently US scientists have made nano-scale devices they claim could one-day replace current transistor technology. The tiny devices called, "crossbar latches", are made up of a combination of crossed-over platinum wires with steric acid molecules set at their junctions. It is still some way off practical use and will certainly not be commercially viable in this decade.

Nanotechnology promises also to bring about new levels of technical progress through Nanoscale catalysts and filters, making fuel cells and Photovoltaics. Nanotechnology also offers major improvements through enabling the development of new drugs, diagnostic tools, and a great variety of other uses.

2.2.2 Molecular Electronics and Organic Material

More than a quarter century ago, scientists of Bell Labs suggested the use of molecules for electronics. Molecules are only few nanometres in size, and it appears feasible to make elements containing billions or even trillions of switches and components. This would enable small devices with supercomputer capabilities on your wrist or within your shirt. Molecular memories could have a million times the storage density of today's most advanced chips. If molecular computing on its own becomes feasible, it would mark a leap beyond silicon. Engineers could pack more circuitry onto a microchip than silicon ever dreamed of, and do it much more cheaply.
The first widely used molecular electronic devices will probably not compete with silicon devices; they are more likely to be sensors rather than logic devices. Also memory devices based on organic materials are under development around the world. However, molecular devices must not only

compete with a rapidly advancing silicon technology but as well with host of bi-stable materials systems also under development. They are only likely to be successful if their manufacturing costs are significantly lower. The solution might be to prepare many copies of the same molecule in parallel or in self-assembly concepts in which the shape of molecules dictates that they will form themselves in regular assemblages. [26]

But there are many problems still to be resolved as interconnection between devices, long time memories or defect correction, but the highly attractive price/performance of such devices will continue to instigate further research.

High carrier mobility organic thin-film transistors are comparable in performance to amorphous silicon. Potential applications are in large area electronics (e.g. electronic paper, print circuitry, displays, bulletin boards, and smart cards etc.). They can be fabricated on flexible substrates at low cost, as 100 million transistors in postage stamp size, or as large flexible plastic displays driven by plastic transistors or in futuristic sounding applications like a wall or car that change colour upon request. Organic electronics may also lead to circuits stamped on rolls suitable for small data volume and short time memory applications (supermarket, product labelling or maintenance tags) produced with ink jet technologies. Before its commercial use problems like adequate drive technology or its slowness of have to be solved.

These outlooks would include equally futuristic manufacturing outlooks like inkjet printer or "stamping" technologies replacing the clean room fabrication or a "fab-in-a-box" or chemical factory on a chip. [15]

2.2.3 Organic Materials

A wide variety of materials ranging from Rotoxane and Benzenetiol nitroamina (shown below) to Bacteriorhodopsin, Nitroaminobezothiol, OLEPs (Organic Light Emitting Polymers) and other bistable molecules are under investigation. The realignment within the molecule serves as reversible switch changing with the internal structure also physical properties.

Organic nanoelectronics has been again drawing attentions at the end of 2003, when IBM demonstrated an alternative method for microchip fabrication that used polymer molecules that naturally arranged themselves into hexagonal patterns. Sticking points remain lifetime of the devices, and their switching speed since, the devices work currently only for 100s of computing cycles, and switching speed is still many thousands of times slower than silicon technology.

The history of silicon technology has consistently demonstrated that all these obstacles and showstoppers of the past could be overcome by the ingenuity of researchers and engineers.

The argument that no exponential growth is sustainable forever is certainly true but does not automatically mean that there will be room for molecular devices to take over. Recent demonstrations of research silicon based devices approaching the size of few nm in critical dimensions, seaming to leave only economic costs as true roadblock Any new technology has only be scientifically appealing but also to meet and excel challenging yardsticks [22]:

- Intrinsic switching speed > 5 THz

- Power consumption < 6μW per MOP/s

- Reliability > 10^5 hours ~10 ys

- Cost < 0,5 mcents/logic gate

- Density > than 4x18^8 logic gates/cm2 and 10^{10} switches/cm²

- Cost < 50 ncents/bit per bit of memory

- Mass production capability (> 1Munits/day)

- Integration of logic, analog, RF, memory etc.

2.2.4 Spintronics

Spintronics can be defined as based electronics where it is not the electron charge but the electron spin that carries information.

The research efforts in spin-physics have dramatically increased during the past years. Spin-based electronics offers opportunities for a new generation of devices combining standard microelectronics with spin dependent effects. Semiconductor based spintronics could combine logic, storage and communications on a single chip.

Magnetism has always been important for information storage and information storage industry has provided the initial successes in spintronics technology. High-capacity disk drives using spintronics effect to read such data with will come within the next few years to the market, increasing storage density by 300%.

A spin device would have several advantages over a conventional since flipping spin takes much less energy and can be done much faster then pushing an electron out of a channel. There are even hopes for the use in quantum computing. Electron spin qubits interact only weekly with the environment surrounding them, principally through magnetic fields, which can be effectively shielded. [3]

2.2.5 Optical computing

Optical computing is attractive because it would solve several problems of silicon based computing, as the power problem, cross-talk interference, and the marriage of computing and communications. This is not just wishful thinking. In February 2004 demonstrated the photonics technology laboratory of Intel a modulator made from common silicon that can process one Gbits/sec making it 50 times faster then previous devices and being crafted on the high volume production line.

2.2.6 Quantum computing

Quantum computing is often heralded as the ultimate technology bringing about properties unmatched by any other technology. For this reason we discussed it at the IDIMT 2004, and gave it the special attention in spite of the rather low expectation that we will see a quantum computer in the next decade.

But there might be an application within near reach: quantum cryptography. In the eighties it has been proposed that as stream of photons could create unbreakable keys. If an eavesdropper attempted to observe the photons that act would alter the key making it thus impossible to steal and the receiver would know a breach was attempted. But it took until last year to transform it into a practical devise, when a company with the name MigiQ-Technologies Co. announced its cryptographic system.

How could a scenario for a roadmap for realization a molecular electronics look like?

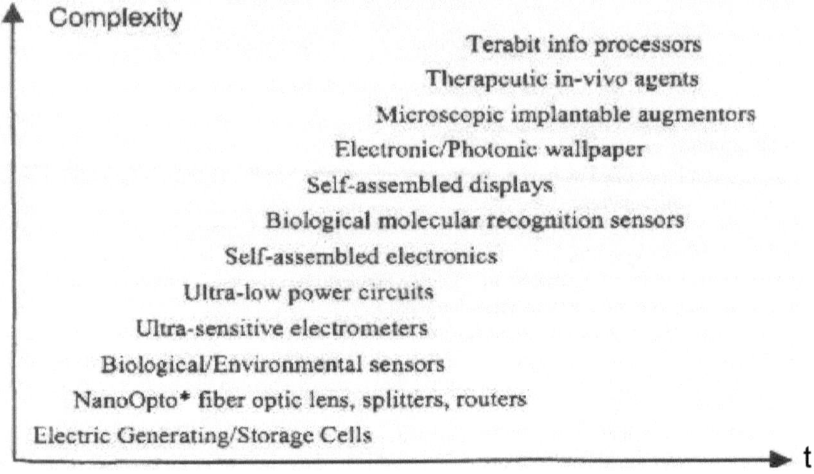

Complexity

Terabit info processors

Therapeutic in-vivo agents

Microscopic implantable augmentors

Electronic/Photonic wallpaper

Self-assembled displays

Biological molecular recognition sensors

Self-assembled electronics

Ultra-low power circuits

Ultra-sensitive electrometers

Biological/Environmental sensors

NanoOpto* fiber optic lens, splitters, routers

Electric Generating/Storage Cells

t

8]

3. Information Technology and our Environment

Microprocessors are increasingly playing a major role in the modern life. The use of microprocessors has increasingly perpetrated all kinds of equipment with computers being increasingly inferior in numbers but spearheading the technology. The use of microprocessors can be put in two classes: The "visible" ones used to build the different classes of computers, today mostly the personal ones, and the "invisible" ones used for controlling and monitoring machine tools, cars, aircraft, consumer electronics and many other electronic equipment. The class of invisible microprocessors is the most important one in term of the number of microprocessors in use. They are gradually changing the relationship we have with these devices. We might be at the beginning of this cultural evolution.

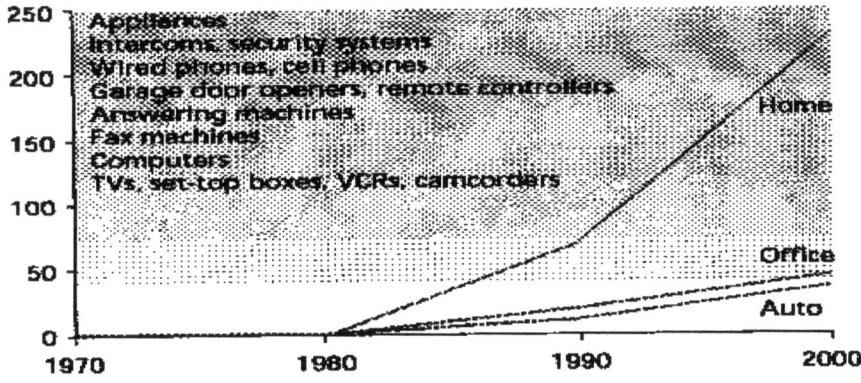

Micro processing's changing eenvironment [Source: Bell Labs]

3.1 The "Great Challenge Exercise"

The British Computer Society in a project called Great Challenge Exercise] tried to identify major directions challenges for the future. This inquiry resulted into seven proposals displaying an interesting perspective for computer technology and applications [11]:

- In Vivo - in Silico
- Science for global ubiquitous computing
- Memories for life: managing information over a human lifetime
- Scalable ubiquitous computing systems
- The architecture of brain and mind
- Dependable systems evolution
- Journeys into non-classical computation

3.2 The Networks and Sensors Revolution

The visible face of computing, the ubiquitous PC, is nowadays generally networked. In contrast, embedded computing systems have largely been stand-alone (e.g. in the brakes of a car), replacing analogue control systems. Increasingly, however, they may become integrated into a whole. Sensor networks are emerging as the next technological thrust in the global area ranging from simple video cameras to micro and nano-structures, RFIDs or hyper spectral optical sensors. These sensors are being imbedded in both ad-hoc and static networks that in turn exploit the Internet. Within the next decade these sensors might be shrinking to the size of sand corn will be scattered across farms, industrial parks, or battlefields. Attached to containers, train cars, trucks and all kind of goods they will become an invisible extension of Internet coupled with distributed or grid computing to handle the enormous data flood with but most traffic flowing from machine to machine.

Autonomous self-aware sensors, capable of gathering information about their physical and digital environment might recognize events, identify threats and take appropriate actions. Intelligent spaces will be created by positioning sensors in the environment, all wirelessly connected and capable of monitoring working conditions and access to restricted parts of the buildings by automatically sensing radio tags in clothing. Medical treatment could be more specific personalized, based on genetic make-up and factors such as age, and even delivered directly to our bodies by wearable devices.

Does this seem too futuristic? Not so, if one considers that already there are hundreds of embedded processors in modern cars, wireless 'motes' are deployed in environmental monitoring and industrial control, intelligent buildings are a commercial reality and first successes have been reported with 'medibots'.

What are the essential features of an infrastructure to support such a scenario?

Firstly, an Internet like enabling global connectivity, by means of wires, radio and satellite communications.

Secondly, each node on the network, either sensor or device, is capable of computation, communication and information processing, as it shrinks in size to the microscale, possibly nanoscale.

Thirdly, the devices should be increasingly self-aware, space and location conscious, able to interact with the surrounding environment and exhibiting introspective behavior and control. The size of the network, and the complexity of the interactions within it, demand that they be capable of cooperation, self-organization, self-diagnosis and self-repair.

Finally, trust, privacy, security and dependability must be assured, as the cost of malfunction or breach of contract can be very high.

This will lead to a new dimension of system complexity, as systems become more integrated more numerous, smaller and more deeply embedded, for example in our clothes and even our bodies. Faced with designing such populous systems, engineers can conquer complexity only by evolving scalable design principles, applicable at each level of population magnitude. The core of this challenge is therefore to abstract engineering design principles, reach via a process of 'build and learn' a more systemic point of view. [11, 24]

3.3 Function and Emotion

This combination builds upon the assumptions of on ubiquitous computing a future where progress is no longer driven by ever better performance of existing functionality of the electronic appliances, but envisaging an ambient intelligent world where the digital environment is sensitive and responsive to people some scientists envisage a world of "Layers of ambient Intelligence" [9]

The emotional dimension will become increasingly important. Designing an effective and appealing user interfaces or putting emphasis on emotional aspects has already become fully in line with marketing. But future will extend this concept. Just think of having a cup of coffee at Champs Elysees versus at the coffee machine in the office, or that a photo camera is for the user not a tool to take pictures but preserve memories. This shows that when computing devices become more and more invisible, it will be increasingly more important to find new ways to capture their values in selling experiences rather than products specs.

This paradigm change will create challenges :

- Data and content management
- Connectivity problems pervasive networks ubiquitous communication

- Trust, privacy DRM encryption and biometric identification at a more subtle level
- Interface technologies as speech or vision
- System level challenges as computational intelligence or contextual awareness and technical prerequisites as:
- Ultra-low power, short-range communication, tiny cellular system
- Displays everywhere ubiquitous flexible reflective displays
- Sensing and control
- Energy supply for autonomic devices [9,11]

3.4 Meeting the requirements for the future

3.4.1 The next 10% and their requirements

The future extension is not just improving technological specs at a cheaper price level but also extending horizontally the scope of use and users. To extend the reach for those technologies when talking about the next 10%, it means 10% od the world population, this means 600 million people, who have presently no access to the technologies we are enjoying since years. Studies show that the requirements are different, not so much for better performance but for enabling applications in the field of:

- Health care
- Education
- Political empowerment
- Communications

The access might be more appropriate via sharing technologies between users, an approach used before in Western countries for access to water supplies or phone etc.

3.4.2 Education requirements

There will request be an increasing need for information technology literates, not just in the Western world, to support future developments.

This should be seen in a global context may be characterized be the number of engineering student and therefore future engineers in China outnumbering the USA by a factor of ten, not to mention India and Pakistan, while European students seem to shy away from "hard core science and high threshold" studies.

Since these numbers and quantities can hardly be matches, quality seems to be the way for Europe to hold ground in these developments.

4. Summary

The dramatic increase in performance and the associated decrease in cost as well as the cross industry effects on productivity have had massive impacts on the economy.
Few other technologies ever had a lasting impact on economic development and our way of life.
Now as additional industries are entering downscaling and nanotechnology, one of the questions will be, if they can they can repeat the silicon story?
But the impact is not restricted to industrial and economic achievements.
The broadening from a specific to a systemic view is emerging. Not only from the hardware side expanding silicon technology into a mix of hybrid technologies, devices and uses but on a much broader scope the full impact of IT including communications in for of wireless and sensor revolution will imbedded us into a global communication skin.
We tried to make brief visit to the field of interaction between man and technology, function and emotion and its future symbiosis, the invisible fields of ambient intelligence and the extension from today's Internet to the "Internet of People and Things."
Is not a privilege to have the chance to witness and participate in these developments?

5. References:

[1]   Benshop, J.P.H., Vekdhoven, Limits and Alternatives to Optical Lithography 2004

[2]   CNN Technology, Top 25 Innovations 1/2005

[3]   Dyakonov, M.I., Spintronics, Univ. Montpellier, 2004

[4]   Eagelsham, D.J., Issues in Scale for Semiconductors 2003

[5]   Gelsinger, P., Intel Corp., 2002

[6]   Gershenfeld , N., Krikorian R., Cohen D., The Internet of Thinks, SciAm 10/2004

[7]   Gibbs, W.W., A Split at the Core, Sci Am 11/2004

[8]   Gorokin, H. and Tsui, R.K., Molecular Electronics a proposed roadmap to commercialisation, Motorola Labs, 2001

[9]   Houten, Henk van, The physical Layer of Ambient Intelligence, Philips Res. Labs, 2004

[10]   Hiramoto, Toshiro Extreme Future CMOS Devices using SOI Technology, IIS Tokyo 2004

[11]   Hoare, T., Milner, Robin, Grand Challenges in Computing, Brit. Comp. Society 2004

[12]   Iwai, Hiroshi, The future of CMOS downscaling, Frontiers Collection 2004

[13]   Kim, K., Koh, G., Future Trend in Memory Development, Challenges and Perspectives, Samsung, 2004

[14]   IBM Research, Nanotechnology, 2004

[15]   ISAAC, R.D., The future of CMOS technology, IBM J. Res. Develop. 44, No. 3, 2000

[16]   ITRS, International Roadmap for Semiconductors 2003

[17]   Kuekes, P., Williams S., Crossbar latch, Journal of Appl. Physics Feb,2005

[18]   Loesch, Chr. W., Trends in Technology, Proceedings of Euromicro 2003.

[19]   Loesch, Chr. W. Information Technology from Trend to Horizons IDIMT 2004

[20]   MagiQ Technologies, NYC 5/2004 , Sci Am, Dec 04

[21]   Moore, G., Moore's vision, Intel Corp., 2003

[22]   Nishi, Yoshio Future Challenges and Needs for Nanoelectronic from a Manufacturing Viewpoint, Stanford Univ.2004

[23]   M. Roukes, Plenty of room indeed, SciAm, 9, 2001.

[24]   Smith III, T.P.,Wireless Sensor Networks and the Sensor Revolution, Mc Lean, 2004

[25]   Theis, Th., IBM Research T .J. Watson Res. Centre 3 / 2003

[26]   Zhitenev, N.B. Molecular Electronics: Experiments, Device Concepts, and Architecture

IDIMT 2004

INFORMATION TECHNOLOGY FROM TRENDS TO HORIZONS.

Abstract

Silicon based computer technology has taken us through a period of exponential growth of technological capabilities but also to unprecedented side effects through cross fertilizing and enabling many other areas of science and technology. But as all phenomena of exponential growth, sooner or later this technology trip must come to an end as the technology is increasingly stretched to the limit.

The race is now already on to discover silicon's successor, since to the winner will not only come glory but also inconceivable profits. The search for the post silicon future has led to the exploration of extraordinary possibilities of nanotechnology and molecular computing as well as far-out options as quantum or DNA computing.

We cannot reliably predict many implications of such developments – but since they may shape our future, it could be worthwhile to review, discuss and assess some these developments and their potential impact on a plethora of fields ranging from science to society and economy.

1. Introduction

The impact of the technology revolution is reaching far beyond merely generating products and services, it changes how people interact and live. Increased miniaturization and sensorization of items as clothing, appliances, cars or housing will likely change the way these devices interact with our lifestyle and these effects are not to proceed without issue.

The realization of these possibilities will depend on several factors ranging from infrastructure investments to technology breakthroughs, the advancement of science and technology, and its social acceptance and will additionally vary around the globe, making forecasting additionally difficult.

Let us first peruse where we stand and where the scientific, technological, and economic thrust is going to lead us in the next years. Based on this assessment we will than look at the follow-on potential on the horizon of research endeavours.

2. Silicon Technology

The exponential improvement of integrated circuits has fuelled the growth of economy, science and of course the information technology for nearly half a century and it is obvious that this advance forever. But predictions of limits have been proven wrong in the majority of cases, since the predicted boundaries have been shifting nearly at the same speed as the improvements.

Not the increases in speed or density but that the increase of components and functions is greater than the increase in costs per chip is the key factor for these developments. The information revolution will therefore continue as long as cost per function is declining.

Therefore preference will be given to protect the investments in know-how and equipment and extend the current silicon technology to its limits. This is no constraint since such a development will result in continued exponential improvements and within the next ten years in equipment as PC's 10000 times as powerful as today's advanced models, using no keyboards being a conversation active machine with low power high density features.

The NTRS roadmap for Semiconductors provides a consensus scenario of leading experts of science and industry how parameters will scale today's devices. Additionally it shows impressively how all ambitious forecasts have been surpassed by the actual developments.

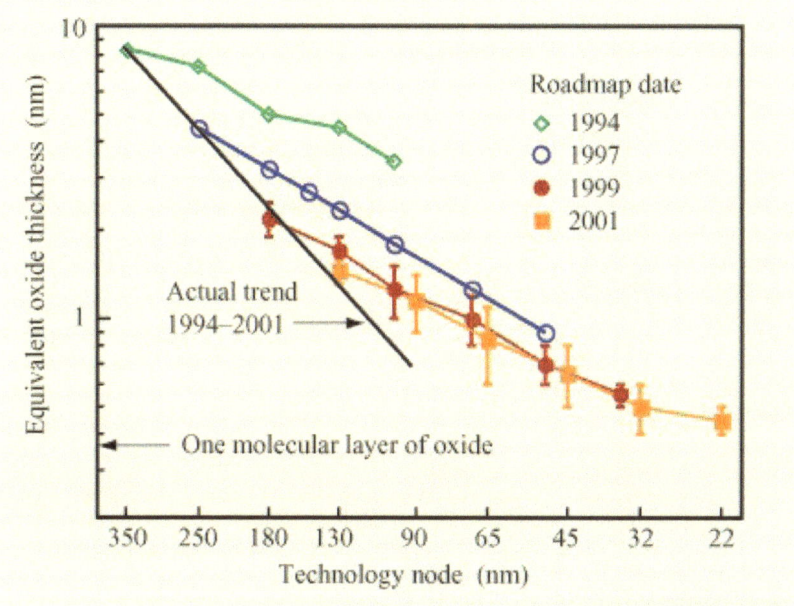

NTRS roadmaps for semiconductors and its adjustments

Decisive for these developments have been and will be:

- Lithography
- Design and Interconnections
- Architecture
- Cost

2.1   Lithography

Photolithography a key process of integrated circuit manufacturing is a combination of optical, chemical and micro mechanical processes to transfer geometric shapes onto the surface of silicon wafer. The steps involved in the photolithographic process are wafer cleaning, barrier layer formation, photoresist application, soft baking, mask alignment, exposure and development and hard baking. This technology is successfully used for more than a billion transistors per second, but it approaches two principal limits.

First for optical lithography – the current workhorse of semiconductor industry – the minimum feature size is closely related to the wavelength of light. Since we are already approaching the short wave edge of conventional optics but even shorter wavelengths will be necessary; but sub-100 nm patterns can only be made by x-rays and electron beam or E(xtreme)UV.

The second limit is cost. Just the tools to produce chips with features under 100 nm will cost up to hundred millions of dollars each. [9]

This explains the efforts to extend the familiar technologies to advanced UV lithography to its limits and explore in parallel improvements possibilities like improved energy management, low temperature operation, the use of superconductivity or materials as GaAs or diamond on silicon.

2.2 Design and Interconnections

System performance of the integrated functionality superseded the pure raw transistor performance as yardstick. Clock rate improvement is not entirely due to transistor performance but also to improved logic design. An optimistic case of continuing improvements would lead to 20+ GHz processors in 2010 and raising the number transistors on a chip from the 170 million (IBM POWER) chip marketed since 2001 to a billion transistor chip envisaged for 2010, or 4,3 billion functions for mass production in 2015. [16]

But there are fundamental limits, as e.g. the tunnelling of electrons since the insulators are 2-3 nm thick today and cannot become less than about 1,5 nm thick while pure extrapolation of the historical trend in dielectric thickness extends below a molecular layer of SiO_2 already in 2006.

2.3 Architecture

Designers of have used the increasing numbers of transistors to improve the performance of a uniprocessor core or by adding caches. Adding transistors to uniprocessor shows diminishing returns, SMP's (shared multi processor) increase the probability that the contents of a requested memory location is in the cache of another processor and thus causes additional traffic between the processors and memory. As a result many applications actually degrade in performance with large numbers of processors. Already years ago H. Grosh pointed out that the performance of paging systems actually decreases with increasing storage.

This has led to alternative architectural attempts as to exploit parallelism at multiple levels at various granularities and migrating from the von Neumann style architecture to cellular architectures and connection machines. Such architecture was proposed for a computer named connection machine, with thousands of processing elements with build-in connections between them or IBM's Blue gene a research computer presently under development, a system, with 32000 chips which may provide one petaflops of computing power.

This approach carries also some other potential advantages as each node becomes an off-the-shelf commodity, tools incl. programming development, testing and debugging programs and program libraries written for the SMP can run unchanged. Combinations of connectionist and von Neumann style of computing architecture would be possible and provide greater overall systems performance than processor performance alone.

In addition we are witnessing a development called lateral integration leading to future electronic elements featuring a mix of technologies on the same chip as high performance logic, low power logic, static RAM, RF, analogue, DRAM (Dynamic Random Access Memory), flash memories, MEMS (microelectronic electro mechanical systems), and a variety of sensors etc. on the same die. [22]

2.4   Cost

The exponential increase in transistor densities and processing speed is being sustained by a similar increase in the financial outlays for tools and facilities that produce these chips. Some expect equilibrium around 2015 - 2020 when a fabrication facility might cost up to 200 billion $. However, since the 90´s the increase of financial outlays to build the facilities has slowed from 20% p.a. to less than 15% p.a. due to better equipment productivity and a slower increase in the number of process steps.

2.4.1 Storage Technology

The pace of storage technology has accelerated to a 60% compound growth rate. Trends for the next few years show no decrease in the pace of technology improvement. Past attempts to predict the ultimate limits have been dismal failures. Today's best disk drives operate at 100 times of the predicted limit of maximum densities. However limits seem also here to be fundamental, like thermodynamics of the energy stored in a magnetic bit, the head to disk spacing only an order of magnitude larger than an atomic diameter or the intrinsic switching speed of magnetic materials or the superparamagnetic limit.

Parallel to the above-mentioned development of magnetic storage devices several other research venues are being pursued as holographic storage or Millipede memories.

2.5   Optical computing

Attractive features of optical technologies are the integration of communication and computing as the absence of cooling problems and cross talk have instigated research into this field.
The ultimate goal is to develop a technology for on-chip integration of ultra-small circuits that can manipulate light signals; similar to the way electrical signals are manipulated in chips. [7]

3. Nanotechnology

Today there is a nanophysics gold rush and scores of researchers and institutions are scrambling for a piece of action. Nanotechnology tries to create materials and system at a length scale of >100nm as shown below and in parallel exploit additional phenomena intrinsic to it.
Some sizing to put things into proportion:

1 Nanometer	10^{-9} (billionth) meter
Human hair (diameter)	10 000 nm
Feature of computer chip	180 nm
Protein, DNA	~ 1 -20 nm
Hydrogen atom	0,04 nm

We are only at the beginning to acquire the detailed knowledge of this future technology, where a complex and rich combination of classical and quantum mechanics govern the properties and behaviour of matter.

The ITRS Roadmap forecasts that by 2014 the minimum feature size will decrease to 20 nm meaning that each switching event will involve only about 8 electrons, so that accounting for single electron charges will become crucial.

The future potential of the current CMOS-technology (Complementary Metal Oxide Semiconductor) should not be underestimated since it is pointing to high performance processors with 20 billion functions and to mass production elements with 4,3 billions functions. However following 2015 limits will be encountered as interconnections between transistors might limit the effective computing speed, thermal dissipation in chips posing another increasing challenge (less a fundamental as an economic challenge).

Another challenge will be surfaces. When we shrink to nano-dimensions much of the foundations of solid-state physics, standing on the premise that the surface to volume ratio of objects is very small i.e. physical properties are dominated by the physics of the bulk, are changing significance. Nanoscale changes effect even classical properties as the melting point and forces as van der Waal forces become important with decreasing scale as illustrated by the surface to volume ratio of a Fe-particle of

- 30 nm particle has   5% of atoms on the surface while a
- 3 nm particle has   50% of atoms on the surface.   [19]

3.1 Microelectronics and Nanoelectronics

Microelectronics and nanoelectronics are different. Thousands of molecules, clustered together can carry electrons from one metal electrode to another. These clustered molecules can be used as on/off switches and might be thus usable as computer memory; it is a well-understood reaction in which electrons shuffle around within the molecule. In the "on"- position conductivity is 1000 times better than in the "off"-position and research is looking for molecules with better properties. The electronics might look more than a chemistry set with new ways of organizing and assembling might be required.

Researchers have created nanoscale electronic components as transistors, relays, logic gates, from organic molecules as well as carbon nanotubes and semiconductor nanowires. The challenge is to connect these components. Unlike the conventional circuit will the design not proceed from blueprint to pattern to chip but from a haphazard jumble of up to 10^{24} components and wires not all of them even working into a useful device.

The age of nanoscience has dawned but the age of nanotechnology – finding practical uses for nanostructures has not fully dawned yet.

3.1.1 Nanomaterials

One of the basic breakthroughs was the Buckyball and its derivatives.

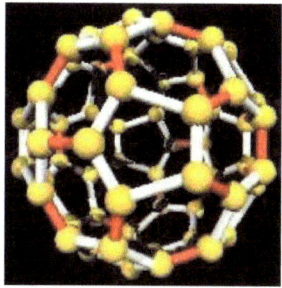

Buckyball or Fullerene (after Richard Buckminister Fuller), diameter 1 nm

A Buckyball or fullerene is a carbon molecule composed of at least 60 atoms of carbon arranged in a ball-like structure. Nanotubes are long drawn fullerenes. The carbon nanotube is the best-known example of inorganic wires, functioning both as interconnections and as components.

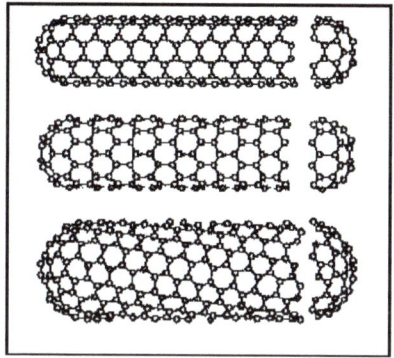

Different structures of nanotubes, Veld, TU Eindhoven.

Carbon nanotubes have been around since 1991, when S. Iijima discovered them. Scientists were excited about their unique qualities. Their astonishing physical properties as 100 times the strength of steel but only of 1/60 weight, as well as electrical properties, their as potential use as RAM's with 1 trillion bit / cm², which could be read 100 times faster than silicon and conduct electricity well made them attractive for intensive R & D.

There are critical voices asking if nanotubes are over-hyped since hundreds of millions of dollars have been awarded to research and developments at more than 1000 universities. Many see in this development not a development of its own merits but as a process that might contribute to prolong the silicon age by another decennium. Probably we are going to see a hybridisation between silicon and nanotube technologies. A major problem with nanotubes is to make them uniformly, reliable and in quantity, since slight differences can make a conductor to a semiconductor.

To overcome the unreliability of individual nanodevices the current work on defect tolerance architecture and self-assembly is critical to future nanoelectronics.

Building an arsenal of molecular and nanoscale devices is a first step, but interconnecting these devices seems to be the even greater challenge.

Nanofabricated devices also reach beyond the scope of computing devices as e.g. quantum dots/wires show. Crystals called quantum dots contain only a few hundred atoms, emit different wavelength of light depending on their size, and will be of use in various applications e.g. as ultra fine biological markers. [7, 28]

4. Molecular computing

Scientists of Bell Labs suggested the use of molecules for electronics more than a quarter century ago. Molecules are only few nanometres in size, and it appears feasible to make elements containing billions or even trillions of switches and components. This would enable small devices with supercomputer capabilities on your wrist or within your shirt. Molecular memories could have a million times the storage density of today's most advanced chips, leaving Moore´s Law a distant memory. If molecular computing on its own becomes feasible, it would mark a leap beyond silicon. Engineers could pack more circuitry onto a microchip than silicon ever dreamed of, and do it much more cheaply. A new and exciting science has emerged in the intersection of Computer Science, Physics, Chemistry, Biology, Material Science and Engineering.

4.1 Molecular Devices

The first widely used molecular electronic devices will probably not compete with silicon devices; they are more likely to be sensors rather than logic devices. In addition, memory devices based on organic materials are under development all round the world. Nevertheless, molecular devices must not only compete with a rapidly advancing silicon technology but as well with host of bi-stable materials systems also under development. They are only likely to be successful if their manufacturing costs are significantly lower. The solution might be the possibilities to prepare many copies of the same molecule in parallel or self-assembly concepts in which the shape of molecules dictates that they will form themselves in regular assemblages may be the solution. [33]

Molecular electronics also encompasses other potential devices as colloid storage or transparent magnet storage devices (where transparency would allow 3D structures) or devices using the molecular cascades like the "linked chevron cascade." [8]

But there are many problems still to be resolved as interconnection between devices, long time memories or defect correction, but the highly attractive price/performance of such devices will continue to instigate further research.

High carrier mobility organic thin-film transistors are comparable in performance to amorphous silicon. Potential applications are in large area electronics (e.g. electronic paper, print circuitry, displays, bulletin boards and smart cards etc.). They can be fabricated on flexible substrates at low cost, as 100 millions transistors in postage stamp size, or as large flexible plastic displays driven by plastic transistors or applications like a wall or car that change colour upon request. Organic electronics may also lead to circuits stamped on rolls suitable for small data volume and short time memory applications (supermarket, product labelling or maintenance tags) produced with ink jet technologies. Before its commercial use problems like adequate drive technology or its slowness of have to be solved.

These outlooks would include equally futuristic manufacturing outlooks like inkjet printer or "stamping" technologies replacing the clean room fabrication or a "fab-in-a-box" or chemical factory on a chip. [13]

4.2   Organic Materials

A wide variety of materials ranging from Rotoxane and Benzenetiol nitroamina (shown below) to Bacteriorhodopsin, Nitroaminobezothiol, OLEPs (Organic Light Emitting Polymers) and other bistable molecules is under investigation. The picture below shows as an example the realignment within the molecule serving as reversible switch changing with the internal structure also physical properties

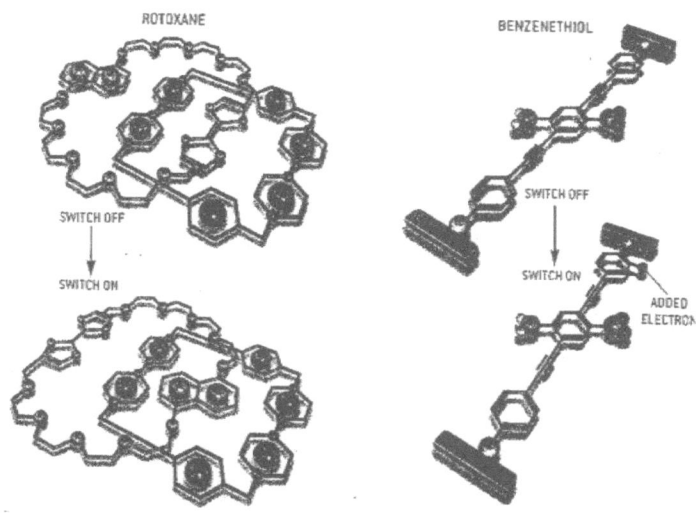

Molecular switches [15]

The two molecules shown above alter their atomic configuration and conduct electricity if the switch is on, and thus be potential building blocks for molecular transistors.

While pure "Molectronics" is still a long way off the hybridisation between silicon and nanotube technologies is a more near term possibility.

4.3   DNA Computing

A special alternative idea to silicon-based computing is DNA-based computing. Over the past fifty years discoveries have shown the extraordinary capabilities of living cells to store and process information more efficient by many orders of magnitude than electronic digital computation.

An example of this is recombinant DNA technology. In rDNA technology, processes inherent to living cells are used to analyse or modify biological molecules, and to select those with desirable properties. In 1994 Len Adleman, performed an experiment in which a collection of DNA molecules was constructed to represent possible solutions to a combinational problem (a simple instance of the Travelling Salesman Problem) and rDNA techniques were used to sift through the molecules to select the correct solution. Besides the novelty value, molecular computing has the potential to outperform electronic computers. DNA computers may use a billion times less energy than electronic computers, and storing data in a trillion times less space. Moreover, computing with

DNA is highly parallel: in principle there could be billions upon trillions of DNA or RNA molecules undergoing chemical reactions, that is, performing computations, simultaneously. [4] It is not surprising that DNA being tiny, cheap and fast, dense packaging and the potential of up to 10^{20} simultaneous operations does attract research worldwide. [15]

4.4. Molecular and Nanomanufacturing

Molecular manufacturing or nanofabrication research features two principal approaches:

- Top down: carving out of material or add aggregates of molecules to a surface
- Bottom up: methods which assemble atoms or molecules into nanostructures.

Molecular computing is in its early infancy but research has demonstrated basic capabilities, but still many questions are open as:

- suitable molecular building blocks must be found, which are stable physically durable, easily manipulated and to a certain extend functionally versatile,
- assembling of complex structures based on a particular design; economically using one of the approaches as AFM, lasers, chemical assembly techniques and
- systems design and engineering ,

have to be resolved. Some of them hold the potential of major shifts in manufacturing technology since they are suited to enable the integration of mechanical, chemical, and electrical components on the same chip; leading chemical manufacturing in the future not to order a chemical but a chemical factory on a chip.

5.   Quantum Coherent Systems (Quantum Computing)

 Scaling further down leads to the dimensions where quantum effects and phenomena of quantum physics as entanglement and quantum coherence will become more and more dominant. Let us look at some phenomena of the quantum world and their as potential relevance for computing and communication.

The first is the notion of quantum "state" as exhibited by the spins of atomic particles. Atomic particles have state also spinning clockwise or counter clockwise - but until that spin is observed, the direction is a probability of one direction versus the other. Thus a particle can be in two states at once; these particles are called qubits (quantum bits). Two qubits can be in four states and 20 particles in a million states. The quantum algorithms as the Shor algorithm have demonstrated that such devices can solve arithmetic problems as factoring numbers and search problems much faster than conventional computers by exploiting these properties of devices being in many states at once. In the steps that a silicon computer uses to seek a single solution for a complex problem, a quantum computer can explore theoretically all the solutions at once - if research will find methods to harness the power of these quantum devices.

The second phenomenon is entangled states. Two particles can have linked spins even though they are at a distance. Manipulating one particle and then reading the spin of the other linked particle is the basis of quantum information teleportation. This has been demonstrated in laboratory conditions and could to be a way to securely distribute cryptographic keys over distances.

The research challenges and rewards of quantum computing are enormous and to date only experiments with few qubits have been realized. The quantum computer would have the simultaneous read, write, and calculate capability, but new types of algorithms are needed that utilize being in multiple states simultaneously, and new devices invented that have coherent spin states immune to environmental hazards. These massive parallel computers would be qualitatively different to the traditional computer and will require new architectures and software for realizing its potential in applications as cryptography, searching large data bases, pattern matching and simulation of molecular and quantum phenomena. So the advantage of speed of quantum computing is counterbalanced by the above-mentioned unresolved problems and the questions of error correction, decoherence and signal input/output. [2]

Only future will show if quantum computing will be able to be practical and assume a major role in information technology beyond its scientific and intellectual attractiveness.
An impressive phenomenon and the application of quantum physics as a potential communication method is called quantum mirage. We are at a scale where the behaviour of electrons changes from particles as described in classical physics to wavelike behaviour as describes by quantum physics.

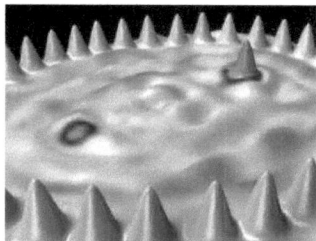

Quantum mirage, IBM Almaden Center D. Eigler, C.P.Lutz and associates

An example of this is IBM's new quantum mirage technique, which may prove to be a fascinating substitute for the wires connecting nanocircuit components as shown in picture 5 where 36 Co atoms on Cu surface forming an oval quantum corral are reflecting the copper surface electrons within the ring. When one single Co atom was placed at one focus a mirage including some of its properties appeared at the other focus where no atom exists. Will this be this information transport with no power dissipation in the transport channel? [8]

6.   Summary

Let a thousand flowers blossom
Mao Tse Tung

The richness of the nanoworld will enrich the macroworld. Presently we enjoy an oversupply of ideas. This richness comes in addition to the ongoing aggressive pursuit of downscaling leading the semiconductor industry from the micro into the nano-domain to Nano-CMOS supplementing the present technology.

We can look forward to a million-fold increase in the power of microelectronics at attractive costs, the integration of different technologies on a chip, and the expansion of the dynamics of the silicon-driven progress to other fields. This will enrich the scientific toolbox resulting in advances that combine the best of each world.

The microelectronic mould is now broken, but cost not only performance will to be the decisive criterion for future success.

The impact of this evolution is reaching beyond merely generating products and services, it changes how people live and interact. Increased miniaturization and sensorisation of items as clothing, appliances, housing or cars will likely change the way these devices interact with our lifestyle.

As technology becomes more interdisciplinary, education and training must adapt to enable participation in this development.

These effects might not proceed without issue. The pace of change is making it difficult for legal and ethical advances to keep up with technology. [3, 4, 6,34].

The race is already on to discover silicon's successor, since to the winner will not only come glory but also fantastic profits.

7. References:

[1]   Ph .S. ANTON et alii, The global technological revolution, RAND, 2001

[2]   R. BAJCSY, Quantum and molecular Computing, Comm. on Science U.S. House of Representatives, 2000.

[3]   J.BEBSHOP, Trends in Microlithography, ASML,AH Veldhoven Nl, Wiley 2002

[4]   C.BORCHARD and M.GROß, Was Bioelektronik kann, Wiley-VCH, 2002.

[5]   C.M.L. DNA Computing, SciAm 9, 2001

[6]   A. DELCHER, L.HOOD and R. KARP, Report on the DNA/Molecular Computing , Comm. on Science U.S. House of Representatives,,2001.

[7]   D.J.EAGELSHAM, Issues in Scale for Semiconductors 2003

[8]   D. EIGLER, IBM Almaden and San Jose Research Centres, 2000 and 2004

[9]   P.GELSINGER, Intel Corp., 2002

[10]   GORONKIN, Motorola Labs, NSF Nanosymposium, 2002

[11]   R. D. ISAAC, The future of CMOS technology, IBM J. Res. Develop. 44, No. 3, 2000

[12]   IBM Research, Nanotechnology, 2004.

[13]   J. JAFFE, Bell Labs perspective on global sc. investment, 2003

[14]   R. W. KEYES, IBM J. Res. Develop. Vol. 44, 1 – 3, 2000.

[15]   L.LANDWEBER, Beyond Silicon Computing, Comm. on Science U.S. H.of Rep.2000.

[16]   E.J. LERNER, IBM Research Magazine, No 4, 1999

[17]   Chr. W. LOESCH, Trend in Information Technology, Proc. of the IDIMT 2001.and
         Chr. W. LOESCH, Trends in Technology, Proceedings of the IDIMT 2003.

[18]   MANDELMANN, Challenges and future directions for the scaling of random access memory devices,
         IBM J. Res. Develop. 46, No 2/3, 2002.

[19]   MEYYAPPAN, NASA Ames Research Center, 2000

[20]   MIT Media Lab, IBM Systems Journal 38, no 2,3

[21]   G. MOORE, Moore´s vision, Intel Corp., 2003

[22]   R.NAIR, Effect of increasing chip density on the evolution of computer architectures, IBM J. Res.
         Develop. 46, No 2/3, 2002

[23]   A. A. NETRAVALI, Bell Labs Technical Journal, 1 – 3, 2000.

[24]   C.M.OSBURN et al., IBM J. Res. Develop. 46, No 2/3, 2002

[25]   R. POOL, IBM Think Research Mag. 3, 1999.

[26]   L. RABBINER, A glimpse into the future, ATT Labs Research, 2000.

[27]   GEORGE A. SAI-HALASZ, RAMAN G. VISWANATHAN, HSING-JEN C. WANN, SHALOM, J.
         WIND AND HON-SUM WONG, CMOS scaling into the nanometer regime, Proc. IEEE 85, No. 4,
         1997.

[28]   M. ROUKES, Plenty of room indeed, SciAm, 9, 2001.

[29]   R.R. Schmidt et al., High-end server low-temperature cooling, IBM J. R&D 46, No 6, 2002.

[30]   NASA improves computers with carbon nanotubes, Space daily, 2004.

[31]   G. TAUBES, IBM Think Research, No 1, 2000.

[32]   Y. TAUR, Y.-J. MII, D. J. FRANK, S.A. RISHTON, GEORGE A. SAI-HALASZ, E.J.NOWAK,
         SHALOM J. WIND AND HON- SUM WONG, CMOS scaling into the 21st century, IBM J. Res. Dev.
         39, No. 1/2, 1995.

[33]   Th. THEIS, IBM Research T .J. Watson Res. Center 3 / 2003

[34]   L.E. THURROW, Die Zukunft des Kapitalismus, Düsseldorf 2002

[35]   P. VETTIGER, M. DESPONT, U. DRECHSLER, U. DÜRING, W. HABERLE, M. I. LUTWYCHE,
         H. E. ROTHUIZEN, R. STUTZ, R. WIDMER AND G. K. BINNIG, The "Millipede" More than a
         thousand tips for a future AFM data storage, IBM J. R and D. 44, No 3, 2000.

[36]   H. - S. WONG, Beyond the conventional transistor, IBM J. Res. Dev. 46, No 2/3, 2002

IDIMT 2003

TRENDS IN INFORMATION TECHNOLOGY

Abstract

It is obvious that the continued exponential advance in the area of technology cannot be sustained permanently, but also predictions of limits have been proven wrong in the majority of cases. The predicted boundaries have been shifting nearly at the same speed as the improvements in technology. But the scenario is changing, physics until now our friend might become the foe as final limits and boundaries are getting more visible and closer.

Additionally we have to realize that we are dealing with an increasing plethora of technologies of different histories merging and enabling other fields of science in an unprecedented way, ranging from a as architecture (smart house) to z as zoology (cloning).

As economic force, the computer might be only at its beginning, becoming all-pervasive and multidimensional, encompassing technologies as sensorics, radio, nanotechnology and others or its extension to ultra-low cost components and devices.

Statements about the future - this paper might be included – have not only misjudged the pace of technology but also its impact on other fields of science, society, and economy.

In this session we intend to address the area of its title but as well pay tribute to the first letter in the title of the IDIMT 03 standing for Interdisciplinary and the meaning of technology as "systematic treatment of an art or craft" inviting contributions on status, interdependence and trends in other scientific disciplines.

1. Introduction

Any attempt to assess trends or future directions enforces learning modesty, in view of its interdependencies spanning the spectrum from philosophy to social sciences, biology and physics, to quote a few. Even restraining us to the field of technology results in an ample short-list of key technologies. Institutions reaching from the Japanese MITI, US Dept. of Commerce, German BMFT to J.Naisbitt or L. Thurow have identified a dozen of basic technologies congruently as the key technologies determining future competitiveness of the economy as the list shows:

Microelectronics
Computer technology
Health technology
Transportation
Biotechnology
Energy
New materials
Sensorics
Micromechanics
Aero/Space technology

Since even this short list would resist any attempt to be covered adequately within a reasonable timeframe, we have to constrain us to a subset [12, 41].

Fuelled by exponential growth of the capabilities of electronic circuitry and the communication fabrics that interconnect them, the technologic future promises a world of pervasive interconnections, customized products and services, and exciting new applications. Although singular projections hold few individual surprises, the totality of what looms likely just few years from today amounts to little less than a fantasy world.

Electronics industry volumes have already outperformed automobile industry volumes in 1998 and could reach 4,5% of the gross world product by the end of this decade and are projected to reach 10% by 2030. [1]

It is satisfying to report that after decennia of exponential growth another phase of comparable progress seem to lie ahead, so we might say "the best is still ahead", in spite of the fact that also limits and boundaries are getting more visible and closer.

2. COMPUTER and COMMUNICATION

2.1 Computer

Futuristic optimists could develop scenarios like:
Today's PC's can perform approximately 1 Mflops that is roughly the operational power of the brain of a lizard. Extrapolating for twenty to twenty-five years, given the continuation of the exponential growth rate, a PC would be able to perform 1 Pentaflops, that is in the range of the estimated operational power of the human brain. Or in other words, should in the next twenty years the growth in computing power correspond to hundreds of millions of years in evolution?
Some scientists forecast advances that would yield low-end computers more powerful than today's workstations for about the price of a postage stamp and in postage stamp quantities.

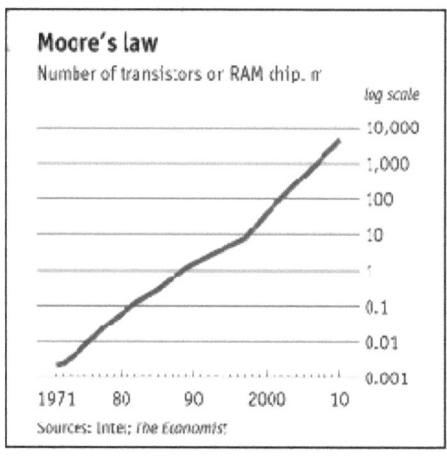

Moore's law
Number of transistors or RAM chip. m
Sources: Intel; The Economist

We do not have not to lean on scientific speculation since ongoing evolutionary R&D is providing with a scientifically founded scenario of comparable fascination.

2.1.1 Silicon Technology

The exponential performance improvement of integrated circuits, matched only by few other technologies has fuelled the growth of economy, science and of course the information technology for nearly half a century. It is obvious that this advance in the area of the transistor of the by the factor two in every three years cannot be sustained permanently, but predictions of limits of pace or size have been proven wrong in the majority of cases. The predicted boundaries have been shifting nearly at the same speed as the improvements. However, a look at the key processes supporting the development of the CMOS technology can give some basis for estimates on future potential. The pre-eminence of CMOS technology invites to take this particular transistor species as example. [14]

Not the increases in speed or density are the key factors but rather the rate of increase of components and functions is greater than the increase in costs per chip. Therefore, the information revolution will continue as long as the cost per function is declining. The NTRS roadmap for Semiconductors provides a consensus scenario of how parameters will scale today's devices.

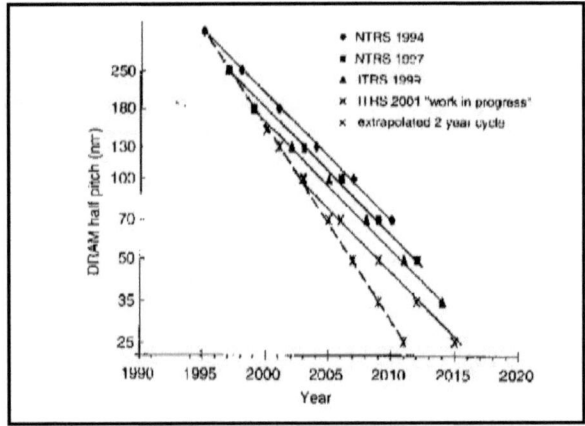

NTRS Roadmaps and its adjustments

Figure 2 shows that progress has outperformed forecasts permanently. However, there are no known solutions for some parameters and pure extrapolation of the historical trend in dielectric thickness extends below a molecular layer of SiO_2 in the year 2006. Areas decisive for these developments are:

Lithography
Design and Interconnections
Architecture
Cost

2.1.1.1 Lithography

Lithography determines the density of the patterns on wafers and is therefore a decisive element for the scaling of transistors. Once estimated to be limited to a >1 μm resolution, the industry has been moving to a 0,13 μm resolution in manufacturing by using DUV (deep ultraviolet) sources like excimer lasers. Moving to 0,13 μm lithography is marking also that features smaller than the wavelength will be patterned, using various techniques as off-axis illuminating and phase shift masking enable the patterning of features smaller than wavelength. Further progress below the 100 nm will require further steps to KrF (248 nm) and further to ArF (193 nm) excimer lasers or F_2 lasers (157 nm). At these wavelengths only few transparent materials are available to be used in lenses or masks. (Calcium Fluoride is a candidate, but it has less desirable properties too, i.e. a thermal expansion 40 times higher than quartz).

The transparency problem might be solved by EUV (extreme ultra violet) mirroring techniques, which could keep further downscaling past 2010 keep on track. [11]

This might mean that we have rarely been in better shape forecasting the future.

Alternative options investigated include non-optical lithography technologies, electron-beam lithography (electron wavelength of about 0,01 nm) or X-ray lithography, exploited for exploratory circuits by IBM at dimensions down to 0,15 μm using 1,1 nm wavelength synchrotron radiation, again involving the problem of lack of lenses and mirrors for these wavelengths and ion-beam lithography or hot electron emission lithography.

It remains to be proven that non-optical techniques will be feasible, meaning as well economically, that the cost of a new system is not greater than the derived improvements. Moore's law will be continuing as long as the cost per component is to declining over proportionally. [14, 39, 40]

2.1.1.2 Design and Interconnections

Two types of transistors have been competing since the late 40´s the bipolar and the field effect transistor. In the early 90´s the greater circuit density of CMOS circuitry transistors outweighed the performance advantage of the bipolar transistor. System performance of the integrated functionality superseded the pure raw transistor performance making CMOS the dominant circuit in production today and for in the next future. There is still a significant improvement potential ahead, but it's not an easy road to success. Let us address some specific areas:

Clock rate improvement is partially due to transistor performance and partially to improved logic design. An optimum case of continuing improvements in both areas would lead to 20 GHz processors in 2010. The increasing clock rate is shrinking the allowable space for a synchronized processor. For a 20 GHz processor the clock rate is 50 ps, so the space reachable by light in one cycle is 15 mm, assuming a medium different than vacuum it is 7,5 -10 mm. [20]

The tunnelling of electrons imposes fundamental limits. The insulator is 2-3 nm thick today; it cannot become less than about 1,5 nm thick; if the silicon dioxide layer is made any thinner electrons can tunnel through it at unacceptable rates. For 2004 the Semiconductor Industry Association (1999) forecasts the 1,5 nm insulators, equivalent to only 5-6 atomic layers.

Channel length is another key parameter. The shorter the less time the transistor takes to switch, but various kinds of so-called short channel effects suggest that the channel length cannot be much shorter then 23 nm that could be attained by 2010. Novel transistor structures might allow shorter channel length to be fabricated and but new materials are needed to enable higher performance for a given channel length.

Recently, there has been renewed interest in the development of BiCMOS, particularly SiGe-base BiCMOS, for mixed-signal system applications. The idea is that the CMOS devices will be used primarily for the digital functions, and the SiGe-base bipolar devices will be used for the RF and analogue functions. For these mixed-signal chips, noise isolation between the digital and the RF analogue parts is critical. SOI (silicon on insulator) or SOI combined with a high-resistivity substrate is advantageous for minimizing noise coupling through the wafer substrate. Once device isolation is not an issue, one can contemplate integrating various devices on the same chip. In particular, the integration of high-performance npn and pnp bipolar transistors and CMOS devices on the same chip will enable mixed-signal systems that provide higher performance and/or lower power dissipation. With the recent rapid growth of the wireless and communication system markets, research and development of SOI BiCMOS technology is likely to grow. [27, 44]

Silicon-on-sapphire (SOS) is seen as an alternative combining the advantages of SOI technology with others relevant to microwave circuitry, enabling in the form of thin film SiGe or SOS a new technology, that if fully integrated, would be attractive because of less cost, less power and less volume requirement and its compatibility to the Si CMOS IC manufacturing infrastructure. [13]

There are already new devices demonstrated like Terahertz-Transistor, featuring a depleted substrate transistor structure and a new high-k gate dielectric material, this experimental device can turn on and off one trillion times per second. [14]

Power supply voltage is critical. Addressing power we differentiate dynamic power, proportional to CV^2f (with C capacitance, V supply voltage and f clock frequency) and static power dependent on the amount of holding logic states between switching events. The nature of Si requires a minimum of approx. 1V. At present the level is between 1,2 - 1,5 V, which leaves room for one more round of reduction possible by 2004. [20, 31]

Threshold voltages of the transistor cannot be scaled down without lowering the operating temperature. Low temperature operations could lead to an improvement by 200% at liquid nitrogen temperature (-195°C), but cost and practical considerations will most probable continue to be prohibitive for large-scale use. With increasing difficulties of further scaling and improvements in refrigeration, low temperature operation might become economically feasible for high performance products at a cost to performance optimum in the range of –50° C.

Wiring is another constraint where the industry is moving from Al to Cu technology because of the lower resistance and capacitance; similar moves from silicon dioxide insulators (between the wiring levels) to low-k (dielectric constant) insulators are under investigation.

DRAM economics may impose a different scenario. If lithography or process technology becomes more and more expensive than justifiable by the resultant bit-density further improvements may not meet the economic test. Such problems have been predicted in the past for several DRAM generations, but never occurred yet.

Superior design can elicit more functions on a chip without increasing the number of transistors, leading to the thought that it could be more appropriate to transform Moore's law reference system into increased function instead of number of transistors. [14, 39, 40]

2.1.1.3 Architecture

Both transistor architecture as well as chip architecture are offering improvement potential, this "Moore by other means" endeavours as novel transistor structures encompass e.g. switch from metal gates to polysilicon gates, transition from diffusion to ion implantation, FinFET's double-gated FET's of IBM or Intel's tri-gate transistors.

There is confidence in improving further from the 2001 170 mio (IBM POWER chip) to the billion transistor chip envisaged for 2010, supported by wafer size increases to 400 mm² and to 800 mm² projected for 2008 or even sooner. This raises the new questions, how to use the billion-transistor chip and the space available effectively? Answers are opening fascinating and additional opportunities as:

- Embedding the memory subsystem on the same chip
- Multiple processing units on a chip,
- Heterogeneous systems on a chip
- 3D integration of active device layers to improve execution speed, power

Until now, designers of have used the increasing number of transistors to improve the performance of a uniprocessor core either through sophisticated micro architecture techniques or by adding SRAM caches. Adding transistors to uniprocessor trends to show diminishing returns. The proportion of transistors essential to the processing of each instruction has become a smaller fraction of the total number of transistors on the processor – many transistors are needed to ensure that added parallel units are busy. In order to improve the performance of widespread superscalar machines it is necessary to increase to the performance of the memory subsystem. Simply increasing the sizes of caches provides no return in small applications and diminishing returns in large commercial and scientific applications. Would the situation improve if the level of parallelism were increased by increasing the clock frequency through increased pipelining?

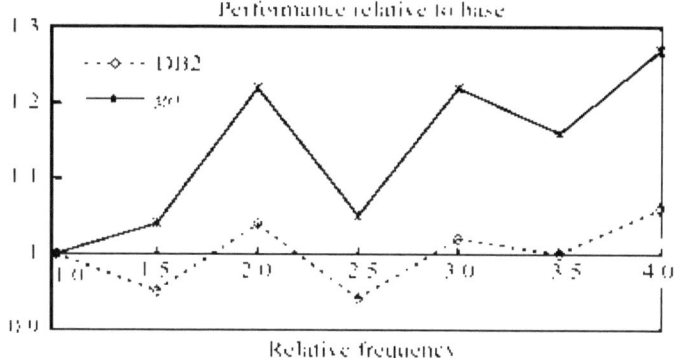

Effect of increase of pipeline depth on performance (R. Nair, IBM J. of R&D., Vol. 46 No 2, 02)

Little seems to be gained by increasing the frequency for the transaction-processing benchmark further. The complexities associated and problems like heat dissipation might be detrimental to increase the pipelining for workloads of this type. Asymptotic performance of the *go*-benchmark does improve with frequency but the fourfold frequency provides less than 30% improvement.

In many commercial applications the biggest detractor to good performance is the response time (latency) of access to the main memory, having increased over the years from few to several hundred cycles. Relief can be expected from reducing latency and increasing the bandwidth to memory by bringing memory and processors together on a die. However, until now technology has not allowed reasonably sized MPs on a die. By 2008 a 400 mm² chip would easily accommodate 16 processors running at >6 GHz or higher (each 5 mm²).

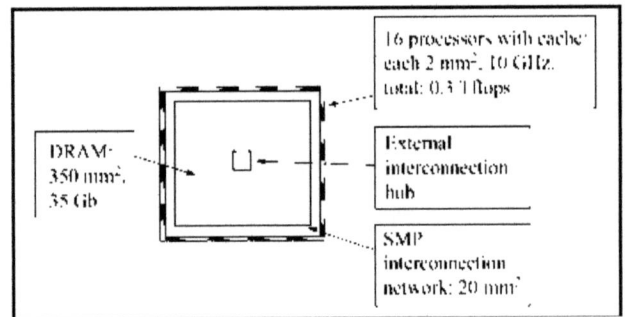

16 way SMP 10 GHz 50 mm² + 35 Gb DRAM (R. Nair, IBM J. R&D, Vol. 46 No 2, 02)

Problems arise from the fact that SMP´s (shared multi processor) scaling increases interconnections and cost as well as the probability that the contents of a requested memory location are in the cache of another processor and causing additional traffic between the processors and memory. As a result many applications actually degrade in performance with large numbers of processors. An appropriate future general-purpose chip may be therefore a small SMP (16 way) with a fair amount of DRAM rather than a large single chip uniprocessor.

Migrating from the von Neumann style architecture

Many researchers see the above-mentioned SMP 16 as potential architectural turning point. The separation of an expensive computing element from an inexpensive memory is a heritage of the von Neumann architecture. Von Neumann model provides a balanced machine in an economical sense as long as the cost-to-utilization ratio of the computing structure is similar to that of the memory structure. However complex superscalar processors are becoming increasingly costly to develop and less effectively utilized. The computing element is declining in its efficiency due to inefficient use of transistors and increasing latency to main memory, so processors spend more and more time waiting for data to move back and forward from memory.

Cellular architectures and Connection machine.

These findings have led to architectural attempts to exploit parallelism at multiple levels at various granularities. One of such architecture was proposed for the connection machine. .

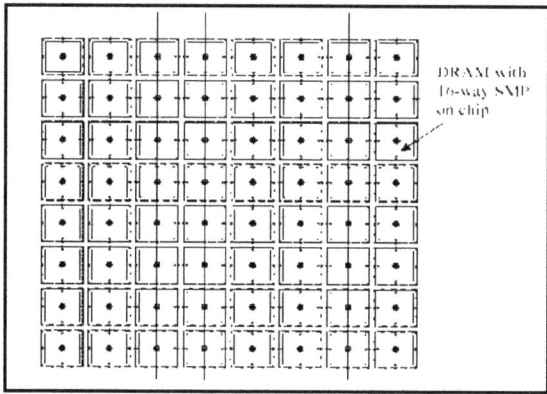

Cellular Computer with processors 256 GB DRAM, peak performance 20 Tflops each a 16-way SMP, (R. Nair, IBM J. R&D., Vol. 46 No 2, 02)

Thousands of processing elements with build-in connections between them, but the optimal interconnection needed between the processing elements configured by the application depending software.

IBM's Blue gene is a research computer presently under development. Based on 150 nm technology with relatively low memory requirement 8 MB DRAM, 32 Gflops, this system with 32000 such chips may potentially provide one petaflops of computing power.

This approach carries also some other potential advantages as each node becomes an off-the-shelf commodity, tools incl. programming development, testing and debugging programs and program libraries written for the SMP can run unchanged and combinations of connectionist and von Neumann style of computing architecture would be possible.

But there are challenges as well associated with, since with a higher level of integration the MTBF decreases unless redundancy is incorporated from the beginning. Reliable computation is a problem that has been already encountered with DRAM design (esp. manufacturing damages to cells) and more will by adding built in self-test structures (BIST) to test detect and reconfigure around faulty processors and around chip defects.

The billion-transistor chip, SOC and SMP.

SMP on a chip offers also an alternative to a billion-transistor uniprocessor by offering reduced communication cost between the integrated elements and providing greater overall systems performance than processor performance alone. It might feature and depend on a mix of technologies on the same chip as high performance logic, low power logic, static RAM, RF, analog, and DRAM. Before 2010, we might see the integration, flash memories, MEMS (microelectronic electro mechanical systems), FRAM (ferroelectric solid-state storage RAM) technologies, and a variety of sensors on the same die. To make SOC competitive it is important to allow to snap together items from a library of carefully designed and tested components, consistent design ways to create easily configurable SW development tools, debuggers, compilers and operating systems.

Success of this approach will strongly depend on the availability of configurable SW development tools, debuggers, compilers, and operating systems.

Convergence of processors

SMP on a chip could become low cost commodity and workhorse e.g. for game industry, low cost desktop WS at next level of hierarchy and a low cost interconnection technology could be the fabric for cellular organization using these commodity SMP chips. This development would consolidate the market for processors except the enabled microcontroller market that is already moving to adopt the SOC paradigm.

Diminishing returns from increasing the width of today's superscalar chips or from increasing the number of processors in today largest SMP's might also lead to shifts in programming paradigms but continuing to be based on the knowledge and tools of the last decades. [25]

2.1.1.4 Cost

Decisive for the viability of new technologies is cost reduction and including capital cost as well, e.g. the total cost of producing a silicon wafer must increase less rapidly than the density. The exponential increase in transistor densities and processing speed is being sustained by a similar increase in the financial outlays to build the facilities that produce these chips. Some experts expect equilibrium around 2015 - 2020 when a fabrication facility might cost nearly 200 Mia $. The rapid increase of the capital cost during the '80s of a silicon manufacturing line amounting to 25% p.a., led to concerns of the diminishing returns in cost per circuit. However since the 90's the rate of increase has slowed to less than 15% p.a. due to better equipment productivity and a slower increase in the number of process steps.

To overcome the impediments for the next rounds of improvements will require significant investments in R&D and technology:

- Optical lithography to new levels and possibly replaced by non-optical techniques.

- Transistor structures replaced with new structures using new materials.

- DRAM cells designed to unknown structures to achieve economically viable   increases in integration.

- Wires shrunk to a tenth of a micron dimension with novel dielectric materials in carefully designed hierarchies.

- Integrating more function on a chip to reduce cost further and increase productivity.

- Major advances in design automation and testing tools.

All these modifications and cooling (to -50° C) might keep progress going for several years but these tricks might be exhausted by 2010.

System integration might result in a performance increase by 500 % even if performance of the individual elements remains the same.

2.1.2 Beyond Transistors

The slope of Moore will change as it has changed in the past without significant impact on the industry due to the tremendous opportunities available for creative design and adding more function per number of transistors on a chip.

Scaling means also freeing room for new devices as MEMS, RF, antennae, fluids, wireless connectivity, selfconfiguring sensor networks, optical transmission and processing and also biological technologies [24, 26].

This does not come without major advances, e.g. wireless, to implement the ubiquitously radio on the chip we need about 5 different technologies as MEMS, little cantilevers to be used for switching (may be switching antennas), capacitors, filters, selectors etc. This means a dramatic reduction of size and cost of the passive components in radio circuits, or sensor networks, not only self-configuring networks, but a new class of sensors networks to be employed for applications like energy sensing, raising efficiency in manufacturing (motors that control themselves, structure who tell when they are ailing).

2.1.2   Post – Silicon

In the timeframe around 2020 the approaches mentioned in the chapters above will not no longer be able to improve performance further.

Opinions on a potential successor of silicon are divided. Some say there is no replacement for silicon or CMOS but with lead times between laboratory and production of more than a dozen years we have to get serious about new ideas. [20] Some lines of long-term research, novel materials and devices are:

- *Perovskites*
- *Nanoscale Computing*
- *Nanotubes and carbon circuits*
- *Molecular and supramolecular systems*
- *Organic computing/components (DNA, Proteins, Rotaxane)*
- *Quantum computing and others (e.g. Josephson junction, cold cathode emitters).*
-

There is no shortage but rather an oversupply of ideas of different realistic chances in the medium and long term. Let us now turn to the second key development arena the field of storage technology.

2.2   Storage Technology

The pace in the early 90´s of density doubling every 18 months, has accelerated to doubling every 12 months and will continue for the next future. But we let us also examine the physical phenomena that might prevent the continuation of the scaling process that served us so successfully in the past.

2.2.1 Magnetic storage

From the beginning of 1990 the development has even accelerated to a 60% compound growth rate due to factors as the introduction of magnetoresistive recording head, but also due to the increase of competition in the market, the transfer of technological leadership to smaller diameter drives with shorter design cycles, supported by VLSI high performance data channels and other electronics.

There are even industry specialists who attribute some of the increased rate of density growth to IBM's strategy to compete primarily through technology.

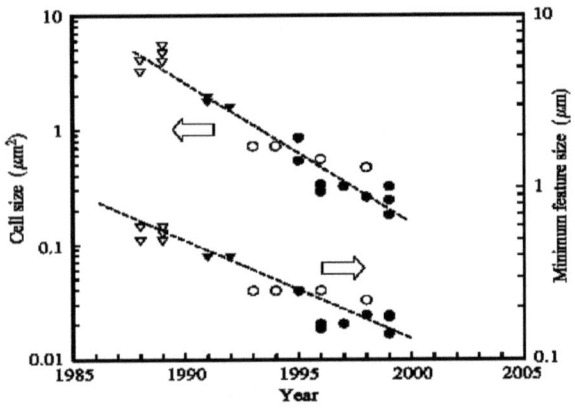

Figure 2

Progression of DRAM scaling.

The current trends for the next few years show no decrease in the pace of technology improvement, we might even expect an increase. Past attempts to predict the ultimate limits have been dismal failures (e.g. today's best disk drives operate at 100 times of the predicted limit of maximum densities).

Collateral achievements as "pixie-dust "are additionally contributing to further improvements of storage density. By placing 3 atoms thick layer of Ruthenium between two magnetic layers and can realize 25,7 Gb/cm² and 5 layers up to 70 Gb/cm².

However, some limits seem to be fundamental, since they include thermodynamics of the energy stored in a magnetic bit, with a head to disk spacing only an order of magnitude larger than an atomic diameter and the intrinsic switching speed of magnetic materials. These are only few of the problems ahead, for others solutions seem to be in sight, as the signal to noise ratio might be improved by tunnel junction heads giving a scaling potential beyond 40 Gb/in². [43, 47]

Another limit of rather fundamental structure is the superparamagnetic limit.This effect can be understood by considering a uniformly magnetized particle that has an anisotropy that forces the magnetization to lie in either direction of a preferred axis. At absolute zero the magnetization lies at one of the two energy minima (0° or 180°). If the direction of the magnetization is disturbed it vibrates at a resonance frequency but settles back afterwards. At higher temperatures, the magnetization direction fluctuates randomly at its resonant frequency with an average energy of kT and the energy fluctuating accordingly to well-known statistics and with each fluctuation will have a finite probability to exceed the energy barrier that exists at 90°. The average time between random reversals is strongly depending on the particle size (a factor of 2 in particle diameter can change the reversal time from 100 years to 100 nsec).

Today's densities are in the 10 Gb/in^2 range and if simple scaling prevails, superparamagnetic effects will appear in few years and become limiting several years after that. By deviation from scaling it can be expected to push the superparamagnetic limit from 40 Gb/in^2 to 100 - 200 Gb/in^2). [47]. Therefore to circumvent the superparamagnetic problem new approaches like perpendicular recording are investigated. [42]

Additionally a factor of 10 could be obtained if the magnetic grain count were reduced to one per bit cell, requiring a photolithographic definition of each grain or of a grain pattern (as used in optical storage disks). It might be difficult but possible, if also the economic i.e. cost side of patterned magnetic media can be solved satisfactorily.

After cost and capacity, the most important attribute is "performance" of disk storage, including access time and data rate. Since the disk drive data rate has been climbing faster than silicon speed this problem is most probably worsening and might lead high performance disks to decrease from 3,5 in. diameter to 2,5 in.

Both heads and media show a change of their magnetic properties below 10 ns switching time. When magnetic field is applied to switch it, magnetization does not start by rotation in the direction of the applied torque but it starts to precess like a gyroscope in a direction rectangular to the direction in which it is pushed and would spin around the applied field without ever switching at a frequency in the MHz-range forever. Since there is some damping it does end in the expected direction but this takes some nanoseconds with eddy currents producing fields in the opposite direction to oppose switching and slow it down.

The rate of improvement will slow down, but it thereafter, which is beyond about a hundredfold improvement of the present levels, but emerging technologies might start to offer potential alternatives.

2.2.2 Non- magnetic storage

2.2.2.1 Holographic storage

Contrary to magnetic and conventional optical storage techniques where information is stored as changes at the surface of the medium; holographic storage has the advantage of being a volumetric technique with potential of huge data rates. In holographic data storage an entire page is stored at once as an optical interference pattern within the material, by two coherent intersecting laser beams. The theoretical limit for this storage technique is in an area density of tens of Tb/mm^3. In addition holographic storage promises fast access times because laser beams can be moved practically without inertia, and by the inherent parallelism of its page-wise storage and retrieval large compounded data rates can be reached by a large number of relatively slow (therefore low cost) parallel channels. Distances between "head" and media are large and media are easily removable. A rather unique feature would be its associative retrieval, since imprinting a partial or search data pattern on the object beam and illuminating the stored hologram reconstructs all of the reference beams that were used to store the data. The intensity diffracted by each of the interference gratings is proportional to the similarity between the search pattern and the content of the particular data page. So the closest match to a search pattern can be found without even knowing its address. But significant problems are still the high component and integration cost characterizing most emerging technologies as well as the placement of the technology in the present storage hierarchy and its market acceptance. [2]

2.2.2.2 AFM (atomic force microscope based data storage) storage

The 21st century the nanometer will be likely play a role similar to the one played by the micrometer in the 20th century.

Emerging technologies can only qualify as serious candidates replacing existing but limited technologies if they offer long-term perspectives.

Such a candidate is probe tip storage. The implementation called "millipede", is based on the operation of arrays of atomic force microscopes (AFMs) and is capable of impressive large information density. One can even imagine extending the approach into an atom-level storage regime. [45]

2.2.2.3 Optical and other storage technologies

An overview of the near and mid-term future has also to include optical storage especially in the form of DVR with improvement potential through spot size reduction, magnetic superresolution and expanding into a third dimension by dual-layer extension, yielding to 20 –25 GB in the near future. [14]

3. Communication

We are already spoiled by getting used to exponential improvement scales but even steeper scales are characterizing the development of communications. Some of this development and trends are commonly called:

3.1 Law of Photonics

The cost of transporting a bit over a network is now decreasing by half every ten months and there is no end in sight.

Results and prospects are promising and laboratory tests show paradigm changes as:

- from one laser for one wavelength, to one single laser for all wavelengths needed, or
- sending 160 Gb/s over >300 km without any repeaters.
- In addition to optical capacity for single fiber doubling every ten months, further acceleration is coming from Dense Wavelength Division Multiplexing (DWDM) increasing the number of modes supported on a single fiber to hundreds or thousands.
- One fiber could carry as many as 15000 wavelengths on single strand.
  Up to 1000 Tbit/sec over fiber seem reachable within ten years.
- Integration of electronic and photonic components eliminating the bottleneck to convert signals from optical to electronic and back to optical as well as micro-electromechanical systems faster then as electronic switch capacity or developments. [11,30,33]

These developments have become know as the "law of photonics".

3.2 Bandwidth

The costs per bit of global communication have dropped by three orders of magnitude or bandwidth has increased by the factor 10^3 in the last ten years and will continue to do so if required.

This is a modest estimate, since cyberspace enthusiasts project annual tripling of bandwidth over a 25 years period. However, even in the modest case, assume one billion on-line households each of them able to command more communication capacity than the entire Internet offered its users when it when global.

Bandwidth will not only become cheap but might even become to cheap to meter. [26, 30]

3.3 A "Global Communication Skin"

The pervasiveness of C & C might lead to an extrapolation only short of science fiction, to a "global communication skin." The "global communication skin" might not only consist of the network of networks but also comprise countless sensors and other devices connected to it. Highly directional smart antennas and advanced signal processing will complete the connection. The interfaces will become so cheap that anything that can be connected to the network - such as thermostats, pressure gauges, pollution detectors, cameras, alarm systems, household appliances, and automobiles. They will also gather information, monitoring people's hearts, children, pets, cars, the traffic, homes, and the environment. In addition, all that with single universal natural addresses with individualized applications and services (P2P) in an open but secure environment.

Internet, telecommunications, broadcast entertainment, as well as tele-sensoring will converge into a single environment.

The work done over the next decade might have greater impact on people's life then anything that happened in the last century of communication history [26,41].

4.   Further Scenarios

Double speed at half the price will not be sufficient to satisfy the users of the future. Cost might even decrease more dramatically. The Billion-transistor chip for less than 100 $ is not beyond reach. The slope for cost of bandwidth is extending to other elements as well. Just within last few years transponder prices fell from 40k$ to 2k$, interconnects on CMOS and SiGe bases from several thousands to 100$, filters will fall from 10k$ to pennies when on the chip. The dimensions are moving from to count to complexity and on to convergence. [25, 39]

Other R & D avenues as ink-jet printing circuits in high volume at ultra low cost and all this programmable or plastic screen technologies might even lead to produce electronic circuitry with wall-paper-abundance thus enabling all pervasive ultra-low cost devices. Research is continuing to use inkjet printing to fabricate plastic transistors, similar to the e-ink efforts currently on going. [33]

Potential for these of areas of development is not anymore one-dimensional. R & D in the area of organic computing have brought potential areas of extremely low cost high volume interfaces and devices into future reach. Combine this with the power and innovation of silicon technologies into integrated electronics and photonics capabilities, with ubiquity of networks and optical connections future, equipped with rf on every chip, sensors and sensor networks and optical technologies as optiprocessor (or opti-puter). You will arrive at a scenario with utopian features suddenly not looking so utopian anymore as smart farmlands or "intelligent" medicine or computing tags.

 But challenges remain as manufacturing techniques need to be developed and critical metrics like power consumption, performance and reliability satisfied, before they can emerge as preferred choice in applications and computing elements and displays.

But we might also be heading to live in a glass-village. Except for those willing to go to much trouble and expense large portions of what we regard now as privacy might diminish greatly or disappear altogether. [26, 30]

5. Predictions Revisited

Each of the projections presented holds few revolutionary surprises, but the total or better the product of what we have perused in the previous chapters and looms likely in few years amounts to little less than another decennium of impressive developments.

Not too long ago it took three years to move the Intel 486i from 25 MHz to 50 MHz, today we are adding 25 MHz a week and in few years, it will be 25 MHz a day.

We can look forward to an million-fold increase in the power of microelectronics, further empowered by the "law of photonic"-driven communication technology developments, and all this at very attractive costs with a new dimension added by the integration of different technologies on a chip, introducing the dynamics of silicon-driven progress into other fields moving from count to complexity and convergence on a single chip. [39]

After decennia of exponential growth another phase of comparable progress seems to lie ahead, so we might say " the best is still ahead", and this in a even richer and more multidimensional scenario as ever envisaged, but also serious and difficult problems have to be overcome, as final limits and boundaries are getting more visible and closer.

Prediction about the future - this paper might be included - have often underestimated the ingenuity of scientists and engineers thereby the pace of technology and as well as its impact on human society, since many developments starting out as evolutions have finally changed the fundamental fabric of their host society.

It would be gratifying if some contributions to the IDIMT 03 can shed light on some of these facets.

6.   References:

[1]   Annual Report 2000 on the Semiconductor Industry, Industrial Res. Institute, Hsinchu, 2000.

[2]   J. Ashley, M.-P. Bernal, G. W. Burr, H. Coufal, H. Guenther, J. A. Hoffnagle, C.M. Jefferson, B. Marcus, R. M. Macfarlane, R. M. Shelby, and G. T. Sincerbox, Holographic Data Storage, IBM J. R&D 44 , No 3,2000.

[3]   Battelle Memorial Institute, Innovation, Strategic Technologies for 2020, 1999.

[4]   J.Bebshop, Trends in Microlithography, ASML,AH Veldhoven Nl, Wiley-Interscience 2002

[5]   Bell Labs Technology, Vol. 4, No.2, 2000.

[6]   B. Beyers, Die Zukunftsmacher, Campus N.Y München, 1999.

[7]   J. F. Bobo, F. B. Mancoff, K. Bessho, M. Sharme, K. Sin, D. Guarisco, S.X. Wang and B.M. Clemens, Spin dependent Tunnelling Junctions with hard magnetic layer pinning, J. Appl. Physics 83, 1998.

[8]   M. Dertouzos, What will be, Harper Collins, Springer. 2000.

[9]   W. D. Doyle, S. Stinnett, C. Dawson, and L. He, Magnetisation reversal at high speed,   J. Magn. Soc. Jpn. 22, 1998.

[10]   Economist, Bioinformatics the race to computerize biology, 2002

[11]   P.Gelsinger, Intel Corp., 2002

[12]   M.Horx, Die acht Sphären der Zukunft, Signum, 2000.

[13]   P.R. de la Houssaye and I. Lagnado, ‚Silicon...beyond Silicon, SPAWAR Syst.Center, San Diego,

[14]   H.v.Houten, Evolution of Optical Data Storage, Philips Research Labs, Eindhoven, 2001.

[15]   R. D. Isaac, The future of CMOS technology, IBM J. Res. Develop. 44, No 3, 2000.

[16]   D.Isenberg, The rise of the stupid network, Computer telephony, 8/1997.

[17]   H.Kirchner, Technologische Grundlagen, IBM Lab Böblingen, 1991.

[18]   R. W. Keyes, IBM J. Res. Develop. Vol.44, 1 – 3, 2000.

[19]   R. Kurzweil, The age of spiritual machines, Viking Press London, 1999.

[20]   E. J. Lerner, IBM Res Mag., No 4,1999

[21]   Chr. W. Loesch, Trends in Business, Technology and R&D, Proceedings of the IDIMT, 2001.

[22]   Mandelmann, Challenges and future directions for the scaling of random access memory devices, IBM
            J. Res. Develop. 46, No 2/3, 2002,

[23]   R. McGinn, Lucent Chairman

[24]   MIT Media Lab, IBM Systems Journal 38, Nos 2 and 3, 1999.

[25]   R.Nair, Effect of increasing chip density on the evolution of computer architectures, IBM J. Res.
            Develop. 46, No 2/3, 2002

[26]   A. A. Netravali, Bell Labs Technical Journal, 1 – 3, 2000.

[27]   T.H. Ning, Why BiCmos and SOI BiCMOS

[28]   OECD, Information Technology outlook 1997, OECD Paris, 1997.

[29]   C.M.Osburn et al., IBM J. Res. Develop. 46, No 2/3, 2002

[30]   A. Penzias, Bell Labs Technical Journal, p 155 – 168,1997.

[31]   R. Pool, Think Research Mag. 3, 1999.

[32]   N. Postman, Technopoly, Vintage Books,N.Y.,1993.

[33]   L. Rabiner , A glimpse into the future, ATT Labs Research, 200.

[34]   J. Rifkin, The age of access, Putnam N.Y., 2000.

[35]   George A. Sai-Halasz, Raman G. Viswanathan, Hsing-Jen C. Wann, Shalom, J. Wind and Hon-Sum
            Wong, CMOS scaling into the nanometer regime, Proc. IEEE 85, No. 4, 1997.

[36]   R.R. Schmidt et al., High-end server low-temperature cooling, IBM J. Res. Develop. 46, No 6, 2002

[37]   P.M. Soloman, IBM T.J. Watson Res.C'tr,Yorktown Heigths

[38]   B. Sellin, Aventis Forum Uni München, 12, 2000.

[39]   Y. Taur, D. A, Buchanan, Wei Chen, D. J. Frank, Kh. E. Ismail, Shin-Hsien Lo, G. A. Sai-Halasz , R. G. Viswanathan, Hsing-Jen C. Wann, S., J. Wind ang Hon-Sum Wong, CMOS scaling into the nanometer regime, Proc. IEEE 85, No.4,,1997.

[40]   Y. Taur, Y.-J. Mii, D. J. Frank, S.A. Rishton, G. A. Sai-Halasz , E.J.Nowak, , S..J. Wind and Hon-Sum Wong, CMOS scaling into the 21st century, IBM J. Res. Develop. 39, No.1/2, 245-260, 1995.

[41]   T. N. Theis, The future of Interconnection Technology, IBM J. Res. Develop. 44, No 3, 2000.

[42]   D. A. Thompson The role of perpendicular recording in the future of hard disk storage, J. Magn. Soc. Jpn. 21, Suppl. S2, 1997.

[43]   D.A. Thompson and J.S. Best, The future of magnetic data storage technology, IBM J. Res. Develop.44, No 3, May 2000.

[44]   J.W. Toigo,. Scientific Am., May 2000.

[45]   P. Vettiger, M. Despont, U. Drechsler, U. Düring, W. E. Haberle, M. I. Lutwyche, H. E. Rothuizen, R. Stutz, R. Widmer and G. K. Binnig, The "Millipede" More than a thousand tips for a future AFM data storage, IBM J. Res. Develop. 44, No 3, 2000.

[46]   C.C.Walton, P.A. Kearney, P.B. Mirkarimi et al. EUV lithography reflective mask technology, SPIEE emerging lithography. Techn. IV,Vol.3397,496 (2000)

[47]   D. Weller and A. Moser, The thermal effect limits in ultrahigh density recording, IEEE Trans. Magn. 35, 1999.

[48]   R. L. White, R. M. H. New, and R. F. W. Pease, Patterned Media: A viable route to 50 Gbit/in^2 and up for magnetic recording?, IEEE Trans. Magn. 33, 1997.

[49]   H.-S Wong, Beyond the conventional transistor, IBM J. Res. Develop. 46, No 2/3, 2002

[50]   W. Zulehner, Historic overview of Si crystal pulling development, Materials Sci Eng 1373,7 (2000)

IDIMT 2002

SAFETY, SECURITY and PRIVACY IN IS / IT

1. Introduction – Status and Scenario

Everybody is aware of the importance and contribution IS/IT are making. As for all valued assets is their safety and security of paramount importance and so becomes their defense. Today most governments, businesses and many individuals are depending on the integrity of their computer systems and networks. Hardware and software problems are not new and known since more than half a century and MTBF and similar measures are familiar to those in relationship with these industries. However, hardware and software have always been and continue to be „hurt and hurting technologies" as some incident remind us:

- Venus mission Marines failure

- US early warning system 1979-1980 triggering 140 wrong nuclear attack alarms

- Wall Street black Friday Institutional Investors sold 'automatically' for 2 billion $

Nevertheless, obviously we have been able to contain these problems and to live with it and in spite of this IT/IS have taken an unprecedented upraise. What has changed?
Has Gerhard Chroust's, idea proposing this subject had the quality of a farsighted prediction, months before Microsoft after nearly 25 years of writing software code will stop writing code for a month and try to close security holes in their existing products. [6]

The reason might be found in the additional dimensions of safety, security and privacy exposures have developed over the last years. Transactions and data are increasingly vulnerable to assaults from both casual and malicious sources.

In view of the level of knowledge represented in IDIMT, we will of course abstain from describing extensively the general basic spectrum from viruses to Trojan horses and firewalls and rather focus on some areas of special relevance.

2. Security and Technology

In the early days of computing, computer security was of little concern. The first computer security problems, emerged in the 1950's, when computers began to be used for classified information, and the primary threats were espionage, computer security was primarily a military problem. By the late 1960's, the sharing of computer resources and information across networks, presented additional security problems and potential avenues of attack that could not generally be secured physically. Disclosure of information was no longer the only security concern. Added to this was concern over maintaining the integrity of the information.

When the economic scale of financial losses reached threatening dimensions, an additional dimension was added. The CSI / FBI Survey of 2002 of government, academic and commercial institutions in the sentative but gives an indication of structure and size of the problem. [24, 25]

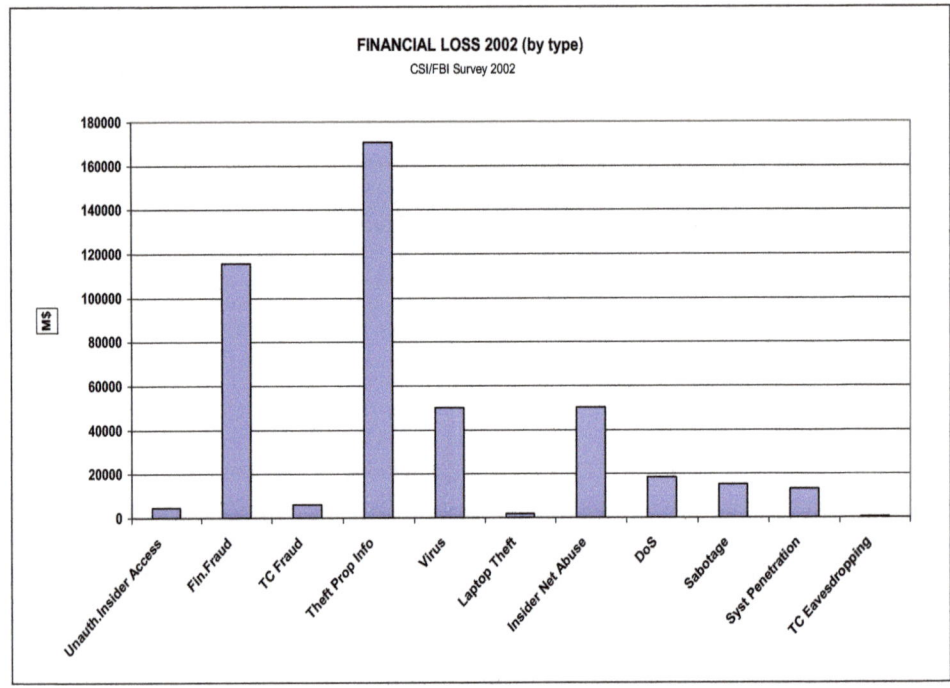

This triggered a higher level of attention and awareness and finally yet importantly a higher level of allocation of resources at the user level parallel to creating a business opportunity.

A plethora of shortcomings characterize the present scenario:

- The increasing number of warnings, updates and complexity, (complexity being the main enemy of safety)
- Attitudes like "install hundreds of patches and call the system secure."
- Hotline load e.g. MS HQ in Redmond receiving 40 000 calls per day
- CERT's documented 130 cases in '89, 3734 cases in '98 and 21700 cases in 2000. [18]
- The exponential growth of registered known viruses as stated by McAfee with 57000, Symantec 74500 and Sophos 61000 viruses.

- IT safety and security business showing in midst of the stagnation of IT industry a growth of 22% last year and may reach 7 billion $ in 2004.

But security continuous to be and will always be predominately a people problem

17% technical failures 16% sabotage, viruses, etc. 67 % human failure >60% data integrity attacks   from inside the network

2.1 Exposures and Countermeasures

2.1.1 Hardware

Hardware reliability is a familiar problem both for computers and communications equipment. Here a successful arsenal of measures on various levels has been developed to ensure availability and minimize threats to the level of service. Examples of such measures to protect the level of service are configuration redundancy, (coupling, tandem etc.), hard and software embedded with digital signatures verified before execution, dynamic reconfiguration, graceful degradation, site hardening. Nevertheless, there is the new phenomenon appearing mini and microcomputers with millions of poorly educated users. Will they be at risk in the near future, or will we be, by integrating them into networks? This might become relevant because of the "Moore progression" of pushing the transferal of the role of today's PCs to smaller portable equipment. What will 387000 laptops stolen and 250 000 mobile phones lost on airports in the US only mean for security in the future? With a password, inflation leading to 70 % of help desk calls related to passwords or a productivity loss of 44 h / year for password, login etc.

The objective is still to reach optimal security with minimal costs. However, the defence against viruses etc. will become much more complex and expensive. Who is willing to spend 10 % or more of his budget for safety for security in the long run?

2.1.2 Software

"One of the most dangerous things that can be done with a computer connected to the Internet is to download an arbitrary piece of software."
The entire idea of network computing is based on the idea of well-written and well-intended software, but the average of one error per 5000 lines of code, has to be seen in context of e.g. Windows 2000 with 50 million lines of code.
Below some facts, illustrate the problem:

- 75% of all complex software systems do not function on due date and on average are

- 50% cost over plan and

- 33% stopped before completion

- The "everything beta" effect, applications depending on beta test code only.

- The "Vendor sponsored incompatibility" effect, using a standard as a market share   lever,

- The "security in V 2.0 "effect.

The lifetime of a product is often short; many products are unsuccessful - so why invest much into security in the first place. However, if the product is successful and builds rapidly a large installed base, it is difficult to add security in a later version,

or let us look at availability of systems. [14]

Availability of systems		
Server 4.0	98,0 %	10000 min / yr
Server 4.0 + SQL server	99,01%	5000
Server 4.0 + SQL server + nonstop SW (Tandem-Compaq)	99,8%	1000
Server 4.0 + SQL+ nonstop SW (Tandem-Compaq)+ ns kernel	99,98%	200

From a theoretical point of view, the security and vulnerability problem related to executable or active content arises because there is no fundamental difference between a program and data components. This relates to John von Neumann's fundamental principle that programmes and data are treated equally and stored in the same memory, thus allowing programmes to modify both data and programmes and itself.

Proliferation of viruses

The proliferation of viruses has lead to a virus-count high in the five-digit figures as stated above (of which estimated 10% are from Bulgaria), but also including also very 'effective' viruses as e.g. the Dark avenger virus. In the future countermeasures will be eased by the expiration of patents in this area, but future viruses will be even more dangerous by becoming Internet-based, self-updating, and metamorphous. Corresponding assumptions may be valid for Worms, Trojan Horses, Brute force or DDoS attacks, or fraudulent programs.

2.1.3 Communications Systems

ECHELON

The public debate on Communications systems security has sparked the setting up of a Temporary Committee of the European Parliament investigating an interception system known as 'ECHELON'. This system differs from other intelligence systems in that it possesses three features that make it quite unusual: First, the capacity to carry out quasi-total surveillance. Satellite receiver stations and spy satellites in particular are alleged to give it the ability to intercept any telephone, fax, and Internet or e-mail message sent by any individual and to inspect its contents. Second,

ECHELON is said to operate worldwide based on cooperation among several states (UK, USA, Canada, Australia and New Zealand), to ensure that both sides of a dialogue in international communications can be intercepted. Third, it operates in a largely legislation-free area. Systems for the interception of international communications are not usually targeted at residents of the home country. The person whose messages were intercepted would practically have no domestic legal protection, not being resident in the country concerned. Parliamentary supervision would be inadequate, since the voters, who assume that interception 'only' affects people abroad, would not be particularly interested in it, and elected representatives chiefly follow the interests of their voters. The hearings held in the US Congress concerning the activities of the NSA were confined to the question of whether US citizens were affected by it, with little concern expressed regarding the existence of such a system in itself. [3]

CLIPPER CHIP

The Clipper Chip is a cryptographic device promoted by the U.S. government. Its purported advantage is that it provides a standard for securing private voice communication. With Clipper, however, the government has the opportunity to obtain decryption keys that are held in escrow by two government agencies. Although the Clipper proposal requires legal authorization to obtain these keys, the existence of this "back-door" decryption channel is a cause for concern.

After the announcement by the US Government originally planned for safe telephones a

Public and customers have not accepted crypto chip with possible listing in potential. An alliance of computer manufacturers and civil rights organizations as CFSR formed against it. J. Gage (SUN) summed the industry position up „You are asking us to ship millions of computers abroad with a stamped „J. Hoover inside" We refuse to do it." [22]

However, this attitude might have changed after September 11, 2002 as reflected in the Patriotic Act legislation.

DOT PROGRAM

Washington Post reported of (DOT) Department of Transportation plans for a "trusted traveler" program for airline passengers to Track, Profile Airline Passengers. The program would involve the use of public and private database to profile passengers. In parallel tests for automatic biometric recognition systems are ongoing.

PASSPORT

is a system that may enable profiling of individuals' browsing and online shopping behaviors. Microsoft has indicated that the company's goal is to have every Internet user possess a Passport account, thus raising the possibility that Passport may become the tollbooth that controls Internet access and online ordering for millions of consumers. Microsoft is said to have already acquired over 200 million Passport accounts. The privacy and security risks include online profiling made possible by the requirement that individuals sign on to Passport before viewing web content,

A special security topic is radiation security

TEMPEST (Temporary Emanation and Spurious Transmission)

i.e. is a codeword for registering unintentional radiation leakage of information from electronic equipment, most likely from displays, less likely but not confined to screens, impact printers, LCD screens and even domestic wiring or plumbing; with normal equipment up to 100 m, with sophisticated equipment the range can be extended to some miles and several screens in the same room. Countermeasures require significant more technical effort as the use of fiber optics, spread spectrum, frequency hopping, steerable antennae and burst transmission.

After the cold war period many of the available capacities are said to have been redirected to other areas as

Industrial Espionage

In view of the high number of unrecorded cases, it is difficult to determine precisely the extent of the damage caused by competitive intelligence/industrial espionage. In addition, some of the figures quoted are inflated because of vested interests. Security firms and counterintelligence services have an understandable interest in putting the losses at the high end of the realistically possible scale. Despite this, these figures do give some rough sizing of the problem. As early as 1988, the Max Plank Institute estimated that the damage caused by industrial espionage in Germany to at least DM 8 billion. The chairman of the association of security consultants in Germany quotes a figure of DM 15 billion a year. The President of the European police trade unions, Hermann Lutz, put the damage at DM 20 billion a year.

To ensure that the benefits and conveniences of networked computing continue to outweigh the risks of operating in an open networked environment a significant research work is dedicated to it. Intrusion detection techniques as VulDa (IBM Zurich Global security Analysis), distributed intrusion-tolerant intrusion detection systems as TIVOLIS´ Webld or Sniffer detectors to detect passive intruders by simulating network traffic using intentionally false information as bait.

2.2 Personal Safety and Security

Security is a subjective feeling perceived differently by different people.
Even the famous definition of the 1890 Harvard Law review is "the right to be let alone" (Louis Brandeis & Samuel Warren) is disputed by some U.S. feminists calling it "la liberté du renard libre dans le poulailler libre"or "espace de inégalité entre les sexes" [2].
A more formal triple definition would be the right:
• To control the diffusion of personal information
• To live without observation
• To be anonymous
While for some the protection of privacy and personal security is in importance equivalent and analogous to the protection of the environment, it is for others just an inevitable consequence of progress or a feature of changing political beliefs or sensitivities.

2.2.1 E-commerce and security

Since e-commerce did not realize its full potential yet, additionally efforts are made to address main impediments as lacking customer confidence and trust. This can be verified by the growth of privacy statements, governmental support as OECD providing a privacy statement generator, or technologies like P3P (platform for privacy preferences), a standard as established by W3C consortium are some of these initiatives. Figure 2 shows how strongly e-commerce transactions might interrelate with improving customer's confidence [2].

However, the ambiguity of this topic is demonstrated by the statement showing the possibilities of personalized marketing: "Tell me where you live and I will tell you what you buy".

This statement for is for many a classical intrusion into privacy and personal security but contradicted by the widespread acceptance of "Permission marketing" rewarding the individual for giving up its anonymity. Personalized marketing is also for many a desirable synonym for „good old times" when the butcher knew you, knew what you bought usually and reserved it for you in advance.

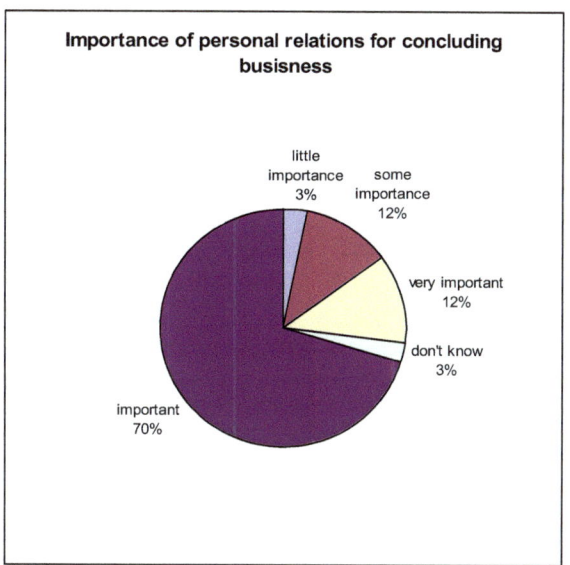

At the same time is the anonymity of large cities attractive to many people or according to an EPIC study 40% of Internet users use false names.

2.2.2   Database Building

We all know of many indispensable and helpful applications of DB/DC but critics see databases as base for of the information level imparity between consumer and seller.

DB CUSTOMER CONCERNS

64%	afraid of files exchanged
59%	personal information collected w/o consent
53%	abuse of credit card information
90%	data protection the most important issue when on line purchasing

Consumer advocates raised concerns about some controversial developments in Data Base building in recent years are mentioned in publications as e.g.:

Double Click acquired AbacusDirect for 1,7 billion $ and with it data on 90 million households, cookies to trace users activities ("Big brother award" 2000 Toronto). How to make this investment profitable?

Toy Smart went bankrupt in 2000 and wanted to sell its database containing 250.000 profiles of children. [2]

Amazon suppressed the "opt out" option for the clients to object to transmission of data.

LOTUS and Equifax wanted to market in 1990 "Lotus Market place". It would have offered to each potential buyer a database comprising: 7 million businesses, 120 million Internet users and 80 million households. Due to the negative public reaction, the project was dropped one year later. [9]

Many have foster the opinion that auto-regulation by industry will bring the solution. But is auto-regulation the solution or only a smoke screen? Cynical critics compare the newly emerging CPO´s (Corporate Privacy Officers) to a "health director for Phillip Morris". But there are signs of a rising the privacy consciousness as security and statements on websites, the wide spread of labels, the establishment of organizations as TRUSTe or the creation of dedicated positions as the above mentioned CPO´s (Corporate Privacy Officers).

2.2.3   Personal Surveillance

Personal surveillance on the job is another security issue getting more attention since companies as GE fired 18 people for distributing pornography in Internet, or Orange, UK 40 employees. The issue resembles in some parts the problem of telephone abuse, raising productivity concerns, as before-weekends-peaks, or up to yearly 115 h per employee are found to be lost for private and unsolicited email according to a study by Ferris Research and this issue is extended in US by the sexual harassment and "political correctness" issues.

2.2.4   Access Control

Access control encompasses identification, authentication as indispensable prerequisites. We are familiar with some of these features as passwords, TANs, PINs, tokens etc. But with the growths of the number of users, of transactions and their value and importance better, more reliable and faster systems are needed. Developments with identity and authentication checking, based on passwords, tokens (e.g. smart cards, keys) and biometric access control devices might enhance these future access-control devices. Many of these systems have yet to become more reliable and economic, but hold a lot of promise. E.g., the current development in the areas of biometrics looks at

Fingerprint
Iris recognition
Face recognition
Voice print
Hand (palm) recognition
Ear recognition

Biometrics-based authentication has many usability advantages over traditional systems; the intrinsic strength of a biometrical signal can be quite good especially for fingerprints, when compared with traditional passwords.
Biometric authentication systems can already support error rates in the range of $10^{**}-6$ for false accept and $10^{**}-4$ for false rejects [12].

Some advantages and weak points of biometric systems are compared below:

ADVANTAGES	WEAK POINTS
Difficult to share	Replay attacks using data hiding techniques
Repudiation unlikely	Fake biometrics (mask, fake finger, copy of signature)
Forging more difficult	Submitting previously stored signals (e.g. previously recorded voice signal)
Cannot be lost or stolen	Tampering with stored templates

2.2.5 Privacy Protection

The drive to maximize user's privacy is antagonistic to business' basic need to minimize fraud. Although Web browsing gives the feeling like an anonymous activity, it is hardly that way. The Web server logs reveal the date and time of each HTTP request, the IP address or DNS host name of the client, the URL of the previous resource requested by the client and some more information is available to the ISP (Internet service provider) whose HTTP proxy server may keep track of every

Web site and URL visited by their subscribers. The potential of traffic analysis has been largely ignored outside the military, but can be used to track the shopping habits, money spending patterns and personal data and HTTP data traffic can reveal a companies focus.

This gave rise to services and organizations like TRUSTe , BBBOn Line Privacy Program, W3C project P3P (platform for privacy preferences). Applicants for a certificate have comply with requirements, as a publishing a privacy statement, or having an opt-out option and others. However, it is yet not clear if these initiatives will be successful in the marketplace.

2.2.6 Censorship and the WWW

Today the Internet in general and the WWW in particular is criticized for providing an information structure that can be used for illegal or offensive content. Measures include content blocking (responsibility ISP), blocking at the packet level, IP address blocking, or URL blocking) Forcing users through a proxy server is commonly used for corporate intranets (blocking sites as www.playboy.com).

In the past many states have developed highly refined systems of censorship and law enforcement agencies mandate ISPs to keep a log of all sites accessed by their customers in spite of the increased operational cost associated with the creation, maintenance and distribution of black lists as well as the configuration of the corresponding screening routers.

2.2.7 Encryption

As computers became widely available in the 1970s, the need for the standardization of encryption systems grew, since in this way firms could communicate securely with business partners without incurring disproportionate costs. Since powerful encryption systems can also be used for unlawful purposes or by potential military opponents, US government agencies urged that firms should be offered a sufficiently secure encryption standard, but one which they could decrypt by virtue of their exceptional technical capabilities, thus the length of the key was restricted to 56 bits. In 1976 the so-called Lucifer key was officially adopted in its 56-bit version under the name Data Encryption Standard (DES) and represented for the next 25 years the official American encryption standard, also adopted in Europe and Japan, in particular in the banking sector. To the contrary of media claims, the DES algorithm has not yet been broken, but hardware now exists which is powerful enough to try all possible keys (brute force attack). In contrast, Triple DES, is still regarded as secure. The successor to DES, the Advanced Encryption Standard (AES), is a European process developed under the name Rijndael in Louvain, Belgium. It is fast and regarded as secure, since it incorporates no key-length restriction.

Standardization makes it much easier to employ encryption. What remains, however, is the problem of key exchange.

A public key cryptosystem can be used to protect the confidentiality of a message but to protect its authenticity and integrity as well. Digital signatures shall provide an analogue of handwritten signatures for documents. As long as a system works with a key which is employed both for encryption and decryption (symmetric encryption), it is difficult to use with large numbers of communication partners.

Asymmetric encryption offers a solution: two different keys are used for encryption and decryption. The message is encrypted using a key which may well be in the public domain (public key). This process works only in one direction, with the result, that decryption is no longer possible using the public key. Anybody who wishes to receive an encrypted message may send a communication partner via an unsecured route the public key required to encrypt the message. The received message is then decrypted using a different key, the private key, which is kept secret and which is not forwarded to communication partners. Although linked, the private key cannot be calculated based on the public key.

By comparison with symmetric processes (e.g. DES) however, public-key encryption requires much more calculation time or the use of fast, large-scale computers.

Therefore to make the public-key process generally accessible, P. Zimmermann came up with the idea of linking the public-key process, which involves a great deal of calculation, with a faster symmetric process. Zimmermann developed a user-friendly program PGP (Pretty Good Privacy) which created the requisite key and carried out the encryption at the push of a button. Implementations of the OpenPGP Standard as GnuPG offer the same encryption methods as PGP. There are also rival standards to OpenPGP, such as S/MIME, which are supported by many e-mail programmes.

2.2.8 Security of Encryption Products

The question is the security of the security measures i.e. of encryption products and processes. The accusation made is that certain products contain backdoors and it made headlines when it was suggested that in the European version of a program revealed half the key in the file header. Microsoft also gained media attention when a hacker claimed to have discovered an 'NSA key' hidden in the program, a claim that was of course strongly denied by Microsoft. The earlier versions of PGP and GnuPG can be said with a great degree of certainty not to contain such a backdoor, since their source text has been disclosed.

2.2.9 Electronic Payment Systems

Electronic payment systems and securing e-transactions as key to and backbone of e-commerce as described in many publication. Detailed descriptions are filling books. This subject will be addressed in an especially in this session.

2.2.10 E-Mail

During the past few years, three primary schemes for e-mail security have emerged on the net. Privacy enhanced mail (PEM), Pretty Good Privacy (PGP) or secure MIME (S/MIME), with the latter emerging as the leading one for e-mail security, being recognized by commercial vendors like Microsoft and Netscape.

However, theoretical discussions and business reality diverge sometimes. The market for e-privacy has proven difficult. Yahoo's e-mail encryption service made only 7 million $ p.a. and e-Nonymous, specialized in privacy seal activities, went even bankrupt.

2.2.11 Procedural Security and Customer Perception

Home banking and on-line shopping show thanks to intensive promotional efforts impressive growth but most of business is still done in conventional methods as shown below and has to improve its acceptance by the public to reach the desired volumes. [14]

It is much too early to make a final assessment, but the development of overall cost should be monitored as well. The claim was to minimize cost of a secure communication path between parties that share no prior administrative relationship. However, with no shared administrative structure to connect the parties many things like certificate chaining, revocation and directory services are established, that is the very thing that PK claimed not to need, namely administrative overhead. There are signs that normal users will use PK to a larger extend only when the problems related authorization and cost have been resolved. This might explain why in the US only 9% use cryptography and 5% use anonymization.

2.2.12 Technical Implementation of Information Security

To complete the overview few remarks should be made regarding the technical implementation i.e. the question which layer is best suited to provide security. There are different schools of thought. The proponents of placing security lower in the stack argue that lower-layer security can be implemented transparently to users and application programmes effectively killing many birds with a single stone. Contrary to the above proponents of placing security higher in the protocol stack argue that lower-layer security attempts to do too many things simultaneously, and that only protocols that work at the application layer or above can actually meet application specific security requirements.
Both arguments are somewhat true, so there is no best layer [16].

2.2.13 Future Processes

Future quantum cryptography may open up new prospects for secure key exchange. The interception of a key exchange could not pass unnoticed, because if polarized photons are transmitted, their polarization cannot be established without altering that polarization. Eavesdroppers on the line could thus be detected with 100% certainty. Only those keys, which had not been intercepted, would then be used. Basic experimental transmission via fiber-optic cable and in through the air have already been successfully done.

Another potential are "DNA-computers". The principal feasibility of this concept has been claimed to be demonstrated, but as for the above the principal question remains if they ever will become practical.
Similar assumptions may be valid for "spintronics".

2.3 Legal Security

2.3.1 General Situation

The legal situation is varying from country to country and slowly adapting to the new scenario. In spite of many initiatives, national legislation differs from country to country and especially when adapting existing legal, historical, and cultural difference come into consideration and is of importance. There is also a problem within the countries caused by the inflation of the legal system in the last years. In Germany to quote an example from the largest EU country a multitude of laws ranging from BDSG, BGB, StGB, UWG to copyright laws have to be considered and be quoted as being relevant and nevertheless many "gray" areas are still left.[15]

Presently there ongoing efforts in Austria to reduce and structure these gray areas and holes. New constituent facts for criminal offences are being defined like malign use of data (§51 DSG), data damage (§126a STGB) or interference with the right of access control (§10 ZuKG).

2.3.2 Digital Rights Management and Copyright Protection

Digital rights management was first proposed with little success some ten years ago, but is increasingly considered as last line of defence against Napster-like activities. Solutions based on watermarking, copy protection, conditional access and older style digital rights exist. Approaches range from usage control, e.g. for viewing pay-TV on demand, to allowing unlimited copying but use digital copyright labelling techniques as watermarks or others allowing trace to back to the original recipient (fingerprints), to tracing schemes or "Webcrawlers" to detect copyright violations. ut Watermark detection is a delicate and complicated task and the detection algorithm is often not sophisticated enough to deal with a downgraded version of the signal. Copyright infringement of though illegal copying could develop into a economic-technology war. Absolute robustness seems to be impossible and none of the systems can claim that its labels will survive all major signal processing operations and transformations. However, it is felt to be to a certain extend useful since it makes tampering and removal a more time-consuming and costly task and thus less rewarding. Next generation digital rights management will likely combine conditional access and copy protection with watermark flavours. But several factors might slow it down as lack of interoperability between systems and lack of standards, as well as sufficiently robust and tamper resistant software solutions, consumer ergonomics, bandwidth insufficiency and the likely challenge by hackers [16, 17].
In parallel to the technical endeavours there are legal initiatives as the World intellectual property treaty (protection of literary and artist work) exists but it does not specify enforcement provisions and restrains itself to requests member states to adopt appropriate measures.

2.3.3 ECHR (European Convention for Human Rights) and the fundamental right to respect for private life.

Any interception of communications represents serious interference with an individual's exercise of the right to privacy. (Article 8 of the ECHR), which guarantees respect for private life, permits interference only in the interests of national security. Interference must be proportionate, thus competing interests need to be weighed up and it is not enough that the interference should merely be useful or desirable. An intelligence system, which intercepted all communications without any guarantee of compliance with the principle of proportionality, would not be compatible with the ECHR. If a signatory state to the ECHR were to promote such a system, this would constitute a violation of the ECHR.

3. Some Conclusions

We tried to make an partial overview of the wide area of safety, security and privacy in IS/IT reviewed status and challenges, addressed ways and means and measures for improvements, both already being deployed and just invented or being studied. Looking at trends one can recognize increasing emphasis being given to these areas by R & D, education and business to improve of confidence, higher quality standards and 'trustworthiness'. One can expect the situation to improve over time additionally since IT security is being taught at an increasing number of universities, polytechnics and research laboratories, consequently the next generation of engineers will have a good chance to positively influence future developments. Keeping this in mind, we could argue that the security problems of the Internet will be overcome.

However, there are other views as well.
Nothing can protect us against new types of attacks. However, we can raise the technical, financial, and legal threshold by making it difficult and unrewarding for potential aggressors. Because of the accelerating development cycles of the IT industries, increasing competition of many start-up companies, aggressive marketing and concept products the situation might even get worse if not counterbalanced. It is difficult to belief in a slow down and prolongation of the development cycles with more time and resources allocated to security and safety without some external pressure to do so. This might support the assumption that security problems will not disappear in the near future.
Both arguments have their merits, but let us look on what could be done in the next future.
There is no one set of a solution that is going to solve the problems, but we can only speculate on some future scenarios:

- Change of the fundamental attitude and to seek proactive, preventive approaches instead of not just reactive, curative approaches (e.g. make high secure/default configurators, or out-of-the-box configurations with enabled security options rather than require the user to enable them in tiresome efforts).

- Virus resistant software with self repair and fail soft features.

- Development of Software development and testing tools

- End of special "legal exempt status" for software and TC products

- Customer / Consumer organizations as advocates.

- The evidently major task is to drive for higher quality products, reducing implementation errors by two orders of magnitude.

- Change in the consumer preferences to high quality and stability (durability) products

- Revitalization of the "old engineering quality" standards and ethics

The field is open for further ….

4. References

[1]   A CAMPO, M., PC-Sicherheit, bhv, 2001.

[2]   BELLEIL, A , e-Privacy, Le marché des données personnelles, Dunod, 2001.

[3]   EUROPEAN PARLIAMENT, PE 305.391, 2001.

[4]   FONT, A., Seguridad y Certificacion en el comercio Electronico, fundacion retevision 2001.

[5]   GARFINKELS, Unix Security 96:11;

[6]   GATES B., Memo to employees, 2002.

[7]   GAULKE M. Digitale Abgründe, Moderne Industrie, 1996.

[8]   GIESEKE W. Anti-Hacker Report, Data Becker 2001

[9]   GURAK L., Persuasion and Privacy

[10]   HIMANAN D. and PALMER C:, The Hacker Ethic, ethical hacking, IBM, 2001.

[11]   IBM Journal of R&D, 4/2001

[12]   IBM, End-to-end Security Systems Journal Vol. 40, 2001.

[13]   MARKUS, G., Digitale Abgründe, Verl. Mod. Industrie 1996.

[14]   MATZER, M., Sicherheitsrisiko Internet, DTV 1999

[15]   MEDOSCH, A., Netzpiraten, Telepolis, H. Heise, 2001.

[16]   OPPLINGER, R., Security Technology for the WWW, Artech House, 2001

[17]   PETHA, R., IT Essential but vulnerable, Testimony to House Committee on Govt. Reform, 2001

[18]   RAEPPLE, M., Sicherheitskonzepte für das Internet, dpunkt, 2001.

[19]   ROBERT, A., The key to your content, Comm. Technology, Feb. 2002.

[20]   SINGH R., Secret Messages , 1999.

[21]   THALLER, G., Computersicherheit, DUD Fachbeiträge

[22]   UNI BIELEFELD, Der aktuelle Stand der Clipper Chip Initiative, 1996.

[23]   WOBST, Abenteuer Kryptographie, On quantum cryptology, 1998.

[24]   2002 CSI/FBI Computer Crime and Security Survey, 2002.

[25]   2002 CYBER EXPO, Encuentros Profesionales, Las Palmas 2002.

IDIMT 2001

TRENDS IN BUSINESS, TECHNOLOGY, AND R & D

Abstract:

Based on reliable projections 01 status and trends in R & D, we will discuss what looms likely in few years from today. It is fascinating and challenging to evaluate based on decennia of exponential growth the prospects and repercussions of another phase of exponential progress, may be we could say: „the best is still ahead"! However, we have to discuss as well that serious and difficult problems have to be overcome, as final limits and boundaries are getting more visible and closer.

1. Prediction about the future - this paper might be included - have also often misjudged the pace of technology and its impact on human society.

2. What are realistic assumptions out of all the predictions? We can look forward to an additional million-fold increase in the power of microelectronics further empowered by the "law of photonic" driven communication technology developments and all this at very attractive costs.

3. Computers and their networks can help humans to reach many goals, but tools supply the power but humanity must supply the direction. Technology therefore will likely make us what we already are - only more so.

1. Introduction

Determining trends or directions necessitates taking stock of the status quo and the direction developments leading to and its interdependencies. Any attempt to match this endeavour enforces learning modesty, in view of its scope spanning the wide spectrum from philosophy to social sciences, biology and physics, just to quote a few. Even restraining us to the field of technology results in an ample short-list of key technologies. Such key technologies have been listed by institutions reaching from the Japanese MITI, US Dept. Of Commerce, NY Times, German BMFT to the Trend Letter of J. Naisbitt. Basically the same dozen of basic technologies were identified congruently as the key technologies determining future competitiveness of the economy as the list shows:

Microelectronics

Computer technology

Health technology

Transportation

Biotechnology

Energy

New materials

Sensorics

Micro mechanics

Chemistry

Laser technology

Space technology

Even this short list would resist any attempt to covered it adequately within a reasonable timeframe so we have to constrain us to a subset [13].

What does computer and communication technology hold in store for us in the second half century of the transistors existence?

Fuelled by exponential growth in the capabilities of electronic circuitry and the communication fabrics interconnecting them, the future promises a world of pervasive interconnections, customized products and services, much help with complexity and exciting new applications. Although singular projections hold few individual surprises, the totality of what looms likely just few years from today amounts to little less than a fantasy world.

It is highly satisfying to report that after decennia of exponential growth another phase of comparable progress seem to lie ahead, so we might say, the best is still ahead, but also that serious limits and boundaries are getting more visible and closer.

2. Computer and Communication

2.1 Computer

Today's PC's can perform approximately 1 Mflops. For comparison, that is roughly the operational power of the brain of a lizard. Extrapolating twenty to twenty-five years and given the continuation of this growth rate, a PC would be able to perform 1 Petaflop, that is in the range of the estimated operational power of the human brain, or in other words, the in the next twenty years the growth in computing power would correspond to hundreds of millions of years in human evolution.

Or some scientists believe that the advances would yield low-end computers more powerful than today's workstations for about the price of a postage stamp and in postage stamp quantities.

We do not have not to lean on scientific speculation since ongoing evolutionary R&D is providing with a scientifically founded scenario of comparable fascination.

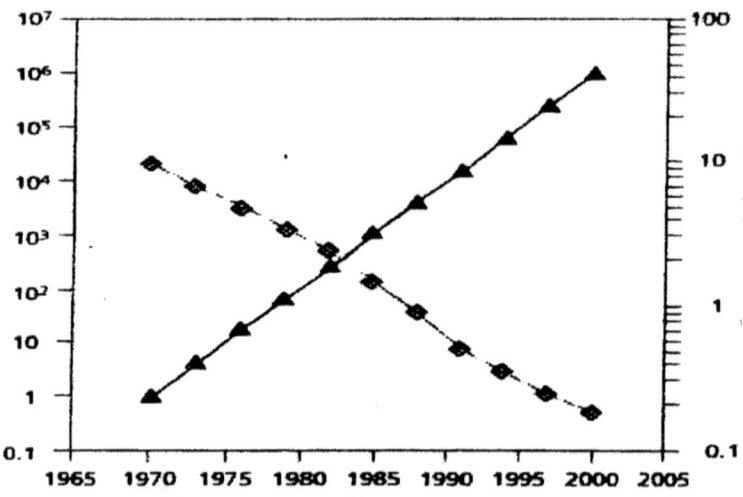

DRAM cell count [K=1024 bits] and desgn rule [microns] (W.F.Brinkman , M.R. Pinto)

2.1.1 Silicon technology

2.1.1.1 Future of CMOS

The exponential improvement of performance of integrated circuits, matched only by few other technologies as magnetic storage, fuelled the growth of the information technology for nearly half a century. In spite of the fact that it is obvious that this continued advance in the area of the transistor of the by the factor two in every three years cannot be sustained permanently, predictions of limits have been shifting nearly at the same speed as the improvements in size speed or other relevant properties of the semiconductors. This could shed a light on the accuracy of predictions even by prominent scientists. However, a look at the key processes supporting the development of the CMOS technology can give some basis for estimates on future potential. The pre-eminent use of CMOS technology invites to take this particular transistor species as example.[12]

Not the increases in speed or density are the key factors but rather that the rate of increase of components and functions is greater than the increase in costs per chip. Therefore, the information revolution will continue as long as the cost per function is declining.

Areas decisive for these developments are:

Lithography
Design & Interconnections
Capital Costs

2.1.1.1.1 Lithography

Lithography determines the density of the patterns on wafers and therefore is a decisive element for the reduction of the size of transistors. Once estimated to be limited to a > 1 μm resolution the industry is already moving to a 0,13 μm resolution in manufacturing by using DUV (deep ultraviolet) sources like excimer lasers.

Moving to 0,13 μm lithography is marking the first time that features smaller than the wavelength will be patterned. 'The use of various techniques as off-axis illuminating and phase shift masking enable the patterning of features smaller than wavelength.

Further progress below the 100 nm will require further steps to KrF (248 nm) and further to ArF Eximer lasers. Only few transparent materials are available to be used in lenses or masks (Calcium fluoride is a candidate, but has a less desirable property too, i.e. thermal expansion 40 times higher than quartz). For further scaling non-optical lithography technologies ranging from electron-beam lithography (electron wavelength of about 0,01 nm) or X-ray lithography has been already exploited for exploratory integrated circuits by IBM at dimensions from 1 um down to 0,15 μm using the 1,1 nm wavelength produced by synchrotron radiation. This involves the problem of lack of lenses and mirrors for these wavelengths. X-ray projection lithography tries to avoid that issue by using 11 – 13 nm wavelength light and the use of a reflective 4 times dimension reduction system (layers of 2-3 nm films with uniformity at atomic dimensions.)

More explanatory approaches include ion-beam lithography or hot electron emission lithography.

Non-optical techniques remain to be proven feasible – meaning economically feasible – the main Risk is of business or economic character – that the cost of any new system might be greater than the derived density improvements. In addition, here Moore's law will only be continuing as long as the cost per component is continuing to decline more rapidly. [12,30,31]

2.1.1.2 Design

Two types of transistors have been competing since the late 40's the bipolar and the field effect transistor. But it took until the early 90's when the performance advantage of the bipolar transistor was outweighed by the greater circuit density of CMOS circuitry transistors. System performance of the integrated functionality superseded the pure raw transistor performance leading to making CMOS the dominant circuit in production today.

Clock rate improvement is partially due to transistor performance and partially due to improved logic design. The optimum Case of continuing improvements in both areas would lead to 20 GHz processors in 2010, with ongoing transistor improvement but without further logic and circuit design improvement 1,5 GHz processors will be attained.

The increasing clock rate is additionally shrinking the allowable space for a synchronized processor. For a 10 GHz processor the clock rate is 100ps so the space reachable by light in one clock cycle is 30 mm, assuming a medium different than vacuum it is 15 -20 mm about the size of a chip! [15].

Fundamental limits are coming from the tunnelling of electrons.

The insulator is 2-3 nm thick today, it can not become less than about 1,5 nm thick, because if the silicon dioxide layer is made any thinner electrons can tunnel through it at unacceptable rates. For 2004 the Semiconductor Industry Association (1999) forecasts the 1,5 nm insulators – equivalent to only 5-6 atomic layers.

Channel length, the distance between source and drain (the two points between which a current flows during operation of the transistor). The shorter the less time the transistor takes to switch, but various kinds of so-called short channel effects suggest that the channel length can not be much shorter then 23 nm, A size that could be attained by 2010. Novel transistor structures might allow shorter channel length to be fabricated and materials to enable higher performance for a given channel length as the SOl (silicon on insulator) with an improvement potential of 20% or SiGe dispositions to enhance the mobility of either electrons or holes with an performance improvement potential of 30 - 60 %. The recent announcement by IBM of a 210 GHz SiGe- transistor for2003/2004 seems to have come just in time to support these assumptions. "Strained silicon" is another recently presented improvement to enhance electron mobility.

Power supply voltage is critical. The nature of Si requires a minimum of approx. 1 V. At present the level is between 1,2 - 1,5 V, which leaves room for one more round of reduction possible by 2004.[15,25]

Another factor is threshold voltages in the transistor cannot be scaled down without lowering the operating temperature. Low temperature operations could lead to an improvement by a factor 2 at liquid nitrogen temperature (-195°C). But cost and practical considerations will most probable continue to inhibit the large scale use of this approach for the time being, but with increasing difficulties of further scaling and improvements in refrigeration, low temperature operation might become economically feasible for high performance products but with a cost 1 performance optimum in the range of -50°C.

Wiring is another constraint where the industry moving from Al to Cu technology because of the lower resistance and capacitance; similar moves from silicon dioxide insulators (between the wiring levels) to low-dielectric constant insulators are under investigation.

DRAM economics may impose a different scenario.

If lithography or process technology becomes more and more expensive than justifiable by the resultant bit-density further improvements may not meet the economic test. However, such problems have been predicted in the past for several DRAM generations, but never occurred yet.

Superior design can elicit more functions on a chip without increasing the number of transistors. , May be it would be appropriate to transform Moore's law reference system into increased function instead of number of transistors. [12, 31, 32]

2.1.1.3 Cost

A decisive factor for the viability of new technologies is cost reduction and economic viability, including capital cost as well. It is obvious that the cost of producing a silicon wafer must increase less rapidly than the density to achieve cost reduction. The rapid increase during the '80s of the capital cost of a silicon manufacturing line amounting to 25% p.a., led to concerns of the diminishing returns in costs per circuit. However, since the 1990 the rate of increase has slowed to less than 15% p.a. due to better equipment productivity and a slower increase in the number of process steps.

To overcome the impediments for the next rounds of improvements will require significant investments in R&D and technology:

- Optical lithography must be extended to unanticipated levels and possibly replaced by non- optical techniques.
- Transistors must be replaced with a new structure using new materials.

- DRAM cells must be designed to unknown structures to achieve economically viable increases in integration.
- Wires must be shrunk to a tenth of a micron dimension with novel dielectric materials in carefully designed hierarchies.
- Integrating more function on a chip will also mean to cost reduction and productivity increase.

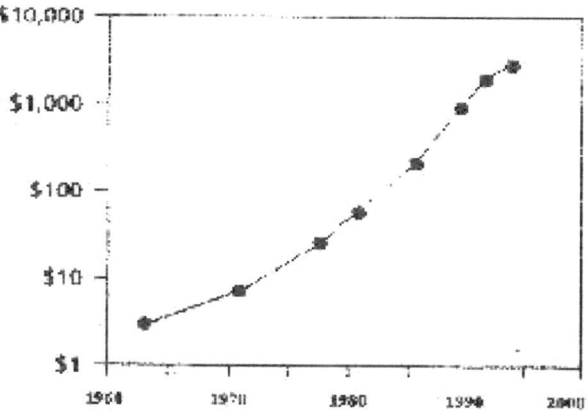

Cost of JC manufacturing clean rooms (J.T. Clemens, Bell Tec Journal 1997)

Productivity is a product of a many variables. All this is resulting in the requirement for major advances in design automation tools, changing the direction from having a microprocessor to having a micro-system on a chip.

The exponential increase in transistor densities and processing speed is being sustained by a similar increase in the financial outlays to build the facilities that produce these chips. Many experts expect equilibrium around 2020 - 2015, when a fabrication facility might cost nearly 200 Mia $.

Modifications of the structure, cooling (to -50^0 C) might keep progress going for some years but such options might be exhausted by 2010.

Further options might appear through other types of measures, such as optimizing overall systems performance, since we are far from optimizing how processor, memory and 1/0 system work together or integration since except for small amounts of high speed cache the key entities of the computer are on different chips. These system integration steps might increase performance by 500% even if performance of the individual elements remains the same.

Another way to boost performance is parallel processing, as we do in today's supercomputers by linking together 100's or 1000's processors, if this is proven successfully it will migrate downwards and we will see multiprocessing for PC's too. The IBM's supercomputer-project BlueGene in process, designed to achieve 1 quadrillion flops, by advanced systems integration and on chip DRAM will test the viability of the above.

2.1.1.2 Post - Silicon

In the timeframe around 2020, parallelism and other approaches mentioned above will not no longer be able to improve performance further.

Opinions on a potential successor of silicon are divided. Some say there is no replacement for silicon or CMOS but with lead times between laboratory and production of 15 - 20 years we have to get serious about new ideas.[15]

Some lines of long-term research, novel materials and devices are:

Perovskites

Molecular electronics

Molecular computation

Nanotubes and carbon circuits

Nanoscale Computing

Quantum computing

In the very long range still more radical concepts may come up, looking up to the achievements of evolution keeping in mind that. a mosquito brain can control navigation, vision, smell, mating, feeding etc.

Let us now turn to the second key development arena the storage technology.

2.2 Storage Technology

As shown below in the years 1991 to 1997 density has been doubling every 18 months, but the pace has quickened to doubling every 12 month and will continue to do so for the next future. But we let us also examine the physical phenomena which might prevent the continuation of the scaling process which served us so successfully in the past.

2.2.1   Magnetic storage

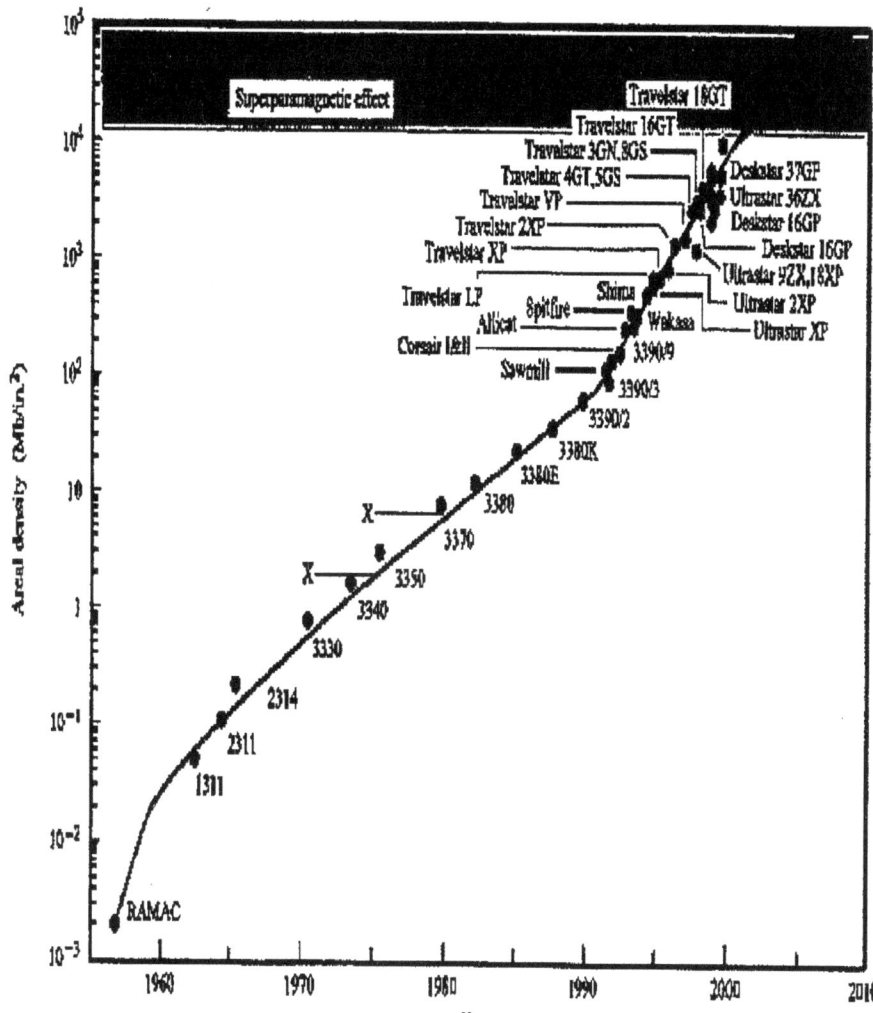

Thomson, IBM J.of R&D, Vol 44, 00 Disc storage density vs. year of product introduction (up to superparamagnetic effect)

From the beginning of the 1990s, the development has even accelerated significantly to a 60% compound growth rate due to several factors as the introduction of magnetoresistive recording head, the increase of competition in the market, the transfer of technological leadership to smaller diameter drives with shorter design cycles, being supported by VLSI high performance data channels and other electronics. There are even industry specialists who attribute some of the increased rate of areal density growth to IBM's strategy to compete primarily through technology. It is worth noting that the two X's mark two levels of density previously predicted as ultimate density levels attainable

The current density improvement rate of a factor 10 every five years may be higher than expected even by optimistic observers, but the current trends for the next few years show no decrease in the pace of technology improvement we might even expect an increase. Past attempts to predict the ultimate limits have been dismal failures (e.g. today's best disk drives operate at 100 times the predicted limit of maximum densities).

However, the present problems seem to be more fundamental than those envisioned earlier, since they include thermodynamics of the energy stored in a magnetic bit, head to disk spacing only an order of magnitude larger than an atomic diameter and the intrinsic switching speed of magnetic materials.

This are only few of the problems ahead, for others solution seem to be in sight, the signal to noise ratio might be improved by tunnel junction heads giving us scaling potential beyond 40 Gb/in^2 .[34, 37]

A limit of rather fundamental structure seems to be the superparamagnetic limit.

This effect can be understood by considering a uniformly magnetized particle that has an anisotropy that forces the magnetization to lie in either direction of a preferred axis. At 0°K (absolute zero), the magnetization lies at one of the two energy minima (0° or 180°). If the direction of the magnetization is disturbed, it vibrates at a resonance frequency but settles back afterwards. At higher temperatures, the magnetization direction fluctuates randomly at its resonant frequency with an average energy of kT and the energy fluctuating accordingly to well-known statistics and with each fluctuation will have a finite probability to exceed the energy barrier that exists at 90°. The average time between random reversals is strongly depending on the particle size (a factor of two in particle diameter can change the reversal time from 100 years to 100 nsec.

Today's densities are in the 10 Gb/in! range, if simple scaling prevails, superparamagnetic effects will appear in few years and become extremely limiting several years after that By deviation from scaling it can be expected to push the superparamagnetic limit from 40 Gb/in> to 100 - 200 Gb/in" [37].

Therefore, other measures to circumvent the superparamagnetic limit problem are investigated like perpendicular recording. [33]

Another factor of 10 could be obtained if the magnetic grain count were reduced to one per bit cell, requiring a photolithographic definition of each grain or of a grain pattern (as used in optical storage disks). It might be difficult but not impossible, if also the economic i.e. cost side of patterned magnetic media can be solved satisfactorily.

After cost and capacity, the most important attribute is "performance" of disk storage, including access time and data rate. Since the disk drive data rate has been climbing faster than silicon speed

this problem is most probably worsening and will force high performance disks to decrease from 3,5 in. diameter to 2,5 in .

Both heads and media show a change of their magnetic properties below 10 ns switching time. Due to the fact that when magnetic field is applied to make it switch, magnetisation does not start by rotation in the direction of the applied torque, but it starts first to precess like a gyroscope in a direction a right angles to the direction in which it is pushed and would spin around the applied field without ever switching at a frequency in the MHz range forever. Since their is some damping it does end in the expected direction but this takes some nanoseconds with eddy currents produce fields in the opposite direction to oppose switching and slow it down.

There are serious limitations to the continued scaling but there is also time to explore alternatives. The rate of improvement will slow down in the next ten years. But it can be expected that after this time, which is beyond about 100 times improvement of the present levels, technologies like holography or probe-based technologies might offer potential alternatives.

2.2.2 Non- magnetic storage

2.2.2.1 Holographic storage

Contrary to magnetic and conventional optical storage techniques where information is stored as changes at the surface of the medium, holographic storage has the advantage of being a volumetric technique with potential of huge data rates. In holographic data storage, an entire page is stored at once as an optical interference pattern within the material, by two coherent intersecting laser beams. The theoretical limit for this storage technique is in an area density of tens of Tb/mm^2,

In addition holographic storage promises fast access times because the laser beams can be moved fast practically without inertia, and by the inherent parallelism of its page-wise storage and retrieval large compounded data rates can be reaching using a large number of relatively slow (therefore low cost) parallel channels.

Distances between "head" and media are large and media are easily removable.

A rather unique feature would be its associative retrieval, since imprinting a partial or search data pattern on the object beam and illuminating the stored hologram reconstructs all of the reference beams that were used to store the data. The intensity diffracted by each of the interference gratings is proportional to the similarity between the search pattern and the content of the particular data page. So the closest match to a search pattern can be found without even knowing its address.

But significant problems are still stemming from the high component and integration costs as most emerging technologies have to overcome as well as the placement of the technology in present storage hierarchy and its market acceptance.[1]

2.2.2.2   AFM (atomic force microscope based data storage) storage

The 21st century the nanometer will is likely play a role similar to the one played by the micrometer in the 20th century.

Emerging technologies can only qualify as serious candidates replacing existing but limited technologies if they offer long-term perspectives.

Probe tip storage, one method is millipede based on the operation of arrays of atomic force microscopes (AFMs) is capable of large densities. One can even imagine extending the approach into an atom-level storage regime. [36]

2.3   I/O Interfaces and Transparency

The basic idea known variously as pervasive or ubiquitous computing or life networking was perhaps first articulated at Xerox Palo Alto Research Centre in the late 80's.

The ongoing move to "people technologies" means:

- Easier to use
- Easier to retrieve

- Easier to communicate
- Easier to maintain

Responsive to word and gesture, future interface technologies will permit to focus on tasks instead on technologies. Examples of technologies under development are for example: eye tracking, screen technology, conversing with machines or the "right" information at the right time and location. [15, 28]

These developments and trends will not only supplemented but accelerated by the developments in communications.

3.   Communication

We are already spoiled by getting used to exponential improvement scales but even steeper scales are characterising the development of communications.

Some of this development and trends commonly called:

3.1   Law of Photonics

The cost of transporting a bit over a network is now decreasing by half every nine months and there is no end in sight. These developments have become known as the law of photonics.

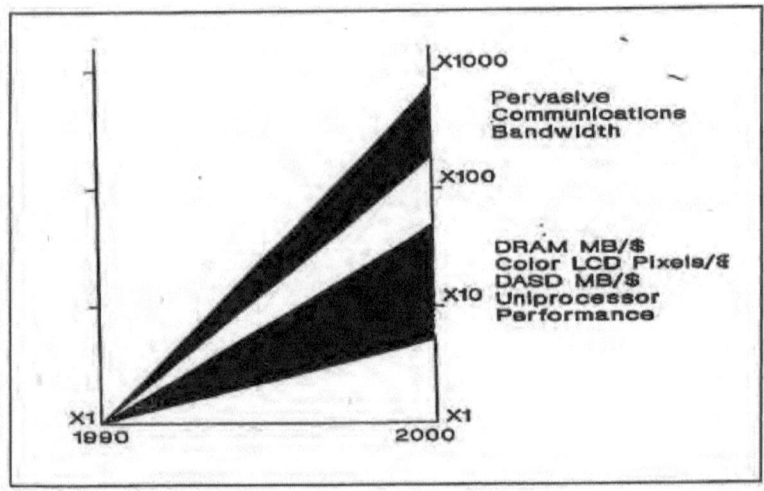

Figure 4: Relative technological improvements 1990 – 2000

Results and prospects are promising and supporting the further continuation of this development since laboratory tests show that e.g.

- One fibre could carry as many as 15000 wavelengths on single strand.
- Paradigm changes as from one laser for one wavelength, to one single laser for all wavelengths are feasible, or
- Sending 160 Gb/s over >300 km without any repeaters, describes a system that could be in service in the near future.

Looking further out, we can see developments are on the way as:

- Tbit/see over a single strand of fibre in ten years seems reachable.
- Integration of electronic and photonic components eliminating the bottleneck to convert signals from optical to electronic and back to optical as well as
- micro-electromechanical systems faster than as electronic switch capacity.[17]

3.2   Bandwidth

The per bit cost of global communication has dropped by three orders of magnitude or bandwidth has increased by the factor 10 to the 3rd power in the last ten years and will continue to do so.

An example should illustrate the economic significance. Today Internet connectivity costs about 1c/MByte. under a conservative assumption of improvements, at a thousandth of this amount a full time video connexion between any to points of the world might cost less than 300 $ year. This is a modest estimate, since cyberspace enthusiasts project annual tripling of bandwidth over a 25 years period). However, even in the modest ease, assume one billion on-line households each of them able to command more communication capacity than the entire Internet offered its users when it went global.

Bandwidth will not only become cheap, but might even become to cheap to meter. [20,24]

3.3   A "Global Communication Skin"

The pervasiveness of C&C might lead to an extrapolation only short of science Fiction, the "global communication skin".

The "global communication skin" might not only consist of the network of networks but also comprise countless sensors and other devices connected to it, Highly directional smart antennas and advanced signal processing will complete the connection. The interfaces will become so cheap that anything that can be connected to the network - such as thermostats, pressure gauges, pollution detectors, cameras, alarm systems, household appliances and automobiles - and you will be able to access what is in your fridge or if your car is locked from anywhere including your office --assuming you still go to an office.
They will also gather useful information monitoring people's hearts, the traffic, homes and the environment. In addition, if desired keep track of children, pet and ears through an omnipresent positioning system and all that with single universal natural addresses with individualized applications in an open but secure environment

All these trends will cause internet to converge with the mega-network and transform it into a broadband "Hi-IQNet".

3.4   The HI-IQNET"

The Hi-IQNet will respond to the spoken voice without regard to language or accent and provide also a degree of natural intuition, finding the. Information and services people want even if they only have a vague idea of what they are seeking. Servlets will enable an individual to embed his personal preferences not only create a personal Web site but his own Web persona.--- Web will become an appendage to a person's daily activities almost a human process akin breathing or thinking.

The work done over the next decade might have greater impact on people's life then anything that happened in the last century of communication history [20].

Internet, telecommunications and broadcast entertainment will blend into a single environment. Nevertheless, we might also be living in a glass-village. Except for those willing to go to much trouble and expense large portions of what we regard now as privacy might diminish greatly or disappear altogether. The average citizen would encounter a level of recognition (name, face, GPS recognition etc) hereto only experienced by celebrities or in very small villages. [20, 24]

4. Business and e-Economy

Since this area will be covered in an excellent and exhaustive way in the preceding sessions this chapter confines itself to few remarks on some business aspects intrinsic to R&D and technology since some business and economic aspects have already been incorporated into the preceding chapters.

In midst of all this euphoria a balanced picture necessitates some objective distance too.

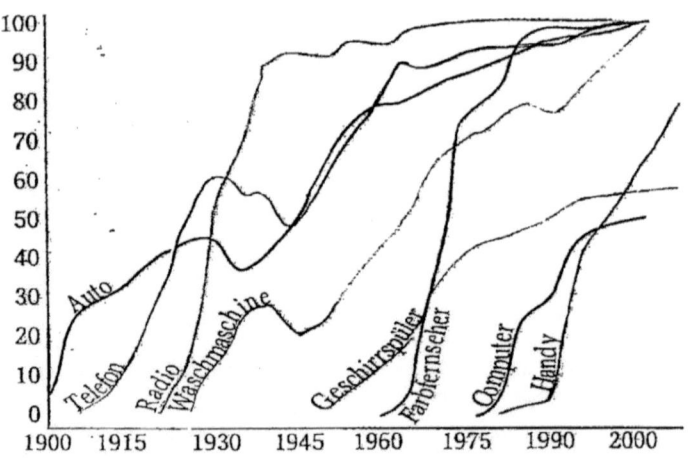

Figure 5: US market penetration of different products [in %] (Fed Res. Bank, Dallas)

As shown above, some technologies, which are today regarded as shining examples of successful technologies, have highly different developments. We will discuss some of the prerequisites interdependencies.

In the 1980's Solow wrote, that we could find computers everywhere but in the productivity numbers.

After languishing for years in 1995 American productivity growth suddenly doubled to 3%, with this productivity miracle the US have outrun all major industrial powers and we have witnessed one of the longest periods of economic upswing in US history.

Recalling the electric motor analogue - it did very little the first 40 years after it was invented (1880), reminds us that it took long to standardise it, build the economic infrastructure around it and last but not least hook it up to the electrical grid network. [19 et alii]. This underlines that just buying computers and attaching it to the Net is not enough to make business smarter, the sensation of the all pervasive technological revolution on its own merits only would prove statistical wrong.

Also we should recall that the automotive industry in its early phase had start-ups in the hundreds, now we have three major companies in the US left, so we might go through a quasi-normal early infancy process of e-business, Of special attraction is that the investments new start- up companies are relatively modest in relation to the potential pay-off.

While for corporations MIT's Sloan School of Management argues that hard- and software accounts only for a minor portion of true corporate investment in information technology. A significant portion of the investment goes into new business processes. i.e. reorganizing the business from new products to training of employees and since this spending does not show up in the corporate account as investment, it is can only be estimated and major benefits might be rather attributed to these accompanying activities.

The remarkable phenomenon is still that one industry generated and generates so much growth.

5. Predictions revisited

We tried to present that each of the projections holds few individual surprises, but the total or better the product of what we have perused in the previous chapters and what looms likely in few years from today amounts to little less than another decennium of impressive developments.

After decennia of exponential growth, another phase of comparable progress seems to lie ahead, so we might say, „the best is still ahead", but also serious and difficult problems have to be overcome, as final limits and boundaries are getting more visible and closer.

Prediction about the future - this paper might be included - have often underestimated the pace of technology and its impact on human society.

What are realistic assumptions out of all the predictions? We can look forward to an additional million-fold increase in the power of microelectronics further empowered by the "law of photonic" driven communication technology developments and all this at very attractive costs.

Computers and their networks they connect to, can help humans to reach many goals.

Tools supply the power but humanity must supply the direction. Technology therefore will likely make us what we already are - only more so.

6. References

[1]   J. Ashley, M.-P. Bemal, G. W. Bure, H. Coufal, H. Guenther, 1. A. Hoffnagle, C.M. Jefferson, B. Marcus, R. M. Macfarlane, R. M. Shelby, and G. T. Sincerbox, Holographie Data Storage, IBM J. Res. Develop.44, No 3, 2000.

[2]   Bauelle Memorial Institute, Innovation, Strategie Technologies for 2020, 1999.

[3]   B. Beyers, Die Zukunftsmacher, Campus N.Y München, 1999.

[4]   1. F. Bobo, F. B. Mancoff, K. Bessho, M. Shanne, K. Sin, D. Guarisco, S.>X. Wang and B.M. Clemens, Spin depend Tunneling Junctions with hard magnetic layer pinning, J. Appl. Physics 83,1998.

[5]   W. F. Brinkman and M. R. Pinto, The future of Sloid State Electronics, Bell Labs ournal, Aut. 1997.

[6]   CEDEFOP, Europ. Center for the Development of Vocational Training, 1999.

[7]   J.T. Clemens, Silicon Microelectronics Technology, Lucent Technologies Inc. 1997

[8]   M. Dertouzos, What will be, Harper Collins, Springer. 2000.

[9]   W. D. Doyle, S. Stinnett, C. Dawson, and L. He, Magnetization reversal at high speed, J. Magn. Soc. Jpn. 22, 1998.

[10]   Economist, Survey: E- Commerce, 2000

[11]   M. Horx, Die acht Sphären der Zukunft, Signum, 2000.

[12]   R. D. Isaac, Tbe future ofCMOS technology., IBM J. Res. Develop. 44, No 3,2000.

[13]   H.Kirchner, Technologische Grundlagen, IBM Lab Böblingen, 1991.

[14]   R. Kurzweil, Tbe age of spiritual machines, Viking Press London, 1999.

[15]   E. 1. Lerner, IBM Res Mag., No 4,1999

[16]   G.E. Moore, Elecronics, Vol. 38,1965

[17]   Ira Matathia and M.Salzman, Next, the flow of future, Uitgeverij,1998.

[18]   R. W. Keyes, IBM J. Res. Develop. Vol.44, 1 - 3,2000.

[19]   MIT Media Lab, IBM Sysztems Journal, p.155-168,1997

[20]   A.A. Netravali, Bell Labs Techn. Journal, 1-3,2000

[21]   R.M.Ginn, Lucent Chairman

[22]   NZZ Dossiers, New Economy, Die Entwicklung des E-Business – Mythos und Realität, 2001

[23]   1997, OECD Information Technology Outlook, OECD Paris, 1997.

[24]   A. Penzias, Bell Labs Tecbnical Journal, p 155 - 168,1997.

[25]   R. Pool, Think Research Mag. 3, 1999.

[26]   Neil Postman, Technopoly, Vintage Books,N.Y., 1993.

[27[J. Rifkin, TIle age of access, Putnam N. Y., 2000.

[28]   G. Taubes, Think Research, Nol, 2000.

[29]   B. Sellin, Aventis Forum Uni München, 12, 2000.

[30]   Yuan Taur, Douglas A, Buchanan, Wei Chen, David 1. Frank, Khalid E. Ismail, Shin-Hsien Lo, George A. Sai-Halasz , Raman G. Viswanathan, Hsing-Jen C. Wann, Shalom, 1. Wind and Hon-SumWong, CMOS scaling into the nanometer regime, Proc. IEEE 85, No.4,,1997.

, E.J.Nowak, , ShalomJ. Wind and Hon-

Sum Wong, CMOS scaling into the 21" century, IBM J. Res. Develop. 39, No.1I2, 245- 260,1995.

[32]   T. N. Theis, The future of Interconnection Technology, IBM J. Res. Develop.44, No 3, 2000.

[33]   D. A. Thompson The role of perpendicular recording in the future of hard disk storage, J. Magn. Soc. Jpn. 21, Suppt. S2, 1997.

[34]   D.A. Thompson and 1.S. Best, The future of magnetic data storage technology, IBM J. Res . Develop.44, No 3, May 2000

[35]   J.W. Toigo,. Scientific Am., May 2000.

[36]   P. Vettiger, M. Despont, U. Drechsler, U. Düring, W. E. Haberle, M. I. Lutwyche, a E. Rothuizen, R. Stutz, R. Widmer and G. K. Binnig, The "Millipede" More than a thousand tips for a future AFM data storage, IBM J. Res. Develop. 44, No 3, 2000.

[37]   D. Weller and A. Moser, The thermal effect Iimits in ultrahigh density recording, IEEE Trans. Magn. 35, 1999.

[38]   R. L. White, R. M. H. New, and R. F. W. Pease, Patterned Media: A viable route to 50Gbit/in^2 and   up for magnetic recording, IEEE Trans. Magn. 33, 1997

IDIMT 2000

ETHICS, ENFORCEMENT AND INFORMATION TECHNOLOGY

Abstract

Ethics and Information Technology have become increasing frequently used terms both as cause and as solution of problems of various kinds.

It is a known phenomenon that whenever a significant new development emerges a period of uncertainty follows and manifold efforts are made to incorporate the new phenomenon into the present system. In cases where these endeavours do not seem to be successful within a short timeframe the desire increases to emphasise and anchor during these periods of change and uncertainty in more enduring value systems of proven stability and familiarity.

This should not belittle or negate the task to incorporate developments into our society in a symbiotic ways encompassing the whole spectrum from education to business and law etc.., but rather emphasise the necessity to implement it expeditious in an pragmatic and efficient way to overcome interregnum-like periods .

Therefore, it might be advisable to take stock preceding the extension of the horizon from the reliable grounds of ethics to some areas of the pending issues and "work in progress" for which we propose to selected topics as:

1. Ethics

Ethics, the Encyclopaedia Britannica refers to it as from the Greek ethos, "character", as the systematic study of the nature of value concepts "good," "bad", "ought", "right"," wrong" etc. and of general principles which justify us in applying them to anything; also called "moral philosophy" from the Latin " mores " customs.

At a first glance it seems redundant to discuss something so obvious to everybody, nobody will ever state that he wants to be unethical himself and everybody wants all the others to be ethical in interpersonal relations and especially to him.

Latest since the Ethica Eudemeia (pursuit of prosperity) or Ethica Nikomacheia of Aristotle's as "Idea of a good live", "good" meant as intrinsically good or good-in-itself, Aristotle's ethics or Kant's deontological ethics are well established and have almost become a household words.

Many think or feel that there is one universal ethics, but multiple schools of thought developed with views on ethics far from homogenous ranging from Aristotle to Machiavelli.

They range from ethics being something to be dealt with by the Marketing departments of large corporations to perceiving ethical and moral issues among the most vital aspects of IT, business, medicine, biology etc. They range from interpreting the moral sense in each of us as a proof for the existence of God, to the proposal to substitute religious by ethics education in schools to various attempts or to construe ethical obligations of different kinds where no legal obligations exist.

If helplessness triggers the quest for ethics this might be a phenomenon worthwhile further study.

Are we for the first time in history entering a period of global culture and want ethics to fill gaps?

1.1 Information Technology and Computer Ethics

In the 60´s science turned to the field of ethics – a field which was dying according to some- and asked the question "what exactly should we do" from this introspection the field of bio ethics emerged (Bartels et alii.)

Contrary to respectable intellectual attempts, the computer or information ethics (CE or IE) seems not to have succeeded in achieving the status of philosophically respectable topic.

Why should be any such thing as Computer Ethics?

Since ethics became such an in–word in the world of science, institutes, publications, committees papers and statements have been growing at an astonishing indicating that there must be some unsatisfactory situation driving this or some demand behind this development.

A leading advocate of Computer ethics concludes that IE does not provide a library of error proof - solutions to moral problems but it fulfils an important missing role within the spectrum of macroethics. What IE and CE can achieve is the shift from an anthropocentric to a biocentric to an onto-centric view, which is more suitable to an information culture and society. (L. Floride).

There were many developments that had an significant impact on society over the centuries.
The invention of the printing press was a singular outstanding event, but there was no such thing as printing-press ethics.
The steam engine revolutionised industry but there was not such thing as steam engine ethics
The telephone changed the way we live and communicate but there was no ......
The combustion motor revolutionised, but was no....   (D. Gotterbarn)

2. Scenario

Let us take some selected glimpses at the scenario we are encountering at present.

There are a rights, believes and values we are proud of and regard them as basic to the quality of our life and society. Let us address some.

2.1 Freedom of expression

Freedom of expression is one of the fundamental rights, engraved in many constitutions, the US constitution is an important and prominent example.

"We the people of the United States of America, in order to form a more perfect union, establish justice, insure domestic tranquillity, provide for the common defence, promote the general welfare, and secure the blessings of liberty to ourselves and to our posterity, do ordain and establish this Constitution of the United States of America.

Amendment 1: Congress shall make no law respecting an establishment of religion, or prohibiting the free exchange thereof; or abridging the freedom of speech, or of the press; or the right of the people to peaceably assemble, and to petition the government for a redress of grievance. "

(The Constitution of the United States of America)

Freedom of speech is for many people synonymous with freedom from censorship and protection of privacy.

2.2 Censorship and Information Acquisition

But we encounter censorship in various forms expressions: open, intrinsic or camouflaged. The list runs from
- Censorship by Government (in many countries from Australia to Russia or UK),
- Censorship by ownership (Decoder, Media, SW, in eligendo) to
- Censorship by technology, (hardware and software technology as well as agent technology).

Let us review some examples in connection with the privacy question

2.3 Privacy

To illustrate the prevailing situation some examples:

- ECHELON Project of the NSA (National Security Agency, 20000 HC budget 8 Mia $ pa) has raised several question since it is a world-wide communication monitoring system operating from US but also from Europe. It stems from the cold war period and is capable to intercept communications of various kinds around the globe.(R.Windram)

- MICROSOFT software was accused of containing a code with the name NSAkey as tool to read confidential industrial information (according to Liberation, Focus, French Min. of Defence) Microsoft rejected this and told Washington Post that NSAkey was only a notation that conforms to the technical standards set by the NSA.

- LOTUS Notes had disclosed 24 of the 64-bit encryption key to NSA so it would have to crack only 40 bits which was in NSA capabilities in that time (1996).(Graham Lea)

- Further examples would be the Clipper chip and cryptography as well as the past 128-bit code export license issue.

But there is also the strong governmental argument in favour of these activities stating that modern crime using newest technologies can only be fought be using adequate technologies as well.

DOUBLECLICK and AUREATE.COM, companies offering freeware were accused of infiltrating software into users PCs, which would monitor the surfing of the user as well as investigating the system and transmit the data obtained. The user is said to receive software that could be used to transmit passwords and system data as files. The accusation were never proven but under public protest the project was stopped. (CNET)

But there is also growing strong interest both from the public as well from industry to stem inadequate developments.

Since a study cited b the FTC found that consumer privacy concerns resulted in as much as $ 2,8 billion in lost online retail sales last year, while another suggested a potential loss of as much as $ 18 billion by 2002. So we can assume that commercial interests will strongly drive and support the improvement of the prevailing situation. (Labaton)

2.3.1 Electronic voting

Electronic voting will add a new challenge to this area. Will the elections in the 21st century be carried out over the Internet? If so, how will secret-ballots elections work with an untraceable universally verifiable voting scheme?

2.4. Pornography and sexual harassment

Even within the so-called Western culture the sensitivity levels differ significantly, e.g. in the

US on sexual harassment and pornography emphasis seem to be higher than in Europe.
Similar sensitivity level differences seem to prevail on topics as "child safety in Internet"
For example, the penalty for transmitting indecent material to minors is up to $ 100000 or two years of imprisonment.

Sensitivity levels are not simply related to the quantitative size of the problem. While not yet being a dominant issue in Europe, it is in the US in spite of the fact that only 3 % of USenet newsgroups (representing only 11,5% of traffic) therefore chances are very slim to come across them randomly and of US 800 000 children reported missing p.a. there are 10 –12 cases where children have been lured online into illegal situations.(Elmer-Dewitt)

The discussion arguments run from, the "First Amendment should not end where Internet begins, to the problem "education but no porno for children to " raise them in a way that they find it as distasteful as you do" or the position of the US Supreme court, that obscenity is not protected by first amendment; it is the right of the nations states to maintain a decent society.

2.5 DB and DM

Knowledge discovery and Data Mining means access to individual date also indirectly, stereotypes, combination of patterns, both legal and illegal as well as combination of files and patterns and record matching. In an environment, where even within the EU only in a third of the countries an adequate level of data-protection is ensured.

A prominent, disliked, but legally correct and effective example of the above is the implementation at the IRS (Internal Revenue Service of the US). For checking the tax declarations living style patterns, car ownership, living area, credit card and other data are matched.

Quoting examples from the USA we have to bear in mind the differing cultural sensitivity, as well as the fluctuating sensitivity due to the prevailing "Zeitgeist". In Asia, privacy was almost no issue but signs of change are demonstrated by examples as the failure of the National ID Initiative in Taiwan or the German census problems in recent past are showing the above.

More issues are rising from areas where the legal situation and the sentiments of the people affected are not matching in spite of the legality of the projects. Examples are the creation of the Australian Geographic DB or Iceland genetic DB.

Are these experiences calling for injection of ethics in DB design and for a stronger vicarious responsibility of the DB designer?

The importance of trust shows the existence of private initiatives like Privacy TRUSTe or the speeding up of the electronic signature legislation.

2.6 Cyber crime

Hacking, DOS (denial of service) etc. have ab obvious negative connotation but some authors see it as well as also as theatre for political protest and electronic civil disobedience. This is made more attractive by the high attention this area receives in the media; but sometimes damages seem to be highly exaggerated. For the recent DOS attack on AMAZON/eBAY, a damage of 1,2 billion $ was quoted, compared to the three month income of Amazon 1.7.99 – 30.9.99 and eBAY of 964 Mio /151 Mio $ including sales and advertising (banner), an of out of service period of few hours would result in 10,7/1,7 Mio $ only.

Opinion surveys on hackers and their image show that them as:

48 % technology freaks

23 % robin hoods

22% no goods / criminals.

Recent statistical data from the BKA (Federal Criminal Office) regarding on-line criminal offences (under German law, 1999):

2795 cases of which 80 % led to foreign countries.

2245 pornography cases

120 fraud cases,

57 inciting of people (Staatsschutz/Volksverhetzung)

37 copyright

30 drug prescription law (Arzneimittelgesetz)

287 defined as others (acquiring or possession of pictures or material of   glorification of

violence, sodomy, sex with minors is in Germany a criminal offence).

(BKA)

A major obstacle is prosecution on a worldwide scale and as mentioned below in the Law-Section, prosecution is in many cases impossible as in the case of an US hacker who in 1993 attacked a system in Australia. Under German law, pure intrusion without data acquisition is said to be no criminal offence.

This should in no way excuse criminal acts committed nor belittle the danger resulting from such activities. To underline the high level of attention it should be mentioned that The US Presidents Commission on Critical Infrastructure Protection states that a failure of two major internet providers in NY area would create a nation-wide dangerous situation and the UK Ministry of Defence expects widespread Information warfare attacks by 2005. (Marsh)

3.   Law and Enforcement

The thesis is that moral self-constraint is rational, in some sense it does pay to be good.

- Law does not automatically embody moral principles (Slavery laws, DDR, etc)
- Bribes are in some countries even tax deductible.

It is necessary to promote an ethical approach too, since problems cannot be legislated out of existence. The problem of Internet abuse cannot be solved by legislate it out of existence.

(Computer and Security, 1995 Elsevier Press)

3.1 Conflict of values and the legal prosecution

Looking at the scenario several emerging phenomena will get our attention:

- Law suits triple in US since 1970's.
- Group cases bring big rewards for law firms.
- Consumer activities and other US activities move us closer to US legal system.
- The discussion in the Internet community assumes US legal framework
- In which framework are we going to discuss what in the future?

The major obstacles in legal prosecution are questions as:
Which law? Which jurisdiction? How to allocate of responsibility? How to implement a sentence?
Is e.g. blockage of illegal content only reasonable if technical possible and economically feasible?

The questions of e-commerce and valid declaration of will, will be addressed later in this session in the context of the e-signature.

The legal environment can be characterised by a plethora of legal systems, as the Austrian example should demonstrate:

1. EU primary law (Primärrecht)
   Human rights (human rights convention)
   Protection of the private sphere
   Freedom of opinion

2. EU Data protection and other guidelines

3. Constitutional laws of countries
   Right for information and official secret

4. Simple locally differing law
   DSG (data protection law), social security, industrial code

   5.   Federal state legislation (different Federal states have different DSGs)

Local variations in jurisdiction add to this, for comparison:

Switzerland: ETH Zurich, a Professor who installed in a web site a critical explaining context a link to other web sites including extreme right web sites, has been charged of racism.

Germany: The person who established a link to newspaper "Radical" featuring instructions to sabotage the railway network has been acquitted.

Consider gambling, being legal in some place but illegal in others, this might result in a multi-billion dollar industry in a virtual location or legalization.

Germany law (EGBGB) grants parties free selection of the legal system for contracts, as far the application does not lead to essentially incompatible results with the German law basic principles of "ordre public".

The US Department of Commerce in 1990 found that international systems administrators have an affirmative obligation to locate improper or illegal traffic, specifically traffic in programs which have controlled export under the Export Administration act or Arms Control Act.

But there are frightening scenarios construed as the failure of the NYSE related computer systems (which could be contained in the past), but consider the medical use of AI systems, the APACHE III medical diagnosis system, a system to help doctors calculate patient's chances of survival .
Who is responsible for systems access, for the quality of the total system including input sensor, software skills required to handle it and to whom which advice is given failure is there a "culpa in eligendo" and what happens in case of …?

3.2 Intellectual Property Rights (IPR)

It is said that Intellectual Property may become the currency of the 21st century.
But it is far from a simple, both legally and ethically.

Intellectual Property Right encompasses

- Copyright (Urheberrecht) and
- Industrial property rights (Gewerblicher Rechtsschutz) patents, registered industrial design, patterns, trademarks and the protection of Semiconductor (protection of the design of semiconductor surfaces)

The principal difference is the establishment:

Copyright is established automatically with the creation of the work, while industrial property rights and the protection of semiconductor come only into existence by the appropriate registration.

One of the problems is that copyright is not internationally standardised, and there are differing interpretation in addition to two WIPO (World Intellectual Property Organisation) standards.
In May of this year, the EU parliament decided to try to unify the legal situation among the member countries for the E-commerce. It states that independent of the location of the server the law of the place of business of the offeror is prevailing. It also restricts the responsibility of the online servers for content of third parties. To caching and hosting, but the key question how illegal content should be identified, reported and eliminated remains open.

At the same time, an Italian court acquitted an executive who had copied software for his companies' internal use. This contradicts the planned intentions of the EU copyright directive to block all copying for private use of films, music etc on tape or CDs. While in the Copyright, fair use doctrine of the US has been called the murkiest of the limitations on the copyright owners' exclusive right.

To size the copyright problem using the example of SW- Piracy some estimate that up to

75 % of students in Western world,

90 % in some countries use illegally copied software.

What about countries like Russia or China ?

What about cultures that do not share our view? There are cultures, which know communal ownership and where Western traditions are unethical e.g. medical knowledge in tribal cultures in South America. They feel that ownership can be destructive for their development, and property rights are subordinated to social well-being (different level of Maslow pyramid).

There are thoughts on Property Rights in personal information, advocating that consumers retain some property rights in the personal information that they provide to vendors and hence ought to be compensated accordingly. Our names, addresses, and personal transactions are valuable information assets worthy of recognition that we have the property rights in them. Unless we assert those rights, we will lose them. If such information has economic value, we should receive something in return for its use by others. [Anne Branscomb]

Corporations would argue that they have exclusive property rights in the information they collect.

Japan being one of the major players in international business, technology and finance had a different view on the role of imitation in Japanese culture. Japan has borrowed extensively from foreign cultures. Hokusai and Hiroshige learned by imitating. A pupil's training in fine arts consists in copying and recopying his master's work, according to "Six Canons "(a classic guide to Japanese painting). Copying old masters was not intended to mere copying but should be rather interpreted as emphasising the importance of preserving that part of tradition which ever lives as an eternal principle and of transmitting to the next generation.

Thus, we can imagine the long way and from which different point of departure the adaptation of Japanese laws and Western laws had to go. Just two examples: Japan (and most industrialised countries) gives priority to the first applicant to file an application for the patent while the US grants the patent to the first to invent the technology.

Japan permits the government to grant to others the right to use it serves public interest, therefore the tendency in Japan to make a patent as narrow as possible.

3.3   US Developments of world-wide international impact

Antitrust Jurisdiction

The US Antitrust legislation has been and is a major shaping force in international business.
Major Antitrust cases as Standard Oil, AT&T, IBM or presently Microsoft have a world-wide impact.
The basis of US legislation is the Sherman Act 1890, the Clayton Antitrust Act 1914 and the Federal Trade Commission Act 1914 as well as the precedence jurisdiction. A person guilty of

violating the Sherman Act may be fined and/or imprisoned.. In addition, a company can face for antitrust violations severe additional penalties.

Recent definitions are:

A monopolist is a company that can significantly raise the barrier to entry within the relevant market (US v.du Pont).

The possession of monopoly power in the relevant market and the wilful acquisition or maintenance of that power as distinguished from growth or development as the consequence of a superior product, business acumen or historic accident. (US v. Grinnell Corp.)

Nevertheless, there are also benefits of market leadership as standards or unified approaches e.g. compatibility.
Another newly arising term for a well known anti competitive practise is "vaporware".
Vaporware is a practice that is deceitful on its face and everybody in the business community knows it (Judge Sporkin)
This is no intellectual fiction. Dell was fined $ 800 000 for ´95 sale of vaporware (FTC charged Dell for not delivering the SW- bundle to accompany the Dell Dimension Series S marketed in 1995) as announced.

4. Business and Fiscal Law and Enforcement

The pure market is an effective method, a good servant, but a bad master and a terrifying religion, but a society which tries to replace economy by ethics, politics or religion is bound to encounter problems.
Under the assumption that large corporations regard long term profit maximisation as their most important strategic objective, there is a high rational interest in ethical conduct on the international and national theatre. In addition trust lowers the cost of doing business thus we may find interesting evidence that some forms of morality are rational policies for companies.

The problem is how to tax what where under which law. Consider a business transaction with the Sales company in A, the Server in B, the Store is located in C, the advertisement coming from D, with a customer in E. However there are ongoing attempts to resolve this, like the UN purchase contract law or several initiatives in the EU area, but tax-havens boom and enjoy more business than ever before.

This might lead to "The phenomenon of the vanishing taxpayer." [Economist]

4.1 Codes of Conduct and other regulations (CoC)

Professionalism and Code of Conduct are not new ideas, many companies, associations, universities etc. have policies, beliefs, code of conducts etc.
The Oath of Hypocrite, ABA, IEEE (institute of Electrical Engineers), ACM (assoc for computing machinery) are some examples.

Technical and General Assemblies of the IFIP urge

1. all computer professionals to recognise the disastrous potential of computer viruses

2. all computer educators to impress upon their students the danger of virus programs

3. all publishers to refrain from publication of details of actual virus programs (IFIP)

One factor behind the rise CoC might be the lingering suspicion that computer professionals may be unprepared to deal effectively with ethical issues in their workplace. Codes of behaviour can be looked to as an ethical solution but cannot be vowed as a method for instilling ethical behaviour in a group. Thus, the conviction that influencing is the remedy and could be successful, like the famous campaign on drinking and driving did.

In business or in finance scientification of life and the emotionalization of ethics might have contributed to a development, which led to a gap between two cultures as C.P. Snow (20) addressed.

5. Social Issues

While trying to address some issues more questions are emerging and the scope of the endeavour becomes larger and larger, far beyond the framework of this short note.

5.1 Accessibility

Accessibility of IT is an ethical question too!
What about ethics and accessabily of IT, for the underprivileged or handicapped?

Whom do we address today?
Optimistic estimates range from a percentage of the one billion people out of six billion people or 16 % of the population, out of the minority of the richest 20% of the population with 85% percent of the world income.
If 2% of the population in South Africa have a telephone, what about the discussion of Video On Demand and its effects on minors in the USA?

5.2 Electronic monitoring

The feat of electronic monitoring the "big brother syndrome" has been spread, but in many western countries legal and contractual regulation have been set up especially for the working environment to handle this situation.
For example, no monitoring of web-activity is permitted, except if it has explicitly agreed upon in the working contract. E-mail and addresses can be monitored only if the employees have been informed in advance or it is part of the employment contract.

5.2.1 Transparent person

Some estimates say that every person in the so-called Western world is registered in about 300 databases. The idea of linking some of these databases could lead to a transparent person especially with the increasing quality of information available. What will this do to society, is this nightmare ethics should beware us of?
Solidarity, will it stay and survive the transparent person?

5.3 Deskilling effect

Many still question claims that the patterns of working life are changing, but the anecdotal signs are increasing. We are encountering the phasing out of the tradition of corporate paternalism. More frequent job changes, more freelancing, more working at home more opportunity mean also more uncertainty. Independence and self-reliability are on the upswing versus loyalty, job security to company or country. There are concerns about the future of push-button jobs and the future of those who will fill these jobs and the qualification profile requested, will it be the lowest common denominator or a highly qualified specialist for a technology with a lifetime of few years only? The old social contract between employers and workers is being shredded. It is still unclear what will replace it. (Economist)

Is this one of the future major challenges to our education system?

6. Summary

We have covered a wide spectrum reaching from philosophy, technology to law and sociology. We have seen that Information Technology is pervading nearly all areas of our being. Are we asking for too much? Is Levy Strauss right, stating that it is highly questionable if ever all people can be happy?

The problem is similar to the problem Kelsen faced when he studied the philosophical rules of the International Law. He proposed an ethical (i.e. non-juridical) background for the International Law, comparing it to a primitive juridical system since with no coercion and no boundaries present in it like an ethical system. (Marturano)

What are the options ? We might do nothing and rely on self healing processes, governments or other regulatory institutions, or leave it to the business corporations or to the market to regulate it or believe that ethics is something we might want to reintegrate, in a non-coercive way, by teaching, by integrating it into education, business and social processes and, last but not least, by living an authentical example.

If in doubt, we have only to ask the old question:
Would it be better with or without it?

Preparing to address a subject is normally helping to clarify an unclear cloud of thoughts, make some analysis, and finally approach the point of suggesting a convincing recommendation or solution.

This time it was the other way round.

I do hope it did not have the same effect on you.

7. References

Bartels, Smith and Gustavson ,Technologically Enabled Crime Shifting Paradigms for the year 2000

Börner, Heitmann, Sengpiel, Srunk, Zöllau, Der Internet Rechtsberater, Bundesanzeiger, Köln 1999

Branscomb Anne,Who really ownes public information, Harvard Program lectures, 1991

CNET, March 3, 2000,New York

The Constitution of the United States of America (1791)

Encyclopaedia Britannica

The Economist, The future of work Jan 29,, 2000

Phillip Elmer-Dewitt, TIME Domestic Vol. 146, No 1

L. Floride: On the Philosophical foundation of computer ethics 1999

Shifting Paradigms for the year 2000, Elsevier Press 1995

Sarah GORDON Computer and Security 1995

David Gotterbarn (1991 p.27)

IFIP Technical Committee TC 11 Computer security and IFIP TC-9 Computer and Society

P. Kemp, Das Unersetzliche. Eine Technologie-Ethik, Wichern Verlag Berlin 1992

Stephen Labaton, Report on FTC and White House split on Internet privacy, May 23, 2000

Thomas Marsh, President's Commission on Critical Infrastructure Protection, Dec.4, 1997

Antomio Marturano, Institute of Philosophy of Law, La Sapienza University, Roma 1999

Graham Lea, The register 12/4/2000

M.T, Siponem, Aston Univ. UK and J.Kajava ,Univ. of Oulu Finland Computer Ethics, 1998

R.A. Spinello, Case studies in Computer and Information Ethics, Prentice Hall N.J.

Judge Sporkin, WSJ March 15, 1969

US v. Grinnell Corp. 1966

US v. E. I. du Pont de Nemours and Company ,1956

Robert Windrem, NBC News April 14, 2000

IDIMT Conferences containing Papers by C.W. Loesch

[IDIMT- 20] P. Doucek, G. Chroust, and V. Oskrdal, editors. Proceedings of *IDIMT-2020, 28th Interdisciplinary Information Management Talks*. Trauner Verlag Linz, Sept. 2020

[IDIMT- 19] P. Doucek, G. Chroust, and V. Oskrdal, editors. *IDIMT-2019, Innovation and Transformation in a Digital World, 27th Interdisciplinary Information Management Talks*. Trauner Verlag Linz, Sept. 2019.

[IDIMT- 18] P. Doucek, G. Chroust, and V. Oskrdal, editors. *IDIMT-2018, Strategic Modeling in Management, Economy and Society*. Trauner Verlag Linz, no 47, Sept. 2018

[IDIMT- 17] P. Doucek, G. Chroust, and V. Oskrdal, editors. *IDIMT-2017, Digitalization in Management, Society and Economy*. Trauner Verlag Linz, no 46, Sept. 2017..

[IDIMT- 16] P. Doucek, G. Chroust, and V. Oskrdal, editors. *IDIMT-2016, Information Technology, Society and Economy, Strategic Cross-Influences*. Trauner Verlag Linz, Sept. 2016,

[IDIMT- 15] P. Doucek, G. Chroust, and V. Oskrdal, editors. *IDIMT-2015, Information Technology and Society - Interaction and Interdependence*. Trauner Verlag Linz, Sept. 2015

[IDIMT- 14] P. Doucek, G. Chroust, and V. Oskrdal, editors. *IDIMT-2014 Networking Societies - Cooperation and Conflict*. Trauner Verlag Linz, Sept. 2014

[IDIMT- 13] P. Doucek, G. Chroust, and V. Oskrdal, editors. *IDIMT-2013 Information Technology, Human Values, Innovation and Economy*. Trauner Verlag Linz, Sept. 2013

[IDIMT-12] C.W. Loesch and G. Chroust (ed.). *ICT Trends and Scenarios: Lectures 2000 - 2017*. Books on Demand, Norderstedt, Germany, 2017 (hard copy and e-book), 2017.

[IDIMT- 11] P. Doucek, G. Chroust, and V. Oskrdal, editors. *IDIMT-2011 Interdisciplinarity in Complex Systems, vol 36, Sept 2011*. Trauner Verlag Linz, 2011

[IDIMT- 10] P. Doucek, G. Chroust, and V. Oskrdal, editors. *IDIMT 2010 Information Technology - Human Values, Innovation and Economy, Sept 2010*. Trauner Verlag Linz, 2010

[IDIMT- 10] P. Doucek, G. Chroust, and V. Oskrdal, editors. *IDIMT 2010 Information Technology - Human Values, Innovation and Economy, Sept 2010*. Trauner Verlag Linz, 2010

[IDIMT-09] P. Doucek, G. Chroust, and V. Oskrdal, editors. IDIMT 2009 - System and Humans - A Complex Relationship, Sept. 9-11, 2009. Trauner Verlag Linz, 2009,

[IDIMT- 08] G. Chroust, P. Doucek, and J. Klas, editors. *IDIMT-2008 - Managing the Unmanageable - 16th Interdisciplinary Information Management Talks*. Verlag Trauner Linz, 2008

[IDIMT-07] C. Hoyer, G. Chroust, and P. Doucek, editors. *IDIMT-2007 - 15th Interdisciplinary Information Management Talks*. Verlag Trauner Linz, 2007

[IDIMT-06] C. Hoyer and G. Chroust, editors. *IDIMT 2006 - 14th Interdisciplinary Information Management Talks*. Verlag Trauner, Linz, 2006

[IDIMT-05] C. Hoyer and G. Chroust, editors. *IDIMT 2005 - 13th Interdisciplinary Information Management Talks*. Verlag Trauner, Linz, 2005

[IDIMT- 04] C. Hofer and G. Chroust, editors. *IDIMT 2004 - 12th Interdisciplinary Information Management Talks*. Verlag Trauner Linz,2004

[IDIMT- 03] G. Chroust and C. Hofer, editors. *IDIMT-2003, 11th Interdisciplinary Information Management Talks, Sept, 2003, Budweis*. Verlag Trauner Linz, 2003

[IDIMT- 02] C. Hofer and G. Chroust, editors. *IDIMT-2002, 10th Interdisciplinary Information Management Talks, Sept, 2002, Zadov*. Verlag Trauner Linz, 2002

[IDIMT- 01] C. Hofer and G. Chroust, editors. *IDIMT-2001, 9th Interdisciplinary Information Management Talks, Sept, 2001, Zadov*. Verlag Trauner Linz 2001

[IDIMT- 00] S. Hofer and M. Beneder, editors. *IDIMT-2000: 8th Interdisciplinary Information Management Talks, Trauner, Linz*, 2000

Curriculum Vitae:

Christian W. Loesch

Dipl. Ing. Dr. techn. TU Wien (applied mathematics and physics)

Unversität Wien and TU Wien (Research assistant)

CERN Geneva (Fellow)

OECD Paris; Direction des Affaires Scientifiques

International IBM career path:

> IBM Austria
>
> IBM Assistant to the President of the ibm
>
> IBM Director of Business Development
>
> Member of Executive committee IBM Austria
>
> Asist. Gen. Mgr. Central and Eastern Europe
>
> Gen. Mgr. IBM Academic Initiative

Some special assignments:

> IBM PC introduction in Europe
>
> EARN (European Academic Research Network)
>
> Super Computing Project Austria and establishment of network hub at Uni. Vienna
>
> Academic Initiative for Central and Eastern Europe
>
> Establishment of competence centers in Prague, Warszawa, Budapest, Belgrade and integration into the WW network.

Invited Lectures at the IDIMT Conferences since 2000